MW00655508

FALL OF THE DOUBLE EAGLE

Fall of the Double Eagle

The Battle for Galicia and the Demise of Austria-Hungary

JOHN R. SCHINDLER

POTOMAC BOOKS
An imprint of the University of Nebraska Press

© 2015 by the Board of Regents of the University
of Nebraska
All rights reserved. Potomac Books is an imprint
of the University of Nebraska Press.
Manufactured in the United States of America.

Library of Congress Cataloging-in-Publication
Data
Schindler, John R.
Fall of the Double Eagle: the Battle for Galicia
and the demise of Austria-Hungary /
John R. Schindler.
pages   cm
Includes bibliographical references and index.
ISBN 978-1-61234-765-3 (hardcover: alkaline
paper)
ISBN 978-1-61234-804-9 (epub)
ISBN 978-1-61234-805-6 (mobi)
ISBN 978-1-61234-806-3 (pdf)
1. World War, 1914–1918—Causes.   2. World
War, 1914–1918—Campaigns—Eastern Front.
3. World War, 1914–1918—Campaigns—Galicia
(Poland and Ukraine).   4. Galicia (Poland and
Ukraine)—History, Military.   5. Habsburg,
House of.   6. Austria—History—Franz Joseph
I, 1848–1916.   7. Russia. Army—History—World
War, 1914–1918.   I. Title.
D512.S34 2015
940.4'22—dc23
2015013277

Set in Minion by Westchester Publishing Services.

CONTENTS

ACKNOWLEDGMENTS

As with any work years in the making, this book only came to fruition thanks to the encouragement and support of many people not the author. I want to thank my two academic mentors, Mark R. Peattie and John C. Campbell, who sent me down this road more than two decades ago, no more certain than I was where it might lead. Their wisdom about history taught me the profession, and I will be forever grateful. Thanks are also due to my friend and colleague Thomas M. Nichols, who provided counsel when it was needed, countless times, in good humor. Gratitude is also due to my friend Tim Hadley, whose contributions to this field have helped my own, proffering important wisdom when it was required.

Additionally, I want to express my gratitude to the Naval War College for its support of this book, including time and money to pursue research. Let me also extend a hearty thanks to the NWC Library for their unfailing help in tracking down ever more obscure books and articles from all over the world. No less, archivists and librarians at the Austrian State Archive deserve my thanks for their help during my multiple visits there.

Lastly, I want to express my profound gratitude to my family for all their love and support. My sons, Jack and Will, were unfailingly understanding about the many hours their father needed to spend time "in World War One," as they put it, while my wife, Anna-Lena, may rightfully consider herself the last victim of the Galician campaign. Her love and support, emotional and material, made this book a reality, and I can never fully explain my thankfulness for her help with this effort as it came to completion, most gradually, amidst countless interruptions great and small, in Vienna, Newport, Florida, and Switzerland.

FALL OF THE DOUBLE EAGLE

Introduction

There were three great battles fought at the beginning of the Great War: the Marne near Paris; Tannenberg in what would today be northeast Poland; and Galicia, waged five hundred kilometers south of that, in the border region of present-day Poland and Ukraine. The first two battles have inspired voluminous literature practically since their conclusion, including recent quality monographs in English on both the Marne and Tannenberg.[1] The significance of Germany's defeat at the Marne was evident from the moment it happened, because it ensured that Berlin's hope of a quick, decisive victory over France evaporated; the result was the conflict became protracted, leading to four more years of the bloodiest war the world had ever seen. The compensatory German victory at Tannenberg, which broke Russia's invasion of East Prussia into pieces, was less significant militarily, but it was a much-needed boost to German propaganda as well as a painful humiliation for the defeated. Both battles became the stuff of nationalist mythmaking, which would take historians decades to unravel.

By contrast the epic defeat of Austria-Hungary in Galicia has been consistently ignored by scholars and popular writers alike. This book is the first work in English to focus solely on the campaign, which despite its historical significance has been nearly forgotten. Yet its import was immense. For the Russians, this victory offset their debacle at Tannenberg and ensured that, despite whatever the Germans had won in East Prussia, they now had to contend with an ally that was militarily on the cusp of dissolution, needing major assistance. For Austria-Hungary, the defeat brought not just human catastrophe, including a hundred thousand soldiers killed in just three weeks but also the shattering of its standing army, the ultimate bulwark of the Habsburg monarchy. Military unpreparedness and deeply flawed generalship had engendered a defeat of unprecedented proportions. In the aftermath of its Galician debacle, Vienna had to raise a new army, one that survived until the end of the Great War, almost miraculously; but in the war against Russia this new army was only a ward of the Prussians and eventually their satellite. The outcome of the battle waged in Galicia in the late summer of 1914 thereby determined not only the course of the war on the Eastern Front, but also the ultimate demise of Austria-Hungary in the autumn of 1918.

How such an important battle has been all but forgotten seems to be an enigma, but upon closer examination the causes of this historical amnesia come into focus. In the first place, histories of the Great War in the English-speaking world focus overwhelmingly on the Western Front. In popular accounts, other fronts, where millions fought and died, customarily make an appearance only if they feature interesting English-speaking characters. The Eastern Front in particular has been underserved by historians, both popular and academic, and despite some progress in recent years it remains too much the "unknown war" that Winston Churchill famously termed it back in 1931.[2] To be fair, the vast war waged in Eastern Europe from 1914 to 1918 is difficult for most English-language historians to unravel: the languages are obscure, the places are unfamiliar (and have often changed names several times since the war), and the characters seem unpronounceable and usually unheard-of to boot. However, with the centenary of the Great War, it is hoped that this persistent inattention to the Eastern Front will change permanently. If this book assists that effort, it will have served its purpose.

Even the Russians have shown scant interest in the momentous Galician campaign, despite their once-heralded victory there. This is perhaps not surprising, as the war's aftermath brought even greater horrors in the East: the Civil War, the Red Terror, then Stalinism, finally the enormously bloody Second World War, remembered as the Great Patriotic War by Russians. During their seventy-three year rule, the Communists forbade dispassionate examination of the Great War by historians, preferring clichéd emphasis on class struggle. After Communism's fall, there were encouraging developments in the 1990s that proved short-lived. Since the rise of Vladimir Putin, Russian reexamination of the 1914 to 1918 period, like history generally, has emphasized patriotic themes at the expense of serious analysis, with the result that a century after the Great War's onset "Russian historiography has not produced a comprehensive and dispassionate account of this conflict."[3]

Understanding of the Great War in the dozen countries that succeeded Austria-Hungary after its demise has been even more complicated over the last hundred years. In the first draft of history, Viennese wartime propaganda was countered by nationalist narratives bemoaning Austro-Hungarian oppression, and in the long run these narratives found a bigger audience thanks to the collapse of the Habsburg realm at the war's end. Novels such as *The Good Soldier Švejk* by the anarchist-turned-Czech nationalist-turned-Bolshevik Jaroslav Hašek created an indelible image of malignant incompetence on the part of the Habsburg military that was more important for many audiences than historical facts. It did not help serious historiography that the nationalist, anti-Habsburg regimes that governed in most of the former Dual Monarchy after 1918, notably Czechoslovakia, Yugoslavia, and Greater Romania, offered accounts similar to Hašek's, minus the biting humor, depicting oppressed soldiery eager to desert to the Allies.

To make matters worse, many accounts from the republic of Austria after 1918 echoed similar themes, namely that brave German-Austrian soldiers had been left in the lurch by traitorous Slavs who had been disloyal from the start of the war. Hence ethnicity, not military factors, stood at the core of Habsburg defeat, a point that nationalists of all stripes could agree upon. That this peculiarly Austrian "stab-in-the-back-legend" ignored many realities mattered less than the fact that some former Austro-Hungarian generals publicly took a similar view. As had been the case during the war, it was always easier to find fault with the troops than with top leadership to explain away defeats. Similar trends were in evidence in Horthyist Hungary, with the "heroic Magyar race" being substituted for brave Germans, naturally.

The fall of nearly all the former Habsburg lands to Communism in 1945 hardly helped the writing of accurate history. Official accounts continued to emphasize the alleged oppression at the heart of Austria-Hungary, with yesterday's nationalist heroes resisting all things Habsburg being relabeled as proletarian vanguards. The essential willingness to resort to clichés at the expense of inconvenient facts remained the same. After the collapse of Communism around 1990, serious analysis of the Great War in Central Europe again became possible, and there are encouraging signs that balanced assessments are emerging, including ones that debunk century-old myths depicting ethnic disloyalty as the core failing of the Habsburg military. Historians are belatedly realizing that even among Czechs, Austria-Hungary's most disaffected minority, the majority of Czech troops remained loyal, doing their duty to the end of the war.[4] This constitutes part of a broader trend in which historians are dispensing with decades of propaganda by reexamining complex notions of identity and loyalty among fissiparous ethnic groups in the militaries that waged the Great War, discovering that even armies that went down to defeat in 1918 inspired considerable fidelity among supposedly "disloyal" elements.[5] It is again politic to note that while Tomáš Masaryk, the father of Czechoslovakia, agitated throughout the Great War against Austria-Hungary, his son Jan, the future Czechoslovak foreign minister, served honorably throughout that war as a Habsburg frontline officer, and spoke fondly of the former empire and its army down to his death in 1948, a probable victim of Communist murder.[6] Nevertheless, it remains the case that across the former Habsburg lands the Great War remains forgotten or remembered selectively, thanks to a century of historical confusion about what actually happened and why.[7]

Historians who are not masochistically inclined prefer to write about the victories of their country rather than defeats, and notwithstanding the tendency to emphasize the horrors of the war that became prominent in the 1960s in the West among popular historians, it is only recently that serious analysis of battlefield setbacks has come into fashion, even in countries where the Great War brought more victories than defeats.[8] The desire to explain away, rather than explain, battlefield reverses has long been especially marked in Austria, perhaps not surprisingly, as there were so many defeats to take account of, starting from the very beginning of the war. The Great War ended in complete defeat for Austria, with the loss of its ancient empire and its venerable institutions, with all the traumas that entailed, particularly for former army officers. None of this was conducive to balanced or dispassionate analysis, neither did the reality that after 1918 cadres of wartime General Staff officers, who had waged the doomed conflict, were re-created as the historical office assigned the task of writing the Official History of said conflict.[9] It is no overstatement to apply the word *conspiracy* to their effort, which aimed at covering up the deeply flawed generalship that brought disaster to Austria-Hungary, particularly during the Great War's critical opening weeks.[10]

Austria's Official History of the war, consisting of seven weighty volumes published between 1930 and 1938, was written under the supervision of Edmund Glaise-Horstenau, a wartime General Staff officer who grew sympathetic to National Socialism in the 1930s.[11] It cannot be considered especially biased compared to other official accounts of the war prepared by Europe's militaries after 1918, and it is actually less skewed than some. Nevertheless, there is no denying that it went to considerable lengths to obscure facts that put the old, defunct army in a bad light. There is a detectable tendency to shift blame for defeats onto soldiers, especially Slavs, deemed of questionable loyalty, while the intent to protect the reputations of top Habsburg generals resonates even more prominently in the Official History.

No general was better shielded by the Official History, and by Austrian historiography broadly, than the most senior one, Franz Conrad von Hötzendorf, who was the professional head of the army from 1906 to 1917, with only slight interruption. Conrad prepared the Austro-Hungarian Army for war, helped considerably to engineer that war, then oversaw the shattering of his force in the war's first month. Despite his huge role in the causes and course of the Great War, Conrad remains an undeservedly obscure figure outside Central Europe.[12] Wartime Habsburg propaganda that depicted Conrad in heroic terms held currency for much longer than it should have, thanks in large part to the efforts of official historians in Vienna, the General Staff veterans who dominated studies of the Great War in Austria into the 1950s and continued to propagate flattering views of Conrad that some of them privately knew were erroneous. As a result, Conrad's reputation among scholars in the English-speaking world, who based their views on official Viennese accounts rather than original research, was higher for decades than it deserved to be, including praise of his alleged strategic genius, leading to widespread misunderstandings about Conrad's actual part in the catastrophic events of 1914.

Things would not begin to change until the 1960s, when a new generation of historians emerged in Austria, no longer beholden to official accounts, yet all the same, honest reassessment of Conrad and the Galician campaign took longer than it should have. Political factors were not irrelevant here. Whatever his myriad flaws as a general, Conrad was untainted by National Socialism, and postwar Austria, traumatized by the Anschluss and the Second World War, needed heroes after the Allied occupation ended in 1955. Thus for the re-created Austrian military, the Conrad cult retained currency for another decade at least. In recent decades, Austrian historians, above all Kurt Peball and especially Manfried Rauchensteiner, have unmasked the Conrad myth by digging deep in the archives, exposing his true role behind the military unraveling of Austria-Hungary.[13] American historians, lacking the ethnic biases that are the bane of historical analysis in the region, have provided important support to this long-overdue revisionism.

Nevertheless, the Galician debacle of late summer 1914 remains unjustifiably obscure, given its historical impact. The campaign never generated the writings it merited, scholarly or popular, even in Central Europe. This can be partly attributed to the fact that the defeat suffered by Habsburg arms in Galicia at the beginning of the Great War was but one trauma among many for the peoples of the Danubian monarchy, not to mention the first of three major defeats inflicted by the Russians on Conrad's forces in Galicia over three consecutive summers between 1914 and 1916. One suspects that, for many in the region, it became difficult to differentiate between these disasters in popular memory. Neither did the desire of official historians in Vienna to deflect attention away from what really happened in Galicia in the summer of 1914 promote a climate of healthy inquiry. There are very few books of any sort that have seriously delved into the details of that campaign. An exception consists of two books written not long after the war by Maximilian von Pitreich, a wartime General Staff officer and dissenter from the Conrad clique, who painted a detailed portrait of Austro-Hungarian military incompetence (his unpublished studies, hidden away in the Viennese archives, are even more scathing).[14] Never intended for a mass audience, Pitreich's books included a plethora of military details—strategic, operational, and tactical—that renders them inaccessible to nonspecialist audiences, while the inattention paid to them by Conrad's protectors in Vienna ensured those volumes would remain obscure to the public.

Promoting confusion about what happened in Galicia, where most of the fighting in the late summer of 1914 between Russians and Austro-Hungarians took place, is the obscurity of the region itself, which has not existed as a political unit since the autumn of 1918 and the collapse of the Habsburg monarchy. Today, Galicia appears as a Ruritania of sorts, difficult to discern by postmoderns. It has fallen to twenty-first century scholars to "reconstruct" that nearly forgotten region, which has seen its contested legacy subsumed into nationalist narratives, both Polish and Ukrainian.[15] While there is considerable agreement in the lands of former Galicia today about the essentially positive nature of Habsburg rule, including its genuine tolerance of diversity in race and religion, despite the mutual antipathies between the Polish and Ukrainian historical narratives that prevailed until quite recently, trying to recapture the mentalities that prevailed in Galicia a hundred years ago remains a daunting task.

Nostalgia, that bane of rigorous history, cannot be avoided either. Decades of nationalist mythmaking across Central Europe have taken their toll, making it difficult to assess the late Habsburg period altogether dispassionately even a century on. In reaction many popular authors as well as some scholars have created a Habsburg counter myth of sorts, particularly in recent decades, portraying Austria-Hungary as a greater oasis of multiethnic functionality than it actually was. This has impacted military history too, with some authors attempting to counteract acid-etched portrayals of Austro-Hungarian inefficiencies, the inevitable by-product of a fractious polity possessing a dozen nationalities, with accounts emphasizing decency and tolerance above all.[16] Moral factors cannot be avoided altogether, and it remains a fact that Austria-Hungary represented a more decent and humane governance than anything experienced by most inhabitants of Central Europe for most of the twentieth century. The well-honed Habsburg tendency to red tape and appearance-over-reality known as *Schlamperei* (slackness) that did so much to undermine effectiveness at war must appear almost quaint compared to Nazi or Bolshevik thoroughness, and historians who leave out this consideration should be questioned, given the last century's sad status as one of "burning flesh," to cite Elias Canetti.

Researching the fateful events that transpired in Galicia in the late summer of 1914 presents its own challenges. In the first place, the strong Habsburg tendency to thorough recordkeeping was undermined by the enormous losses sustained by Austro-Hungarian forces in the opening weeks of the war. Units battling the Russians took so many casualties, especially among the officers assigned to recount such events, that a surprising number of regiments and divisions have hardly any records to plumb in the famous War Archive (*Kriegsarchiv*) in Vienna. I was shocked to discover how the exact fate of so many Habsburg regiments was lost to history because no officers survived to update the unit's war diary (*Tagesbuch*), which recounted actions and losses.[17] It was even more depressing to encounter how the surviving records of numerous Habsburg regiments and divisions remained sealed in the original twine-laced dossiers where they had lain for nearly a century, untouched by uninterested historians.

To compensate for frequently inadequate official records, I have consulted memoirs and secondary accounts in a dozen languages. It is a sad fact that far too few of the survivors of Austria-Hungary's defeat in Galicia in the summer of 1914 left behind memoirs; among common soldiers, the infantry rankers who fell in such vast numbers, hardly any wrote up their ordeals in a manner that historians can track down. As a result, reconstructing what happened to the Austro-Hungarian Army in Galicia has been difficult, not helped by the fact that hardly any "action" photographs were taken. The lack of sources, written and visual, to help capture what actually happened when the Russian and Austro-Hungarian armies collided with full force a hundred summers ago, helps explain why so few accounts have been published. Readers should dispense with any notions of trenches or other Great War clichés: on the plains and rolling hills of Galicia in the late summer of 1914, two enormous armies, millions strong, collided on a vast front in huge encounter battles, featuring great columns of infantry, eager battalions stacked deep, meeting each other with bayonets fixed as mounted cavalry dueled and artillery decided the day with fire. This was a spectacle unprecedented in warfare, lost to history for a century, that this book tries to recreate.

My own career path has impacted how I view this campaign and choose to present it here. Unlike many military historians writing today, I have served as a military officer myself, which has given me an understanding of how difficult it can be to make and execute decisions upon which lives hinge, not to mention grasping that war is inherently the most inefficient of human endeavors. I first did research in Vienna's *Kriegsarchiv* in the early 1990s as a young graduate student tearing into records with eager yet inexperienced eyes. Over the succeeding two decades, however, my perspective shifted thanks to my service in the U.S. Department of Defense, in two distinct phases. The first involved nearly a decade in intelligence work, which bequeathed me a secret viewpoint rather different from most scholars. That intelligence matters in war (and peace) is reflected in my analysis in this book, yet neither is espionage alone a panacea: it cannot compensate for manifest military weakness. Moreover, having been an intelligence officer who created records on a daily basis taught me that such files are also valuable for what they do *not* say: with such opened eyes, I would never look at archives quite the same way again.

Then I took a professorship at the Naval War College, the oldest continuously operating institution of its kind on earth, where I spent nearly a decade teaching students about war, peace, and the sometimes hazy place between them. This experience forced me to think systematically about these issues in a fashion few civilian academics encounter. It has enabled me to see many things, not least Austria-Hungary's Galician debacle, with fresh eyes. As a graduate student, I could hardly grasp how Vienna's military elite could leap into the abyss so forthrightly in 1914, without pondering consequences. Experience, however, has taught me differently. As head of an intelligence task force, I witnessed my country embark on Operation Iraqi Freedom in 2003 in a similar manner, ignoring obvious evidence that it was headed into long-term failure. Happily for the United States, its avoidable errors in Iraq cost it only prestige, money, and a few thousand American lives, unlike Austria-Hungary in 1914, which would never recover from its military mistakes. Yet the basic impulses, rooted in institutionalized escapism, appear similar. In the aftermath of the September 11, 2001, terrorist attacks on the United States, decision makers in Washington, DC, opted for a war plan that addressed preexisting political goals more than present realities. The consequences of this strategic miscalculation would prove severe. In a similar fashion, Austria-Hungary's top officials, military and civilian, seized on the assassination of Archduke Franz Ferdinand to launch an ill-fated war to save their country from its political problems. From this miscalculation, there would be no return, however, only disaster. To sum it up, the Galician campaign of 1914 offers scholars as well as security practitioners ample lessons in conducting civil-military relations and matching strategy to policy, mostly as a guide of what to avoid, as well as insights into the limits of the military instrument in solving political problems, particularly in fractious multinational societies.

As a historian, it is impossible to eliminate current events from the story altogether. There has been a gradual reassessment of the Galician campaign after the Cold War, politically as much as militarily, in light of the trajectory of events in the region. The simple categories of nationalism and tribe, presumed by so many previously, do not fit so easily in postmodern Europe. As was the case a hundred years ago, Galicia again appears as a bulwark of European values against Russian intrusion. As I write, Ukraine—led politically by its western region, what was once Galicia—is attempting to define its European future under Russian pressure. It is not a coincidence that this movement derives its strength from the city of L'viv—once the Austrian Lemberg, Galicia's capital—as an outpost of Central European history, culture, and values, juxtaposed against Moscow's authoritarianism. Putin's Russia today, with its aggressive emphasis on unitary nationalism, politics, and religion, would seem familiar to any observer of a century ago.

A Polish historian not long ago explained that Austria-Hungary's doomed Galician campaign nevertheless achieved what it intended, which was protecting Central Europe against "a permanent deluge of Eastern barbarism," borne by Russian bayonets.[18] Although Austria-Hungary disappeared from the map of Europe nearly a century ago, aided by its Galician debacle, some of its values seem to have endured, even under great stresses. What Habsburg arms could not protect by force—which is the story presented here for the first time—may in the long run have been defended by civil society and average people, even under decades of pressure from multiple repressive regimes.

1 AEIOU

The cryptic vocalic motto had existed for nearly half a millennium, but no one was exactly certain what it stood for. Some believed it represented *Alles Erdreich ist Österreich untertan* (All the earth is subject to Austria), while others preferred the more classical *Austria erit in orbe ultima* (Austria will stand until the end of the world); there were other options too, and the arcane debate had continued for centuries, without resolution. Regardless, AEIOU—whatever it really meant—was found prominently on edifices all over the vast Habsburg realm, as a symbol of that family's ancient and enduring power and prestige.[1]

The Habsburgs had burst upon the European scene out of the Swiss Alps in the eleventh century, gaining the crown of Austria in 1282 and the crown of the Holy Roman Empire in 1452. Between its Spanish and Austrian wings, the Habsburgs at their zenith controlled most of the West and much of the New World too; surely none of Europe's great royal houses thought of itself in grander terms. None could deny that it had saved Europe from the Turk. It was very much a family firm, a *Hausmacht*, leading to truisms such as the quip that other royal houses were periods in the history of nations, while nations were periods in the history of the Habsburgs. There was no doubt that the Habsburgs had been ensconced in their Danubian principalities for centuries when the Hohenzollerns and Romanovs were mere border-runners. Well known too was the saying, "Let others wage war; you, happy Austria, marry!" (Bella gerant alii, tu felix Austria nube!), which implied that the

Habsburg patrimony had been assembled through matchmaking rather than conquest, which was, generously, a half-truth. Most potent perhaps was the "Habsburg myth" that embodied the belief in the mission of the family and its subjects, a mystical union with religious overtones whose hold lasted centuries, longer even than the dynasty itself. In a manner that postmoderns have difficulty grasping, the Habsburgs, a distinctly German dynasty for all their polyglot holdings, represented a *Reich* in the ancient, non-Hitlerian sense, a throwback entity that defied easy definition as Europe became dominated by nation-states more than multinational dynasties.[2]

Napoleon had set the Habsburgs on the path to perdition in 1806 when he disbanded the Holy Roman Empire, forcing the family to redefine itself as the emperors of Austria. Franz II, the last Holy Roman Emperor and first emperor of Austria, claimed the titles of three dozen Central European kingdoms and principalities, plus the crown of Jerusalem for good measure, but what exactly was "Austria"? That was the question that would take a century to answer, and some remained unsatisfied with any answers the Habsburgs could proffer. Having outlasted Napoleon, who with his aggressive Enlightenment views, particularly anticlericalism, represented all that the devoutly Catholic Habsburgs despised, Vienna stood as a bulwark of reaction, guided by the gifted Prince Metternich in staving off modernity in all its forms, until the revolutions of 1848 nearly destroyed the whole Habsburg edifice.

The conflagration that engulfed much of Europe in 1848 spared hardly any part of the Austrian Empire. Vienna was convulsed with social unrest from which the Habsburgs fled to the safety of the Alps, while the rest of the realm was shaken by revolts both social and national. These were crushed one by one by the army, the only element to remain mostly loyal throughout the crisis. Most consequentially, Hungary, the largest of the Habsburg dominions, engaged in open revolt led by the firebrand Lajos Kossuth, a direct challenge to Habsburg dominance in the Danubian space that was subdued only with great difficulty, including Russian military assistance, by the autumn of 1849. Hungary was brought to heel by brute force, aided by competing nationalisms: while Magyars (that is, ethnic Hungarians) believed they ought to dominate Hungary, that country's many minorities—Slavs, Romanians, Germans, amounting to half its population—did not wish to live in a Magyar ethno-state, and in considerable numbers they were willing to support the Habsburgs to avoid Magyar domination.[3]

The new emperor who witnessed Hungary's submission was Franz Joseph, who was crowned at the end of 1848, aged eighteen, succeeding his severely epileptic uncle Ferdinand on the throne. His realm was in dissolution, and from its salvation by bayonets the teenaged monarch learned that his army was the ultimate defender of the Habsburg inheritance, and that the rising force of nationalism endangered the stability and even existence of the empire. The remedy suggested by counselors was absolutism, keeping power firmly in the hands of the monarch, his ministers, the army, and the police. Alexander Bach, the interior minister, played a key role in suppressing dissent through police measures, both overt and secret. Absolutism, however, alienated those who longed for liberty, both personal and national; and Slavs, Magyars, and Italians alike, whatever their mutual antipathy, commonly despised the Bach system, as did no small number of Germans. The rise of the bourgeoisie and educated classes to prominence and aspirations to power sharing with the monarch, a pervasive phenomenon in Central and Western Europe by the mid-nineteenth century, imperiled such throwback political systems.[4]

The deficiencies of absolutism were laid bare by Austria's brief, painful war against the joined forces of Piedmont-Sardinia and France, waged in northern Italy in May and June of 1859. The aim of the conflict, to guard the empire's Italian province of Lombardy from the greedy hands of the house of Savoy, was not achieved thanks to French aid to the Piedmontese. Moreover, the Habsburg edifice demonstrated inefficiency, while the military showed serious weaknesses, not least the shaky performance of regiments comprised of unwilling Hungarians and Italians, and after the bloodbath at Solferino, where scenes of slaughter moved Henri Dunant to found the Red Cross, Franz Joseph sued for peace. He gave up Lombardy, allowing Piedmont to soon create the kingdom of Italy. In the wake of defeat, to shore up the realm and appease discontent, Vienna experimented with constitutionalism and limited concessions to Budapest, but it was not enough to satisfy critics, nor could it heal pressing problems of state finance. When the empire went to war again in the summer of 1866, defeat was awaiting once more. It was over in just six weeks, the Prussians defeating Habsburg forces in Bohemia, with the army proving weak and plagued by morale problems among Hungarians and others. Salving Vienna's relationship with Budapest, a wound unhealed on the heart of the realm since 1849, was now imperative if the Habsburgs wished to preserve their patrimony.[5]

Habsburg territorial losses in 1866 were not crippling, amounting to the surrender of the province of Venetia to Italy notwithstanding the fact that Habsburg arms had defeated the Italians at Custoza on land and at Lissa on the Adriatic, but the political implications of humiliation by Prussia were immense. The Six Weeks War settled the longstanding question of who would dominate the German lands—Habsburgs or Hohenzollerns—decisively in favor of the latter. Henceforth, Austria would be the "other" German state, while Prussia would take the lead politically, militarily, and economically in Central Europe, forcing the Habsburgs to look south and east to maintain their geopolitical relevance. It was a humbling experience for the family that only six decades before still wore the crown of the Holy Roman Emperor.

Nevertheless the need to placate the Hungarians was urgent, and the outcome of the sea change in Vienna's strategic position in 1866 after defeat at Königgrätz was the Compromise (*Ausgleich*) with Hungary in May of the following year, the official birth of Austria-Hungary. Shepherded through Budapest by Ferenc Deák, the veteran fixer of Hungarian politics, the compromise granted Hungary what its moderate nationalists craved, self-rule and independence from Vienna in most matters, while maintaining union with Austria through the person of the monarch, the Austrian emperor and Hungarian king. Budapest was made master in its own house of all internal matters of governance, law, finance, education, and commerce. What united Austria and Hungary after 1867, aside from Franz Joseph himself, were the military, foreign affairs, and a joint finance ministry to fund the forces and the diplomats; all else was left to the Hungarians themselves. While hard-line nationalists would settle for nothing less than complete independence from the Habsburgs, their protests were drowned out by the Magyar "political nation" that ran the country and understood what an estimable deal they had obtained thanks to Prussian arms. Yet the *Ausgleich*, far from solving the problems of the Habsburg realm, ultimately created new ones that proved intractable and would lay paths to the disaster of 1914.[6]

While the compromise understandably pleased the Magyars, it was anything but pleasing to the other groups that made up half of Hungary's population. In the first place, large tracts of territory, Transylvania and the Military Border on the southern flanks of Hungary were incorporated fully into the kingdom, losing their separate status, and placed under Budapest, to the chagrin of many who lived in them. Croatia-Slavonia, which had been nebulously part of Hungary since 1102, had its status ratified with its own compromise (*Nagodba*) in 1868 negotiated between parliaments in Budapest and Zagreb, which left the Croats in partial control of their own affairs, though bickering between the capitals, over issues great and small, continued nonstop for the next five decades. The last Habsburg census in 1910 revealed that—despite decades of Budapest's gerrymandering plus efforts to turn Slavs and Romanians into Magyar speakers—out of the population of almost twenty-one million in Hungary, barely ten million listed Magyar as their primary language; even subtracting Croatia-Slavonia, which had few Magyars, ethnic Hungarians made up less than 55 percent of the population. There were huge communities of minorities in Hungary proper, including almost three million Romanians, nearly two million each Slovaks and Germans, plus three-quarters of a million South

Slavs, predominately Serbs, and almost a half-million Ruthenians (that is, Ukrainians), and in many regions of the country the minorities dominated numerically, if not politically.[7]

Efforts by Budapest to transform the country's demographics by using the schools to Magyarize promising pupils—almost any young Slav or Romanian who went to high school or university emerged a Magyar in language and thought—were deeply resented by the minorities. In addition, the "political nation" kept non-Magyars away from power through skewing voting districts, while Budapest resisted universal manhood suffrage mightily for decades, on ethnic more than social grounds. Every decade, the compromise required official reapproval by Vienna and Budapest, and without fail the Magyar elite used this opportunity to demand more perquisites while explaining how charitable they had been to agree to the *Ausgleich* in the first place, amidst reminders that Hungary was not wedded to the union forever, and that the 1867 agreement represented only Hungary's minimum demands. Budapest was a showcase for the worst kind of lawyerly showboating by nationalist parliamentarians who demonstrated no concern for issues beyond their own bailiwick. It drove ministers and bureaucrats in Vienna to distraction and tested Franz Joseph's famous tolerance for Hungarian antics, as he viewed the *Ausgleich* as his reign's greatest accomplishment and the guarantor of the dynasty. The deleterious impact of Budapest's politicking on the military was profound, since the defense budget was held hostage every decade to Hungarian demands, while by the early twentieth century Hungary's disaffected minorities despaired of any aid from Vienna.[8]

Austria-Hungary, alternately called the Dual Monarchy—Hungarians disavowed the Teutonic term "Reich" since it implied a unitary state, which did not exist after 1867—was a unique creation born in response to the internal problems of the multinational empire, one that was difficult to explain to outsiders. In the first place, officially Hungary was termed Transleithania, since it stood across the small Leitha river that was the historic border between Hungary and the Austrian lands, though most people of course called the country what it was: Hungary. Cisleithania was the Austrian half of the empire, which was not officially given the name Austria until 1915; before that it was formally "the kingdoms and lands represented in the Imperial Council" (*die im Reichsrat vertretenen Königreiche und Länder*), that being the parliament for so-called Cisleithania located in Vienna. There was no denying that the Austria half of the Dual Monarchy lacked the coherence, historical and political, of Hungary, comprising as it did fifteen different crown lands, from Dalmatia on the Adriatic, to "holy" Tyrol in the high Alps, to the industrial heartland of Bohemia, over to Bukovina, Austria's easternmost outpost. The 1910 census showed a population of thirty million, consisting of ten ethnic groups, the biggest being Germans (36 percent), Czechs (23 percent), Poles (18 percent), and Ukrainians (13 percent).[9]

The relationship between the dominant ethnic groups, Germans and Magyars, and the minorities in the Austrian and Hungarian halves of the monarchy was fundamentally different. At root Austria was no German ethno-state (contrary to the wishes of German nationalists) and was considerably more tolerant of non-Germans than Hungary was of non-Magyars in matters of language and cultural policy; there was no official effort to turn minorities into Germans; on the contrary, Austria allowed its Slavs and other minorities considerable leeway to be educated and receive government services in their own languages. This is not to deny that ethnic rivalry was problematic in Austria too—the struggle between Czechs and Germans in Bohemia was poisonous, serving to paralyze parliamentary life in Vienna—but Austria did offer a more diverse, if bumpy path to modernity than Hungary chose to take after 1867.[10]

Nevertheless, the fate of fellow Slavs, particularly Slovaks, in Hungary, where they faced national oppression and their gradual absorption into a Magyar sea, served as a constant irritant among Czechs. For many of them, it was transparent that by accepting the *Ausgleich* Vienna had sacrificed the rights of Slovaks and many others on the altar of placating

Magyardom. Standing at the middle of this controversy was the pro-found disconnect between historic political units and current-day populations inside Austria-Hungary. Budapest claimed the "historic" boundaries of Hungary as her own, even though these feudal-era frontiers trapped millions of unenthusiastic non-Magyars in the country; following the logic of nation-states that was becoming norma-tive in Europe, there existed five or six ethno-states-in-waiting inside Hungary, only one of which was Magyar. However, Czech nationalists undermined their arguments by advocating the same thing in their own lands, wanting to keep millions of Germans under Prague's rule inside the "historic" boundaries of Bohemia.

Had there been options other than the Compromise of 1867? To many Habsburg Slavs the road not taken was the open embrace of the empire's essentially Slavic nature: after all, the seven Slavic nations nested together in Austria-Hungary together came to 45 percent of the monarchy's population, twice the number of either Germans or Magyars (and roughly equal to the population of the Dual Monarchy's dominant races put together). This possibility, termed Austroslavism, came to prominence in the tumult of 1848 and was hardly anti-Habsburg; indeed it envisioned reimagining the realm on the basis of nationality rather than feudally derived political models.[11] One of its proponents was the Czech historian and politician František Palacký, who saw the Habsburgs as the defenders of the smaller peoples of Central Europe, Czechs included, against hungry neighbors. As he wrote in 1848, "Assur-edly, if the Austrian state had not existed for ages, in the interests of Europe and indeed of humanity itself, we would have to endeavor to create it as soon as possible." However, enthusiasm for Austroslavism waned in the 1860s, as its advocates waited for signs of compromise from Vienna that never came, while the *Ausgleich* drove many to despair. As Palacký observed, "We existed before Austria, and we shall exist after it," and in 1867, he attended a Panslav congress in Russia. Like many Czech nationalists, he began to ponder options beyond the Habsburgs as Austroslavism's moment passed, unfulfilled.[12]

Reform ideas continued to percolate inside the Dual Monarchy as the congenital defects of the compromise became plain for all but Hungarian nationalists to see. Here the doomed Archduke Franz Ferdinand played a role. Franz Joseph's nephew became heir to the throne in 1889, after the death of Crown Prince Rudolph in a bizarre murder-suicide pact with his teenaged mistress, which, in trademark Viennese fashion, was covered up imperfectly. Relations between the monarch and his successor were far from warm, not helped by Franz Ferdinand's insistence on marrying a mere Bohemian countess, in a morganatic love match—an unthinkable breech of Habsburg protocol for an old fashioned stickler like the emperor. After 1900, when Franz Joseph passed his seventieth birthday, Franz Ferdinand's residence at Vienna's Belvedere Palace became a government-in-waiting, where reformers went to pitch their ideas to the future emperor. He took his position seriously, energetically traveling some two hundred days a year, seeing the Dual Monarchy and its peoples for himself amidst much hunting of any animals that crossed his voracious path. The heir's loathing of Magyars was deep and well known, and there is little doubt that, had he ever ascended the throne, Franz Ferdinand would have forced alterations on the compromise, perhaps breaking it altogether, by force if necessary.

What path such reform might have taken remains difficult to establish. One option was Trialism, which would convert Austria-Hungary into a Triple Monarchy with a self-governing South Slav unit, basically a greatly expanded Croatia, to placate Croats, Serbs, and Slovenes who were becoming attracted by the rise of an independent Serbia out of Ottoman ashes. Hungary was vehemently opposed to such ideas, and it is far from clear that Trialism would have actually deterred Habsburg Serbs from desiring union with Serbia, as advocates expected. Another possibility was more radical, abandoning all "historic" units in favor of federalizing the realm by recognizing fifteen self-governing ethno-states subject to the Habsburg throne. Its architect was Aurel Popovici, a Romanian lawyer from Transylvania who had Franz Ferdinand's ear. He grandly termed his concept the United States of Great Austria; his book explaining the concept became a sensation.[13] Popovici, who loathed Budapest but was loyal to the monarchy, crafted the most forward-looking reform proposal, which, in its acceptance of universal ethnic rights and national equality, remains pleasing more than a century later, in the era of the European Union. For exactly that reason, however, it generated vociferous opposition, notably in Hungary, and Popovici's plan came no closer to realization than the Trialist option, remaining an important what-might-have-been in the history of Central Europe.

That said, Franz Ferdinand's political views were admirably clear and thoroughly reactionary. An ultramontane Catholic who despised modernity in all its forms, the emperor-in-waiting understood that by the twentieth century, in a Europe dominated by nation-states, Austria-Hungary was an "anomaly," as even Franz Joseph conceded, and the time to reform it before disaster encroached might be limited. Franz Ferdinand saw his salvific mission with clarity and understood the role of the Habsburg myth behind it: "it is not, as elsewhere, where the state carries the dynasty—here the dynasty carries the state," he explained.[14] His views were so backward-looking that Franz Ferdinand had no sympathy with the main European political currents of his age—including liberalism, nationalism, and socialism—that were tearing the Dual Monarchy apart. This alienation, however, may have allowed him to leapfrog over them. Shorn of its Catholic traditionalism, Franz Ferdinand's belief in the importance of multinationalism over ethnic politicking would be heartily endorsed by any Eurocrat in Brussels today—had he ever ascended the throne: it is all speculation.

Franz Ferdinand's deeply retrograde attitudes made him immune to the aggressive views about war, rooted in social Darwinism, that were all the rage in early twentieth-century Europe. Unlike many of his generals he viewed war as a horror and something that the fissiparous Dual Monarchy needed to avoid at almost any cost. While he was passionate about the military, and sought to protect it from Hungarian meddling, he saw it as primarily an instrument of internal security and dynastic preservation. He had no time for talk of saving Austria-Hungary through making war on neighboring states, and Franz Ferdinand especially wanted peace with Russia, a reactionary monarchy he admired in some ways. He eschewed war even against troublesome little Serbia, which many political and military leaders in the Dual Monarchy itched to crush to stave off further collapse of Vienna's position in the volatile Balkans, particularly when it became clear that Belgrade was an implacable opponent of Austria-Hungary after the 1908 Bosnian crisis. Franz Ferdinand added a moment of clarity the following year, when plans for war against Serbia were the talk of the war ministry in Vienna, telling the Habsburg military commander in Bosnia that war with Serbia would gain Austria-Hungary "nothing but a bunch of pigs and swine herders."[15]

Yet there could be no avoiding the reality that for Austria-Hungary, more than for any other country in Europe, foreign and domestic problems were deeply, intractably interwoven. To Vienna, there were hardly any purely domestic issues anymore, as all the major ones had ramifications abroad, while nearly all the empire's foreign concerns impacted its internal politics too. The gradual collapse of the Ottoman Empire in Southeastern Europe, the growth of which the Habsburgs had resisted for centuries, now exposed the Dual Monarchy to strategic hazard. Romanians, Hungary's largest and unhappiest minority, could not fail to seek ties, if not political union, with neighboring Romania once it achieved independence from the Turks. The threat posed by Serbia loomed larger still in Vienna and Budapest. Particularly after 1903, when a bloody palace coup installed an openly anti-Habsburg monarch and government in Belgrade, Serbia became the *bête noire* of Austro-Hungarian functionaries who feared that a rising Serbia might fatally undermine the loyalty of the Dual Monarchy's 5.6 million South Slavs. It did not help matters that Serbian officials talked openly about doing exactly that, while the Bosnian crisis of 1908, caused by Vienna's formal annexation of the once-Ottoman provinces of Bosnia-Hercegovina, which Austria-Hungary had occupied de facto since

1878, caused outrage in Serbia. Liberation of the Serbian lands from foreign occupation, as nationalists viewed it, required the eviction of both the Ottomans and the Habsburgs from South Slav territory, a seemingly impossible dream given the size of tiny Serbia compared to two great empires. Yet these empires were aged and increasingly infirm, and the verdict of the two Balkan Wars of 1912–13, which created an enormously expanded Serbia and evicted the Ottomans from Europe almost altogether, gave optimists in Belgrade the dangerous notion that, given sufficient firmness and risk taking, even the impossible could be realized.

Although there were still more Serbs found in Austria-Hungary than in the expanded Serbia, the collapse of the Habsburg strategic position in the Balkans engendered by the wars of 1912–13, caused genuine panic in Vienna among the generals and bureaucrats charged with defending the Dual Monarchy from threats both foreign and domestic. Particularly worrisome was Russia's open, indeed enthusiastic embrace of victorious Serbia. The Bosnian crisis encouraged anti-Habsburg feelings in St. Petersburg, which felt humiliated by Vienna's breach of diplomatic norms, while Slavophil politicians, who viewed the Serbs as Orthodox brothers and the Habsburgs as oppressors of Slavs, encouraged aggressive attitudes toward the Dual Monarchy among Russian diplomats and generals alike. Although no traditional foe of the Habsburgs, by 1913 Imperial Russia was unmistakably allied with Serbia and seemed to share Belgrade's view that the Dual Monarchy represented the last obstacle to realizing Greater Serbia.

Rising rivalry with Russia involved the customary Habsburg admixture of internal and external worries, intertwined. These played out in Galicia, the largest and most populous of Austria's provinces. It bordered Russia and had been joined to the Habsburgs in 1772, out of the carcass of Poland. Its population of eight million was largely Slavic, divided roughly 60-to-40 percent Poles-to-Ukrainians, with a significant minority (12 percent) of Jews. West Galicia was overwhelmingly Polish while the East was heavily Ukrainian, though even there cities and towns were occupied mostly by Poles and Jews, while Ukrainians, with few exceptions, lived in urban areas mostly as the servant class. Galicia was desperately poor—the most impoverished of the Habsburg lands and perhaps the poorest in all of Europe. Despite the growth of an oil industry in southeast Galicia—by the early twentieth century, it made Austria the world's third-largest oil exporter, though lagging far behind America and Russia—this was practically the only industry in the province, and oil did little to create general prosperity.[16] As a result of this intractable poverty, emigration was a mass phenomenon, particularly to North America, in the decades before 1914, by Poles, Ukrainians, and Jews alike.

National rivalry between Poles and Ukrainians was the preeminent factor in Galician political life after 1867. While the Poles were not unreservedly happy with Habsburg rule, that was far preferable to the fate of their co-nationals abandoned to Prussia and Russia after Poland's disappearance from Europe's map at the end of the eighteenth century. While most Austrian Poles wanted to see their ancient country eventually reborn, life under the Habsburgs was far from uncongenial, particularly for the elites who were granted considerable political autonomy by Vienna. The Poles enjoyed a degree of independence in "their" province of Galicia that was not significantly less than what Budapest had, while the powerful "Polish club" in the Austrian parliament customarily played a kingmaker role, ensuring that the concerns of Galician elites always had an audience in Vienna.[17] The bureaucracy and the schools were firmly in Polish hands after 1867, and Ukrainians who received an education not infrequently emerged speaking Polish words and thinking Polish thoughts.

This was galling to the relatively few educated Ukrainians in Galicia who had aspirations to political life independent of their Polish overlords. Most Ukrainians were poor and illiterate, yet loyal to the Habsburgs. The primary vehicle for their national identity was the Greek Catholic Church, Eastern in rite yet subservient to Rome, which emerged in the nineteenth century as a specifically Ukrainian institution, indeed the only one of any note in Galicia. It was able to shield its flock from both the Poles, who were Roman Catholics, and the Russians, who were Orthodox (the Russians had a particular hatred for the Greek Catholics, whom they viewed as renegades from Orthodoxy, and sought to bring them "home," coercively if necessary); as such, the Greek Catholic Church occupied a position of far more than spiritual import in Galician life.[18]

However, the emergence of a Russophile tendency among Galician intellectuals in the nineteenth century caused alarm in Vienna, not least because it made inroads even among some Greek Catholic clergy. St. Petersburg employed means, both overt and clandestine, to support pro-Russian views in the province, with the Orthodox Church acting as the most important vehicle for propaganda and agitation. While most Ukrainians knew that life in Galicia, for all its grave problems, offered more political liberty than that enjoyed by their co-nationals living inside the Russian Empire in the last decades of peace, their long-standing reputation as the "Tyrolians of the East," pious and steadfastly loyal to the Habsburgs, seemed to be at risk.[19]

Galicia was home to a large portion of the Habsburg Army, with three army corps stationed in the province: I (Cracow), X (Przemyśl), and XI (Lemberg). Large garrisons were found all over Galicia, particularly in areas close to the Russian border. Cavalry and infantry patrols of the frontier were a regular sight in Galician villages, while major maneuvers brought out spectators in large numbers. The population's relationship with the military was ambivalent. The numerous barracks did bring funds into depressed areas, but as with armies everywhere much of the soldiers' money was spent on liquor and prostitutes. Nor were soldiers necessarily enamored with Galicia; many officers viewed an assignment there as a hardship, since outside a few cities, life offered little but gambling and the aforementioned alcohol and women as diversions. It was a place where many officers got into debt and trouble. Bemoaned as "our Siberia," a desolate land of poor villages, illiterate peasants, and medieval shtetls, Galicia was a posting that socially connected

Habsburg officers sought to avoid or at least to make their tours there as brief as possible. Nevertheless, some soldiers felt that duty in the province, where the Russian threat loomed as more than notional, offered opportunities to escape the boredom of normal barracks life, and the army, which was tolerant in matters of language and national identity, was viewed as "theirs" by Galician subjects in a way that Poles, Ukrainians, and Jews never looked at the Russian military.[20]

That Russian espionage and covert action were rising dramatically in Galicia in the run-up to the Great War was not the figment of overactive imaginations of worried counterspies in Vienna. For St. Petersburg, intelligence activities formed a critical component of its foreign policy, particularly in Galicia, where tsarist spymasters saw a potential fifth column against Austro-Hungarian rule in the form of Russophiles who, given proper incentive—often but not invariably financial—would secretly serve Russia. Habsburg counterintelligence saw unmistakable signs of increasing clandestine activities by Russian spies and sympathizers. They arrested four suspected Russian intelligence operatives in Galicia in 1908, seven the following year, seventeen in 1910, thirty-seven in 1912, and fifty-one in 1913, leading to major trials that exposed part of the spy network, which was both broad and deep, encompassing political activists, businessmen, students, Orthodox priests, even bureaucrats. The Russians were secretly funding clubs and newspapers to disseminate propaganda, often of a religious nature. The Russian Orthodox Church in particular served as a vehicle for espionage and subversion in Galicia and was considered by Habsburg security officials to be the linchpin of secret Russian activity in the province. That said, while the bulk of Galicians who were clandestinely serving St. Petersburg were Ukrainians of Orthodox affinity if not necessarily affiliation, there were many exceptions, including those whose motivations were pecuniary, among them Poles and Jews.[21]

The decade before 1914 witnessed a full-fledged spy war emerging in Galicia. Austro-Hungarian intelligence was increasingly active there too, not solely in counterespionage. Galicians of all nationalities judged reliable were on the payroll of military intelligence, monitoring Russian subversion, while Vienna's efforts at positive intelligence and subversion against Russia centered on the Poles. Its main vehicle was the Polish Socialist Party, which was vehemently anti-Russian, particularly its rabble-rousing leader, Józef Piłsudski, a firebrand revolutionary and whose hatred of tsarism knew no bounds. After years of underground life on the run inside Russia, Piłsudski settled in Galicia, choosing Cracow as his base of operations for the eventual liberation of Russian-occupied Poland. His first contacts with Austro-Hungarian intelligence dated to the Russo-Japanese War, which Piłsudski viewed as an opportunity to foment national as well as social revolution (he reached out to the Japanese for help as well); he had regular discussions with intelligence officers assigned to Cracow's I Corps. Beginning in early 1909, the General Staff's main espionage office in Vienna got involved, giving financial and logistical support to Piłsudski's plan to create cadres of trained revolutionaries for intelligence and diversionary missions inside Russia. This paramilitary-cum-espionage group was termed the Riflemen's Association (*Związek Strzelecki*), and by the time the war with Russia did arrive, which Piłsudski both predicted and welcomed, there were eight thousand trained Riflemen on hand to carry the war into Russia. Austria-Hungary's struggle and Poland's against the tsar would be complementary if not identical.[22]

Austria-Hungary would not survive that war, though by the struggle's end, Poland did reemerge on the map of Europe, just as Piłsudski had predicted. The fact that the Dual Monarchy succumbed in late 1918 and the Habsburgs lost their ancient empire dictates that the issue of inevitability cannot be avoided. Predestination is a matter for theologians, however, not historians. The issue remains complex and polemical even a century later. In economic matters, endemic Galician poverty aside, Austria-Hungary after the *Ausgleich* represented a more positive story of growth than was realized at the time. Although the Dual Monarchy ultimately failed, its collapse ought not be written farther back into the history books than is appropriate.[23] While the matter of Hungary was intractable as long as the Compromise of 1867 prevailed, other national struggles demonstrated visible signs of improvement in the decade before the Great War. The Moravian Compromise of 1905 pacified the bitter conflict between Germans and Czechs in that province, and in the long run might have proved a template for Bohemia too. Even in Galicia, on the eve of the war Ukrainians gained significant concessions from the Poles, particularly in education, that ameliorated the worst aspects of their national rivalry. In the end, Austria-Hungary was destroyed not by internal politics and nationalist passions, but by military defeat. Vienna effectively lost that war, the Habsburgs' last, at the very outset, thanks to poor preparation and military incompetence. That is the story you are about read.

2   The Most Powerful Pillar

Befitting Austria-Hungary's status as the most complicated state in Europe, it also boasted the most complicated military. The Habsburg Army was a unique force, an ancient institution bound to a dynasty, not a state. Comprised of men from all the nationalities of the Dual Monarchy, it was a jumble of languages, cultures, and confessions, and above all the guarantor of unity in a divided polity. Yet in the era of the nation-state it was an anachronism. In the years before the Great War, many observers, including more than a few of its own soldiers, questioned its viability in peacetime, and its potential durability in war.

Nevertheless, the army was "the most individual creation of the dynasty," as remembered by Oscar Jászi, a prominent Hungarian social scientist who lamented much about the Habsburg state and its army while they existed, but after their collapse in 1918 looked back with more admiration.[1] Like the dynasty it faithfully served, the military was bureaucratically complex and often unwieldy, marked by congenital inefficiencies that were the natural accompaniment to any institution made up of a dozen ethnic groups, countless dialects, and a half-dozen major religions. The army had its share of *Schlamperei*, a trademark Habsburg sort of slackness, and throughout its long history of more than a little red tape and mismanagement had gotten by on *fortwursteln* (muddling through), a sort of improvisational art to take the place of skilled leadership and proper strategy, which more often than not were lacking.

Certainly the history of Habsburg arms, despite much glory in the heady days of Prince Eugene in the early eighteenth century and his epic struggles against the Ottomans, left much to be desired in the next century for anyone seeking quick, decisive victories. Although Habsburg forces comprised the steady bulwark against Napoleon, resisting the Corsican and his revolutionary tide longer than anyone else, the actual performance of the military had been mixed during the generation-long Revolutionary Wars, demonstrating more determination than inspiration.[2] The same could be said of Habsburg military efforts throughout the nineteenth century. With the exception of the suppression of the revolutions of 1848–49, when forces in Italy, led by the energetic octogenarian Field Marshal Radetzky, decisively smashed the revolt and thereby saved the dynasty, other wars had ended in varying degrees of woe.[3] The 1859 campaign in Italy was a bloody defeat, despite bravery and grit, while the war against Prussia in 1866 constituted an unexpected thrashing from which the morale of Habsburg arms can be said to have never fully recovered.[4] Throughout his reign, Franz Joseph's wars had seldom ended successfully. The invasion of Bosnia-Hercegovina in 1878, a sort of colonial campaign waged in Europe, was a bright spot, but was really the suppression of a rebellion and could not be considered on a par with Aspern or Custozza. It was also the last time Habsburg forces had gone to war.[5]

For the army dynastic ideology made up for the ties of shared ethnicity or identity that bonded soldiers in most European states, but that in multinational Austria-Hungary were impossible. "Lacking all cohesive basis for a state," explained the General Staff chief succinctly in 1911, "the army can only rely on the dynastic principle."[6] The Habsburg cult witnessed its fullest embodiment in the military, where troops swore an oath to the emperor-king, not to any state or constitution, and the uniforms bore the insignia of a family. Soldiers marched under flags bearing the Habsburg double-eagle, and their caps bore the monogram FJI for *Franz Joseph Imperator*, the elderly monarch whose portrait hung in every barracks and officer's casino. On the eve of the Great War,

Franz Joseph had been on the throne for over sixty years, having already outpaced Queen Victoria's impressive reign; no Austro-Hungarian soldier on active duty had served another monarch.

Franz Joseph's affection for his army was legendary. Taking his role as first soldier of the monarchy seriously, he was seldom seen in anything but a uniform. He kept soldier's hours, rising at four in the morning and working long days at a simple army desk, going through stacks of correspondence wearing a cut-down army greatcoat, which served as the imperial robe in the drafty Hofburg palace. Franz Joseph had little interest in strategy or modern tactics, and he was positively averse to new technologies, civilian or military, but he was always interested in uniforms, parades, and old-fashioned field maneuvers—his much-noted eye for such matters being at the level of a career sergeant-major. He believed in the old virtues of order and discipline, and after so many military setbacks in the opening decades of his reign, Franz Joseph was against wars unless they were unquestionably necessary. Like many of his generals, he saw the army primarily as a domestic instrument—had it not saved his reign just as it started in 1848 by crushing rebellions in Hungary, Italy, and Bohemia?—only secondarily as an arm of foreign policy.[7] The army reciprocated Franz Joseph's affection with deep loyalty and a pride that those in uniform were the ultimate bulwark of Habsburg rule. Soldiers, officers especially, would have embraced Jászi's retrospective assessment that the army constituted "the most powerful pillar of the Habsburg fortification."[8]

The emphasis on dynastic devotion and the unified vision of the monarchy which that entailed was not just psychologically comforting for Habsburg soldiers, but a political necessity, since it compensated for the actual unity in military-political matters which was sorely lacking. Thanks to the 1867 *Ausgleich* with Hungary, the Dual Monarchy was unique in that it had not one army, but three: the joint or common army, plus nascent national armies for the Austrian (properly, Cisleithanian) and Hungarian halves of the monarchy. While the common force, the Imperial-and-Royal Army (*kaiserlich- und königliche*, henceforth *k.u.k. Armee*), was viewed by Habsburg patriots and the vast majority of officers as the "real" army, it looked different in Budapest, where so many things looked different, and for Hungary's political elite their own Home Guard, the *Honvéd*, was where their military interests resided.

The birth of national armies for Austria and Hungary was the result of the military aspects of the 1867 compromise that created Austria-Hungary. Indeed, military matters had played an outsized role in the difficult negotiations that gave birth to the Dual Monarchy. Budapest was eager to win as many concessions from Vienna as it could, especially in the symbolically important military sphere. Nothing less than "the future existence of the monarchy," according to War Minister Franz Kuhn, depended on "a successful solution of the army question."[9] Yet most officers disliked the compromise that was reached in 1868, which in exchange for Budapest's acceptance of peacetime conscription and maintaining German as the language of the joint force, created a small Hungarian national army. It would carry national colors and use Magyar as the language of command and service, plus bearing the title, *Honvédség*, and wearing more or less the uniforms of the revolutionary army of 1848, which the Habsburg military had fought hard to defeat. The agreement provided for two national war ministries in Budapest and Vienna as subordinates to the joint ministry as well as requisite national staffs and schools. From 1872, the *Honvéd* had its own military academy, the Ludovika in Budapest, to train officers for the force.[10]

As created, the *Honvéd* was very much a second-line army, with small active-duty cadres. To the *k.u.k. Armee*, it was an also-ran, something to be tolerated, and for decades it barely featured in war plans. The Austrian half of the monarchy gave scant thought to its national army in waiting, the *Landwehr*, and showed little interest in increasing its size or armaments. The ruling elite in Budapest, however, considered the *Honvéd* a point of national pride and the embryo of a future Hungarian army fully equipped for war. Parliamentarians in Hungary consistently showed more interest in funding "their" army than the joint forces. Consisting initially only of infantry and cavalry, and with no units larger than a brigade, the *Honvéd* lacked heavy armaments, above all artillery, and no one in Vienna wanted to give it heavy guns. Almost from the establishment of the *Honvéd*, Budapest agitated for artillery, a political campaign that irritated the *k.u.k. Armee*, poisoned the already choppy waters between the two capitals, and took decades to pay off; beginning in 1907, the *Honvéd* was permitted artillery units, raising eight field artillery regiments and a battalion of horse artillery, making it closer to a first-line army.[11] The *Landwehr* slowly began adding its own artillery battalions to maintain the all-important appearance of symmetry. By the eve of the Great War, the *Landwehr* and *Honvéd* supplied a total of eighteen combined-arms divisions—eight infantry divisions for the former and eight infantry plus two cavalry divisions for the latter—to Austria-Hungary's order of battle. These second-line armies had grown into something larger, more powerful, and more politically complicated than anyone had imagined when the compromise was reached in 1868. Right down to the fall of Austria-Hungary, the three-part army constituted the major liability of the *Ausgleich*, rendering military matters "the Achilles' heel of the dualistic system," in the words of Gunther Rothenberg.[12]

Adding to the complexity of it all, the military compromise of 1868 included a series of reforms involving Croatia and its relationship to both Budapest and Vienna. Hungary had long advocated the elimination of the Military Border, a unique organization that for centuries had guarded the monarchy's volatile southern frontier from Ottoman raids, employing farmer-warriors in an almost Cossack fashion, but that by the second half of the nineteenth century was an anachronism. Nevertheless, many Croats, both Catholic and Orthodox, had a strong attachment to their *graničari*, as well as suspicions regarding Hungarian intentions. Budapest indeed wanted to gain power over the Military Border, which was ruled directly by the joint army, and therefore beyond its grasp.[13] Croatian nationalists opposed any concessions to Budapest, and the announcement in 1869 that the Military Border would be disbanded was met with anger, and even a small revolt in October 1871 that had to be put down with force, although it was more anti-Hungarian than anti-Habsburg in character.[14] The actual disestablishment of the Military Border took over a decade, with the control of the frontier returning to civil authorities, and joint army regiments raised from the historic *graničari* forces. As a concession to Zagreb, elements of the *Honvéd* recruited in Croatia were titled the *Domobranstvo* (Home Guard in Croatian), were commanded in their own language, and marched under Croatian colors; by 1914 they constituted a single infantry division plus a hussar regiment.[15]

However, the military reforms of 1868, rather than resolving tensions between Vienna and Budapest, merely added another venue for endless argumentation over army matters. Some of the debates seemed symbolic yet had important implications. Hungarian agitation made certain that the joint forces were referred to as Imperial-and-Royal, not merely Imperial-Royal as had been the custom, since that critical conjunction matched with Hungary's vision of two separate states united by one monarch. Similar Magyar logic required the alteration of the joint war ministry's title from *Reichskriegsministerium* to merely *k.u.k.* in 1911, since the original name implied there was a unified Reich, a position no Hungarian patriot would countenance. Debates inevitably followed about the color of official twine—black-yellow for Habsburg or red-white-green for Hungary?—used to bind military paperwork.

Yet behind such silliness lay the critical issue of what actually did bind Vienna and Budapest in military affairs after 1867. While the creation of the *Honvéd* was expected by most officers and politicians in Vienna to have resolved Hungary's demands in the military sphere, from Budapest's viewpoint that was only a starting point. What Hungary's ruling elite wanted was a full-fledged national army based on the *Honvéd*, the heir of the revolutionary tradition of 1848, which was something that few Habsburg loyalists, and hardly any in uniform, would tolerate. The result was decades of political debating, browbeating, and deadlock, all at the expense of military strength and readiness.

The military aspects of the dualist system required renewal every ten years, with approval from both national parliaments, so once a decade at least Budapest collided head on with Vienna's requests for more military funds with a list of nationalist demands of their own.

By the beginning of the twentieth century, it was apparent that political gamesmanship between Vienna and Budapest, and the resulting roadblocks, had real costs for the army, particularly as Europe increasingly girded for war. As friends and adversaries alike increased military budgets and raised conscript calls, Austria-Hungary kept the 1889 law on the books, which annually brought 103,100 conscripts to the joint army, 19,970 to the *Landwehr*, and 12,500 to the *Honvéd*. Because of perennial budget shortfalls, many conscripts were released from service after two years, rather than the mandated three, while reservist training was rare, and for the third-line militia (*Landsturm*), essentially nonexistent. Men who avoided active duty by serving in the *Ersatzreserve*, who were supposed to receive regular refresher training, received none.[16] The joint War Ministry understood the readiness implications of all this, but Budapest blocked efforts to increase the annual conscript levy. A request in 1898 for a small increase in the call-up, to bring units to intended peacetime strength, encountered over seven years of Hungarian obstructions. Only in 1907 did Budapest give its assent to this, a boost of just 23,000 to the annual conscript numbers.[17]

More serious was the political confrontation beginning in 1903 and lasting three years, when the joint War Ministry requested Budapest's approval to raise both military spending and conscription levels above the 1889 levels. As usual parliamentarians responded with a range of theatrics and technical obstructions, even though there was agreement among the major parties in Budapest that the increases were necessary on security grounds. Nevertheless, in exchange for more men and money for the military, Hungary demanded a wide range of sops to nationalist sentiments, including more use of Magyar in the joint army, national symbols for *k.u.k. Armee* units recruited in Hungary, plus transforming the *Honvéd* into a first-line force complete with artillery.[18] Bolstering Hungary's pet army was something the generals in Vienna could live with, but anything that threatened the symbolic unity of the joint forces was another matter. Similarly, while Franz Joseph was customarily tolerant of Hungary's "political nation" and its perquisites, he was no more willing to Magyarize the *k.u.k. Armee* than his top generals were.

Efforts during the winter of 1903 to enact a military reform bill in Budapest met with political turmoil, then crisis; by the summer the Hungarian coalition government had fallen, and Viennese whispers had it that the army was readying to take matters into its own hands to break the deadlock. As the crisis dragged on without resolution, the General Staff indeed commenced planning an invasion of Hungary, a massive operation by eight corps of loyal *k.u.k.* troops, as a solution to the perennial crisis in Budapest, but Franz Joseph considered this plan a truly last resort.[19] In September 1903, the emperor issued an order while observing maneuvers at Chłopy in Galicia, where he issued an edict, aimed at Budapest, clarifying his position as supreme war lord and the role of the military in the Dual Monarchy: "My Army shall remain as it is: common and united." This raised ire in Hungary but assured the army of his position, age notwithstanding, and signaled to other nationalities that Budapest could not simply get whatever it wanted.[20] Franz Joseph, backed by top generals, then took the offensive, threatening to bring universal suffrage to Hungary, which terrified its ruling magnates into an eventual compromise. Months went by, but Budapest in the end agreed to leave the *k.u.k. Armee* as a joint institution without an explicitly Hungarian character—since, as the emperor made clear at Chłopy, the army belonged to all his peoples, not any particular one of them—in exchange for a small increase in the conscript levy and artillery for the *Honvéd*, which from 1907 would be recognized as a first-line force. The joint army was left without the major boost in men and money it wanted, while Vienna was left sufficiently shaken by the crisis that it would not be until 1911 that the joint War Ministry would again propose serious revisions to the 1889 law.[21]

While Hungary played politics, the rest of Europe armed, and the Dual Monarchy's military position was eroding rapidly. Between 1907 and 1910, France conscripted 0.63 percent of its population annually, while Germany called up 0.46 percent, and Russia and Italy, the Dual Monarchy's major rivals, conscripted 0.40 and 0.41 percent each; Austria-Hungary called only 0.29 percent to the colors annually, and considering that as much as 30 percent of conscripts were dispatched to the *Ersatzreserve*, where they saw no active service, only one Habsburg man in eight received serious military training.[22] Thus while the population of Austria-Hungary ballooned from forty million in 1890 to fifty-two million in 1910, the conscript levy hardly increased. The result was a force of too few active units, with low peacetime strengths, backed by a reserve that was likewise small and significantly lacking in skills and readiness.[23]

The budgetary predicament, with spending frozen at 1889 levels, was just as parlous. Austria-Hungary's military budget for 1911 came to 420 million crowns, while Germany's was the equivalent of 1.79 billion, Russia's was 1.65 billion, and even Italy spent 528 million.[24] In 1903, Habsburg subjects spent three times as much on beer, wine, and tobacco as they did on national defense, and a decade later that ratio had not changed much. Between 1908 and 1912, the overall military budget increased slightly, but that was mostly absorbed by the cost of new ships, as the navy's outlay more than doubled while the army's stayed close to stable.[25] Officers were frustrated as the army stagnated while rivals armed. When asked about Austria-Hungary's participation in The Hague disarmament conference of 1907, General Staff chief Gen. Franz Conrad von Hötzendorf replied that "the present condition of our army already has an appearance of a permanent limitation of armament." His churlish remark echoed a common sentiment.[26]

Mounting crises close to Austria-Hungary overcame the resistance in Budapest as nothing else could. Hungary's leaders watched their southern border quake with wars and rumors of wars. The Bosnian Crisis of 1908–9 raised awareness of how unstable the region had become, but it was the Balkan Wars of 1912–13 that created an enlarged, triumphant, and aggressive Serbia, and finally opened up the state's coffers for the military. In June 1912, a new army bill passed through Budapest and was quickly endorsed by Vienna. This at last boosted conscription significantly, with a rise of 42,000 to bring the annual call-up to 181,000: 136,000 for the joint army plus 20,715 for the *Landwehr* and 17,500 for the *Honvéd*. This was conceived as the first in a three-stage personnel increase that would result in a call-up of 236,000 annually by 1918, backed by trained primary reserves of 450,000 by 1924.[27]

Military spending rose concomitantly, particularly in weapons procurement. Counting the costs of the partial mobilization during the Balkan Wars, an emergency allocation of 250 million crowns, increased spending during 1912–13 came to 123 percent. Included in the 1912 defense bill were provisions for the allocation of all labor, goods, and services to the state in time of war. The only concessions made by the joint War Ministry to obtain these long-desired goals were a curtailing of conscript service from three years to two—the admission of a long-standing reality—and the recognition of the *Landwehr* and *Honvéd* as co-equals in the Dual Monarchy's first line of defense.[28]

Although political elites eventually found their courage, after more than a generation lost, change came too late to make the Habsburg military ready for war. Although Austria-Hungary conscripted a record 227,000 soldiers in the last year of peace—amounting to almost 167,000 for the joint army versus 25,000 each for the *Landwehr* and *Honvéd*—leading to an active force of 414,000, this had little impact on overall strength, counting reserves.[29] The results of years of underfunding were soon apparent. In August 1914, when Vienna mobilized all classes of reservists, it fielded a force of 2,265,000 (of which only 1.4 million were fully trained)—yet that same month France, with a population ten million smaller than Austria-Hungary, was able to mobilize an army of four million.[30] On the eve of the war, the Dual Monarchy was the third-largest European state by population, behind only Russia and Germany, but its military spending ranked as the lowest of any major power: a mere quarter of what Russia or Germany spent, a third of Britain's defense outlays, and even less than Italy.[31]

The Austro-Hungarian military would pay a terrible price in blood in the summer of 1914 for decades of underfunding. A generation of officers had come of age knowing nothing but austerity while rivals armed. This was the result of endless and ultimately pointless political gamesmanship, especially in Budapest, where the elites were willing to sacrifice all, including military readiness, on the altar of nationalism; and in 1912, when Hungary's political class at last realized the extent of the danger and began to meaningfully cooperate with the army, it was a case of too little, too late. Norman Stone's acid observation, "The weakness of the Habsburg Army in 1914 stemmed not from the disaffection of its soldiers but from the intransigence of politicians in Hungary," seems essentially correct, notwithstanding that many generals would later excuse their failures in battle with similar statements.[32] While the flawed concepts—strategic, operational, and tactical—of Habsburg generals at the outset of the Great War were bad enough on their own, as the following chapter will elaborate, the congenital defects of the dualist system when it came to military matters meant that it is questionable whether Austro-Hungarian arms ever truly had a chance to prepare themselves for the war they encountered in 1914. Alan Sked's assessment that the Habsburg Army on the eve of that fateful conflict was "badly equipped, under-financed, technologically backward but splendidly uniformed" appears more right than wrong.[33] Politicians, above all in Budapest, precluded any different outcome. Hungarian elites in the decades after the *Ausgleich* desired a joint army that was undermanned and underfunded, which would pose a diminishing threat to Hungary's ambitions inside the Dual Monarchy. They got what they wanted—and more.

Funding shortfalls aside, Austro-Hungarian forces were undoubtedly among the best turned out in Europe, with colorful uniforms across the arms. Infantry regiments each had a unique combination of facing colors and buttons to distinguish them, and those raised in

Hungary had their distinctive cuff decoration, the "bear's paw," plus tight, embroidered trousers. Rifle (*Jäger*) battalions had a unique gray uniform complete with bowler hats accoutered with cock feathers, while the Bosnian infantry wore Turkish-inspired uniforms complete with tight trousers and fez. *Honvéd* troops had a uniform based on the national costume, as did all hussar regiments. Similarly, lancers wore Polish-inspired kit, while dragoons were splendidly outfitted with outsized shiny helmets. Considering that the army's mission included a significant domestic component—what strikers or rioters would not be impressed, and perhaps cowed, by the appearance of a squadron of mounted cavalry adorned in bright red and deep blue?—such attention to colors made sense, not least as a bolster to troop morale. No soldier has ever felt badly about looking sharp. Whether such dandyism made sense in the face of modern weapons was another question altogether.

Eye-catching uniforms aside, what foreign observers never failed to notice about the Habsburg Army was the astonishing array of ethnicities, languages, religions, and cultures found there. With the imposition of conscription in 1868 on the Prussian model, the army was a faithful representation of Austria-Hungary in all of its breathtaking diversity of tribe and tongue. For every hundred soldiers in the *k.u.k. Armee*, there were twenty-five Germans, twenty-three Magyars, thirteen Czechs, nine Serbs or Croats, eight Poles and Ukrainians each, seven Romanians, four Slovaks, two Slovenes, and one Italian.[34] These were also the "national languages" recognized by the army.

Because the army after 1868 recruited on a regional basis, units took on distinct ethnic characters. Vienna's famed Fourth Infantry Regiment was almost entirely German, while Prague's Twenty-eighth was almost entirely Czech; Trieste's Ninety-seventh was a mix of Slovenes, Croats, and Italians; but Temesvár's Sixty-first was almost evenly divided between Romanians and Germans, with a strong admixture of Magyars and Serbs. To accommodate this linguistic diversity, the army enforced a policy of requiring German for basic functioning and the troops' own tongues for almost everything else. In all units of the joint army and *Landwehr*, German was the language of command (*Kommandosprache*), consisting of some eighty parade-ground phrases, as well as the language of service (*Dienstsprache*), about a thousand terms, mainly technical, so for instance a gun captain could command an polyglot artillery crew since all soldiers knew the German words for breech, shell, load, fire, and so on. The most important tongue, however, was the regimental language (*Regimentssprache*), the unit's vernacular. Any language spoken by at least 20 percent of a unit's men was accorded this official status, and officers were required to establish proficiency as proven by exams. Given the army's diversity, many units had more than one regimental language, and some had several. Throughout the army, 142 units had a single *Regimentssprache* while 163 had two, twenty-four had three, and several had four or even five. Of the 102 line infantry regiments of the *k.u.k. Armee*, only 15 were considered "race pure" (*reinrassig*), deriving 90 percent or more of their troops from a single ethnic group. Nineteen *Landwehr* regiments had a single *Regimentssprache* while forty-four had two and one boasted three of them. In the Fifth Dragoons, composed of half Slovenes and half a mixture of several ethnicities, the regimental doctor routinely conducted exams in seven languages.[35]

Hungary's *Honvéd* adopted a distinctly different language policy from the rest of Habsburg forces, employing Magyar for all purposes. While this was in keeping with Budapest's general policy of using all state organs as engines of Magyarization, this policy was unpopular with many of Hungary's minorities, most of whom preferred to serve in the more tolerant joint army over service in the monolingual *Honvéd*. Befitting their status as Hungary's most disaffected minority, Romanians in particular found service in the *Honvéd* nationally onerous yet had few complaints about their treatment in the *k.u.k. Armee*.[36] Similarly, *Domobranstvo* units employed Croatian for all purposes, though this was less of an irritant as Croatia had few minorities who did not speak Croatian, or the closely related Serbian language.

Having such polyglot forces brought endless possibilities for com-plications, offense, and sometimes dark humor. Misunderstandings were commonplace, though the system functioned well enough in peacetime. Sergeants, usually of the same ethnicity as the rank and file, functioned as translators for officers who had trouble communicating, but there were never enough long-service noncommissioned officers (NCOs) to go around. Educated and literate soldiers willing and able to be effective sergeants were in short supply, and the prewar army averaged only three career NCOs per company, compared to a dozen in the German military (versus six in the French Army, three in the Italian, and but two in the Russian).[37] To compensate, officers who lacked the gift for languages got by with various pidgins, most famously "Army Slavic," an ungainly mélange with Czech predominating that was alleged to work well enough on troops from all the army's seven Slavic ethnic groups.[38]

Fortunately for military effectiveness, the Habsburg Army, save the *Honvéd*, dealt with ethnolinguistic matters in a generally tactful man-ner, and the friction caused by miscommunication was manageable in peacetime. The dominance of German reflected historic practice and the need to have a unifying language—not prejudice. Even critics on the left praised the army's "delicate and tactful handling" of touchy matters such as ethnicity and language, which proved so deleterious in civil society, where nationalist backbiting was far from uncommon, and in politics constituted the norm.[39] While the peacetime army coped well enough with its diversity, possibilities for misunderstand-ing were ubiquitous, particularly where ethnic frictions preexisted. In a typical case, a newly raised *Landwehr* artillery battalion in 1909 which had a mix of Germans and Czechs, plus a minority of Slovenes, tried to improve the unit's morale and effectiveness by making Czech a regimental language. But this was not particularly necessary since most of the Czechs knew German already, as the artillery generally got better educated conscripts, and instead the gesture offended the battalion's Slovenes, who felt unfairly left out.[40]

There was a certain ethnic division of labor in the army. While the infantry recruited from across the empire, the prestigious rifle (*Jäger*) battalions were disproportionately German, and the famed *Kaiserjäger* recruited exclusively from the Tyrol and Vorarlberg, and constituted the army's *corps d'élite* (anomalously, Habsburg forces had no guards regiments). Yet the four regiments of *Kaiserjäger*, which averaged about 60 percent Germans and 40 percent Italians, took men from across the Tyrol, not a particular district, to ensure no regiment became too Italian.[41] A newer elite, the army's four infantry regiments from Bosnia and Hercegovina, were a jumble of Croats, Serbs, and Muslims, like their homeland; despite their youth—they had only been raised by Vienna after the conquest of the provinces by the *k.u.k. Armee* in 1878— and far from infrequent problems among the different ethnoreligious groups in their ranks, the *Bosniaken* regiments would win a reputation second to none in the Great War.[42] Dragoons were mostly Czech and German, while lancers recruited in Galicia and were heavily Poles and Ukrainians (though two regiments recruited in Croatia), while hussars came exclusively from Hungary.

Jobs requiring better educated soldiers were filled disproportionately by Germans and Czechs, reflecting that ethnicity was far from the only dividing line in the military. While western parts of the Dual Monarchy were as well educated and developed as anywhere in Western Europe, regions to the south and east of the Habsburg domains reflected far lower levels of social progress. Some recruits seemed to emerge from an earlier age "utterly alien to the world of discipline, timetable, and hygiene," and conscripts unable to tell right from left were encountered frequently.[43] On the eve of the Great War, just 3 percent of the population around Vienna was illiterate, while among Ukrainians in Galicia the rate was 61 percent, and among Croats and Serbs from Dalmatia the rate was three points higher still. A popular army joke had it that Ukrainian peasants made the best infantry but first needed three years to become human, then another five to master being a soldier.[44] Many were the officers who discovered that training methods that worked effectively with recruits from Vienna or Prague got nowhere with conscripts from the Balkans, Transylvania, or Galicia.

Religion was another marker of identity that the Austro-Hungarian military did its best to accommodate as well as employ as an engine of cohesion. To counter the Dual Monarchy's remarkable ethnic diversity, there was at least more unity in faith, and some 77 percent of the population consisted of adherents of the Church of Rome. As the army of the last Catholic great power and the final remnant of the Holy Roman Empire, Habsburg forces relied heavily on Catholic rituals and beliefs to bolster spirits and loyalties. Field mass was an indelible part of the army experience, and chaplains regularly gave sermons hailing "Emperor, King, Fatherland," a message that, given its frequent incantation, cannot have failed to make an impression.[45] Certainly the pious peasantry who made up much of Franz Joseph's infantry during their army service entered a world where matters of faith and dynastic loyalty were inextricably linked. Yet other religions were more than tolerated. There were chaplains for all soldiers—priests for Orthodox, pastors for Protestants, rabbis for Jews, even imams for Muslims—all of them preaching a gospel of loyalty unto death to the Habsburg throne.

Supplementing religious piety were regular doses of unit pride. "Regimental ideology," though more commonly associated with long-service professional armies, played a major part in building morale. Each regiment had its own flag, its own traditions and uniforms, its own special days, and its own honorary colonel (*Inhaber*), a legacy of the time when commanders owned their units. These prestigious posts were held by senior generals, royal personages (sometimes foreign), in a few cases by long-dead greats who were named *Inhaber* in perpetuity.[46] The Habsburg Army's notion of *esprit de corps* was expressed in the 1807 field regulations as consisting of "The confidence of a regiment in its capabilities, pride in its tradition, and the determination to safeguard its reputation." It was the same a century later.[47] Lacking ethnic cohesion, the army relied on religion, regimental ideology, and overarching dynastic devotion.

How average soldiers reacted to this can be difficult to assess a century and more later, though it is clear that peacetime conscription after 1868 created a new Habsburg military, and tensions along lines of ethnicity and identity that permeated civilian life could not be kept out of the army.[48] Bad blood in the barracks was far from unknown, especially in ethnically mixed units recruited from regions where tensions were high (for example, between Germans and Czechs in Bohemia, between Magyars and Romanians in Transylvania), but it is important to note that after 1918 nationalists of all stripes had incentives to magnify incidents of anti-Habsburg agitation as alleged precursors of independence. In the decades before the Great War, the Austro-Hungarian military suffered from few notable problems grounded solely in ethnicity. Brawls were commonplace, but they are in all barracks, and it is difficult to ascertain how these were grounded in ethnicity, rather than the normal tensions involved when large numbers of young men are placed in tight quarters. While ethnic tensions certainly existed, evidence for ethnic violence is mostly absent before 1914. Instead, commentators at the time were struck by the army's high suicide rate, but that must be viewed in a broad Danubian pattern of heightened suicide and appears not to have been specific to the military.[49] Following a common pattern, young men did their time with the colors, complained about it—though in Austria-Hungary it was not especially difficult to get out of military service if one wanted to—and in later years considered it to have been a positive experience. Not to mention that for many peasants, army service represented their first, and often last, experience outside their native village, the source of stories to last a lifetime.

One of the important by-products of peacetime conscription after 1868 was the creation of large groups of veterans who liked to reminisce about their service together. As in most European countries at the time, veterans formed clubs, some of which grew to impressive size, and in time they constituted a political factor that mattered, especially at the local level. While Austria-Hungary lacked veterans' groups with the clout found in Imperial Germany, such societies played an important part in inculcating dynastic patriotism, playing roles in patriotic parades and commemorations. By 1912, there were 2,250 such clubs in the Austrian half of the monarchy alone, with several hundred thousand members, and that may be an understatement. Even in regions where *schwarz-gelb* ("black-yellow" for the dynasty's colors) loyalty was challenged by rising nationalism, veterans' clubs served as an important symbol of imperial unity in towns and villages across the Dual Monarchy, showing the flag and demonstrating the power of loyalism, regardless of ethnicity.[50]

Recent research into the role of veterans' groups in Austria-Hungary demonstrates that traditional views of loyalty, emphasizing soldiers who were *kaisertreue* (loyal to the emperor) on one side versus ardent nationalists on the other, are far too simple. In practice, moderate nationalism coexisted alongside dynastic loyalty, even in the military, and more than a few soldiers played the role of "amphibians": loyal to nation and monarch simultaneously, though their views would have been considered somewhat insufficient by both sides. "Despite the unrelenting efforts of nationalists," concluded a recent study of veterans, "there was apparently still more than enough room in Imperial Austrian society and its institutions for national indifference, bilingualism, Austrian patriotism, dynastic loyalty, and similar practices."[51] Yet maneuver room for moderate nationalism in the military context could be limited, and veterans' groups frequently walked a fine line under the watchful eye of the army, whose officers defined acceptable displays of patriotism. A revealing incident came in September 1908, when riots in Laibach (Ljubljana) left two Slovenes dead, shot by the army. This stoked the fires of Slovenian nationalism, and a prominent veterans' group raised funds for their dead and wounded countrymen. Additionally, the group voted to change its language of command from German to Slovene. That the army would not tolerate, perceiving a direct attack on the unity of the forces, and the commander of the local III Corps, Gen. Oskar Potiorek, ordered the group disbanded at once, with the support of the civil authorities, citing "treacherous articles" in a liberal newspaper that the army believed had influenced the veterans. Veterans groups took part in the struggle over identity in the late Dual Monarchy, often seeming too nationalist for the army yet too dynastic for the comfort of nationalists.[52]

Rising nationalism was not a figment of the officer corps' imagination, oversensitivities notwithstanding, and incidents that deeply troubled the army mounted in the years before the Great War, mainly involving Czechs, who had not failed to notice that nationalist antics worked for Hungary. It began in 1897, when reservists of Twenty-eighth Regiment, the famed *Pražské děti* (Prague's Children), refused to call out *hier* (here) on the parade ground, opting for *zde*, in their own language. Challenges to the army and its Germanic character started small but grew, and by 1905 Czech nationalists were protesting with signs stating, THE ARMY IS THE GRAVE OF OUR YOUTH, THE PRISON OF OUR FREEDOM.[53] Such sentiments could not be isolated from the ranks for long, and there were several troubling incidents during the partial mobilization of autumn 1908 during the Bosnian Crisis. Czech reservists showed open sympathy for Serbia, carrying black flags and shouting Serbian slogans; the all-Czech *k.u.k.* Thirty-sixth Regiment was so bumptious that the army declared a mutiny and rounded up miscreants for court-martial.[54] Things got worse during the 1912–13 preventative mobilization during the Balkan Wars, when numerous Czech units reported disturbances. These ranged from the singing of "anti-military" songs, nationalist and socialist, to outright disobedience. Reservists of two Czech cavalry regiments refused to board trains and had to be forced on like cattle, at bayonet-point. The Thirty-sixth Regiment was again a source of nationalist commotion, as was the heavily Czech Eighteenth. The army made its point by court-martialing troublemakers, though few heavy sentences were handed down.[55] The General Staff considered removing Czech regiments from their home districts, to prevent further "contamination" by civilian agitators, but ultimately demurred.

On the eve of the Great War, it was widely accepted among senior officers that nationalism had infected the ranks, and that in the event of war many Slavic soldiers—Czechs above all but there were doubts too about Serbs and Ukrainians—would refuse to follow orders; large-scale mutinies were anticipated. In 1911, the commander of XI Corps in eastern Galicia reported, "as matters now stand, the entire Ukrainian population must be considered unreliable." Fears about the "internal enemy" were pervasive among the generals, and not confined to Slavs. During the Bosnian Crisis, the commander in Trieste explained that, in the event of war with Serbia, Habsburg Italians would stage an armed revolt.[56] Such pessimism was a complex phenomenon, grounded in a deep distaste among Habsburg officers for ethnic nationalism, not to mention an inability to distinguish between moderate and disloyal national sentiments, yet in the years before 1914 it grew into a genuine *déformation professionelle* for many officers, influencing minds and policies. The 1907 book *Unser letzter Kampf* (Our final struggle), written anonymously by General Staff officer Hugo Kerchnawe and part of a European trend of best-sellers foretelling future war, prognosticated doom for the Dual Monarchy, beset by foes on all sides and crippled from within by nationalism and disloyalty. Kerchnawe's views were typical of many Habsburg officers, who in the last decade of peace saw mounting threats on every front, including inside the state and even in the ranks of the army.[57]

The views of the officer corps held particular importance, and not just in the military, as the Habsburg officer occupied a unique place, as the ultimate guarantor of the dynasty and its institutions. As the officer corps proved in 1848, it alone was unshakably loyal, and led by Field Marshal Radetzky had saved the dynasty and the state. Down to the collapse of the Habsburg edifice in late 1918, the Radetzkyean cult imbued the officer corps in story and song, and the old *Vater*, who conveniently was of Czech origin too, was the model of an officer, loyal unto death not to a nation or even a state, but rather "patriots for me" in the formulation of old Emperor Franz.[58] In no European army did the officer corps occupy such an exalted place in the imperial identity as in Austria-Hungary, and fatefully, in the run-up to the Great War, in no other European state did senior officers have such a powerful role in determining policies of war and peace.

This special position was both the product and cause of the officer corps' sense of identity in the Dual Monarchy. Career officers were not particularly representative of the diversity of Austria-Hungary, being overwhelmingly German, but the issue of their actual identity is difficult for postmoderns, accustomed to the centrality of ethnicity, to unravel. At a distance, the dominance of Germans in the professional officer corps appears daunting, with 79 percent claiming German as their primary language—though only a quarter of the monarchy's population consisted of Germans—the next biggest groups, far behind, being Magyars at 9 percent and Czechs at a mere 5.[59] Yet many of those officers functioned in a German-speaking world but were not necessarily German by ethnicity. They lived in the world of *ärarisch deutsch*, the rootless language of the Habsburg bureaucracy, and many had grown up in it, as the sons of soldiers—including many sons of junior officers and NCOs—and knew no other reality than the anational existence of Habsburg garrison towns experienced by "knapsack kids" (*Tornisterkinder*). It is significant that an officer's personnel file (*Qualifikationsliste*), which included voluminous details about education, service, health, even personal lives, made no mention anywhere of an officer's nationality. Often modern questions about ethnicity evade a firm answer. The case of August von Urbański, a General Staff officer who rose to major command in the Great War, is illustrative: born to a Polish father, a career officer, and a Dalmatian mother, he grew up all over the Dual Monarchy, marrying into a Romanian family and speaking several languages fluently, yet considered German to be his first tongue.[60] For such officers, questions of personal ethnicity seldom came up, and their sense of identity was rooted in the dynasty and the army, not any particular nation.

Indeed, among career officers nationalism of any sort was considered bad form at best, traitorous at worst. Anything that smacked of modernity was eschewed, and overt nationalism in all forms was considered contemptible, while officers viewed themselves as the last bastion of old values that were under mounting threat in the civilian world. The more that nationalism, socialism, and threatening ideas took hold outside the army, the more that career officers clung tightly to resistance, "black-yellow in their bones, dynastic to the point of excess."[61] That the officer's mentality was increasingly at odds with the values of the wider world did not concern careerists, who ignored changes when they could, and denounced them when they could not. The idealized vision of the Habsburg officer was captured in 1900 in a newspaper that catered to them:

> There are no nationalities, no racial differences, and no religious disputes in the Imperial Army. In one rank Germans, Slavs and Hungarians stand together as brothers, in the other Catholics, Jews, Orthodox, Protestants, and Muslims raise their hands in prayer and an oath of loyalty to Emperor and Fatherland, ready to march together when ordered unto death, with the blood of Christians and Jews, of Germans and Slavs, flowing together on the battlefield, building a great stream, and after falling as one for Emperor and *Reich*, resting in peace side-by-side, regardless of race or religion, until they are all called to a better life with the Almighty, where there is no more racial inequality, no more anti-Semitism, and no more religious strife.[62]

Officers were able to maintain such idealized visions since their careers set them considerably apart from the civilian world, which was viewed with a cultivated distaste. Many entered the barracks as young teenagers, as cadet schools were the dominant commissioning source. Although the army's two joint military academies, the Theresian at Wiener Neustadt (for infantry and cavalry) and the Technical Academy at Vienna (for artillery and engineers), offered a prestigious route into the officer corps, which conferred career advantages, they only graduated 250 new lieutenants annually. In addition, however, the nineteen cadet schools gave the army a thousand ensigns every year, who after completing a four-year cadet program followed by two years of probationary line service, received their lieutenancies.[63]

There was considerable flux in the social background of career officers in the late Habsburg Monarchy. The Austro-Hungarian aristocracy, itself in a period of transformation after 1867, had once given the army most of its generals, but increasingly sent its sons elsewhere.[64] Professionalization of officer education after the Austro-Prussian War debacle of 1866 opened opportunities to the middle class and their lessers, and the aristocracy gradually lost interest. In 1896, of 15,580 regular officers, only 3,534 were nobles of any sort, with 1,374 being *vons*, the lowest rung and probably the sons of officer who were ennobled at the end of a long career, and the percentage of nobles continued to drop steadily down to the Great War. None of the ten chiefs of the General Staff from the *Ausgleich* to the fall of the Dual Monarchy was a member of anything but the service nobility (*Dienstadel*): none were actual aristocrats, while only one of the dozen war ministers after 1867 was. During the period, fully 89 percent of General Staff officers came from the middle or lower-middle classes—in the middle of the nineteenth century only 10 percent did—while by 1918 so did three-quarters of the army's general officers.[65] Even the *arme blanche*, the traditional preserve of the nobility, was leveling, and of the forty-two cavalry regiments in 1914, only nine were commanded by bona fide aristocrats.[66] On the other end of the social spectrum, the requirement for more formal education for officer cadets after 1868 meant that commissioning from the ranks, which had been commonplace for long-service NCOs who had distinguished themselves in battle, essentially ended. For promising enlisted men without secondary education there were hardly any possibilities to win an officer's saber, a development that enhanced social stratification in the army and would have important effects during the Great War.

The retreat of aristocrats from the professional officer corps, coupled with the fact that many officers had social backgrounds nearly as modest as their men, had unintended consequences on relationships in the army. Moritz von Auffenberg, a top general who served as joint war minister in 1911–12, decried the increasing proletarianization of the officer corps; like many senior officers, he viewed socialist propaganda as even more dangerous than nationalism. Auffenberg's solution, never implemented, was to get boys into cadet school as young as possible, and to shield them from family and social circles in an army cocoon to stave off negative influences.[67] To compensate for a lack of social standing, would-be officers were instructed to maintain a strong distance from the men at all times; this essentially artificial prestige was puzzling to some, irritating to others. Otto Bauer, a socialist politician who was a reserve officer in the Great War, noted of his prewar training how his commanding officer warned the class to strictly separate themselves from the men at all times: "The NCOs are peasants; an educated person has no social contact with a peasant. If I should learn that one of you talks to an NCO outside of military duty, shakes hands with him or even joins him in the pub, he will lose eligibility to become an officer!"[68] While such efforts to maintain class differences were tenable in peacetime, when war came they would collapse.

A special place was occupied by reserve officers, who were needed in large numbers after 1868 when the army became dependent on reservists to flesh out the order of battle; upon mobilization they would form the bulk of subalterns at the company level. Liberals in Vienna and Budapest agreed to the creation of a new system whereby any young man who had passed his secondary school exams and possessed sufficient means could become a one-year volunteer (*einjährig-Freiwilliger*, EF in army shorthand). After a year's active service, during which he acted as a junior NCO, paying his own expenses, the EF could take courses and apply for a reserve commission. While by no means all candidates passed the required exams, many did, and the program became the main source of reserve officers, particularly as bourgeois families sought

EF status for their sons, seeing it as an honor worth attaining, not to mention a way to complete their military service obligation that was preferable to two years with the rank and file. While the EF program succeeded in bringing the Dual Monarchy's rising intelligentsia into the army, its effects were complex and at times ambivalent.[69]

To start, reserve officers often enjoyed higher social standing and accomplishment than their active duty counterparts. Fritz Kreisler, a well-known violinist and reservist, observed of his prewar militia battalion that its officers included, in addition to himself, "a famous sculptor, a well-known philologist, two university professors (one of mathematics, the other of natural science), a prince, and a civil engineer at the head of one of the largest Austrian steel corporations."[70] The reserve officer corps, while still strongly German in character, was less so than the active cadre, with 59 percent in 1906 claiming German as their primary language, compared to 26 percent for Magyar and almost 10 percent for Czech. The number of non-German EFs was rising significantly in the decade before the war, and not just among Magyars and Czechs, as Poles, Romanians, Ukrainians, Croats, and Serbs accepted reserve commissions in previously unseen numbers, due to an effort to broaden the EF base, which was helped in 1912 by opening up of the program to schoolteachers.[71] (National minorities were rising slowly in the active army too: the last peacetime class at the elite Theresian Academy was "only" 63 percent German, while 16 percent Magyar, with increasing numbers of Slavs.[72]) While many generals quietly fretted about the rise in the number of non-Germans in the reserve officer corps, particularly those with socialist inclinations, most EFs seemed eager to ape the traditionalist ways of the regulars. Also, the increase in the number of non-German reserve officers was important, as one of the critical defects of the EF program was the fact that candidates had little time to learn the languages of their men, unlike active officers, which would have significant ramifications during the Great War.

Given the importance of anti-Semitism in the history of modern Central Europe, mention must be made of Jews and the army. The professional officer corps was overwhelmingly Catholic, 87 percent in 1911, and Jewish career officers were uncommon outside the medical corps, where the Jewish army doctor was a cliché (for example, Sigmund Freud, who did a year as an EF with the medical corps), but in the reserves the numbers of Jewish officers were enormous, indeed without precedent in European history. On the eve of the war, Jews represented less than 5 percent of the population of the Dual Monarchy but 17 percent of reserve officers and 23 percent of reserve officials (that is administrators with officer rank): there were six Jewish officers for every Jewish ranker in the Habsburg military. The numbers were even higher in the *Honvéd*, where as many as one-quarter of commissioned reservists were Jews.[73] The influx of Jews into the reserve officer corps during the *Ausgleich* era had many causes, not least a desire by bourgeois Jews for assimilation or at least social respectability, and it set Austria-Hungary apart from many European armies. From 1885 to 1914, the Prussian Army trained some thirty thousand Jewish officer candidates, yet deemed not one worthy of a commission.[74]

Ethnicity had little impact on an officer's career, and racial background played a scant role, if any, in advancement. Of the nine officers promoted to field marshal during the Great War, three—Eugen, Joseph, and Friedrich—were Habsburg archdukes, Conrad and Rohr were Germans from Austria; Böhm-Ermolli and Kövess were part-Germans from outside Austria, while Krobatin and Boroević were Czech and Croatian Serb, respectively. The army was anything but top-heavy by modern standards, with only 1.4 percent of officers in 1911 wearing generals' stars, while 86 percent were lieutenants and captains.[75] As the figures bear out, promotion for line officers was slow, and for arms like the artillery downright glacial. Long hours were spent on preparing for language exams, as an inability to speak regimental languages was a career-ender. Habsburg regular officers mostly served their careers in garrisons, many distant from fashionable cities and socially undesirable, with companies, batteries, and squadrons, waiting patiently for promotions to come. For many, boredom led to gambling, drinking, whoring, and debts. A particular burden was the hefty marriage bond required to wed, to ensure a proper living standard for an officer's family, particularly in the event of his death, which meant that many officers lived the solitary bachelor's life into middle age, and some never married at all.

To compensate for the relative social isolation of army life and the somewhat low pay, officers cultivated an *esprit de corps* with many manifestations in an effort to ward off modernity and all its concomitant social trends that they loathed. Officers addressed each other with the informal you, regardless of rank, *duzen* being an archaic custom that enhanced a feeling of belonging across the officer corps. A rigid sense of honor was another point of pride for all officers, as unshakable a part of their near-medieval self-perception as the saber and yellow sash. Their oath included the promise "to live and die with honor," and these were more than words. In a manner that befuddled civilians, Habsburg officers adhered to a rigid and thoroughly outmoded code of honor, which mandated a range of reactions that appeared quaint, at best, to the outside world—most of all, a penchant for dueling. While dueling was a crime, officers were expected to be ready to defend the honor of the army, the emperor, their regiment, and themselves at all times, with pistol or sword. Woe to the civilian who insulted the army or the dynasty within earshot of an officer, as a duel was the likely outcome. Although officers in theory could be prosecuted for dueling, passing on a challenge to honor was a surer way to end one's career, as the army took a dim view of any officer who failed to uphold the code of honor.[76]

The only certain way to escape the sometime dreary life of a line officer was via admission to the elite General Staff, the self-appointed brains of the army. Although the Habsburg military went to some length to ensure there was no discrimination on the basis of ethnicity, there was great discrimination in favor of the General Staff, as entry into it opened the door to the senior ranks. After the defeat in 1866, the army remodeled its General Staff on the Prussian model, making it a small, self-assured body of the best officers who would run the military; its special role reflected the hand-picked nature of admission to its exalted ranks. In the run-up to the Great War, the number of officers assigned to the General Staff ran only in the low five hundreds, under 3 percent of the active officer corps.[77]

The gateway to the General Staff was the War College (*Kriegsschule*), established in 1852 to train the army's best, brightest, and hardest-working junior officers. Every year, hundreds of lieutenants, most in their mid-twenties, sat for the initial examination. Officers who passed went to Vienna to take the second-round exam, an arduous event that lasted four days and served to whittle away all but the sharpest and most ardent officers. Those then matriculated at the War College in Vienna, where they underwent two years (by the twentieth century it had been expanded to three) of education in warfighting and staff procedures. Not all completed the program successfully, but those who did were accepted into the General Staff and entered the Habsburg military's leadership cadre, where they would remain for the remainder of their careers.[78]

In an illustrative case, an officer who entered the War College in 1896 recounted that more than 300 officers sat for the first round of exams, of whom 200 advanced to the second round, with 103 admitted to the War College; of those, nearly all were from the joint army, with eight from the *Honvéd*, and two from the *Landwehr*. Sixty-two of the students were infantry, the cavalry and artillery had sixteen each, while nine came from the technical services; 72 percent were graduates of the Theresian Academy, nearly all were bachelors, and only a few had claim to nobility. Of the ninety-nine students who completed the two-year course successfully, eight-four were detailed to the General Staff. This class would serve throughout the Great War, often in senior positions. Significantly, the War College curriculum that they studied, while unquestionably arduous, emphasized tactics and military history, yet strategy received very little attention, with less than 10 percent of the curriculum having anything to do with strategic questions, while issues of grand strategy were wholly absent.[79]

General Staff officers lived a life apart from the rest of the commissioned corps, enjoying accelerated promotion, with long stints in Vienna punctuated by relatively short periods in command of line units. They enjoyed a charmed life, albeit one devoted to hard work, and were the source of resentment and envy by officers who failed to make the cut. Competition to enter the General Staff was suitably intense, so much so that in 1909 First Lt. Adolf Hofrichter, who had graduated from the War College but failed to find a place on the General Staff, killed a fellow officer with cyanide to create an opening.[80] General Staff officers wore more elegant uniforms than line officers, in striking green with plumed hats that made a captain look like a general, reinforcing their sense of being a caste above and apart from fellow officers, whose views of the "bottle-green-boys" were invariably negative. The General Staff's advantages in promotion and position were there for all to see. On the eve of the Great War, 72 of 142 colonels, 110 of 183 one-star generals, and eighty-seven of 101 two-stars were graduates of the War College. While it was possible to reach the senior ranks without admission to the General Staff, those who wore the bottle-green uniform got there faster and in much higher percentages. The access that General Staff officers had to jobs in Vienna, close to top generals and the court, conferred advantages that were frequently career changing.[81]

The nexus of General Staff and court proved the key to success in the Habsburg Army in the decades before 1914. For any officer seeking admission to the best positions at the commanding heights of the military, a network of supporters among top generals and royals, what they termed *Protektion*, was a requirement. Examining the careers of senior leaders of the *k.u.k. Armee* in 1914 reveals how the system worked. Oskar Potiorek was practically the model of the successful Habsburg officer before the Great War.[82] The son of a civil servant, he entered the engineers and gained admission to the War College at the tender age of twenty-two, following only four years of line service, passing into the General Staff at twenty-four; his ambition was noted by all who encountered Potiorek, whose staff work was exemplary. Although he traveled all over the Dual Monarchy on special-duty assignments, he missed the invasion of Bosnia-Hercegovina in 1878 and the 1881–82 rebellion, his generation's only war service. Potiorek was known for his laconic statements, taken as wisdom by his admirers, and workaholic ways; he seemed to have no life outside his career. Spending many years with the General Staff's Operations Bureau, the destination of choice for high-flying officers, Potiorek was promoted to lieutenant colonel at thirty-six, a decade before most officers of his cohort were, and served a short stint in battalion command. He was promoted to one-star general in 1898, taking over an infantry brigade, his last troop command. Potiorek received his second star, and appointment as deputy chief of the General Staff, only four years later, while still in his forties. Although he had never commanded a regiment or a division, careerism and cultivating court connections had paid off handsomely for Potiorek, who had his detractors; the bachelor's absent personal life, combined with a lack of social graces and overt misogyny, led to whispers. He was admired, if not universally liked, at court. The 1907 assessment of Archduke Friedrich is revealing: "superbly prepared, a good commander, but unworldly, gullible, without manners or an understanding of human nature."[83]

Such sentiments played a part in Potiorek being passed over in autumn 1906 for chief of the General Staff, in favor of a rival, Franz Conrad von Hötzendorf, whose career had largely paralleled his own, and who had gained the support of Archduke Franz Ferdinand, the heir to the throne. Potiorek received command of III Corps and a third star as a concession, but he remained bitter and schemed for a better job. Being named army inspector in April 1910, a fine-sounding position but one without much power, did not quench his ambition. He wanted a job with real power and importance, so he campaigned to be named commanding general and governor of Bosnia and Hercegovina, a politically sensitive post with high visibility. Potiorek gained Conrad's support, with the chief of the General Staff citing "his certain nature and his enormous work ethic" as reason to send him to Sarajevo—which was conveniently far removed from Vienna. At last Potiorek had a job which he felt to be commensurate with his abilities and which could serve as an ideal position to win back the court's full favor. He was named governor in Sarajevo in March 1911, a selection that would have far-reaching consequences.[84]

The life and career of Potiorek's rival are not sufficiently well known outside Central Europe, yet merit attention given the enormous role Franz Conrad von Hötzendorf would play in the coming of the Great War, and Austria-Hungary's performance in it.[85] The son of a hussar colonel who was elevated to the *Dienstadel* for long service—there was neither family manor nor money—Conrad displayed a drive to succeed almost as impressive as Potiorek's. Commissioned into the infantry from the Theresian Academy, he attained admission to the War College at twenty-two, just like Potiorek (they matriculated one year apart); unlike his rival, Conrad had a serious scholarly interest in his profession, becoming a noted writer on military affairs, and he participated in the Bosnian campaigns of 1878 and 1881–82, and wrote about his combat experiences, including astute recommendations for tactical improvements.[86]

Conrad spent the mid-1880s on the Operations Bureau of the General Staff, serving alongside Potiorek, but was dispatched to the War College in 1888 for a four-year stint as an instructor in tactics. He was popular with the students, and the experience cemented his reputation across the army as a forward-looking thinker on military matters, tactics foremost, as well as a mentor to rising officers; Conrad was approachable, even charismatic, and cared little for formalities. Also unlike Potiorek, Conrad served as a dedicated commander of a battalion, a regiment, a brigade, finally a division: his command of the Eighth Division in the Tyrol was considered highly successful, an experience which culminated in a refinement of the views on warfighting he had been pondering for decades. The stellar performance of his division in 1905's grand maneuvers caught the attention of Archduke Franz Ferdinand, who had been watching the rising officer since the late 1890s, resulting in an unexpected offer to become chief of the General Staff in November 1906, once the heir to the throne had decided not to elevate Potiorek to the position.[87]

In the last years of peace, the role of Franz Ferdinand in army politics proved critical. In 1906, Franz Joseph permitted the heir to the throne to form his own military chancellery at Franz Ferdinand's Belvedere Palace in Vienna, which soon became a rival power center in all military matters.[88] A staunch traditionalist, indeed a confirmed reactionary whose views were of a piece with the "conservative revolution" that would take Central Europe by storm a decade after his death, the heir to the throne displayed minimal interest in matters of tactics and organization, yet he was acutely aware of the key role of the military in the Dual Monarchy. Understanding that the army constituted the last bulwark of unquestioning support for the Habsburg throne and dynasty, Franz Ferdinand took the General Staff's side in the never-ending squabbling with Budapest, favoring a strong and united army, and positioned himself as an advocate for officers whom he deemed reliable.[89]

Although Franz Ferdinand enabled the rise of Conrad to the heights of the army, there were significant differences between the men, and over time they became onerous. While the heir to the throne was a devout Catholic of ultramontane disposition, Conrad's beliefs were more complicated. Though it was politic to appear a faithful Catholic, the top general's actual worldview reflected a deep social Darwinism and disdain for rigid beliefs of any sort: "the proper philosophy would be to have none," as he liked to say. He was enamored with aspects of Eastern religions, Buddhism and Shinto especially, and indulged in cultural pessimism, under Nietzsche's influence. Of the inevitability of conflict Conrad was certain, and he envisioned preventative wars as the only salve for the Dual Monarchy's grave and mounting problems.[90] As a hunter Franz Ferdinand displayed epic bloodlust, taking an astonishing 275,000 trophies around the world, to the extent that he permanently harmed his hearing, but he feared major wars, seeing in them nothing but destruction of life and order; Conrad, who never hunted, viewing it as inhumane, desired wars as the sole solution to what ailed Austria-Hungary.

Personal life became another sore subject between the heir to the throne and the top Habsburg general. No misogynist, Conrad was devoted to his mother and sister, and had a normal marriage with offspring until his wife's untimely death. Lonely, the widower maintained an active social life which brought him into contact with Gina von Reininghaus, half his age and the mother of six, not to mention the wife of one of Austria's wealthiest industrialists. An awkward relationship commenced soon after Conrad assumed his position at the top of the army, and over time it became a full-blown affair that increasingly obsessed Conrad, who catalogued his despair over the fact that Gina would not leave her husband in his "Diary of my Woes." Franz Ferdinand, devout Catholic and firm family man, approved of none of it.

Yet in many ways the two men got along well, their broad political goals, based on saving the Habsburg edifice in a world of rising crisis, seeming compatible. There was a shared pessimism: both felt foreboding about the Dual Monarchy's future. While Conrad viewed the European situation with fear and loathing, Franz Ferdinand felt the same about Austria-Hungary's domestic scene. As he wrote to Conrad in early 1908: "The root problem is that today the monarchy is totally in the hands of Jews, Freemasons, socialists, and Hungarians, and these elements make the army, especially its officers, unhappy . . . in a crisis I don't know if I can rely on the army!! That's the main thing."[91]

An important intermediary between the archduke's military chancellery and the High Command was Alexander Brosch von Aarenau, a thirty-six-year-old major and General Staff up-and-comer when he came to Vienna, fresh from battalion command with the *Kaiserjäger*, in early 1906 to establish the heir to the throne's new military office. There he would stay for almost six years, serving as Franz Ferdinand's factotum on defense matters, developing a close personal relationship with the archduke. Brosch, who thanks to his office in the Belvedere enjoyed access to top politicos far beyond what his rank would suggest, established a parallel network throughout the army to agitate for the reforms Franz Ferdinand desired; he was seemingly also the only person who could talk the heir to the throne out of some of his less inspired ideas, serving as a stabilizing influence on the sometimes hot-headed archduke. The men became close, Brosch being able to calm Franz Ferdinand down when he grew distraught over his treatment by the emperor ("I'm more out of the loop than the most junior servant at Schonbrünn" was a frequent complaint), battling together against Budapest's demands and trying to keep the army intact as crises, foreign and domestic, mounted. Brosch was devoted to Franz Ferdinand and only went back to line service at the end of 1911 reluctantly, to a colonelcy and command of a regiment of his beloved *Kaiserjäger*. Franz Ferdinand did not want to give up his trustworthy aide-partner, and did so only with the provision that Brosch would return to him once his command tour ended.[92]

Conrad could have benefited from his own Brosch, as his behavior, personal and professional, grew more erratic as war drew nearer. While his affair with Gina became more publicly visible and more privately torrid, the Balkans grew increasingly unstable. During the Bosnian Crisis of 1908, Conrad counseled war against Serbia, the rising threat to the south, getting ahead of the cautious emperor, something that would have been unthinkable under his predecessor, General Friedrich von Beck, who served as General Staff chief for an astonishing twenty-four years, all of them peaceful. Conrad pushed for war against Italy, his other obsession, in 1911, during that country's Libyan campaign, even though Rome was ostensibly an ally. Conrad did not get along with Alois Lexa von Aehrenthal, the foreign minister, which combined with his ceaseless agitation for preventative wars resulted in his dismissal in December 1911. Yet he was back in the job only a year later: Franz Ferdinand wanted him reinstated, his nemesis Aehrenthal had died, and his replacement, General Blasius von Schemua, proved to have few of Conrad's gifts and a stranger personality; a religious mystic, Schemua was a member of an occult order with proto-Nazi beliefs that practiced its rituals at a castle under a swastika banner.[93] Conrad reassumed his post as General Staff chief just in time for the Balkan Wars of 1912–13, which would see an irrevocable erosion of the Dual Monarchy's position in the region, bringing with it the strategic peril Conrad had long feared.

Conrad's defects were many, yet he had undeniable gifts. His work ethic was impressive, and he was a tireless advocate for his causes, worrying little about their popularity. His view of future war was more perceptive than many, and his pessimistic assessment of the Dual Monarchy's international position was proved correct by events. That said, his blind spots were numerous. It is doubtful whether he really understood strategy deeply, his concepts seldom seeming to rise above grand tactics; important matters such as logistics aroused none of his interest, and he was quick to dismiss subjects that did not inspire him with a curt, "I've got no time for that." Perhaps most important, his understanding of human nature was poor, and his relations with fellow generals were often testy. While he was not a cold fish like Potiorek, neither was Conrad a savvy chooser of personnel, a fault that generals who fell out of his favor noted frequently.[94] Above all, how well did Conrad, who headed the Habsburg Army for seven of the last eight years of peace, actually prepare his forces for the war he so ardently sought?

3   War Plans

The Austro-Hungarian Army in 1914 was organized along standard continental lines of the era. Reforms in 1868 had built the modern Habsburg military, and thereafter the overall organization experienced alternations but no fundamental changes. The largest peacetime formation was the corps, of which there were sixteen. Field army headquarters were only mobilized for war, and the first fourteen corps (eight for Austria, six for Hungary) corresponded to territorial regions where the local regiments recruited; most units served in their home districts, which made mobilization simpler: XV (Sarajevo) and XVI (Ragusa) Corps, guarding the southeastern frontier, were exceptions, being comprised mainly of mountain formations recruited from across the Dual Monarchy.[1]

The line corps, I through XIV, consisted of two or sometimes three *k.u.k.* infantry divisions, an infantry division of the *Landwehr* or *Honvéd*, often a cavalry division, an artillery brigade, plus battalions of sappers and support personnel. On mobilization, a corps was a powerful force of sixty thousand troops and more, the size of whole armies during the Napoleonic era a century before. In peacetime cadres were smaller, and the life of the corps was closely linked to the surrounding population, which experienced the army's calendar with parades, exercises, reservist recalls, and maneuvers great and small.

With mobilization the Habsburg military would come to 50 infantry divisions and 11 cavalry divisions, some 927 infantry battalions (counting the third-line *Landsturm*), 383 cavalry squadrons, 483 field artillery batteries with 2,610 pieces and 76 fortress artillery batteries with 280 heavy guns, backed by 24 engineer battalions.[2] Although this was by far the largest Habsburg Army ever fielded, it was dwarfed by its potential adversaries. In 1914, Russia would mobilize 93 infantry divisions, while Italy could manage 46, and even Serbia could muster 10. Efforts to seriously increase the military finally overcame Hungarian obstructionism in 1912 but arrived late, and even then Austria-Hungary was still lagging behind its rivals. Call-ups rose beginning in 1912, rising to 159,500 in 1914, a jump from 22.7 percent of available men in that year-group to 29.7 percent (compared to 37 percent in Russia, 40 percent in Germany, and 86 percent in France), but that was too late to have much effect on the mobilization strength of the army. Had Budapest acquiesced in a similar reform plan in 1900 when the High Command began demanding it, and not a dozen years later, Austria-Hungary would have mobilized 22 additional infantry divisions in 1914.[3] Conrad planned a Prussian-style reserve force to quickly supplement the order of battle. Implemented at the end of 1913, it would add many new reserve formations—14 infantry divisions, 14 mountain brigades, plus 16 infantry brigades from the *Landwehr/Honvéd*—but the scheme was not slated to be in effect until 1915, thus bringing no benefit when war actually came.[4]

Given the deterioration of Austria-Hungary's Balkan position in the decade before 1914 and the close ties between Russia and Serbia, it was likely that Habsburg forces would confront a two-front war, without having the means to fight one. This was the essential challenge facing Conrad and his planners on the General Staff before 1914, thanks to a generation and more of Hungarian obstructionism on military matters. While the dilemma of a two-front war with too few troops would have challenged even a Radetzky, Conrad dealt with the fundamental strategic problem by mostly ignoring it.

The question of how to defeat Russia had been debated by the General Staff's Operations Bureau since the 1880s, when the odds were more even. As Russia's strength grew, particularly after its army's recovery from the 1905 defeats in Northeast Asia, the numbers grew worrisome. Russia's military expansion and modernization program was outpacing Austria-Hungary's by a distressing margin. Yet Conrad's real interest lay elsewhere, having spent much of his career commanding units facing Italy, which he loathed, and his obsession with Serbia after 1908 became pronounced. Russia was not his dreamland of victory, as the enormous tsarist empire, with its vast spaces and seemingly unlimited manpower, was no candidate for a quick, decisive war of the sort Conrad sought as solution to the Dual Monarchy's problems.

The General Staff had a monopoly on war planning, and interference from outside its Viennese corridors hardly existed, which combined with Conrad's indefatigable energy translated into dozens of studies and proposals emanating from the Operations Bureau annually, without any outside review. All plans for war were offensive; under all circumstances the fight was to be taken to the enemy.[5] In 1908, Conrad's vision for War Plan "R" (for Russia) called for a small, two-division attack northward from Cracow, a feint, with the main force of three dozen divisions moving northeast between the San and Sereth rivers, aimed northwest into Russia. Over the next two years, Conrad's concept evolved into a sweeping half-circle between the Bug and the Vistula that, again, would seek decisive battle against the Russians, this time in central Poland.[6]

Conrad had fully imbibed the European-wide tendency of the period in favor of great offensives as the only acceptable form of warfare. It was an essentially utopian vision, filled with hopes for a Cannae-like grand encirclement, sweeping flanking actions that would defeat the enemy in one grand tactical exercise, causing him to sue for peace in a matter of weeks. How this could be executed in the vast spaces of Eastern Europe against a numerically superior enemy was never clear in Conrad's plans; neither was there much appreciation for the difficulty of translating tactical victories into strategically important results. The General Staff chief's thinking rarely ascended beyond higher tactics, and his appreciation for logistics was even more limited.[7] It ought to be noted that Conrad's concept of operations, while consistent with European military thought of the era, represented a clean break with centuries of what can be termed Habsburg "strategic culture," which emphasized a fundamentally conservative, often defensive, approach to war-making that prioritized dynastic preservation over quick, decisive victory or operational panache.[8]

For any strategist, the Serbian problem offered a seemingly insurmountable challenge. The political need to reassert Habsburg power and prestige in the Balkans at the expense of the upstarts in Belgrade, to crush their "mortal enmity" in the words of Vienna's ambassador, was a project Conrad dearly embraced—but how to do it?[9] Although a two-front war could be assumed after 1909, once Russia's support for Serbia was clear to all, how War Plan "B" (for Balkans) could be executed with success simultaneously with War Plan "R" remained an unanswered question, despite thousands of pages on the subject churned out by the Operations Bureau. The bulk of the army would be gathered in what the General Staff termed A-Group, nine corps with twenty-eight infantry and ten cavalry divisions, plus numerous militia brigades—the main strike force against Russia. The monarchy's southern frontier would be guarded by *Minimalgruppe* Balkan, eight divisions to conduct defensive operations and perhaps limited probes into Serbia. The army's swing force would be B-Group, four corps with a dozen infantry divisions plus one of cavalry. Flexibility was the key to all Habsburg planning on the eve of the Great War, as the ominous numbers combined with the fragile situation at home and abroad demanded it. B-Group would be used against Serbia, or for War Plan "I" against Italy, the war Conrad really wanted, or against Russia, depending on circumstances.[10]

Surveying the order of battle, it was evident that there simply were not enough forces available to fight a two-front war offensively. A "win-hold" strategy might have been feasible, meaning taking the offensive against either Russia or Serbia, while defending against the other. However, any Balkan war involving Austria-Hungary mandated a quick offensive, to crush Belgrade before Serbs inside the Dual Monarchy could stage a revolt as well as before Romania jumped sides and backed Serbia with force. Conrad, with one eye on domestic threats and the other on Austria-Hungary's deteriorating position in the Balkans, would accept no discussion of defense to the south. Similarly, a defensive strategy against Russia did not simply go against all of Conrad's soldierly instincts, it also subjected the army to an agonizing wait while Russia marshaled its vast forces and marched westward, an unstoppable steamroller. Striking before the Russians were fully assembled seemed to offer the only remedy to the numerical imbalance, not to mention that Austria-Hungary did not have the option to wait. Berlin, its only dependable ally, demanded an offensive to tie the Russians down while the Germans were first winning the war against France, per its Schlieffen Plan.[11]

Rather than accept that years of political squabbles and underfunding had left the army unprepared to fight a two-front war, Conrad and the General Staff, confronting an array of seemingly unanswerable strategic riddles, engaged in institutionalized escapism, particularly after 1910. Under Colonel Joseph Metzger, head of the Operations Bureau and a Conrad protégé, war plans evolved to include moving four corps of B-Group against Serbia before they were required against Russia. This concept required a great deal of optimism about the speed of mobilization and railway timetables, but it seemed to be the only way to conceive of any "win-win" moves at the outset on both critical fronts. More flexibility in the mobilization scheme after 1909, allowing for corps to be called up and deployed individually, made the concept seem plausible, if only just barely.[12] Whether this was a reasonable strategy remained to be seen.

The alliance with Germany lay at the heart of the Dual Monarchy's strategic dilemmas. Berlin and Vienna had discussed joint war planning against Russia ever since 1882, and for years the rough-sketched concept called for Germany and Austria-Hungary to conduct mutually supporting offensives into Russia out of East Prussia and eastern Galicia, respectively. After Alfred von Schlieffen became chief of Berlin's General Staff in 1891, joint planning with Vienna, never very detailed, became hazy; Schlieffen lacked faith in the Habsburg Army, viewing it as brittle, having witnessed its defeat at Königgrätz in 1866. More interested in his war plans in the West and uncertain of Austria-Hungary's value in the East, Schlieffen explained laconically, "The fate of Austria will be decided not on the Bug but on the Seine."[13]

The departure of Schlieffen and his replacement by Helmuth von Moltke in 1906 heralded rejuvenation in the relationship between the two General Staffs.[14] In the aftermath of the Bosnian Crisis, Conrad and his counterpart exchanged letters, which gave a sense of each side's war plans at least at the strategic level; Conrad's subsequent complaints that he was not aware of the implications of Berlin's strategy, particularly the Schlieffen Plan, do not hold water. Although the information exchange did not give away much about operational matters, it revealed that Germany intended to seek a decision in the West at the outset, and that Austria-Hungary would need to face the Russians without significant German aid for six weeks.

A "systematically developed war plan" of the sort considered second nature in later alliances did not exist between Berlin and Vienna.[15] Yet the understandings between the allies were really no more fragmentary than what transpired between St. Petersburg, Paris, and London before the war; much was taken on faith, not always wisely. While the Germans expected the Austro-Hungarians to keep the Russians at bay while they crushed France, Vienna expected Berlin to commit sufficient resources to an offensive out of East Prussia to give Conrad's attack into Poland a reasonable chance of success: in the end, both allies were disappointed. In the run-up to 1914, both sides overpromised, since each needed the other to do more in the East than it really could. No one in Berlin or Vienna sought to ask troubling questions, which no one really wanted to be answered. "This lack of a critical assessment of one's ally was not just a question of politeness," observed Günther

Kronenbitter, "It was essential to believe in the alliance because otherwise there would not have been any way out of the strategic impasse."[16]

Thus was self-deception in Vienna matched in Berlin, and Conrad was far from the only general willing to bend the facts after everything went awry in the summer of 1914. "The Danube monarchy's strength and armed forces were adequate for a campaign against Serbia but inadequate for a war against major European powers," was the assessment of August von Cramon, a Prussian general who spent most of the Great War as Berlin's representative to the Austro-Hungarian General Staff.[17] While Cramon was an expert witness, and his retrospective assessment of Habsburg arms is in accord with events, he likewise created a more palatable narrative in which Berlin had been deceived by Vienna about the true condition of the Austro-Hungarian Army in 1914. The Germans were taken aback when war came, when the weaknesses of their Habsburg ally were revealed painfully, according to Cramon.

Yet Cramon's depiction of sly Austrians was no more accurate than Conrad's image of deceptive Prussians. In truth, Berlin was well informed about the shortcomings of the Habsburg military thanks to its productive military attaché, Carl von Kageneck, who arrived in Vienna in late 1906 and stayed there until the war's outbreak.[18] Diligent and personable, Kageneck developed a close relationship with Conrad, and he sent reams of reports to Berlin on the whole range of issues indicating serious problems with the Habsburg Army: nationalist politics, budget shortfalls, the lack of trained reserves, outmoded weaponry, flawed tactics, plus the worries of top generals that minorities would revolt against the dynasty in the event of war. In Berlin and Vienna during the run-up to the Great War, generals looked away from problems they did not wish to see; hope triumphed over facts, becoming the backbone of strategy.

Even Conrad was daunted by the scope of the challenges he found, writing to a fellow general shortly after assuming the top job in late 1906, "I knew that the army was in a poor way, but I had absolutely no conception of how bad it really was."[19] Tactics were Conrad's *métier*, having enjoyed a reputation as a leading thinker on such matters since the 1880s, and it was here that he intended to enact change where the budget allowed it. He could not fix the Dual Monarchy's broken politics, he could not make Budapest behave responsibly, and there was little he could do about Austria-Hungary's eroding strategic position, but tactics were something Conrad had it within his power to improve, and so he did.

Conrad's views were shaped several decades before, particularly by his only combat experience, in Bosnia in 1878 and again in 1881–82, in mostly small engagements against rebels. His tenure as a War College instructor cemented his faith in the offensive, and his views were of a piece with the 1889 Infantry Regulations, which advocated the primacy of infantry fires culminating in bayonet charges; artillery, while valued, was not considered a decisive arm on the battlefield.[20] Conrad's faith in the offensive and the power of the bayonet against firepower remained unchanged even as technological advances—including machine guns, smokeless gunpowder, and especially rapid-fire artillery—were rendering the modern battlefield an ever-deadlier place. As he wrote of his experience as a junior officer under fire in Bosnia, "Forward! What magic there is in that word! Wherever you go, only move forward!"[21] Yet more than three decades later, Austro-Hungarian infantry would encounter a far more lethal battlefield than anything Conrad had witnessed.

To prepare the troops for combat, Conrad pushed for more staff rides, more exercises, and more realistic maneuvers. The annual *Kaisermanöver* was more a military pageant than preparation for the twentieth-century battlefield, so Conrad changed that as soon as he became chief of the General Staff. Henceforth, the annual grand maneuvers were more realistic, with enhanced free play for commanders, more critical umpiring, even night combat. The emperor and the heir to the throne disapproved of the changes; being traditionalists with scant interest in tactical innovation they felt Conrad had ruined the show. Forward-thinking officers, however, were encouraged by the alterations.[22] No Luddite like Franz Joseph, Conrad embraced technological change, advocating for new weapons systems of all kinds, including aircraft, though Austria-Hungary's parsimonious budgets made that mostly wishful thinking. In a typical case, in 1906 a junior officer named Günther Burstyn demonstrated his working model of the first armored car, but when it scared the emperor's horses during its first public showing, it became a nonstarter, not to mention that the budget lacked money for fundamentals, much less novel experiments.[23]

Conrad forced the army, or at least most of it, into its first drab field uniform beginning in 1907. The new uniform, in a shade termed pike gray (*hechtgrau*), constituted an improvement over the dark blue tunics previously worn by the infantry, but its blueish tinge was better suited to the Alps, which Conrad knew well, than to the plains of Galicia. Conrad's efforts to induce the cavalry into the new uniforms got nowhere, however, and Habsburg mounted troops would go to war in 1914 in what amounted to full-dress uniforms, all bright reds and blues. This was thoroughly unsuited to the modern battlefield, but the cavalry lobby was powerful in the Habsburg Army—it would provide a dozen senior generals during the war, including two field army commanders at the outset—and as in so much of Europe before 1914 it was fighting a retrograde action to maintain its relevance to warfighting in the twentieth century.[24]

Recent conflicts, the Anglo-Boer War of 1899–1902 but especially the Russo-Japanese War of 1904–5, had sparked robust debate in the Habsburg military about what to expect in the next war. The army's observer with the Russians in Manchuria, Lt. Col. Maximilian Csicserics von Bacsány, returned brimming with ideas about the carnage he had witnessed.[25] A talented General Staff officer, he encapsulated his thoughts in a 1908 brochure *Die Schlacht* (The battle), which was widely read in the army and was at least implicitly critical of Conrad's outmoded views on tactics. Like Conrad, and practically every other officer in the army, indeed across Europe at the time, Csicserics retained his faith in the power of the offensive; but what he saw in Manchuria gave him appreciation for the power of artillery and machine guns too, resulting in a need for entrenchments, an appreciation that eluded older officers. Conrad for years had advocated that an infantry unit, if morally prepared, could sustain 50 percent casualties in the attack and still reach its objective, and the Manchurian war seemed to bear his views out. Like most European generals of the day, Conrad considered that Port Arthur and related battles in 1904–5, where infantry units took egregious losses yet defeated the enemy, made their point about the primacy of morale over machine weapons (the esoteric chief also felt the appeal of Shinto, since it seemed to drive the determined Japanese infantry forward even in the face of murderous fire). He allowed Csicserics to publish his findings, but otherwise paid little attention. It had no impact on the formulation of army doctrine before the war.[26]

Conrad's tactical views culminated in the 1911 Infantry Regulations, the last major articulation of doctrine before the war. The chief's views had not changed, and the regulations considered infantry to be the dominant arm on the battlefield, capable of overcoming all obstacles, including machine guns and rapid-fire artillery, as long as it was sufficiently trained and morally prepared to win. Although doctrine called for infantry to attack in open order, to mitigate the effects of enemy firepower that would lay waste to tightly packed battalions, it mandated that battle would be decided at close quarters, with the point of the bayonet, after the infantry had shot its way forward. The regulations, which accepted that casualties would be heavy in the attack, placed great weight on superior morale and the will to win: "Infantry that is filled with an aggressive spirit, physically and morally persevering, properly trained and self-confident, can succeed in battle even under the most difficult conditions."[27]

The strong emphasis on moral factors in the 1911 regulations was impossible to miss, amidst claims that victory on the battlefield would come to the side with "iron discipline and superior willpower," along with "unwavering perseverance," which could overcome all obstacles.

Even when the enemy was well entrenched, it asserted, preparatory artillery fire would not suffice, only aggressive infantry assaults would be able to take the position, since "the attack alone" brings victory.[28] How infantry could be convinced to march into devastating enemy fire was explained forthrightly: "Soldiers must be infused with the knowledge that honor and salvation exist only in FORWARD!—for them there is no RETREAT!"[29]

The new regulations were implemented but were met with questions in certain quarters of the army. Professional journals delved deeply into just how deadly artillery especially had proved in Manchuria, observing that Russian infantry in the attack routinely absorbed casualty rates of one-third, and as high as 40 percent among officers, when confronted by machine weapons; enormous rates of ammunition expenditure were likewise much commented on.[30] Recent improvements in Russian artillery, based on the lessons of Manchuria, were likewise noted, along with detailed observations regarding new weapons and tactics that would prove highly lethal to Habsburg infantry. That Russian artillery was outpacing their own in skill and weight of shell was not doubted by Austro-Hungarian officers who examined the matter closely.[31] How the infantry would fare when confronted with adept enemy gunnery was a problem that vexed forward-looking Austro-Hungarian tacticians on the eve of the Great War; indeed it was the preeminent problem. Gen. Alfred Krauss, the War College head and an astute tactician, was sharply critical of Conrad's theses, believing them to be a generation out of date and lacking appreciation for the lethality of modern weaponry. Reviewing rising firepower on the battlefield since the Franco-Prussian War, he advocated developing light infantry guns, to be pushed forward to clear a path for the infantry with direct fires; otherwise foot soldiers would be stalled on the open battlefield with heavy losses. "Enemy artillery is the most dangerous foe of our infantry," Krauss warned presciently a year before the Great War.[32]

Yet many officers agreed with the essential tenets of the 1911 regulations, or at least knew it was impolitic to say otherwise. An infantry colonel reviewing the new doctrine admonished colleagues, "Let us learn from the examples of the Germans in 1870–71 and of the Japanese in 1904–5," meaning not to pay needless costs in flesh and blood when confronted with firepower, yet nevertheless reminded that morale indeed could work wonders: "The spiritual and moral strength of the individual even on today's nerve-wracking battlefield, despite so many technological advances, remains the best and most successful weapon."[33]

Despite Conrad's much-lauded emphasis on realistic training, there were numerous indications that the army's tactical readiness left much to be desired. During exercises, infantry units from the better-educated regions of the Dual Monarchy often displayed finesse, while those comprised of illiterate peasants, who were notoriously difficult to train in complex tactics, demonstrated a tendency to bunch up in dense columns that would be quickly cut down by artillery and machine guns on any real battlefield. Foreign observers noted that while Habsburg infantry was as tough and uncomplaining as it had ever been, unit skills and readiness varied greatly, depending on ethnicity, training levels, and the quality of officers, with some showing slackness and inattention to detail about tactics that would prove lethal in combat.[34]

Similar observations came from Kageneck, the German attaché, a sympathetic witness who nevertheless was troubled by what he observed at Austro-Hungarian exercises, year in and year out. He found that units from the less developed parts of the Dual Monarchy suffered from many illiterate troops, which only made communications problems in polyglot regiments worse; they were not on a par with Prussians. Kageneck likewise noted a tendency to move sluggishly when under simulated fire, while even some officers displayed a cavalier attitude toward the lethality of modern artillery: "In a real situation they would be shot down in the first few minutes," he reported to Berlin about the 1910 *Kaisermanöver*. March discipline was often substandard, and Kageneck was especially troubled by the Habsburg infantry's tendency to advance over open ground in a single mass, a sure way to invite annihilation, "again, as usual," he rued after watching the summer 1912 maneuvers.[35]

In fairness to Conrad, the persistent lack of funds made institutionalizing realistic training exceptionally difficult. Active-duty cadres were small, with infantry battalions only having an authorized strength of 394 versus war strength of over a thousand—it was but 235 for the *Landwehr* and 208 for the *Honvéd*—which meant that even first-line units were heavily dependent on reservists, whose tactical skills were usually sorely out of date, as refresher training was rare.[36] For the artillery, the shortage of funds for training was acute. Field batteries received only 250 rounds per year for training purposes, while in Germany the figure was 650, versus 730 in France, and between 500 and 600 in Russia.[37] Exercises gave a perfunctory role to the artillery in any event, with barrages over open sights, without detailed targeting, to be followed by infantry charges without fire support. Even the Official History conceded about prewar training, "Doubtless too little attention was paid to the cooperation of infantry and artillery," which was the tactful way of explaining that exercises had hardly any provisions for coordinating artillery fires to support infantry attacks.[38]

War games habitually paid insufficient attention to terrain features, while despite lip service about the importance of entrenchments and the need to protect infantry from enemy fires, they hardly made an appearance in exercises: "trenches had only been marked with strings; to actually *dig* them was seen as a waste of time."[39] Additionally, there were generals who expressed skepticism about any efforts to make training more realistic. Witnessing 1913 maneuvers that made some account of enemy firepower, Karl Tersztyánszky, a cavalry general, explained his dismay: "What you have shown me here does not interest me at all. This slow crawling around, bending, ducking . . . I don't understand it and I don't care for it one bit. What I want to see is a regiment that shows briskly and dashingly how one can attack and fire quickly."[40] Despite his reactionary views on war, Tersztyánszky was one of Conrad's favorites, and he promoted him regularly during the war.

A problem as serious as flawed tactics for the Austro-Hungarian Army in 1914 was the inability to generate combat power on the battlefield. The infantry, despite its shortcomings in doctrine and training, was the best prepared of the combat arms for war. The infantry rifle, the M.95 Steyr-Mannlicher, was a bolt-action weapon with an internal magazine holding five 8 mm bullets; in every way equal to the rifles of allies and adversaries alike, its only shortcoming was a lack of numbers. While there were enough M.95s to equip the first line plus *Landwehr* and *Honvéd* units, some third-line *Landsturm* regiments would have to make do with obsolete Werndl single-shot rifles from the 1880s. The same was true of machine guns. Each infantry battalion had a detachment with two M.7/12 Schwarzlose weapons, an 8 mm belt-fed, water-cooled weapon capable of firing four hundred rounds per minute.[41] It was up to European standards of the day, though there was a limited reserve of machine guns, there not being enough on hand to equip *Landsturm* units on mobilization. Foot soldiers formed the bulk of infantry divisions, which conformed to the standard continental pattern in 1914: two brigades, each of two regiments of three to four battalions, each of four companies (*k.u.k.* infantry regiments had four battalions, though one battalion was often serving with XV or XVI Corps in the Balkans, while *Landwehr* and *Honvéd* regiments had three battalions each), supported by an artillery brigade.

Cavalry divisions were significantly smaller than infantry divisions in both size and firepower. Intended to conduct screening and deep reconnaissance missions, they had two brigades each of two regiments, each of two mounted battalions with three squadrons (that is, companies), supported by a single horse artillery battalion with a dozen cannons. What exact role cavalry divisions would have in wartime remained unclear, not least because the recent conflicts in South Africa and Manchuria demonstrated that while cavalry fighting as mounted infantry had a part to play on the modern battlefield, particularly in scouting and pursuit, the traditional tactics of the *arme blanche*, focused on charges against infantry or artillery, were likely to result in heavy casualties for little effect. However, the cavalry lobby was strong, particularly in Hungary, and ensured that the combat value of mounted regiments was overrated by the Habsburg Army in 1914.[42]

The real problem was the artillery, what Kageneck termed the army's "sick child," a source of endless frustration for the generals since the root of the issue was a lack of money.[43] No branch of the Habsburg Army was as fatefully impacted by financial shortfalls as the artillery, and gunners watched in the last years of peace with mounting frustration, as they fell further behind potential adversaries, while the navy got the funds they needed to modernize. Artillery organization in 1914 conformed to normal continental standards. Field gun regiments had five batteries (some had a sixth to be added on mobilization), while field howitzer regiments had four batteries. Horse artillery battalions had three batteries, while heavy howitzer battalions had only two batteries. Mountain artillery regiments had six batteries, four gun and two howitzer. Fortress artillery was organized differently, with two to three battalions each of several batteries. Generally, field gun batteries had six guns each while horse, howitzer, heavy, and mountain batteries had four pieces each.[44]

Austria-Hungary's artillery park varied widely in terms of quality. The numbers looked impressive on paper: when the army mobilized in 1914 it had 2,154 light guns, 112 medium guns, 296 light mountain guns, 206 medium howitzers, and 72 mobile heavy guns (the fortress artillery had hundreds of nonmobile pieces, mostly obsolete).[45] Upon closer examination, however, problems became evident. In theory, the field artillery brigade belonging to each infantry division had 54 pieces, but due to equipment shortages, in practice few went to war with anything like that many; most were able to muster an average of 42 guns per division, compared to 72 for a German infantry division and 60 for a Russian one. Counting the corps "slice," each Habsburg division had fewer than 50 guns, compared to almost 70 for a Russian division, 78 for a French, and 80 for a German.[46]

The mainstay of the field artillery was the M.5 (and M.5/8, an improved model) field gun. A modern piece by Habsburg standards, this 80 mm weapon (it was actually 76.5 mm) could fire a shell six thousand meters and possessed up-to-date features such as a recoil mechanism and a protective shield for the gunners. However, its rate of fire and range were already becoming obsolescent—the comparable Russian 76 mm field gun, which had a faster rate of fire, outranged the M.5/8 by a thousand meters—and like the whole Habsburg artillery gun park M.5 had an heavy steel-bronze barrel, which was obsolete technologically not to mention metallurgically inferior to an all-steel barrel, yet was cheaper to produce, always a concern in the perennially cash-strapped *k.u.k. Armee*. However, the M.5/8 was among the most modern weapons fielded by the Habsburg artillery in 1914, having mostly—though not entirely—replaced the obsolete 80 mm M.99 field gun, which lacked modern features such as a protective shield or a recoil mechanism, in most field gun batteries.[47]

The situation in field howitzer regiments was much less satisfactory, as they were equipped with the M.99 100 mm (actually 104 mm) howitzer, which lacked features such as a modern recoil mechanism or a protective shield; its maximum range of 6,100 meters was inadequate, far behind comparable Russian or German pieces. The same could be said of the M.99/4 149 mm howitzer that equipped heavy howitzer batteries: its shell range of 6,000 meters was limited, and it was missing a shield for the crew or a modern recoil mechanism.[48]

Even the mountain artillery, a long-standing Habsburg strong point, was short on up-to-date weaponry.[49] Despite Conrad's intense interest in Alpine tactics, only four of the army's fifty-two mountain batteries were equipped with modern pieces (the M.8/9 70 mm mountain gun or the M.8/10 100 mm mountain howitzer); the rest were equipped with the outmoded M.99 70 mm mountain gun or M.99 100 mm mountain howitzer, which, like all guns of the previous generation, were short-ranged and lacked modern recoil mechanisms and protective shields for the crew.[50]

A particular concern was the lack of an adequate shell reserve. Despite warnings from the gunners to expect unprecedented rates of fire, based on combat in Manchuria, Habsburg arsenals had only 650 shells on hand for each field gun, and a little over 500 per howitzer or mountain gun. Russia had a thousand shells for each field gun and 600 per howitzer, not counting rear echelon depots, while the Serbs had an impressive reserve of 1,300 shells for each field piece.[51]

One of the few bright spots in 1914 was the enormous and powerful M.11 305 mm mortar, produced by Bohemia's famed Škoda Works, which could fire a massive 380 kg. shell almost 10,000 meters. It was an ingenious and innovative design that incorporated many modern features; broken into three loads for transport, it was moved by motor carriage, a rarity at the time. Due to inadequate funding, it was secretly ordered by the joint War Ministry in 1911 without legislative approval and paid for out of the army's "black budget," resulting in a scandal and parliamentary uproar. Therefore, there were only twenty-four M.11 pieces—a dozen batteries—available at the war's outbreak, yet they would perform sterling service despite their small numbers; most famously, they shattered several major Belgian fortresses in August 1914 while on loan to the Germans, who lacked a comparable system. Yet two-thirds of the mobile fortress artillery was equipped with the obsolescent M.98 240 mm mortar.[52]

The problem facing Austro-Hungarian artillery was not a paucity of innovative ideas but rather a chronic cash shortage. Habsburg arsenals, above all the Škoda firm, offered cutting-edge artillery designs in the decade before the Great War, yet few went beyond the testing stage, much less mass production. Up-to-date weapons, on a par with artillery anywhere in Europe, had been designed but not purchased and issued to the army. There were replacements available for the obsolete M.99 howitzer and M.99/4 heavy howitzer, which the Technical Military Committee, responsible for keeping the artillery modern, knew were needed, but funding never materialized to begin production. The same could be generally said for the mountain and fortress artillery: the problem was poor funding, not poor designs.[53]

The same could be said about any number of technological innovations for which funds, not ideas, were scarce. Conrad was fortunate that his support for wireless telegraphy units in the army, which would pay huge dividends when war came, was not a big-ticket item, and by 1914 there was a series of permanent radio stations, with fifteen-meter masts with long range, all over the Dual Monarchy (two in Vienna, one for the Eastern Front, two in the Balkans, and one facing Italy), on duty and supplemented by smaller, mobile stations to deploy with the field forces.[54]

Military aviation told a similar tale. Despite Conrad's interest in the potential of flying units on the battlefield, plus civilian advocates for aviation, the Habsburg military found it difficult to make more than a token effort in the air, again thanks to limited funding. Conrad ensured that air units had a prominent place in the summer 1911 maneuvers, their debut event before the High Command and royals, with aircraft being employed by both sides, but despite an expansion plan calling for forty squadrons with 240 aircraft by 1916, he was unable to obtain sufficient funds to come close to his objectives. By 1913 the nascent air arm had a dozen balloons and fifteen fixed-wing aircraft; rapid expansion over the following twelve months added eleven balloons and thirty-six aircraft, but it still fell well short of what Conrad had wanted for the army.[55]

The General Staff was well aware of the shortcomings of the army in men, equipment, and training, above all a lack of divisions and critical shortfalls in modern artillery, but how strong were the Dual Monarchy's potential enemies? Assessing that vexing issue was the job of the intelligence staff, the quaintly named *Evidenzbureau*, buried in the bowels of the General Staff. Although the office boasted some of the smartest of the bottle-green boys, it was small—at the beginning of 1913 it had only thirty-five officers on staff—and, of course, it was short of funds. Its relationship with the Operations Bureau was tricky, thanks to somewhat cumbersome organization, not to mention that intelligence assessments were rarely the source of good news from a planner's viewpoint, but given its limitations, the *Evidenzbureau* did its job well in the run-up to the war.[56]

Most of its assessments were the outcome of judicious use of open sources, supplemented by military attaché reports and sometimes agent reporting, which was the purview of the *Kundschaftsgruppe*, a small office that handled espionage and counterespionage.[57] Although the question always remained where the Russians in particular would deploy their forces against Austria-Hungary, that was not as imponderable a mystery as it might seem, as such huge deployments would be dictated mostly by factors of geography and rail lines, which Vienna knew well. Moreover, the *Evidenzbureau*'s annual classified assessment of the Russian military was the size of a small book, and packed with details that should have caused much consternation on the General Staff. The 1913 study brimmed with details about every aspect of the tsar's army—complete orders of battle, explanations of new technology on land and in the air, profiles of top generals, and much about Russia's fast-growing rail network—and made abundantly clear that the enemy was readying for war and would be formidable foe.[58] Intelligence reporting demonstrated that any hopes that Russian forces remained shaken by defeats in the Manchurian war were wishful thinking. Assessments regarding Russian artillery were particularly troubling, and the last *Evidenzbureau* report before the war elaborated just how outgunned the Habsburg Army would be in battle against the Russians, whose divisions and corps were equipped with new guns, which outranged anything the Austro-Hungarians had. In range and weight of shell, Russian units possessed a major edge.[59]

In the tension-filled years before the war, the army devoted more effort to countering enemy intelligence than to its own espionage operations abroad. Given the generals' acute fears regarding the disloyalty of significant elements of the Dual Monarchy's population, combined with foreign scheming, military intelligence before 1914 spent much time, in collaboration with civilian police special branches, thwarting spies and saboteurs for Russia above all, though Serbian and Italian intelligence were also feared. There was a veritable spy mania beginning after the Bosnian Crisis, with regular arrests and trials that demonstrated beyond any doubt that Austria-Hungary was a major target for espionage. Russian spying aimed at the monarchy was rising fast, with the number of cases uncovered by Habsburg counterintelligence roughly doubling every year beginning in 1910. The tsar's agent network inside Austria-Hungary was wide and, as mounting arrests demonstrated, went ever deeper into sensitive institutions, including the army, than many wanted to suspect. Unsurprisingly, the army had identified many suspected spies and subversives all over the Dual Monarchy, who in the event of war would be rounded up quickly with the aid of the police.[60]

The army's espionage arm, the *Kundschaftsgruppe*, had trouble keeping up, though this had something to do with the inadequate funding that placed limits on everything the General Staff did. Its architect was Alfred Redl, who by 1913 was a colonel and one of the brightest stars of his generation in the army. Redl, a hard charger even by the General Staff's workaholic standards. He compensated for a modest background with grit and determination, coming to the *Evidenzbureau* in 1900, where he quickly became the doyen of matters Russian. He spoke the language well; hailing from Galicia, he had a knack for Slavic tongues, and a year spent in Russia allowed him to learn it fluently. From 1901 to 1907, he headed the *Kundschaftsgruppe*, conducting espionage against Russia but also sharing some information with its intelligence service (the liaison relationship only broke down with the Bosnian Crisis). Based on his successes, Redl was appointed deputy chief of the intelligence service, gaining a reputation for excellence known across the General Staff; he was admired by younger officers, the best of whom he mentored, though few knew Redl well. Like Potiorek, he seemed to have no personal life, only devotion to duty and emperor. When he left for Prague in 1910 to become chief of staff of VIII Corps—the most politically sensitive command in the army, and a natural fit for Redl given the extent of Russian espionage and subversion in Bohemia—he was viewed without exception as a model officer, and a future top general.[61]

However, Vienna's agents inside Russia had been gradually drying up, and with Redl's departure the *Evidenzbureau* began to suffer from a lack of clandestine information about events to the east. Most worrisome were indications that the General Staff itself had been penetrated by the tsar's spies; counterintelligence hands suspected a mole—but where? Investigations culminated in early April 1913 in the arrest of Čedomil Jandrić, a Bosnian Serb officer and a student at the War College. Lieutenant Jandrić had passed very sensitive information to the Russians regarding the army's new heavy mortar, a "black budget" program. Offered a pistol when caught, Jandrić demurred, and instead received a twenty-year sentence for his crimes. Worse, Jandrić had been living a life of ostentatious debauchery, hosting *"grosser Orgien"* at his Vienna apartment, which featured lower-class women for the pleasure of army officers, one of whom was Lt. Kurt Conrad, a War College classmate and the son of the General Staff chief.[62] The matter was quickly hushed up, though the younger Conrad's wild ways were known to many, and some officers suspected Kurt was involved in espionage, though that line of investigation was quickly curtailed, for obvious reasons. With the breaking of the Jandrić ring, Habsburg counterintelligence went into overdrive, and the hunt for more Russian spies was accelerated, with the help of partners in Berlin, who supplied critical lead information. Seven weeks later, police surveillance of Vienna's main post office resulted in the identification of the suspected Russian spy, who had arrived to pick up a clandestine payment. It was Col. Alfred Redl.[63]

Given the profound shock that revelation brought to the General Staff and eventually to the entire Dual Monarchy, the Redl case can still generate headlines in Vienna a century later.[64] For Habsburg loyalists, the date, May 24, 1913, would be regarded with perpetual infamy; by odd coincidence, it was the same day that an embittered young man from Upper Austria, one Adolf Hitler, finally abandoned Vienna for good, after several frustrating years in the imperial capital as a strug-gling artist.[65] Infuriated by Redl's treachery, Conrad demanded a quick resolution to the matter, meaning suicide to spare the army a full-blown scandal: "It all must happen tonight!" So it did. Redl, holed up in his hotel near the Hofburg, was confronted by *Evidenzbureau* officers, led by his protégé Capt. Max Ronge, a future head of Habsburg intelli-gence, who in an Oedipal moment offered Redl a pistol, the same one Lieutenant Jandrić had refused. After long hours of waiting, the colonel shot himself in the early hours of May 25, and there the matter ended, as far as the General Staff and Conrad were concerned.

The High Command mandated a lock-down on the Redl disaster, with only a brief, vague obituary appearing in the Vienna press, though in a trademark case of *Schlamperei* the matter was botched. A young reporter in Prague, Egon Erwin Kisch, who had carved out a reputa-tion as an *enfant terrible* on the Central European journalism scene, managed to get hold of a sensational scoop that he quickly published in a Berlin paper, which Vienna could not censor: the late Colonel Redl had been a notorious homosexual and a Russian spy who had divulged the closest-held secrets of the Habsburg Army. How exactly Kisch obtained this information remains a mystery, yet by publishing the first draft of history only two days after Redl's death he cemented his reputation as "the raging reporter" and thoroughly humiliated Conrad, the General Staff, and the army.[66]

Despite High Command denials, Kisch's account was mostly accu-rate. Redl indeed had lived a secret double life for years, throughout his service on the General Staff, and how he had concealed illicit lovers and hidden wealth revealed many of the defects of the officer corps in general, and the bottle-green mentality in particular. In the first place, Redl was simply above suspicion as the army's top expert in espionage; it can be assumed that when investigators in spring 1913 compiled a list of suspects in uniform who could be Russian spies, the name of Alfred Redl would have appeared last. Moreover, Redl's louche lifestyle, with many lovers, some of them soldiers, was considered off-limits to speculation among officers and gentlemen. Bachelors were commonplace in the officer corps, particularly due to the cost of marriage: before his 1908 wedding, Lt. Col. August von Urbański, the *Evidenzbureau*'s chief, had to post a bond of 50,000 crowns, which equaled half the army's annual intelligence budget.[67] Homosexuality, if discreet, was tolerated among officers and civil servants in the Dual Monarchy, even at senior levels. As for Redl's high life, which included lavish furnishings and expensive jewels and automobiles, the colonel had explained it away as an inheritance; it was a private matter and, as such, off limits for discussion, particularly on the clannish General Staff, which protected its own.

In a panic, Conrad engineered a cover story claiming that Redl had only been spying for the Russians for a couple years, and had betrayed nothing of real consequence, a lie that was presented, in various forms, to Franz Joseph, the Viennese parliament, and to allies in Berlin. Conrad's relationship with the heir to the throne had grown strained anyway, and the Redl disaster worsened their interaction; as a devout Catholic, Franz Ferdinand disliked how Redl had been forced into suicide without benefit of confession, though the emperor, who was sensitive to the army's rigid code of honor, was more understanding. Several careers were damaged by Redl, and Urbański, the humiliated intelligence chief, only kept his commission due to Conrad's *Protektion*. Officers on the *Evidenzbureau* suspected that Redl's treachery went back to roughly 1907, though no one really knew, as there had been no effort to debrief the traitor before death: eager to make it go away immediately, Conrad precluded any real investigation. Research decades later would reveal that 1907 was the decisive year, when large, unexplained payments began appearing in Redl's bank account, but it seems likely that he had dabbled in betrayal well before then.[68]

Redl's motive was nothing other than pecuniary; he was not recruited, rather he offered his services to the Russians simply for cash to finance his expensive lifestyle. He passed information to the French and Italians too, his relationship with Rome being mysterious and profitable to both sides.[69] Exactly what information Redl passed to the Russians is difficult to establish with certainty, though due to his position he had access to virtually anything he wanted, and later accounts have revealed that Agent No. 25, as he was known to tsarist intelligence, was an exceptionally valuable source of war plans, orders of battle, and all manner of classified information about the Habsburg military. His identity was a closely guarded secret inside Russian intelligence, which protected him carefully, and shared some of his information with Serbia.[70]

It is evident that Redl's treachery caused Austria-Hungary real damage in 1914, but exactly how much is difficult to assess, though it is known that 1912 major military exercises in western Russia were based on information about Habsburg deployments that Redl had provided. What is not debatable, however, is that Redl destroyed his service's espionage network inside Russia. He betrayed it *in toto*, rendering Vienna blind in the spy war that preceded the actual one. When Redl arrived at the *Evidenzbureau* at the turn of the century, it had over a hundred active agents inside Russia; by the time the colonel died, there were none left, the clandestine network having drowned in double agents and mysteriously disappeared sources. Vienna had to resort to desperate measures such as dispatching its most gifted Russian linguist, Capt. Hermann Pokorny, on a "private" driving tour across Russia in the spring of 1914, to learn any military information he could while dodging Russian surveillance. As war approached, Vienna and the General Staff were blinded by the reality of the old cliché: they did not know what they did not know.[71]

Moreover, the lack of any real investigation of the Redl case by the General Staff precluded an answer to the most critical question: Was he acting alone? Rumors had it that the colonel had one or more helpers, and later investigation indicates that was true. Russian intelligence archives possess sensitive Habsburg documents, including an original version of war plans against Montenegro from the end of 1912, to which Redl, then in Prague, would not have had direct access. A senior Russian intelligence general cited a Colonel Jandršek as the other Russian agent on the Habsburg General Staff, though this name does not correspond to any officer of the period.[72] Much about the Redl affair is destined to remain unknown in perpetuity.

While its impact on strategy has perhaps been overdramatized—there have been three films about the case, most recently in 1985—the effect of the Redl scandal on the army and its role in the Dual Monarchy would be difficult to overstate. Only a year before the Great War, the confidence of Austria-Hungary's key institution was badly shaken when one of its rising stars was revealed to be a traitor. The implications were stunning. If even top officers on the General Staff were untrustworthy, in whom could anyone have confidence? The young novelist Stefan Zweig, in Paris when he heard of the affair, said it was the first time "terror clutched my throat," a feeling shared by many Habsburg subjects who saw the Dual Monarchy's international position eroding and its internal stability evaporating around them. Franz Joseph was deeply disturbed by the Redl case, even the sanitized version Conrad told him, commenting, "So this is the new age? And these are the creatures it produces? In our old days such a thing would have been unthinkable."[73]

For Conrad there was no getting away from the Redl disaster. It harmed his relations with Berlin and Franz Ferdinand, both of whom questioned his judgment, as Europe drifted toward war, as well as causing backbiting and bad feelings inside the General Staff, which was distracted by the scandal for months. To the end of his life Conrad could not bear to hear the name of "that scoundrel" uttered in his presence, so fresh did the wound of Redl's treachery remain.

4   July Crisis

Although the Redl debacle was a disaster for the Dual Monarchy, not least because it preoccupied the top military leadership during critical months as Austria-Hungary's strategic position deteriorated thanks to the Balkan Wars, the scandal was not without beneficiaries. In Conrad's setback, his rival Oskar Potiorek saw an opportunity. He had nursed grievances ever since being passed over as General Staff chief in 1906 in favor of Conrad, and in the sensation surrounding Redl's demise, Potiorek at last detected a way to re-ingratiate himself at court, particularly with Archduke Franz Ferdinand.

Word soon reached Sarajevo about the falling out between the army's top general and the heir to the throne, giving Potiorek hope that he might be able to replace Conrad, whose already bumpy tenure as General Staff chief now seemed endangered by the spy scandal and its failed cover-up. The relationship between Conrad and Franz Ferdinand bottomed out in the late summer of 1913, and for a time the heir to the throne did contemplate firing Conrad, but his preferred choice was not Potiorek, rather Karl Tersztyánszky von Nádas, the reactionary cavalry general.[1] Undeterred, Potiorek commenced his campaign to win the favor of the archduke, a course of action that would ultimately lead to crisis and conflagration.

As well as being commanding general in Bosnia-Hercegovina, Potiorek was a skilled bureaucratic operator, and he used his court connections to get the attention of Franz Ferdinand and his retinue.

Potiorek's co-conspirator in this was his adjutant and factotum, who never seemed to leave his side, Lt. Col. Erik von Merizzi, the son of one of the general's closest confidants; Potiorek had known the younger Merizzi since he was a boy and trusted him fully. Through the summer and fall of 1913, as Europe girded for war, Potoriek plotted his career restart, all the while privately denouncing the "foul peace" he detested. Ensconced in the Konak, the former Ottoman governor's palace in downtown Sarajevo overlooking the Miljacka river, Potiorek and Merizzi exploited their media connections to make the general seem competent and forceful to Vienna.[2]

That there was something unhealthy about that relationship, and the whole command climate in Sarajevo, was widely noted in General Staff circles, where Potiorek's tendency to ignore advice and even orders from Vienna that he did not like was noted with dismay. Merizzi's deep influence hardly helped Potiorek's difficult working relationship with Conrad. Isolated in the Konak from contrary opinions, the duo seemed to feed off each other's Machiavellian tendencies, resulting in bad feelings on the Sarajevo staff and whispers about both men.[3] Potiorek seldom left his residence and did little to keep contact with his own senior officers, much less the 24,000 infantry under his command in peacetime, to say nothing of the Bosnian population, which he largely ignored in any political sense outside worrying about ubiquitous anti-Habsburg plots he suspected among the populace. In the last months of peace, Potiorek's command was dangerously dysfunctional thanks to its commander's self-removal from decisions and activities that did not interest him.

Here Merizzi's influence must be considered cancerous, since Potiorek's adjutant seemed unworldly and unfamiliar with the troops even by the modest standards of General Staff high-fliers. The forty-year-old officer was "a pure theoretician and bureaucrat," griped Gen. Michael von Appel, the XV Corps commander and Potiorek's top field officer in Sarajevo, who rued how Merizzi's running interference for his boss made him deeply unpopular with senior officers, who fingered him as the main culprit in the inability of anyone to get through to Potiorek about important matters. By the spring of 1914, Appel and other top officers had all but given up trying to connect with the commanding general in Sarajevo, who seemed walled off in an alternate reality in the Konak, a self-constructed world devoted to politicking and getting Potiorek the top uniformed job in Vienna. While Appel respected Potiorek's talents, including his strong work ethic and gentlemanly ways, he considered his superior to be deeply isolated from the deteriorating world outside his palace, evaluating him as "no judge of character, a resident of Mars," as he complained in late October 1913 to Col. Alexander von Brosch, Franz Ferdinand's well connected former military aide. Others were less charitable, including one exasperated general who compared the isolated Potiorek to the Dalai Lama! In the last months of peace, Potiorek was alienated from his own top commanders in Bosnia, including Appel, who had ceased trying to keep the command relationship functional in the face of stonewalling by Merizzi and apparent escapism by Potiorek.[4]

Potiorek was correct that the heir to the throne was unhappy with Conrad in the aftermath of the Redl scandal and the General Staff chief's hotheaded behavior during the Balkan Wars, and by October 1913 informed staffers in Vienna knew that Conrad's tenure was far from indefinite. That said, the sense of mounting crisis surrounding the Dual Monarchy with the emergence of a greatly enlarged and aggressive Serbia that summer, following the Second Balkan War, meant that no decisions about top military jobs were taken rashly. During the last Balkan crisis that October, when Vienna demanded that Serbia evacuate Albania, Franz Ferdinand became exasperated with Conrad's ardor for a conflict that could quickly involve Russia, the European war that the archduke so feared. Yet replacing Conrad, whose judgment he questioned, was a long-term project that the heir to the throne deferred once Belgrade acceded to Vienna's demands regarding Albanian territory.[5]

Frustrated with the archduke, Conrad seriously considered resigning in September 1913, and during the annual *Kaisermanöver*, held in the middle of that month in Bohemia, Franz Ferdinand's right-hand officer, Colonel Brosch, visited the General Staff chief to get assurances that Conrad would not quit in the middle of the exercises, causing bad press for the army and the heir to the throne. The top general agreed to stay in the job and not resign rashly, but he was depressed, not least because Gina von Reininghaus, his longtime mistress, was unenthusiastic about his possible resignation. A few weeks later, during celebrations of the hundredth anniversary of the Battle of Leipzig, the German press reported the peevish comments made by Franz Ferdinand about Conrad in the presence of top Prussian officers, leaving Berlin to wonder about the state of court-army relations in the Dual Monarchy. Conrad ended 1913, by far the toughest year of his career so far, between the Redl and Jandrić spy scandals, the latter involving his own son, unenthusiastic about the future and resigned to the reality that he would not get the preemptive war against rising Serbia that he had so ardently desired, an act that Franz Ferdinand had dismissed as pointless as it would only win Vienna "some pigs and pig herders."[6] Yet to Conrad, his fears for the future of Austria-Hungary seemed increasingly like accurate predictions, made worse by the announcement that, in the event of war, Franz Ferdinand would be named commander of the forces, with Conrad serving as his chief of staff, a position that the latter could not have welcomed, given the two men's parlous relationship. In his annual "Summation of the Situation" report for the General Staff at the beginning of 1914, an increasingly downbeat Conrad concluded that the time for preventative war, his perennial salve for the Dual Monarchy's ills and his personal *idée fixe*, had passed.[7]

In the spring of 1914, Potiorek redoubled his efforts to win the favor of the heir to the throne. His chosen method, which he envisioned months earlier and began planning in May, was a successful run of major maneuvers in Bosnia in late June, where Franz Ferdinand would be the guest of honor. What Potiorek had in mind was nothing short of a military extravaganza, with XV Corps exercises outside Sarajevo that would intimidate Serbia and impress the archduke; what he wanted would consume the army's entire maneuver budget for 1914, one million *kronen*. Franz Ferdinand's staff was sold on the idea, to include an official visit to Sarajevo, despite security concerns, since to avoid the city would insult loyal Bosnians, insisted Erik von Merizzi. This would be a showcase of Habsburg power where and when it was needed. The exercises were scheduled for June 26–27, with a visit to the Bosnian capital the following day. The June 28 stopover was chosen by Franz Ferdinand's military chancery, not by Potiorek's staff, a fateful choice given that it was St. Vitus Day (*Vidovdan*), the holiest day in the Serbian nationalist pantheon that celebrated Serbia's defeat in Kosovo in 1389, though there is no evidence that anyone in Sarajevo pushed back against something that hard-line Serbs would inevitably see as a Habsburg provocation.[8]

Neither is there any convincing evidence that Potiorek intentionally downplayed security during the archduke's fateful visit to Sarajevo, so as to make himself look imposing and able to project his will onto hostile elements of the local population without special measures. Although it would appear self-evident that high security should have been arranged, not least because Potiorek's predecessor, Gen. Marijan Varešanin, was nearly killed by a Serbian assassin in Sarajevo four years before. From the Konak, where reality seldom intruded, it seemed that the unruly provinces were well in hand. Potiorek and Merizzi had managed to wall themselves off from any opinions contrary to their own, and the military had established an impressively comprehensive counterintelligence program in Bosnia-Hercegovina, encompassing border controls with checks on all persons entering from Serbia or Montenegro and supervision of trains and rail stations, as well as cooperation among police, Gendarmerie, state offices, and the army to ensure tabs were kept on suspected subversives and terrorists in the troubled provinces.[9]

Yet, inevitably, Habsburg *Schlamperei* (carelessness) meant that plans were easier to create than to implement effectively, and in the event, the Sarajevo-bound assassins had no great difficulty infiltrating Bosnia, not least because they were assisted by Serbian military intelligence. Despite considerable effort expended by the *k.u.k. Armee* to monitor Belgrade's covert operations in Bosnia-Hercegovina, Vienna and Sarajevo were both in the dark about the assassination plot, despite a general awareness that Col. Dragutin Dimitrijević, the powerful Serbian military intelligence chief known as Apis (the Bull), was running spies inside the Dual Monarchy and was deeply hostile to anything Habsburg.[10] Apis, after all, had supported terrorism in his own country, including his key role in Belgrade's bloody 1903 palace coup, so it hardly should have been a surprise that the ringleader of the "king killers" was capable of backing murderers abroad. Operational security was not a priority for Apis and his coterie, as it dispatched the young assassins into Bosnia in late May armed with pistols from Serbian Army stocks, complete with stamps from the Kragujevac arsenal, thus betraying the actual affiliation of the Black Hand terrorist group as a front for Serbian military intelligence.

Moreover, Apis was no more professionally competent than his Austro-Hungarian opponents in the spy war, as the assassination of Franz Ferdinand was desired because Belgrade's classified assessment placed the heir to the throne at the center of the alleged "war party" in Vienna that wanted to crush Serbia. As Franz Ferdinand was in fact the most antiwar figure inside power circles in Austria-Hungary, this must rank as one of the most consequential failures of intelligence analysis in history. Little new has emerged in recent decades to flesh out the background to the Sarajevo assassination, mostly because relevant paperwork on the Serbian side, if it ever existed, was long ago destroyed.[11] What is not in doubt is that Apis and his staffers were the drivers of the plot, making the assassination an unambiguous case of state-sponsored terrorism. Myths about alleged specific warnings given by Belgrade to Vienna, yet misplaced, have been debunked long ago, but significant questions remain about major aspects of the Sarajevo plot.[12]

Although it has long been apparent that senior members of Serbia's civilian government had foreknowledge of the plot, and the matter was discussed in some fashion *en cabinet* before Franz Ferdinand set out for Sarajevo, details are sparse, though it is evident that Prime Minister Nikola Pašić and Stojan Protić, his interior minister, were aware of Apis's machinations by mid-June, yet they demurred from taking on the fierce colonel, who after all had overseen the brutal murder of Serbia's king and queen a decade before. Less defined and more sensational still is the matter of Russian involvement. While none have questioned that Apis had a close relationship with Col. Viktor Artamonov, the Russian military attaché in Belgrade, accessible records do not explain what role, if any, Artamonov had in the plot. To make matters murkier still, just before his execution by his own government at Salonika in June 1917, Apis boasted in writing of his role behind the Sarajevo plot and admitted that Artamonov funded the terrorist operation, something that Yugoslavia's Communists revealed in 1953 to discredit the royal regime that preceded them in power in Belgrade.[13] Since Artamonov died in exile in 1942 without fully explaining his role in the assassination, details are likely to remain unresolved in perpetuity, especially the tantalizing question of whether Artamonov's support to the plot was his own initiative or something undertaken by direction from St. Petersburg.

Given that Russian radio intelligence was able to read Austro-Hungarian diplomatic ciphers before the war, it seems likely that St. Petersburg was aware of what Vienna's probable reaction to the assassination would be, and, as Sean McMeekin has recently observed, the Russians subsequently acted as if they have something to hide: "gaps in the record strongly suggest a good deal of purging took place after 1914," to cover whatever tracks Artamonov left behind. The attaché conveniently managed to be out of Belgrade on the day of the assassination, yet it was well known in Serbian military circles that, in the weeks before the assassination, he and Apis saw each other almost daily. A Serbian colonel who was close to Apis conceded that Artamonov had encouraged the plot: "Just go ahead! If you are attacked, you will not stand alone!" Although the colonel later retracted his statement, it seems very likely that St. Petersburg knew more about the plot that it later proved politic to admit.[14]

The assassination itself unfolded on Sunday, June 28, in a manner that proved tragic and comic in equal measure. As it was a long weekend, with the feast of Sts. Peter and Paul falling the next day, much of the court as well as many General Staff officers in Vienna had headed to the Alps on holiday. It made no difference anyway, since the assassins had no trouble getting close to their quarry due to lax security in Sarajevo.[15] Fresh from observing two days of successful military exercises in the hills outside Sarajevo, the imperial-and-royal entourage set out from the nearby spa town of Ilidža, where they were lodging, and headed into the city. Franz Ferdinand was in good spirits throughout his Bosnian sojourn, and even Conrad found his interactions with the archduke more pleasant than usual during the maneuvers. The General Staff chief had headed to Zagreb the previous evening, to prepare for a staff ride, and was not present for the fateful visit to Sarajevo.

Although there were six would-be killers in position downtown that morning, the first two failed to act when the three-car motorcade drove right past them at no great speed. The third young assassin, Nedeljko Čabrinović, managed to throw a grenade at Franz Ferdinand's car, but it bounced off and exploded under the following vehicle, wounding twenty bystanders but in no way harming the archduke. Čabrinović also failed with his suicide attempt, his cyanide pill inducing vomiting rather than death, and his jump into the Miljacka river proved anticlimactic as the stream was only a few inches deep in summer. He was beaten by the crowd and saved by the police, who promptly arrested him; embarrassingly, Čabrinović's father was a Sarajevo police official.

Leaving the damaged car behind, the convoy sped up to reach City Hall, where the next event was planned. As the two cars drove past them, with Franz Ferdinand in plain sight, the three remaining assassins, including nineteen-year-old Gavrilo Princip, failed to react. Yet Čabrinović's grenade had impact, since Erik von Merizzi was among the wounded. He had been riding in the damaged car and was taken to the hospital with shrapnel injuries. While Potiorek advocated a quick run to the security of the Konak after the archduke's speech at City Hall, Franz Ferdinand wished to check on the wounded adjutant and, without guidance from Merizzi—who was the action officer for the entourage—the heir to the throne's driver took a wrong turn on the way to the hospital. Correcting his error, the driver placed Franz Ferdinand and his wife, Sophie, directly in front of Princip, who was despondent about missing his chance to make history. With his quarry suddenly before him, the terrified teenager closed his eyes and fired two shots with his Browning 9 mm pistol: both fatal, one felled Franz Ferdinand while the other killed Sophie. Oskar Potiorek, from the car's front seat, watched it all, helplessly. Within minutes both victims were dead. Princip was grabbed by police immediately, while five of the six assassins were in custody within hours. It made no difference now.

As word of the double murder was telegraphed to the world, Potiorek overcame his shock. His grand plan to ingratiate himself with the future emperor had ended instead in Franz Ferdinand's assassination. Potiorek was beside himself with rage and began dispatching cables to Vienna explaining that the assassination was just the beginning of a Serbian uprising against Habsburg rule that must be crushed at once with military force. The commanding general in Bosnia was hardly alone in his anger, and Sarajevo saw spontaneous attacks on Serbs, and Serbian-owned businesses in the city were assaulted by angry mobs. The riots spread across Bosnia and Croatia, and long-festering anti-Serb sentiments burst into the open among average Habsburg subjects. While mourning was muted in Budapest, where the late archduke's anti-Magyar views were well known, in the rest of the Dual Monarchy the double murder was met with sincere outrage. The mordant rhyme *Serbien muss sterbien* ("Serbia must die") quickly gained currency, while among the Slovenes, not previously noted for their anti-Serb views, the poem *Srbe na vrbe* ("Hang the Serbs from willow trees") by the *kaisertreu* politico Marko Natlačen was soon the rage.

Conrad, who was on an overnight train from Sarajevo to Zagreb when the assassination happened, was informed of the news upon his arrival around 2:00 p.m. on June 28, when he reached the Croatian capital. His assessment was a common one in Habsburg power circles: "the murder in Sarajevo was the last link in a long chain. It was not the deed of an individual fanatic . . . it was the declaration of war of Serbia against Austria-Hungary."[16] Conrad accepted that war with a surprising degree of resignation, given the many times as General Staff chief that he had enthusiastically counseled war on Serbia as the salve for the Dual Monarchy's ills. Only hours after the assassination, he confided his deepest thoughts, as was his custom, in a letter to his mistress. He was filled with pessimism, seeing Russia, together with Serbia and Romania, attacking Austria-Hungary now: "It will be a hopeless struggle, but it must be pursued, because so ancient a Monarchy and so glorious an Army cannot perish ingloriously," he wrote to his beloved Gina.[17]

Conrad's letters to his friends as crisis took over Vienna were hardly more optimistic. As he wrote to the jurist Johann von Chlumecký, "In 1908–09 it would have been a game with open cards, in 1912–13 still a game with chances, now we are betting everything (*jetzt ist es ein va banque Spiel*)."[18] The General Staff chief did not meet with Franz Joseph until July 5, two days after the funeral of Franz Ferdinand and Sophie. Conrad, who hardly felt the archduke's death deeply, nevertheless found the old man less in mourning for his nephew than he had anticipated, and mostly concerned with whether Germany would support Austria-Hungary in the event of war. Notwithstanding the fact that the aged monarch feared war's impact, Franz Joseph too did not shy away from war in the aftermath of the assassination. As Manfried Rauchensteiner has uncovered, in the almost daily meetings Franz Joseph had after the assassination with his military and political leadership, the emperor-king did little, if anything, to stymie the many voices counseling war on Serbia and, with it, Russia too. Four days after the assassination, the emperor's foreign minister, Count Berchtold, forthrightly informed him that the Dual Monarchy's status as a great power now depended on directly confronting Serbia. When confronted with the reality of a multifront conflict, Franz Joseph's laconic comeback was trademark: "Well then it's war."[19]

The same day Conrad met with Franz Joseph, Foreign Minister Count Leopold von Berchtold sent Count Alexander Hoyos, his *chef de cabinet*, to Berlin to secure German support for war on Serbia, and likely Russia too. Two days later, Hoyos returned to Vienna with Germany's famous "blank check" in hand.[20] That day, July 7, the relevant ministers met to decide a course of action, based on Hoyos's briefing: Berchtold plus Gen. Alexander von Krobatin (War), Leon von Biliński (Finance), joined by the prime ministers of Austria and Hungary, Count Karl Stürgkh and Count István Tisza. Conrad and Rear Adm. Karl Kailer represented the armed services and participated in the meeting as experts on military matters only, something Conrad made much of in later years, implying his involvement was marginal. In truth, Biliński and Stürgkh had accepted the validity of Conrad's repeated advocacy of war against Serbia long before the assassination, and under the crisis conditions now prevailing, Berchtold agreed, so there was little chance that peace remained a serious option. Only Hungary's Tisza's expressed concern about the rush to war, and his resistance would prove temporary.[21] There was general consensus among the ministers, Tisza excepted, that the time for appeasing Serbian misconduct was long passed, and, with German support received, it would be foolish for the Dual Monarchy to pursue any course but war, as the domestic consequences for the multinational empire of anything less than crushing Serbia appeared dire. In a perverse irony, Princip had taken away the one major leader in Austria-Hungary who would have mightily resisted the rush to war that overtook Vienna in early July. By the evening of July 7, it was clear that the Habsburg Army was going to war.

Yet Vienna did not issue its ultimatum to Serbia until July 23, over two weeks later. Why the Dual Monarchy allowed this strange lethargy to take over in the midst of the rising crisis that was engulfing the rest of Europe remains debated, but it is evident that much of the delay was caused by the army's peacetime personnel policies. It had been the custom for years to give harvest leave in mid-summer to help bring in the crops. This policy was regarded as dubiously valuable for agriculture, as many troops seemed to spend more time carousing than working the fields, but rural politicians demanded the policy be retained, and by early July tens of thousands of troops were already away from their barracks. In a report dated July 6, the General Staff stated that troops had been furloughed for the harvest in seven of the sixteen army corps districts, including three—IV (Budapest), VII (Temesvár), and XIII (Zagreb)—bordering Serbia, and, barring a special order, they would not begin returning until July 19, or as late as July 25 in two Hungarian corps districts. Hence no ultimatum could be delivered to Serbia until July 22, at the earliest, Conrad informed the Foreign Ministry leadership on July 8. With that, the General Staff chief went on holiday—in part because Berchtold suggested that Conrad and Krobatin take some leave to give the appearance of normalcy—and headed to the Alps with Gina and several friends. He would not return to Vienna until July 19.[22]

For once, Conrad did not rank among the biggest fire-breathers in the army regarding Serbia. From Sarajevo, Potiorek throughout July dispatched cables to Vienna pleading for war, arguing that Bosnia-Hercegovina was swarming with enemy spies, saboteurs, and even Serbian troops in disguise, and the provinces would be lost if action were not taken quickly. Indeed, for many Habsburg senior officers, the great fear that July was that there would *not* be war, a worry that rose by mid-month, as no diplomatic action had been taken against Belgrade. It is important to note that, for most of the hard-liners, war against Serbia was fundamentally a matter of domestic politics, a last-ditch effort to save the fragmenting Dual Monarchy from chaos and dissolution. In early July, Appel, the XV Corps commander in Sarajevo, was writing fellow senior officers that only a military dictatorship could now save the realm, "we have to clean up this place," all that was needed was "a tough soldier with an honorable heart, an iron will to serve his Emperor loyally and lift up the country, a year of a state of emergency"—provided, of course, there were victories on the field of battle.[23]

There was the rub. For the army to save the empire it had to win, and many senior officers at least privately knew that the military's readiness for a major war left much to be desired. Yet it was difficult to escape the war euphoria that spread after the assassination, the sense among many in uniform that this was the last chance to set right what had been going so wrong for the Dual Monarchy for decades. As Gabriel Tánczos, military attaché in Athens, wrote to Conrad on July 3, "I have taken into account the possibility of failure: 1. but I believe in success, and 2. even a partial failure would hardly have worse consequences than continuing inaction."[24]

For some officers, the coming war seemed inevitable yet filled with foreboding. None was more despondent than Col. Alexander von Brosch, the former military assistant to the murdered archduke. The two had stayed in close touch after Brosch took command of the elite Second *Kaiserjäger*, a regiment he loved—he was being stashed in the Tyrol, awaiting his call back to Vienna to serve Franz Ferdinand again, as a general—and news of the assassination sent him into despondency. Although Brosch had recently married well, his world crumbled in an instant with the events at Sarajevo: "I lost every hope for the future," he confided to a senior general three days after the murders. "Spiritually at least I am as dead as my old boss," he explained to another friend. All Brosch could now look forward to was avenging Franz Ferdinand's murder by leading his regiment into battle, as "all my hopes for the future have been destroyed." He would soon get his wish.[25]

Conrad returned to Vienna for a secret meeting at Berchtold's home on July 19, where the top ministers convened. Here the ten points for the ultimatum to Belgrade were drafted, while Conrad briefed the Dual Monarchy's civilian leadership on his war plans for Serbia. By now,

Prime Minister Tisza of Hungary had come around to the necessity for war, in part because he was reassured of Berlin's support. Unlike the military leadership in many European countries that fateful July, the General Staff made no effort to mislead politicians about what the military intended to do. However, war plans for Russia got much less attention at that pivotal meeting than they deserved. Conrad continued to treat the likely titanic struggle with Russia as something approaching an afterthought. It certainly interested him less than the prospect of giving Serbia a thrashing. He then returned to Tyrol for two more days of rest, and came back to Vienna late on July 21. Conrad's retinue now included a bodyguard, a logical decision given the events at Sarajevo, yet this development depressed the General Staff chief and contributed to his rising gloom about the war he had done so much to bring about. On July 23, just hours before the ultimatum was sent to Belgrade, Conrad reminded Berchtold that the decision to mobilize the army could not be reversed.[26]

What transpired among Austria-Hungary's military and political elite in July 1914 may be charitably termed groupthink. Not only did Conrad and his civilian counterparts fail to seriously debate the consequences of war against Serbia—any Viennese discussion of what strategic objectives and war termination might look like was cursory at best—they almost wholly ignored the impact of what all-but-certain Russian involvement in the war might mean. Given the Dual Monarchy's military weakness, which Conrad well knew, the General Staff chief must bear primary responsibility for this willful strategic blindness, a desire to avert eyes that would have catastrophic consequences for Austria-Hungary. Moreover, we can dispense with shopworn notions that Berlin was encouraging reckless behavior in Vienna. Conrad from beginning to end was notoriously unconcerned with the thoughts of the Prussians, whom he cordially despised; beyond getting the blank check, the General Staff seemed largely uninterested in coordinating with their allies. "The Habsburgs were making their own decisions about their future," concluded Samuel Williamson, and the decision for war that fateful July would prove to be the last major strategic decision the Dual Monarchy would make on its own.[27]

That Russia was likely to enter the war on behalf of its ally Serbia was understood by many Habsburg officials, though few at the top wanted to admit it. After the fact, War Minister Krobatin conceded that during secret deliberations throughout the July Crisis, "in preparing our measures against Serbia, all competent authorities had counted on the inevitability of Russian intervention."[28] Diplomats noted that Russian counterparts were slow in expressing their condolences about the assassination, while the tsar's embassies all over Europe failed to follow the custom of lowering flags to half-mast out of respect for the fallen archduke. Nikolai Hartwig, the tsar's minister in Belgrade, who was notorious in Vienna for his fiery encouragement of Serbian nationalism, held a party on the night of the assassination and took two weeks to deliver condolences to his Habsburg counterpart in Serbia—at which point he promptly dropped dead of a heart attack (his end, typically, was attributed to Habsburg malfeasance by the Belgrade press).

Within two days of its receipt, Serbia rejected the Austro-Hungarian ultimatum, as Vienna had anticipated. Indeed, the main fear of many Habsburg generals was that, somehow, Belgrade might accede to the Dual Monarchy's demands, thereby cutting short the war that was coming so tantalizingly into focus. From Sarajevo, Appel wrote to Brosch on July 25 of his "feverish longing" for war "to finish off those murder-boys—God grant us only that we remain steadfast . . . oh that we could march forth, we're only lacking faith . . . just let it go (*nur los lassen*)—we'll take care of the rest."[29]

Appel need not have worried. There was never any chance that the Pašić government, which understood some of Belgrade's culpability in the assassination, would agree to all Vienna's demands, especially the requirement that Habsburg investigators have a free hand to pursue leads in Serbia regarding the assassination plot. Serbia's rejection, received on July 25, came as a blessing to many Austro-Hungarian officers. That evening, Franz Joseph authorized a limited mobilization, beginning

July 28, of eight corps—twenty-six divisions—the forces required to execute Conrad's Plan "B" for the invasion of Serbia. The Serbs issued their general mobilization order on July 24, fearing a rapid Habsburg invasion that did not materialize. Military action against the Serbs at the end of July, after Belgrade received Austria-Hungary's declaration of war at noon on July 28, was limited to desultory shelling of Belgrade by Habsburg batteries across the Danube and Sava rivers, and by three monitors of the navy's Danube Flotilla. Its military effect was nil.

Senior officials, worried that the cautious old emperor might be wavering at the eleventh hour, briefed Franz Joseph that on July 27, Serbian troops on a river steamer had opened fire on a Habsburg unit of VII Corps at Temeskubin, in south Hungary on the Danube, in an act of unprovoked aggression. Yet news of this "battle" was not reported through normal army channels—VII Corps command at Temesvár was unaware of it—and the skirmish may never have happened at all; at a minimum, the event was seriously embellished to impress the emperor with Belgrade's aggressive intent as the July Crisis came to its denouement.[30] Austria-Hungary's declaration of war against Serbia soon followed.

How Austria-Hungary mobilized and deployed its forces in August 1914 remains one of the most vexing and consequential historical questions surrounding the First World War. In no other country would the manner in which its armies went to war prove to have such an impact—here, entirely negative—on the course of the conflict. Habsburg weakness at the outset would have vexed even the most seasoned strategist, since the essential problem was that the Dual Monarchy simply did not possess sufficient forces to fight any two-front war, much less execute simultaneous offensives on Serbia and against the lion's share of the vast Russian Army. Yet the ways the General Staff chose to approach this strategic dilemma must rank as one of the greatest debacles in all military history.

Simply put, Conrad took his disadvantages and magnified them through seemingly willful blindness and an intractable escapism that was impressive even by Viennese standards. Conrad's disastrous choices on how to mobilize and deploy his armies that August sealed the fate of his army and with it the Dual Monarchy itself. How the General Staff chief, who for all his weaknesses understood the essential strategic dilemma that his outnumbered army faced in 1914, came to such dreadful decisions has troubled historians for a century. As two eminent scholars recently concluded charitably, "it continues to be puzzling that Conrad made so many decisions that seemed to defy common sense."[31]

Despite the fact that Russia's involvement in the coming war was obvious by late July, Conrad persisted in executing plans based on the assumption that Austria-Hungary would have a free hand to deal with "Dog Serbia." As late as the night of July 31 to August 1, in the face of evidence that Russia had already begun to mobilize its huge army for war, Conrad pushed forward planning solely for War Plan "B" against Serbia. As discussed in the previous chapter, Conrad had long been haunted by the terrible conundrum of a two-front war that Austria-Hungary could not likely win, and his blindness to the realities unfolding before him in late July 1914 would doom his army.

The most fateful act was the decision on the evening of July 31 to mobilize B-Group, essentially the Second Army, and dispatch it to the Balkans to assist in the invasion of Serbia, then quickly ship it northwards to join A-Group in its offensive against Russia. This plan relied on the assumption of glacially slow Russian mobilization—and exceptionally wishful thinking. In the end, it performed the remarkable—and for Austria-Hungary tragic—feat of giving the Second Army the opportunity to participate in two great offensives on different fronts inside three weeks, yet never enough to actually deliver victory in either effort. Winston Churchill's verdict on B-Group is apposite: it "left Potiorek before it could win him a victory; it returned to Conrad in time to participate in his defeat."[32]

When the extent of Habsburg losses in the summer of 1914 became apparent and it became impossible to conceal the impact of terrible deployment decisions at the outset, Conrad and his loyal staffers responded by blaming everyone—the railroads, technical difficulties, diplomats, German allies—except the General Staff chief himself.[33] For decades after the war, General Staff officers, who controlled official military history in Vienna into the middle of the twentieth century, preserved the reputation of their former chief through dissimulation, obfuscation, and outright lying. This process, which caused deep misunderstandings about what actually happened in Vienna in the summer of 1914 and particularly why the Habsburg military performed so poorly in the Great War's pivotal opening campaigns, has been termed "the Habsburg Command Conspiracy" by the American historian who uncovered the relevant evidence.[34]

According to the General Staff–approved version of events, the decision to send the dozen divisions of the Second Army first to Serbia and then rapidly to Galicia was sensible, indeed unavoidable, since the army's Railroad Bureau, which controlled all deployments, determined that, due to the complex nature of preplanned rail schedules, B-Group would reach Galicia at approximately the same time, regardless of whether it had a fighting detour in the Balkans along the way![35] The painful truth is that there was nothing inevitable about any of it, indeed it flew in the face of what some Railroad Bureau officers had counseled, yet the deployment decisions made by August 1 by Conrad doomed his grand offensive against Russia to certain defeat. At the beginning of August there was still time to dispatch B-Group to Galicia, not Serbia, thereby giving the war against Russia at least a chance of success, but for reasons that cannot be satisfactorily answered, Conrad chose to persist with his original deployments.

To be fair to Conrad, the chief of the army's Railroad Bureau was on holiday in Dalmatia while many key decisions were taken in late July, leaving authority in the hands of that office's fourth-ranking officer, Maj. Emil Ratzenhofer (who, not coincidentally, wrote extensively after the war in defense of his bureau's disastrous deployment decisions). To make matters worse, the General Staff went to war against Russia based on enemy deployment plans from 1908 that had been purloined by Habsburg intelligence, despite the fact that the most rudimentary counterintelligence assumption had to be that the Russians knew that plan was compromised as the result of Redl's treachery. Yet nothing was done in this case of Habsburg *Schlamperei* grown Kafkaesque.[36]

Nevertheless, primary blame for the disasters born of flawed Austro-Hungarian deployments in August 1914 must be placed on Conrad, who had planned for this war for years and was unquestionably acquainted with the strategic realities caused by endemic Habsburg military weakness. Why Conrad chose to doom his own war plans at the outset by refusing to accept the inevitability of war with Russia until it was too late perhaps cannot be answered fully. Yet the character of the General Staff chief offers hints, not least Conrad's persistent unwillingness—evidenced painfully many times in the Great War—to accept that his grand strategic concepts simply could not be executed by the army he actually had at his disposal. No less, Conrad's well-honed tendency to ignore vital matters of logistics seems to have played a part, as did his manner of taking as strategy what was frequently just grand tactics.

There is also the complex matter of Conrad's personal life. In the last years of peace, his relationship with his mistress Gina bordered on obsession. One of his staffers noted that the affair "totally absorbed" the general and was "something very unhealthy." As war loomed, Conrad battled depression, confiding to a friend, "I have lost the joy in my profession that has sustained me through everything since I was eleven years old," finding solace only in Gina, a woman he could not truly have. She demurred at the public stigma of divorce, which upset Conrad profoundly, who in his letters entertained the notion that, if he became a successful war leader, Gina then might leave her husband and become truly his. While it cannot be established that this caused Conrad's terrible decisions in the summer of 1914, there seems little doubt that the lovesick general's tempestuous affair only encouraged his desire to seek solution to the vexing problems of the Dual Monarchy—and his own personal life—on the battlefield.[37]

Perhaps fortunately, Austria-Hungary's public knew nothing of Conrad's affairs nor of his deployment mistakes. Word of the declaration of war against Serbia on July 28 was met with euphoria across the Dual Monarchy. The tension that had been building for weeks, indeed years, burst at last. The crimes of Sarajevo would be avenged, a thought that warmed the hearts of Habsburg patriots and was welcomed even by those who had doubts about the empire. Sigmund Freud pronounced, "For the first time in thirty years, I feel myself to be an Austrian, and feel like giving this not very hopeful empire another chance. All my libido is dedicated to Austria-Hungary."[38] In Budapest, Count Albert Apponyi, who headed the parliamentary faction that disliked the *Ausgleich* because it did not give Hungary *enough* power, greeted the news of war by exclaiming, "At last!" The notion that Austria-Hungary could now solve its internal problems through fighting was by no means confined to the Dual Monarchy's military elite.

The Austrian violinist Fritz Kreisler, who was living in Switzerland when the crisis came, quickly headed home to his regiment. Although he had actually resigned his reserve commission two years earlier, he now wanted to take part in the war, as a patriot. He reached Vienna on August 1, the first day of general mobilization. Spirits were not dimmed, despite the fact that the army in a strange legalism turned away enthusiastic reservists who appeared for duty all over the country on July 31, a day early. The capital was bursting with patriotic emotions. Kreisler witnessed a Vienna he had never seen before, filled with troops of many regiments, a city imbued with a patriotic fervor that transcended nationality and even class:

Immediately it was evident what a great leveler war is. Differences in rank and social distinctions had practically ceased. All barriers seemed to have fallen; everybody addressed everybody else.

I saw the crowds stop officers of high rank and well-known members of the aristocracy and clergy, also state officials and court functionaries of high rank, in quest of information, which was imparted cheerfully and patiently. The imperial princes could frequently be seen on the Ringstrasse surrounded by cheering crowds or mingling with the public unceremoniously at cafes, talking to everybody. Of course, the army was idolized. Whenever the troops marched the public broke into cheers and every uniform was the center of an ovation.[39]

Beginning August 1, staff officers everywhere in the Dual Monarchy followed the detailed plans that had been drafted for decades and updated annually by the General Staff on how to call up, organize, equip, feed, and within a few days move all of the sixteen standing army corps, each of which quickly swelled to a strength of more than fifty thousand troops and thousands of horses.[40] The General Staff prepared to enter the field and took on the title of High Command (*Armeeoberkommando*, AOK) for the duration of hostilities. The fifty-eight-year-old Archduke Friedrich, grandson of the legendary Archduke Karl, who bested Napoleon at Aspern, was appointed supreme commander of the forces, but despite the fact that "Fritzl" was a career officer he left nearly all military matters beyond the ceremonial to Conrad and his staff. He did, however, sign off on one of the first orders issued after mobilization, the declaration of martial law (*Standrecht*) over all persons, including civilians, in the zone of field operations, which was defined broadly by the army; this order encompassed a wide array of crimes that could be punished summarily by the military, including "insulting His Majesty."[41] Across the Dual Monarchy, military and police officials collaborated on identifying suspected subversives, particularly in sensitive border regions where the population was assessed as being of questionable loyalty, based on internal security plans drawn up since the Bosnian crisis of 1908. In this way, the military defined "enemy espionage" not only as spying, but rather as a wide range of activities that could impinge on the effectiveness of the army and harm the war effort.[42]

Popular reaction to the mobilization order was far more enthusiastic than most officers had anticipated. Across Austria-Hungary, the appearance of posters ordering general mobilization—in fifteen languages—were met with patriotic cries and toasts from most, with little dissent in public. Despite the confusion caused by the twenty-four-hour delay in report time, depots all over the Dual Monarchy witnessed enthusiastic reservists showing up a day early, eager to rejoin the colors. Decades before, Bismarck had observed, "When Emperor Franz Joseph mounts his horse, all his peoples will follow." The events of early August, played out in hundreds of barracks across the country, seemed to bear out that prognostication better than many Habsburg generals had thought possible. Numerous career officers were startled to see socialist and left-leaning reservists and even Czechs, the most suspect of the army's nationalities, appearing for duty punctually and filled with good spirits.[43]

Loyalism among Czechs surprised many officers, who had been conditioned to expect revolt and revolution from them. Patriotic sentiments were suddenly visible in the unlikeliest of places. That August, troops were surprised to be greeted all over the Czech lands with enthusiastic shouts from civilians of "*Naši vojáci!*" (Our soldiers!), accompanied by gifts of food and liquor, even when the troops were not Czech themselves.[44] A captain of the Thirtieth *Landwehr* Regiment, more than two-thirds of whose troops were Czechs, noted that the pro-Habsburg sentiments he witnessed among Czechs, military and civilian, upon mobilization was something he would never have believed, had he not witnessed it himself. The assassination hurt the fortunes of the pro-Serbian element among the population, and while there was little enthusiasm for war against Russia, there was no antiwar sentiment detectable either. Indeed, the captain noted that he could not tell his Czech and German troops apart in their attitudes toward the army and the empire, and he claimed not to hear "a word against the war nor against the Monarchy—on the contrary." As the regiment waited longer than most units to head to the front, the troops interacted with the locals, and the captain observed that, at the public concerts given by the regimental band, civilians sang the imperial hymn with greater feeling than he had ever witnessed before. Although some of the Czech intelligentsia remained aloof, average people were warm and friendly to the soldiers, while among the troops, some of them fathers and sons serving in the same company, most seemed more worried about missing the war than anything else.[45]

Even Italians, another ethnic group most career officers deemed to be suspect, reported for duty with gusto. In Trieste, where irredentist spirits had seemed commonplace to the local garrison staff, the Ninety-seventh Regiment, which recently had the duty of escorting the bodies of the murdered heir to the throne and his wife through the city after they were brought up the Adriatic on the dreadnought *Viribus Unitis*, seemed to be in high spirits as it readied for war. On August 11, its 4,300 men departed their city singing patriotic songs in their Venetian dialect about the looming fight for Galicia, where so many would soon become casualties.[46]

Upon mobilization, units of the *k.u.k. Armee* expanded enormously, as reservists of all classes fleshed out the ranks. In a typical example, the Fourth Infantry Regiment, Vienna's famed *Hoch-und Deutschmeister*, expanded several times in size practically overnight. Its peacetime cadre was only 1,500 soldiers, but its war strength, counting a replacement (*Marsch*) battalion, came to 6,500 officers and men. Companies tripled in size to 300 strong, while each battalion had two machine guns and dozens of horses; the *Deutschmeister*, like every regiment, had become a mobile town all its own, complete with supply train. Within days the expanded unit attended field mass in Vienna, with all hands reswearing the oath to Franz Joseph at the Prater. For added effect, on August 5, before boarding trains for the ride East, to war, the Fourth Regiment marched in formation down the capital's Ringstrasse, to excited hometown crowds, past the imposing statue of Field Marshal Radetzky.[47]

Everywhere morale seemed high, as the Dual Monarchy appeared to have been turned into one vast army encampment. When the Eighth *Jäger* Battalion left its Carinthian depot on August 10, officers assured the men, "When the leaves begin to fall—or at worst by Christmas—we'll be home." The men entertained themselves in camp on the long train ride east with card games, plus nonstop music played on instruments of all sorts—violins and harmonicas, mostly—while singing army songs from Radetzky's time. Boastful taunts were universal, especially "*Jeder Schuss ein Russ! Jeder Stoss ein Franzos—und Serbien muss sterbien!*" (Every shot a Russky! Every attack a Frog—and Serbia must die!)[48]

Patriotic and religious overtones were intertwined in the army's message to the troops headed to war. In a scene replayed across the Dual Monarchy in every depot, on August 9, Dalmatians of the Twenty-second Regiment gathered in a field at Mostar in Hercegovina under a bright sun and deep blue sky, as the chaplain led the troops, Croats and Serbs, in a restating of their oath to the sovereign and then gave the kneeling thousands general absolution. Then the colonel addressed the men in their own language, unsheathing his sword and saluting the colors while speaking in a powerful voice:

> Soldiers! Our regiment has existed for 205 years. It has participated in countless battles and engagements, it has always fought bravely on the field of honor, it has covered itself with pride, it has earned the thanks of our Emperor and our Fatherland. Here is our brave flag. It's the same flag your fathers and grandfathers fought under . . . and we owe the memory of those heroes (*junaci*) that we also fight for Emperor and Fatherland, and to die bravely if it comes to that.[49]

The army encouraged an explicitly religious understanding of the war getting underway. Rhetoric of "holy war" was commonplace in Austria-Hungary in August 1914, and the righteousness of the cause at hand after the Sarajevo assassination, which was sincerely felt by most citizens in a manner that Americans after the September 11, 2001 terrorist attacks might recognize, was publicly doubted only by those wishing to be seen as subversive. The Catholic Church firmly embraced such heady language, intertwining faith and dynastic loyalty with a strong admixture of desire to punish the Dual Monarchy's enemies, as evidenced in the message from the army's chief chaplain that was read to all Catholic troops in the first week of August:

> Our struggle is a holy and just struggle for sacred right and holy order. It is about the defense of our Fatherland, the defense of our things. It is about the security of our borders. Truly this is a holy war according to the will of God! And if the belligerence of our enemies is brought to shame before the admonishing voice of the angel at Bethlehem: Peace on earth!—so will our struggles be found in the judgment of God even more: You have fought the good fight, a just and holy struggle.[50]

More forceful still was the speech given by Col. Alexander Brosch to the assembled troops of his Second *Kaiserjäger* Regiment as they prepared to entrain for Galicia. At a field mass on Sunday, August 9, held at Brixen, surrounded by high Tyrolean Alps, Brosch exhorted his men to seek nothing less than "the death of the Serbian state." In a bellicose speech tinged with his own grief, he optimistically explained the mighty task before them:

> Soldiers! Today it has been six weeks since the cowards dispatched by Serbia treacherously murdered our dearly beloved heir to the throne, Archduke Franz Ferdinand, the pride and the future of Austria, and his noble, high-minded wife. . . . Our Balkan Army is already marching. Soon it will destroy the Serbian Army and chastise the land of the murder-boys. But the greater and more honorable task falls to us—we are marching against Russia.
> Soldiers! You have heard about Russia's giant army. But do not be dismayed. The Russian Army consists mainly of uncivilized barbarians who know neither love of Emperor nor of Fatherland. Russian soldiers have neither enthusiasm nor confidence in victory, and their military training ranks far behind ours. Internal unrest and vast borders mean Russia cannot deploy its whole army against us. Moreover, Germany's powerful and glorious army is marching with

us. Even more, the enthusiasm of all the peoples of the Monarchy marches with us too, with Justice and God beside. With such allies we must win and destroy our powerful opponents. What little Japan pulled off years ago must also be possible for us.

Tyroleans! We are embarking on a Holy War. We must avenge the blood of our heir to the throne, on behalf of our beloved aged Emperor, the noble scion of the Habsburgs, fighting for honor and the existence of our Fatherland. . . . Victory must be ours! May God grant it![51]

Upon total mobilization of all categories of reservists, the Austro-Hungarian Army, which had a peacetime strength 414,000, rose to 2.08 million soldiers in the field forces (including 53,000 officers), with 1.27 million more troops in rear areas and depots.[52] This meant a frontline strength of 18 corps (including 2 just raised at mobilization), 50 infantry divisions, 11 cavalry divisions, 483 field artillery batteries with 2,610 pieces and 76 fortress artillery batteries with 280 heavy pieces. The infantry came to 110 *k.u.k* regiments plus 30 battalions of *Feldjäger*, 40 regiments of Austrian *Landwehr*, and 32 *Honvéd/Domobran* regiments from Hungary; second line reserves (*Landsturm*) added 40 regiments from Austria and 32 from Hungary, respectively—some 927 infantry battalions in all, which was actually slightly less than the Habsburg military had sent to war in 1866, despite the enormous growth in Austria-Hungary's population in the intervening five decades.

Cavalry amounted to 303 squadrons divided among 42 *k.u.k.* regiments (15 Dragoons, 16 Hussars and 11 Lancers, each of 2 "divisions," i.e., battalions), plus 6 regiments and 2 divisions from the Austrian *Landwehr* and 10 regiments and 10 *Landsturm* divisions from the *Honvéd/Domobranstvo*.[53] Engineers included 14 battalions of sappers (79 companies), 9 battalions of pioneers (43 companies) plus a specialist bridging battalion. There were also 11 battalions of the recently raised Telegraph Regiment to provide communications. Last, the *Landsturm* mobilized 227 battalions to provide rear area security throughout the

Dual Monarchy. With the exception of a small contingent of fortress artillery, the entire *k.u.k. Armee* would be committed at the outset to either the Balkan or Eastern fronts: 4 batteries of super-heavy artillery, 8 M.11 305 mm mortars, one-third of the army's total, were dispatched to Belgium to help the Germans blast their way through fortifications as they executed the Schlieffen Plan. The excellent Austro-Hungarian pieces, more advanced and mobile than anything in German arsenals, did excellent work at Namur, Maubeuge, and Antwerp, among other battles in Belgium that August.[54]

Despite Conrad's support, the army's nascent air arm was far smaller on mobilization than the General Staff chief had wanted. Each field army would receive an detachment of four or five balloons to assist artillery spotting, but the notional establishment of fourteen air companies was cut short by the fact that the *k.u.k. Armee* had only 79 fixed-wing aircraft on hand when war came, only 39 of which were actually deployable in the field. There were only 85 trained pilots, against a requirement for 120. Conrad's ambitious plan for 40 air companies with 240 aircraft by 1916 came nowhere near realization, thanks to limited funds.[55]

First-line units were properly outfitted, although often with out-moded weaponry, but second-line units made do with what was on hand in depots. *Landsturm* regiments were mostly issued the modern pike gray field uniform—though some made do with the obsolete dark blue uniform that was standard before Conrad insisted on drab tunics and trousers for the infantry—but none of them were provided with machine guns or telephones like the first-line forces. Many had obsolete rifles from the 1890s. Moreover, due to a lack of refresher training for reservists, most of the "old boys" filling out *Landsturm* units had never seen modern repeating rifles—much less machine guns. Men in their late thirties and early forties recalled to the colors that August were confronted with a whole range of weapons and equipment they had never seen before, much less learned to use.[56] Perhaps most seriously for *Landsturm* regiments, which thanks to shortfalls in the regular forces would bear much of the fighting in the coming weeks, only the regimental and battalion commanders were regular officers; at the company level all officers were reservists and a high percentage of the enlisted reservists had undergone training in the *Ersatzreserve* for just eight weeks, as long as twenty years before. Their readiness for the modern battlefield was seriously limited.[57]

Knowing these weaknesses, Conrad was sensitive to public perception. As the army girded for war, he established two organizations to help the General Staff manage the information the Dual Monarchy's peoples would hear about the conflict. On July 28, he set up the War Press Office (*Kriegspressequartier*) under Col. (later Maj. Gen.) Max von Hoen to manage press releases about operations. This started as a tiny operation—Hoen and his staff headed east on August 11, headed for Galicia in two cars—but it would soon grow into a vast enterprise employing hundreds of journalists and artists charged with keeping public morale high about the Habsburg military.[58] In a related vein, a day earlier the High Command established the War Supervisory Office (*Kriegsüberwachungsamt*) to deal with censorship and subversion in the Dual Monarchy, though Hungary successfully prevented it from operating on its territory. Planned before the war and based heavily on how the military had stemmed subversion in occupied Bosnia-Hercegovina, this office rapidly expanded into wide areas of civilian life, as officers searched for disloyalty and defeatism among civilians as well as among those in uniform.[59] The struggle against subversion, real and imagined, began at once, and soon there would be unprecedented defeats that Conrad and the army would want to hide their full extent from the public.

5   Disaster on the Drina

"Today my war has begun," wrote Gen. Oskar Potiorek in his private diary on the morning of August 12 from the safety of Sarajevo, where he had opted to remain "for the time being" while his forces, the *Balkanstreit-kräfte*, began enacting vengeance on "Dog Serbia" for the assassination of the heir to the Habsburg throne. For Potiorek, always sensitive to the winds at court and eager to punish Belgrade for ruining his reputation, the stakes could not have been higher, personally as well as politically. He had secured a free hand to crush the Serbs with minimal interference from Vienna, Conrad, or the General Staff, and he intended to do so with speed and determination. Yet the much-anticipated invasion began inauspiciously for Potiorek, who confidently cabled his emperor that morning to announce that "my regiment"—the 102nd, of which he was the honorary colonel—had just crossed the Drina river into Serbia "without meeting significant resistance," only to receive a confused reply from the aged Franz Joseph: "Just one battalion?"[1]

The forces at Potiorek's disposal for the invasion looked impressive enough on paper. These included the Fifth and Sixth Armies, supplemented briefly by the Second Army, which thanks to Conrad's mobilization moves would have to begin departing for Galicia on August 18. Yet the Second Army, with three corps including seven infantry and one cavalry divisions, was the strongest Potiorek had; the Fifth and Sixth Armies were considerably smaller, the former possessing 5 infantry divisions in 2 corps, and the latter with 5 divisions, 4 of which had been garrisoned in Bosnia-Hercegovina and Dalmatia in peace-time as part of XV and XVI Corps, and were organized and equipped to fight in the mountainous local terrain. In all, the *Balkanstreitkräfte* on August 12 totaled 319 infantry battalions, 60 cavalry squadrons, 142 artillery batteries with 744 guns, and 486 machine guns, supported by six monitors and six patrol boats of the navy's Danube Flotilla. It was the most powerful force the Habsburgs had ever marshaled in the Balkans in all their centuries of waging war there.[2]

The departure of the Second Army beginning on August 18 would reduce the forces under Potiorek's command by more than a third, perhaps at the critical moment. Moreover, the *Balkanstreitkräfte* looked more impressive from a headquarters desk in Sarajevo than they appeared close up. Four of Potiorek's divisions were from the second line, *Landwehr* or *Honvéd*, composed of older troops, most of them long out of practice with soldiering; yet they were expected to fight on an equal par with active divisions, which had younger, fitter men and much larger peacetime cadres. Were they ready to take on the battle-hardened Serbian Army, whose veteran regiments were made up of tough peasants defending their native soil?

Potiorek's war plan looked similarly adequate on paper. He intended to send the Fifth Army, his main strike force, across the upper Drina river, advancing southeast toward Valjevo, while to the north the Second Army on the Sava river would conduct supporting attacks as long as it could. To the south, the Sixth Army, initially defending eastern Bosnia-Hercegovina against expected Serbian and Montenegrin probing attacks, would invade Serbia five days after the Fifth Army crossed the Drina, through the Užice mountain gap, advancing into the enemy's rear and causing havoc. Once primary objectives were reached, the Fifth and Sixth Armies would commence mutually supporting offensives toward Kragujevac in the forested central Serbian heartland, where the main body of enemy's field forces, weakened by successive blows on multiple axes of advance, would be annihilated. The plan was to be executed quickly, not merely to provide units for the Eastern Front as soon as feasible, but also to persuade Romania to stay neutral and to destroy Serbia before Bosnian Serbs had any chance to stage a major anti-Habsburg revolt.[3]

This scheme, which looked superficially pleasing to any graduate of Vienna's War College, promised a quick, decisive outcome. But it neglected important factors, above all Serbia's tricky terrain, with its many mountains and few decent roads, which promised to offer the defender significant advantages and make logistical support difficult throughout the operation. Besides, the Fifth and Sixth Armies, separated by over a hundred kilometers at the outset, were too far apart to support each other; the necessarily limited role given to the powerful Second Army, which Potiorek wanted to seize Belgrade, a hopeless task given its imminent departure for Galicia, only worsened the odds.[4] Such topographical blindness is difficult to explain, since Potiorek, as a young General Staff officer, had grappled with war plans against Serbia as far back as the 1880s, yet a will to win, without reference to crucial facts, took over at an early point in Potiorek's planning for revenge on the "murder-boys" (*Mordbuben*) in Belgrade.

The rail and road network in Bosnia and southern Hungary, which the troops would abandon as soon as they crossed into Serbia, was barely adequate, and the Serbs, closer to their supply depots and less road-bound than the invader, would inevitably find it easier to keep their troops provisioned than the Austro-Hungarians would. The logistical problems facing the Fifth Army, which would make the key push across the Drina river into mountainous terrain, were daunting. Especially puzzling was the absence of a powerful drive on Belgrade, for centuries the gateway to the Balkans for invading Habsburg soldiers, most famously Prince Eugene, whose seizure of the city in 1717 broke Ottoman power in the region for good. Although Conrad's 1909 operational concept embraced putting a strong field army on both the Sava and Drina rivers to conduct supporting offensives and the War College's big war game the following year posited a direct attack on Belgrade as the best way to take out Serbia quickly, thus mimicking long Habsburg practice, Potiorek ignored these precedents. Significantly, he too had endorsed a drive on Belgrade as the best way to defeat Serbia as far back as 1891 when he was serving with the General Staff's Operations Bureau. Again in 1903, as deputy chief of the General Staff, Potiorek approved a war plan that placed three corps against Belgrade, supported by a single corps on the lower Drina and another defending against Montenegro. Why these sound concepts were not followed in 1914 can only guessed at, though fears of a Serbian uprising in Bosnia and Hercegovina, shared by Conrad and Potiorek, played a role.[5] Fatal flaws in Sarajevo's strategic concept were met with derision by Gen. Alfred Krauss, who as War College head in 1910 oversaw how to invade Serbia properly. Mocked by some officers as "our Prussian" for a toughness and thoroughness that appeared un-Habsburg, Krauss pointed to Potiorek's basic blindness about the world outside his headquarters as the key problem facing Austro-Hungarian forces in the Balkans in mid-August 1914.[6]

Like his archrival Conrad, Potiorek displayed a cavalier attitude toward logistics that would do enormous damage to his forces when the fight commenced. He was interested in aggressive offensive moves and little else. His devotion to the all-out attack was sincere and no doubt bolstered by his desire to win glory fast to erase the terrible stain of the assassination of Franz Ferdinand. As he explained fully two decades before the invasion, castigating a "blind devotion" to the defense, "seeking to start a major war defensively betrays a basic misunderstanding of the nature of our army."[7]

Importantly, Potiorek's plans took inadequate account of the capabilities of the Serbian military, which the staff in Sarajevo, like most General Staff officers, viewed as a bunch of Balkan brigands better at marauding and murder than modern combat. Yet by regional standards, the Serbian Army was an impressive force. On total mobilization it included three armies (each actually the size of a large army corps) with ten first-line infantry divisions, five of them recruited in the districts won in the recent Balkan Wars. On paper, the armies were roughly evenly matched, with the *Balkanstreitkräfte* possessing 282,000 rifle-men, 10,000 cavalry, and 744 guns, against Serbian strengths of 264,000 riflemen, 11,000 cavalry, and 828 guns.[8] Such figures were deceptive, however, as they did not take into account the irregulars whom the Serbs employed in abundance, nor did they consider that the Serbs, veterans of the two recent Balkans Wars, were better equipped with modern weaponry than their agricultural economy would suggest.

Serbian first-line divisions were slightly larger than their Habsburg counterparts, including four infantry regiments, each with four bat-talions and a machine-gun detachment (sixteen pieces per division), a thirty-six-gun artillery regiment, a cavalry regiment with three squadrons and four machine guns, and two engineer companies. Five second-line divisions, "shadow" formations for the first-line units from Old Serbia, had only three infantry regiments and machine-gun detachments (nine battalions and twelve machine guns in all), one or two artillery battalions (twelve to twenty-four guns), two cavalry squadrons, and two engineer companies. Although the second-line divisions could bring less combat power to bear than first-line equivalents, ample recent combat experience meant that first- and second-line divisions were nearly equal in fighting quality.[9] The army's third line included fifteen supplementary infantry regiments of four battalions each. There were also a small cavalry division and three independent artillery regiments to support the field armies.[10]

Swarms of irregulars assisted the Serbian field forces, protecting flanks, collecting intelligence, and harassing the enemy nonstop. Known as *komitadji*, these bands of guerrillas, operating in anything from handfuls of fighters to company-size units with a couple of hundred men, were frequently armed with modern rifles and hand grenades, and were usually locals intimately familiar with the terrain, thus constituting a menace to any invader. As many of the irregulars possessed ample combat experience fighting the Turks, *komitadji* were especially dangerous to vulnerable Habsburg rear areas and logistical units.[11]

Despite the Serbian Army's peasant origins, it was a well-equipped force, as the small kingdom had invested heavily in armaments from all over Europe. Small arms were modern, at least for first- and second-line divisions, including Mauser M.99 and M.10 rifles, as well as Russian M.91 rifles; there were considerable numbers of modern Maxim and Hotchkiss machine guns too. The artillery park was also quite up to date, including M.07 75 mm field and M.09 70 mm mountain guns and M.11 120 mm and M.10 150 mm howitzers. Although third-line batteries were outfitted with obsolete 80 mm M.85 field guns, there was at least a prodigious ammunition supply.[12]

Overall, Austro-Hungarian forces had no firepower advantage over the Serbs, and in some cases, particularly the artillery, the defenders were equipped with more modern equipment than the invaders. Although the recent Balkan Wars left the Serbian military with serious supply problems, so that extended resistance was impossible—staff officers in Belgrade expected to last a few weeks, at most—they also had given it battle experience that no one in the Habsburg military possessed.[13] Proficient, well organized, well equipped and well administered, led by battle-tried officers, and fiercely determined to defend its homeland, the Serbian Army's only significant deficiency was a logistical inability to sustain a prolonged war. Given the lack of any numerical or firepower advantage, Potiorek's forces had a hard fight ahead of them, particularly considering the difficult terrain of northwest Serbia—hilly, forested, lacking roads and communications—which favored the defender.

These facts were known to the General Staff. As tensions mounted in the Balkans in the years running up to the war, the *Evidenzbureau* did an admirable job keeping track of the growth of the Serbian military into a worthy and wily opponent. Annual reports on the state of Belgrade's forces told the tale. The last intelligence assessment completed before the war, which was available to staffs and headquarters a full year before the July Crisis, charted the Serbian order of battle in detail offering an insightful look at tactics, weaponry, and operations.[14] The study in particular noted the effectiveness of Serbian mobilization, the skills of senior officers (leading generals were profiled in detailed biographies), the battle skills of the first-line units, recent weapons acquisitions, and the impressive capabilities of Serbia's well-equipped artillery, the "best arm" according to the assessment. Although the *Evidenzbureau*'s 1913 report tended to attribute recent battlefield successes as much to Ottoman incompetence as to Serbian skill, mirroring the standard views of Habsburg officers who looked south, the most recent Viennese intelligence assessment left no doubt that Belgrade's forces merited more respect than most General Staff officers gave them. It also noted the poor condition of Serbia's lines of communication, including detailed maps that showed the limited road system, and the challenges this would pose to any invader.

Similar language was used by the June 1913 assessment of Serbian performance in the just-ended Balkan Wars prepared by Maj. Otto Gellinek, the military attaché in Belgrade. Although the *Evidenzbureau* lacked high-placed sources in Serbia, Gellinek was an insightful observer, and his nearly thirty-page report made abundantly clear that Serbia's military had a great deal of combat experience and modern weaponry, and deserved to be taken seriously, especially when fighting in defense of its own soil.[15] Nevertheless, the mostly accurate work of the intelligence staff in Vienna made little impression on Potiorek and his planners, who viewed the Serbs with equal parts contempt and derision. "A brief autumn stroll" (*einen kleinen Herbstspaziergang*) was what staffers in Sarajevo, singing the tune of jingoistic journalists and politicians throughout the Dual Monarchy, expected once the troops crossed into Serbia, a rosy assessment shared even by many well-placed functionaries in Vienna. "We'll be able to chase off the Serbs with a wet rag," promised Lt. Col. Purtscher, chief of the Balkan operations group on the General Staff.[16]

The Serbian high command, in particular, merited more consideration than Vienna and Sarajevo gave it. It was led by the tough *Vojvoda* Radomir Putnik, army commander since 1912, an able tactician and competent strategist. Putnik, a national hero, was the architect of

Serbia's victories in the 1912 and 1913 campaigns and a shrewd planner. Though old at sixty-seven, he possessed an astonishing amount of battle experience, having fought in all Serbia's wars since the 1870s: against the Ottomans twice between 1876 and 1878, against Bulgaria in 1885, and in the two Balkan Wars of 1912–13. In a perverse irony, Austria-Hungary might easily have been spared great difficulties, for Putnik was on Habsburg soil when the war broke out, taking the cure at Gleichenberg. The old general was briefly interned at Budapest, but was soon released as a soldierly gesture by Emperor Franz Joseph, who thought it dishonorable to keep Putnik under such circumstances, thus allowing him to return home to defeat the Habsburg army.[17]

Serbia demonstrated greater effectiveness in mobilization than Austria-Hungary managed that summer. Belgrade mobilized its forces on July 24–25, the call-up proving rapid and efficient, as it had been executed three times in as many years, so that the army was fully ready to fight by August 10. Serbia's three field armies deployed in the north, well behind the frontiers so as to provide strategic depth: the First and Second faced the Danube, and the Third took up positions near the meeting of the Drina and Sava rivers. The independent division-sized Užice Group defended the western frontier, while the southwestern border, where the rough terrain mitigated against invasion, was covered by 35,000 troops of Montenegro's militia, poorly equipped but tenacious soldiers. Putnik's war plan called for active defensive: the invader's initial advances were to be thrown back by rapid and decisive counterattacks. By the time Potiorek was ready to begin his offensive, the Serbian Second Army's four infantry divisions and the Third Army's two infantry divisions were positioned first to absorb and then push back Habsburg spearheads across the Danube, Sava, and the upper Drina.[18] Putnik initially deployed his forces somewhat east of where Potiorek's main blow was set to fall, based on Vienna's war plans before 1912, which Redl had passed to Belgrade; here, at least, Potiorek's disregard for the General Staff's standing plans may have helped his cause, albeit only temporarily.

The Habsburg field army chosen to play the key part in Potiorek's operation was Gen. Liborius von Frank's Fifth (Potiorek retained command of the Sixth Army, as well as serving as the theater commander, a cumbersome arrangement). Its two corps were the heavily Czech VIII (Prague) and the Croatian XIII (Zagreb); army command held a mountain brigade and a brigade of Croatian militia in reserve. The Croatian corps, with two infantry divisions and a separate infantry brigade, was the stronger of the two. The choice of Gen. Arthur Giesl von Gieslingen's VIII Corps for such an important role was perhaps an odd one, given the army's suspicions about its Czech troops.

Headquartered in Prague, the center of Czech nationalism, VIII Corps was considered the most politically touchy command in the *k.u.k. Armee* and originally had been part of *B-Staffel* (Second Army), but was reassigned to bolster the Fifth Army. The corps had lost one of its three divisions, the Nineteenth, which was dispatched to Galicia with the Fourth Army, leaving the Ninth and Twenty-first, the latter a second-line *Landwehr* division. The General Staff had doubts about Giesl's troops, and about Giesl himself: his career had not been helped by the previous year's uncovering of his chief of staff, Col. Alfred Redl, as a notorious traitor and homosexual; no less embarrassing was the fact that Giesl, as army intelligence chief in 1900, had rapidly promoted the promising young Captain Redl.

The Twenty-first *Landwehr* Division of VIII Corps was not especially remarkable, though its prominent role in Austria-Hungary's disaster on the Drina that fateful August requires a closer look. Recruited from ethnically mixed western Bohemia, many of its soldiers were proletarians from Prague, Pilsen, Budweis, and other industrial towns. Its four *Landwehr* infantry regiments were the almost entirely German Sixth from Eger and the equally Czech Twenty-eighth from Prague, plus the Seventh (Pilsen) and the Twenty-eighth (Pisek), which were respectively 60 and 80 percent Czech, the rest being Germans.[19] Divisional artillery, eight batteries in all, plus support and service units were about three-quarters Czech.[20]

The Twenty-first Division's artillery, like the Habsburg Army's whole gun park in 1914, was a mix of pieces, some showing their age and some, like the M.99 100 mm howitzer, thoroughly obsolete. The division's soldiers were older by a decade than in first-line units, and many of the recalled reservists—over 80 percent of the troops in most battalions—were in less than ideal physical condition; the long marches ahead, up mountains in the hot Serbian summer sun, would push many to the limit. Moreover, their commander was not much better prepared for war than his aging reservists. Lt. Gen. Arthur Przyborski was in many ways a typical Habsburg Army high-flier of his era. Though of Polish background, he had joined the army as a teenaged cavalry cadet and had risen quickly in the anational world of the Habsburg officer corps. He had done well enough at the War College to be admitted to the General Staff, spending seven years in various desk jobs in Vienna; his time in command was relatively limited, and like most Austro-Hungarian officers of his generation he had never heard a shot fired in anger. Przyborski's reputation was middling, and it was no secret that his career had prospered thanks more to Viennese connections—his father-in-law was Gen. Franz von Schönaich, joint war minister from 1906 to 1911—than to skill.[21]

The Twenty-first Division's road to war was not without friction. Przyborski's staff in Prague received mobilization orders shortly after noon on July 26, but the actual mobilization was delayed two days to give reservists time to put their affairs in order, which dampened the enthusiasm of many men caught up in the war fervor of that summer. Mobilization proceeded without complications, no morale problems being reported even in all-Czech units, yet there was confusion about the division's destination. As a result of Conrad's mixed-up corps deployments, Przyborski and his staff were still unsure as late as July 31 if they were headed for Galicia or the Balkans. Divisional units were ready to deploy by August 1, but in some cases there were no trains available to move them.[22]

Despite the confusion and red tape, divisional staff moved to Brčko in northeastern Bosnia (also the headquarters of Fifth Army) on August

2, and the rest of the division soon followed, sent on their way from Prague by Prince Thun, governor of Bohemia. There were problems with both rail and road movement, mostly due to Bosnia's inadequate infrastructure, but by the afternoon of August 9 all Twenty-first Division units were settled into the Brčko area near the Serbian frontier, holding the northern flank of VIII Corps and the Fifth Army.[23]

The burgeoning Habsburg encampments on the Drina and Sava rivers, teeming with men eager to take revenge on Serbia, were hothouses of hatred, paranoia, and rumors about the enemy. Newspapers across Bosnia-Hercegovina carried reports of uprisings by local Serbs against Habsburg rule, fueling suspicions about a vast fifth column inside Austria-Hungary.[24] Wild rumors had it that Habsburg soldiers, even officers, were defecting to the enemy; whispers of disloyal generals— some said Gen. Svetozar Boroević, the army's top-ranking Serb, had been arrested and shot for espionage—were rife and inaccurate.

The army and police in Bosnia showed an almost equal degree of suspicion regarding local Serbs. Long a priority, the hunt for spies kicked into high gear, and Serbian civilians, bureaucrats, and even soldiers in Habsburg uniform were scrutinized for potential disloyalty. Serbian Orthodox churches and monasteries, as well as Serbian cultural groups, were placed under close observation for signs of treason, while anyone near the border was intrinsically suspect. Every night border patrols caught Serbs along the Drina river—many were fishermen or smugglers—and hauled them in for questioning. As the Sarajevo assassination had proved, Serbia unquestionably had an espionage-terrorist infrastructure in Bosnia, but ham-handed Habsburg control methods proved better at persecuting discontent than uncovering spies and saboteurs.[25]

Fears of Serb irregulars were universal. Rumors of incursions by *komitadji*, by no means all untrue, put Habsburg troops on edge as they neared the border zone. Gendarmerie posts at the frontier were reinforced, and mobile response platoons were assembled, but this failed to stop raids by irregulars, particularly on the porous border with Montenegro, where incursions by groups of over five hundred *komitadji* were reported.[26]

Habsburg units marshaled on the border were cautioned to be prepared for attacks by Serbian irregulars. Nighttime gun battles were commonplace in early August, not necessarily against the enemy. Illustrating the perils of a polyglot army, on several occasions Twenty-first Division sentries mistook Croats of the neighboring Forty-second Division for the enemy and opened fire—understandably enough, as the Forty-second Division, the Croatian Home Guard, used basically the same language of command as the Serbs. Repeatedly troops of the Twenty-first Division fired on detachments of the paramilitary *Schutzkorps*, local auxiliaries, even in the daytime, as they were clad in civilian garb, identified only by black-yellow armbands; even close up they looked, and sounded, like *komitadji*. Fifth Army headquarters tried to remedy the situation by ordering all sentries to shout basic commands ("Halt!" "Who goes there?") in German.[27]

Potiorek's intent to crush disloyalty was plain from the start, and he placed the civilian population near the border under martial law; as he put it, "to gain the upper hand against subversive elements, a quick and energetic intervention was absolutely necessary." Troops of XIII Corps in Syrmia on the Sava River searched aggressively for possible disloyalty among the local Serb population, arresting or even taking hostage anyone, regardless of age, suspected of treason or even "antimilitary attitudes."[28] The culling of the potential Serbian fifth column extended to politicians and clergy, as well as Serbs in Habsburg uniform. Units recruited in Bosnia-Hercegovina were examined closely for disloyalty before the invasion of Serbia commenced, and Potiorek demanded that the units—all four Bosnian-Hercegovinian regiments were garrisoned outside their home provinces in peacetime—be stripped of their Serbs before they deployed to the Balkans. Yet in a trademark display of Habsburg toughness and slackness rolled into one, the implementation of this order was left to local commanders, so that only some Bosnian units had their Serbs filtered out and dispatched to unarmed labor battalions, as

Potiorek had ordered. While the number of Serbs in Bosnian regiments fell by about 40 percent, the Second Regiment, which would become the most decorated Habsburg unit in the war, maintained a plurality of Serb troops as it went to the front, while the Fourth Regiment, which was considered to have the biggest reliability problem, shed only about twenty Serbs per company, since officers insisted that most of their Serbs were fully trustworthy.[29]

On August 9, Potiorek issued the order for the invasion of Serbia to commence. According to the final plan, the Second Army would shell Belgrade and launch an attack across the Sava River, to support the main drive by the Fifth Army across the Drina on the morning of August 12 in the direction of Valjevo, while the Sixth Army would push toward Užice.[30] No lenience was to be shown to the enemy, particularly not to *komitadji* who violated accepted laws of war. "The Serbian population you will encounter has lost any sense of humanity," informed one corps headquarters on the eve of the offensive, "and is downright pernicious."[31] Yet the *k.u.k. Balkanstreitkräfte* were stronger on propaganda than information about Serbian deployments. Operational intelligence was sorely lacking on the Balkan front. Human intelligence was singularly deficient, and the few agent reports coming out of Serbia provided little that was actionable about where enemy forces were arrayed.[32] Aerial reconnaissance revealed not much more, thanks to the mere handful of aircraft at Potiorek's disposal, all short-ranged and unreliable. As a result, when Habsburg forces crossed into Serbia, they had hardly any sense of where the enemy was to be found.[33] They would find him by probing until battle was joined.

Austro-Hungarian forces of the Second Army crossing the Sava on the morning of August 12 found the enemy without difficulty. Fighting centered on Šabac, a border city of fourteen thousand and a local communications hub that the Second Army had to take and clear. While Serbian regulars contested the invasion, *komitadji* were even more plentiful, and they took a toll on Austro-Hungarian officers, who with their yellow sashes and sabers made easy targets. For Habsburg units attempting to clear Šabac, snipers in civilian garb killed as many, especially officers, as Serbian regular troops did.[34] Col. Oskar Hranilović, head of the *Evidenzbureau*, warned at the outset that *komitadji* enjoyed considerable esteem in Serbian society, including the support of politicians and secret societies such as the Black Hand, and they would prove a serious obstacle to Habsburg forces. The solution for such outlaws, Hranilović explained, was annihilation: *komitadji* were to be summarily executed, as they had no standing under the laws of war.[35] Events in Šabac in the opening days of the campaign seemed to confirm this grim intelligence assessment, and Habsburg units were routinely fired upon by civilians, even women and children. In retaliation, Austro-Hungarian troops executed between one hundred and two hundred suspected *komitadji* in Šabac in the opening days of the campaign. By August 14, troops of IV Corps had established a foothold in Šabac, after intense fighting in the city and its suburbs, repulsing several Serbian efforts to push them back across the Sava. Habsburg forces would maintain their tenuous hold on the city for the next ten days, while events unfolded south of them.[36]

General von Frank's Fifth Army, tasked with breaking the decisive opening in the enemy's front, would bear the brunt of executing Potiorek's war plan. Its VIII and XIII Corps were to cross the Drina and penetrate the Jadar river valley toward the key city of Valjevo. The actual river crossing was anticlimactic, as only in a few places did Serb forces strongly contest the invasion at the water's edge; they planned to fight an active defense further inland. The nearly unopposed Drina crossing by XIII Corps proved easier than the more northerly movement of VIII Corps, which encountered stiff local resistance from Serbian border guards and irregulars. The Ninth Division ran into two reinforced Serbian battalions supported by artillery on August 12, delaying the Fifth Army's advance by a day. The Twenty-first Division's forward echelons, its Sixth and Seventh Regiments, forded the shallow river just before dawn on August 13, reaching the Drina's east bank at 6 a.m. Despite some losses to enemy rifle and machine-gun fire, the division's assault elements had established a foothold inside Serbia by 10:45 a.m. The 11,922 infantrymen of the Twenty-first *Landwehr* Division actually waded across the Drina, as before the autumn rains came it was shallow enough to ford, often no more than a feet deep. Habsburg troops took off their pants and entered Serbia in their underwear.[37]

The Twenty-first Division's progress inland on August 13 was slowed by stiff resistance from Serbian irregulars. Although VIII Corps soon had reliable pontoon bridges over the Drina, the hilly terrain, combined with the lack of good roads or railheads near the front, led to delays and mounting supply problems, not least because service columns moved slowly across the Drina and were vulnerable to *komitadji*. As a result, the Twenty-first Division never established proper supply lines during its push into Serbia, and the troops went without essentials. Its units received some water but no food on August 13; some food reached the infantry on August 14 but no water; by August 15 only a single battalion had established functioning field kitchens, and almost no water made it to the infantry; on August 16 neither food nor water reached the division's combat units, and things did not improve the following day. For the infantry, marching up hills in hot temperatures, crisis was reached almost immediately.[38]

Things were much the same all along the invasion front, as Austro-Hungarian forces were delayed by *komitadji* harassment and supply problems. Rapid advances proved elusive. Further south, the Sixth Army's XV Corps crossed the Drina on August 14, and it too encountered serious logistical problems and enemy resistance. Habsburg mountain troops proved able to push the enemy out of hilltop positions, usually with spirited bayonet charges, but casualties were heavy, and the supply system was breaking down almost from the moment the invaders crossed the Drina.[39] More seriously, the Serbian high command at Kragujevac, having accurately surmised Potiorek's intent to strike farther to the west than Putnik had expected, took advantage of the slow pace of the Habsburg advance by shifting its field forces westward. The Serbian First Army moved to face IV Corps at Šabac, the Second confronted

VIII Corps in the Jadar valley, and the Third stood before the advancing XV Corps. Putnik prepared to strike.[40]

On the morning of August 14, the Twenty-first Division began its advance in a southeasterly direction toward the Jadar valley. Three of its regiments, following the shortest route to their objective, the city of Valjevo, over seventy kilometers beyond, entered Cer mountain, a rugged and roadless plateau nearly twenty kilometers long and seven wide, dominated by undulating hills and ridges ranging to heights of almost a thousand meters. What the Serbs called *Cerska planina* was surrounded by vast cornfields—for many Habsburg soldiers the salient memory of the fight for Cer would be corn and more corn as far as they could see—and towered over the Drina and Jadar valleys. It had to be cleared of the enemy to secure any advance toward Valjevo.

The strenuous march uphill proved trying for the heavily burdened infantrymen, most of them reservists; each infantryman carried in addition to his rifle and bayonet, ammunition, a spade, a knapsack (filled with emergency rations, cooking and eating utensils, extra shoes, an extra shirt, and a change of underwear), an overcoat, a tent quarter, and anything else the soldier might be ordered to carry—in all at least fifty pounds of kit and in many cases closer to seventy. Without the provision of fresh water, which VIII Corps failed to do during the invasion, troops dropped from heat exhaustion in the midday sun when temperatures approached a hundred degrees Fahrenheit. The farther the troops ventured up the rocky and roadless plateau, the worse the supply situation became. Since the Twenty-first Division was not equipped for mountain warfare, the infantry went forward largely without road-bound artillery and logistical support. Additionally, *komitadji* attacks brought wagons carrying food and water to a halt, and infantry and cavalry patrols had to be assembled to protect the supply columns and artillery from Serbian irregulars.[41]

While the Twenty-first Division advanced ponderously southeast on August 14, Gen. Stepa Stepanović and his Second Army prepared to strike. The tough Stepanović, a former Serbian war minister, had been in uniform since 1874 when he entered cadet school, and had been at war most of his life; defending Serbia against the Austro-Hungarian onslaught was his sixth war. He knew his troops and the terrain well, and he was a popular leader; Stepanović had commanded the Second Army in the Balkan Wars, including at the siege of Adrianople, and he was confident in his forces.[42] On August 15, having moved his forces into position, Stepanović was ready to engage the enemy, sending his veteran troops of the Combined and Šumadija I Divisions, supported by the Cavalry Division, to confront Habsburg units that were advancing deeper into the *Cerska planina*.[43]

At 8 a.m., on the opposite side of the plateau, a battalion of the Twenty-first Division's Sixth *Landwehr* Regiment began its march up Hill 630, a peak that stood 2,300 feet above the Jadar valley and dominated the Mačva plain beyond. Soon elements of the Eighth and Twenty-eighth Regiments followed in support. By noon, troops of the Sixth, Eighth, and Twenty-eighth Regiments, plus a cavalry squadron and the Twenty-first Division's headquarters, were surrounding Hill 630, near the village of Skakalište at the eastern edge of the *planina*. Artillery and supply units were held back, at a safe distance from *komitadji* attacks, guarded by three full infantry battalions. The infantry was tiring from marching in the heat up and down mountains, not least because the lead columns had received no fresh water or food in two days. Regular sniping from *komitadji* in the surrounding woods constituted a further irritant for the Habsburg foot soldiers. At 4 p.m., troops of the Twenty-eighth Regiment had reached the summit of Hill 630, where they halted due to exhaustion; after an hour's rest the infantry got on their feet but were halted by a rainstorm. There the Twenty-first Division's advance ended. Knowing his troops were tired, hungry, and thirsty, Przyborski ordered the lead battalion—two-and-a-half companies of the Twenty-eighth Regiment with a company of the Eighth—to hunker down for the night. They established a perimeter, posted sentries, and began a well-earned rest.[44]

The exhausted Bohemians had no idea that Serbian infantry was closing in on their encampment. Four regiments of Gen. Mihailo Rašić's Combined Division, after hours of marching through the rain, were ready to join battle. Two regiments, the spearhead of Stepanović's army, advanced through the cornfields, invisible to Habsburg sentries. Around 1 a.m. on August 16, companies from two of Rašić's regiments approached the Twenty-first Division's lead battalion as it slept. Guards failed to react, as the Serbian infantry announced they were Croats, friends from the nearby Forty-second Division. Rašić's troops opened fire at close range, cutting down dozens of Habsburg troops; most were still asleep when the shooting started. Chaos followed, and in the darkness Austro-Hungarian officers and NCOs tried to rally their groggy soldiers; many were cut down before they could form any coherent defense. Serbian infantry kept coming, as reinforcements surged from the corn, and Habsburg platoons, then companies were overrun and melted away in the darkness.[45]

The Twenty-eighth Regiment's forward positions were shattered before many officers even understood what was happening. In the brutal, point-blank struggle, leaders fell quickly, among them Col. Joseph Fiedler, the Twenty-eighth Regiment's commander and the first of thirty-five Habsburg colonels who would die at the head of their regiments in 1914. Divisional headquarters was nearby, and soon General Przyborski was in action too. As Serbian assaults increased and Austro-Hungarian companies tried to hold their positions and attempt counterattacks, confusion mounted, and before long the Twenty-first Division's command staff was in the thick of the melée. Rifle in hand, Przyborski rallied his startled soldiers as Serbian bayonet attacks grew closer. At one point in the desperate fight, Przyborski had only twenty soldiers around him, but the position held, although the general counted among those wounded.[46]

Several hundred meters west of the divisional command post, the Sixth *Landwehr* Regiment was fighting with the Serbs with bayonets and even hand to hand, as the enemy had used the darkness to infiltrate between Habsburg companies. Adding to the confusion, the Serbs employed Austro-Hungarian bugle calls for deception purposes. The regiment's Third Battalion nearly buckled under the strain, but the First Battalion, roused from sleep, arrived in time to prevent a Serbian breakthrough. Yet losses were steep, as Serbian rifle and machine-gun fire was concentrated and accurate. This meeting engagement, which went on bloodily until dawn, was more a series of firefights than a coherent battle, and casualties on both sides proved steep. The division's Forty-first Brigade formed a lager, a temporary defensive position in all directions, around its commander, Major General Panesch, and his staff, which withstood repeated Serbian bayonet assaults.[47]

By dawn both sides were exhausted, so Rašić committed a third infantry regiment to the fight and moved his artillery into position, which had been delayed by muddy roads. Two batteries deployed forward, close to Habsburg positions, firing over open sights and inflicting heavy losses, their shells tearing gaps in the closely deployed defenders. It was a one-sided artillery duel, as Austro-Hungarian gunnery was inadequate. Most batteries had been kept too far back or were under attack themselves as Serbian infantry and irregulars kept advancing. The Twenty-first Division's guns were mostly out of range, but the neighboring Ninth Division's batteries offered fire support. Yet Habsburg infantry-artillery cooperation was haphazard at best, and a high level of confusion paralyzed coordination; in the chaos, many battalion commanders simply did not know where their companies were. For several hours that morning, the Twenty-first Division ceased to function much above the company level. Przyborski's two brigadiers did not know where he was or even if their commanding general was alive.[48]

By mid-morning, positions had stabilized as exhaustion brought the encounter battle to a close. Word travelled up the Habsburg chain of command about the extent of the Twenty-first Division's losses, particularly the shattered Twenty-eighth Regiment. General Frank at Fifth Army, hearing ominous initial reports and fearing a debacle that

threatened to unravel his entire front, wanted the division to with-
draw, even though Giesl's VIII Corps largely held its ground against
Stepanović; while the Twenty-first Division was in chaos, the Ninth
Division was holding fast. The Serbs had taken grave losses too: the
Combined Division lost forty-seven officers and nearly three thousand
men, and in its Sixth Regiment all four battalion commanders and
thirteen of sixteen company commanders were dead or wounded.[49]

General von Frank and Fifth Army command overreacted to a local
reverse, startled by the ferocity of Stepanović's nocturnal assault, but
there was no doubt that the Twenty-first Division needed relief and
reinforcements immediately. The *Landwehr* division's losses had been
severe and in some units crippling. Further offensive operations were
out of the question: VIII Corps reacted to the setback, and on Giesl's
orders the Sixth and Twenty-eighth Regiments, which had borne the
brunt of the morning battle, were the first to march westward, back
toward the Drina, on the afternoon of August 16. The Bohemians'
retreat was observed by Serbian king Peter, who watched the day's
happy events from a nearby hilltop. The victor kept the pressure on
the Austro-Hungarians as *komitadji* sniped at the ranks of tired and
retreating troops. Constant sharp, small attacks made the Habsburg
troops jumpy, and in some depleted companies panic arose, particularly
because many senior officers—including Przyborski—were incommunicado or casualties themselves. Cavalry patrols could not keep the
komitadji at bay, and supply and artillery units in particular absorbed
rifle fire and raiding from irregulars throughout August 16.[50]

Pursuit by Serbian cavalry and irregulars dogged the Twenty-first
Division throughout August 17 as it made its way back toward Bosnia.
The day saw several sharp engagements that were indecisive but costly
to both sides. Habsburg artillery lost two guns to the enemy at Prnjavor,
while the Forty-first Brigade punched back several Serbian probes at
Petkovica on the north side of the *planina*. Serbian cavalry probed the
flanks of the *Landwehr* division and tried to induce more panic, not
always with success. Troops of Sixth Regiment, which was still mostly

in good order, defeated a charge by an enemy cavalry regiment, using machine guns to wipe out two whole mounted squadrons.[51]

On August 18, Franz Joseph's eighty-fourth birthday and also the day the Second Army began to depart the Balkans for Galicia, all of the Fifth Army was in retreat toward the Drina bridges. Although XIII Corps was in better shape than VIII Corps, the defeat of the Twenty-first Division at Cer meant that the offensive had failed. The *Landwehr* division resisted probes by Serbian infantry, cavalry, and irregulars throughout the day, and attempted to support the nearby Ninth Division, which was under severe enemy pressure.[52] Knowing the Austro-Hungarians were retreating, Stepanović pushed harder. Habsburg troops were tired, hungry, and thirsty, as the struggle for supplies was going as badly as the fight with the Serbs, but the retreat was essentially orderly, considering the difficult terrain. Afraid of being massacred by *komitadji*—rumors were rife of knife-wielding women hacking apart Habsburg wounded—the troops stayed alert and close together. The Twenty-first Division was off the *Cerska planina* by midday on August 19 and prepared to cross back into Bosnia. Pressure from the Serbs was dwindling as Stepanović's forces were nearly as exhausted as the Austro-Hungarians were after four days of nonstop fighting. On the morning of August 20, a relatively quiet day when even the tired *komitadji* were almost silent, Przyborski's soldiers crossed the Drina in defeat. To the end needless chaos erupted, including an attempt by jumpy sappers to blow the pontoon bridges prematurely, before divisional headquarters was certain all its troops were back in Bosnia, but by nightfall no units of the Twenty-first Division remained on enemy soil. The rest of the Fifth Army soon followed. Stepa Stepanović and his Second Army had delivered the Entente its first victory of the Great War.

The vanquished Twenty-first Division established encampments across the Drina as the troops got their first hot meals, fresh water, and real sleep in eight days. Przyborski's staff at Bijeljina counted their losses. Casualties were unexpectedly high among battalion- and company-level officers; Fifth Army termed losses among infantry leaders "nearly colossal." The Sixth *Landwehr* Regiment, which bore much of the Cer fight, lost its commander and four other field-grade officers, fifteen captains, and thirty-three lieutenants. Sergeants were already being appointed acting platoon leaders due to a severe officer shortage.[53]

After only a week in Serbia, the division had lost almost a third of its riflemen. The exact number of dead was difficult to determine due to the confusion attending the retreat; many killed in action were thus listed as missing. In the worst case, the Twenty-eighth Regiment lost 1,700 men, over half its strength, but many of the two-thirds of the casualties listed as missing were dead on the *Cerska planina*, while others were in Serbian captivity. Although losses were heaviest among the infantry, service units had taken casualties too, mostly from *komitadji* attacks, and the artillery was substantially weakened: in all, the division's batteries had lost half their pieces.[54]

The lamentable condition of VIII Corps was captured by Egon Erwin Kisch, Prague's "raging reporter" who little more than a year before had broken the sensational Redl story. A reserve corporal, Kisch went to war with the heavily Czech Eleventh Regiment, part of the Ninth Division, and saw action at Cer. Three weeks before, when his mother pestered him to put more underwear and night clothes in his knapsack, Kisch retorted: "Do you really think I'm going to the Thirty Years' War?" On August 19, he watched his vanquished comrades cross back into Bosnia, "a boisterous horde fleeing in thoughtless panic toward the border," his shattered battalion led by a mere subaltern, its companies led by sergeants. "The army is defeated, on a lawless, wild, hasty retreat," he lamented to his diary.[55]

Things were not much better across the Fifth Army. The Seventy-third Regiment of Kisch's division, which had fought at Cer next to the *Landwehr*, recorded six hundred men lost in Serbia, of whom 150 were missing: half were presumed dead, the rest captured.[56] It was just as gloomy in XIII Corps, whose two divisions each lost over three thousand dead, wounded, and missing. Its Twenty-fifth *Domobran* (Croatian Home Guard) Regiment—which included a Sergeant Josip

Broz, better known in later years as Tito—lost over eight hundred men in Serbia, nearly 60 percent of them listed as missing, leading to suspicions that Habsburg Serbs were deserting to their ethnic kin.[57] The Croatian Sixteenth Regiment recorded losses of 54 officers and 1,004 men as casualties, with almost eight hundred wounded and 140 missing. Doubts about the loyalty of Serbian troops, particularly when fighting against co-nationals, arose from the fact that in the Croatian Thirty-sixth Division, the highest number of missing was found in its most Serbian regiment, the Seventy-ninth.[58]

Since the Sixth Army had also retreated back into Bosnia once the extent of the defeat at Cer became apparent, the only Habsburg troops still fighting in Serbia on August 20 were units of the Second Army, which was supposed to be making for Galicia with all haste but which had gotten bogged down in intense combat around Šabac. Once the Fifth Army had retreated across the Drina, holding on to Šabac made little sense, not least because its divisions were soon to be desperately needed to halt the Russian steamroller in Galicia, but keeping the Serbs out of Šabac was "a matter of honor," said Maj. Gen. Eduard Zanantoni of the Twenty-ninth Division, whose troops, Germans from north Bohemia, had been beating back attempts by the Serbian First Army to retake the city ever since they crossed the Sava almost a week before. "Šabac must be held at all costs," explained the local commander, Gen. Karl Terszt-tyánsky von Nádas, whose IV Corps was holding fast to the city for no clear military purpose—though he, like Potiorek, was eager to inflict losses on the Serbs anywhere Habsburg forces could in the aftermath of the Cer debacle.[59]

The fight for Šabac was bitter and costly on both sides, descending at points into savagery. Spirited Serbian assaults were met with vigorous counterattacks, led with bayonets. Cold steel was commonplace, including against civilians suspected of firing on Habsburg forces. Even Austro-Hungarian units filled with Serbs—in IV Corps, recruited from south Hungary, the Sixth Regiment was 60 percent Serb while the Seventieth Regiment was 90 percent—kept fighting with grit.[60]

Yet courage did not equal competence, and Austro-Hungarian losses at Šabac were needlessly high thanks to a reliance on frontal assaults by infantry battalions, without effective artillery support, on narrow frontages. Tersztyánsky adhered to his prewar belief in mass attacks over open fields, displays of dash, which in the face of machine weapons meant mass death. For the Serbian First Army it was a shooting gallery. One of its majors who fell into Habsburg hands at Šabac praised the courage of the infantry opposite, noting its dash under fire, yet found fault with the overall method. Habsburg commanders, he observed, sent their infantry into the attack without adequate reconnaissance, and artillery support was minimal and ineffective. Once officers were picked off—they exposed themselves to danger and their yellow sashes and sabers made them easy targets—advancing Austro-Hungarian battalions melted into disorganized masses, pushing forward with more *élan* than finesse, and were routinely shattered by machine-gun and artillery fire.[61]

Despite heavy losses IV Corps kept up the fire until it received the order to retreat late on August 23, Potiorek having belatedly accepted the reality that his invasion of Serbia had ended in failure. Down to the end, Tersztyánszky kept pressure on the Serbs and gave no ground freely. Morale, however, had begun to suffer. He ordered one last attack on afternoon of August 23, a show of aggression against "Dog Serbia." His three divisions *en masse* mounted bayonet assaults on the positions of the First Army at 3 p.m., resulting in high casualties for no purpose. As battalions gave way, panicked troops of the Thirty-first and Thirty-second Divisions broke and ran for the Sava, while the Twenty-ninth Division held its ground thanks to fire support from river monitors of the Danube Flotilla. The final pullout on the early morning of August 24 was orderly, but IV Corps was a shambles. The twelve-day fight for Šabac had cost Tersztyánszky 6,700 casualties: 2,917 dead and wounded in the Twenty-ninth Division, 2,075 in the Thirty-first Division, and 1,717 in the Thirty-second Division. Many of the survivors were soon entraining for Galicia.[62]

By the afternoon of August 24, no Austro-Hungarian troops remained on Serbian soil. The extent of the disaster that Potiorek's "brief autumn stroll" had become was impossible to avoid, though the commander of the *Balkanstreitkräfte* did his best to keep the press, the public, and the court in Vienna in the dark about the magnitude of the debacle. There was no escaping the fact that the ancient Habsburg Monarchy had been humiliated by the peasant regiments of a small Balkan kingdom. Austria-Hungary lost more than 23,000 killed, wounded, and missing in the brief campaign. Over four thousand Habsburg prisoners of war, forty-six artillery pieces, and thirty machine guns had been left in Serbian hands.[63] Serbian casualties of 16,000 were considerable, but there was no mistaking that this had been an historic defeat for the House of Habsburg. The loss of prestige for the army and the monarchy was vast, and its diplomatic implications in the Balkans were frightening for Vienna. For Potiorek, the need for a scapegoat was pressing.

Conveniently for the staff in Sarajevo there was the hard-luck Twenty-first Division, licking its deep wounds on the west bank of the Drina river. Conrad was furious with Potiorek for making a hash of the Balkan campaign, but there would be no high-level personnel changes yet; the consummate court general would stay in place for the time being, shielded by *Protektion* through his connections. Potiorek pointed his accusations at the defeated Twenty-first Division rather than at any generals, least of all himself. The narrative quickly assembled in Sarajevo in late August, and soon accepted by the General Staff, was that the *Landwehr* division had panicked and failed to do its duty. Accusations that the Twenty-first Division "simply melted away" and had "abandoned field guns and equipment," began spreading among *k.u.k. Armee* higher-ups, including Conrad.[64]

Worse, the division's defeat was attributed not to military shortcomings but to ethnic disloyalty. Much of the officer corps, mistrusting Czech soldiers before the war, reverted to ingrained prejudices; doing so caused much less embarrassment and soul-searching than finding fault with the army and its leaders. Potiorek insisted that the Czechs of the Twenty-first Division had not done their duty and that their retreat had been unjustified, even cowardly. A board of inquiry was convened at Sarajevo in late August to get at the truth, but it was a rigged game. The defense was presented by Maj. Gen. Alois Podhajský, one of Przyborski's brigadiers, who insisted that ethnicity had nothing to do with the debacle. A Czech himself, like many officers Podhajský was of modest background, his father having been a small-town police-man, and he had made his way up the ranks through merit rather than connections. His conduct at Cer had been exemplary, as even Potiorek conceded. During the battle, Podhajský kept a cool head, and since his divisional commander was incommunicado for much of the fight he took charge and prevented a bad situation from becoming a complete rout. His aggressive leadership, assembling disorganized companies into coherent units, saved the division, and perhaps the whole VIII Corps, from being shoved into the Drina.[65]

Nevertheless, Podhajský could not persuade Potiorek and his staff, who wanted to blame the disaster on supposed Czech cowardice and treachery. While the official report on the Cer battle did not demure from criticism of Przyborski's leadership—there was no way to hide that the ill-fated division's commander, while no coward, was not nota-bly competent, having allowed his division to blunder into an enemy offensive and be caught literally napping—it placed more blame on the alleged cowardice of the Seventh, Eighth, and Twenty-eighth *Landwehr* Regiments, that is, the Twenty-first Division's Czech infantry units. Based on this pretext, Potiorek placed the division under emergency martial law to stave off further treasonous incidents.[66] Following Sara-jevo's cue, both Fifth Army and VIII Corps issued warnings of severe punishment in the event of unit collapses and flight from the bat-tlefield; the death penalty, especially to punish desertion, was noted frequently.[67] Responsibility for firmer discipline was placed on officers and sergeants, particularly when confronted by battlefield reverses. A

Fifth Army assessment advocated "*the strongest obedience to discipline and duty*," notably from officers, adding, "*iron discipline, the strongest discharge of duty* guarantees the success of an army."[68]

The narrative of the Cer defeat that emerged under Potiorek's guidance and became accepted by most Habsburg officers focused on cowardly, even treacherous, Czech behavior, not military incompetence. Potiorek's investigation concluded that in the Twenty-first Division, only the German Sixth *Landwehr* Regiment had done its duty, and as the Official History concluded with a bit more delicacy, "At the least it would be justified to blame the division's mishap—as it occasionally appeared—to national causes."[69] Singling out Czechs, rather than senior officers, as the culprits for the failure of the invasion of Serbia was undoubtedly politically convenient for many generals, but it did not accord with the facts.

While there was no getting around the reality that the defeat of the Twenty-first Division had undone the Fifth Army's offensive, it was difficult to pin that on ethnicity. Though it was clear that some Czech troops had surrendered to the enemy once the reverse began to turn into a debacle, other Czechs fought like lions. The Second and Sixth Armies reported no problems with their Czech troops during the invasion, and in the Fifth Army, the Ninth Division, raised from the same Bohemian districts as the Twenty-first Division, performed much better at Cer, one of its regiments, Potiorek's own 102nd, which was over 90 percent Czech, being praised by the High Command for its vain efforts to assist their *Landwehr* brethren fighting on the *Cerska planina*.[70]

The decisive issues were preparedness and leadership, not ethnicity. An untried, poorly trained division, heavily composed of out-of-shape reservists, with too-small cadres of professional officers and NCOs, tired from long marches and inadequately supplied and nourished, was surprised at night by an equal number of battle-hardened, energetically led enemy soldiers: the result was no surprise to any seasoned or impartial observer. Przyborski and his staff had neglected to conduct reconnaissance of the mountain and its environs, in particular toward the southeast, the avenue of advance, a grave defect that permitted an enemy attack to be a surprise. The divisional commander's leadership once battle was joined was uninspired at best, allowing confusion to reign far longer than it should have. Only aggressive initiative by Przyborski's subordinates, many of whom fell at Cer, allowed the survival of most of the Twenty-first Division.[71]

The Ninth Division outperformed its sister Twenty-first Division at Cer, as it had larger cadres of active-duty officers, NCOs, and men, plus the benefit of more training in small-unit tactics. General Podhajský, surveying the wreckage of his division, noted the inadequacies of prewar training and the needless casualties caused by reckless attacks. Officers were brave and loyal, he felt, but lacked initiative and the desire to close with enemy, and the collapse of the logistical system in Serbia was decisive and inexcusable. The "*komitadji* effect" was lamentable too, as it made tired, hungry, and thirsty troops jumpy and prone to panic, especially at night or in rough terrain, as Podhajský witnessed personally.[72]

The Fifth Army's internal findings of what went wrong in Serbia were more honest than the public pronouncements. Assessments of logistical performance were scathing, and Frank's headquarters cited "disorder and indiscipline" in supply columns as one of the top causes of the Cer defeat.[73] March discipline in all units was poor, and officers were doing a weak job of maintaining order. Reconnaissance was usually inadequate, so enemy attacks were too often a surprise—a tendency not helped by using lanterns profligately at night, which Serbian prisoners observed meant that Austro-Hungarian units could be spotted miles away—as happened at Cer. Artillery support was thoroughly inadequate, and target acquisition was poor: "Artillery should basically only open fire when it has real targets," concluded VIII Corps after the defeat. Perhaps worst of all, "friendly fire" incidents were rampant in Serbia, as jumpy units, fearful of *komitadji*, fired blindly at anything. The Habsburg Army was just beginning to learn painful tactical lessons.[74]

The enemy's unwillingness to play by accepted rules of warfare was likewise condemned by Austro-Hungarian forces in the Balkans. "Savagery" was a word commonly applied to the Serbs in battle, and Fifth Army reports included detailed reports of massacres of Austro-Hungarian wounded and prisoners by Serbian troops, often irregulars. There were also incidents of Serbs—even civilians—showing a white flag falsely to gain tactical advantage, while deception in uniforms, signals, and language was to be expected from the Serbs in battle, based on what was witnessed during the mid-August invasion. Habsburg officers, stinging from defeat, viewed the Serbs with a deep hatred combined with contempt for an enemy who so flagrantly acted with dishonor.[75]

There can be no doubt that Serbian conduct that was perceived by Austro-Hungarian officers as unfair and illegal contributed to the violence visited on Serbs, military and civilian, during the August invasion. Approximately 3,500 Serbian civilians were killed by Habsburg forces during two weeks (to compare, German troops killed 5,000 Belgian civilians over a period of two months in 1914), many of them around Šabac, where both sides seem to have summarily shot prisoners, wounded, and even civilians without second thoughts.[76] Some of this certainly had to do with intense propaganda on both sides that demonized the enemy, while hatred of the Serbs ran deep among Habsburg troops after the assassinations at Sarajevo. It also bears noting that the lines between civilian and soldier was intentionally blurred by the Serbian military, and Austro-Hungarian accounts of being attacked by armed women and even children in Serbia, while perhaps embellished, were not fabricated.

All the same, killing *komitadji*, real or suspected, was no substitute for victory. Morale dropped on the Balkan Front after the unexpected thrashing that Habsburg forces received at the hands of the hated Serbs. While many sought to place blame on disloyal Slavs, or an all-purpose Fifth Column lurking inside the Dual Monarchy, savvier generals were not so easily fooled. Gen. Alfred Krauss, perhaps the army's top tactician and a sharp critic of Conrad and his methods, rued the poor combat readiness and battlefield performance that the disaster on the Drina had laid bare. In the aftermath of the defeat, Krauss confided in his diary: "The fault lies—I say this with clarity and certainty—exclusively on the High Command and the army's top leadership."[77] It was a view that many Habsburg generals would have endorsed, though few would say so openly in the first month of the war.

Potiorek itched for another opportunity to enact vengeance on Serbia, his desire now increased by the humiliating defeat at Cer. Only a truly significant victory could recover his now-tattered reputation at court. But the *Balkanstreitkräfte* needed time to recover from the rough handling they had received on the east bank of the Drina. Potiorek's troops beat back minor Serbian incursions into Bosnia and a local rebellion in Hercegovina in the week after the retreat from Serbia, but launching another major offensive needed more time. Replacement (*Marsch*) battalions at the front made good the recent losses, and barely forty-eight hours after it had reached safety in Bosnia, the Twenty-first Division had made good most of its casualties, at least on paper: its infantry regiments were at about two-thirds strength (except for the Twenty-eighth, which had the biggest losses at Cer, which was only at half-strength even with *Marsch* reinforcements), and the artillery had been partly restocked with new guns.[78]

The quality of the remade division was an open question, particularly because so many trained officers and NCOs had been lost and could not be replaced, and the fresh replacements from *Marsch* units were even less trained than the original *Landwehr* contingent had been. The only comfort for the Fifth Army was that it was not being sent north to Galicia, to confront the Russians, which promised to be a far greater and bloodier undertaking than anything yet seen on the Sava and the Drina.

There can be little doubt that morale among troops of the *Balkanstreitkräfte* left much to be desired in late August, especially among the Czechs of VIII Corps, who had been singled out for blame by Potiorek in the defeat. Confronted by an embarrassing setback, too many Habsburg officers, including plenty on the General Staff, fell back on ingrained suspicions of Slavic, especially Czech, troops. The lesson learned by the bottle-green boys regarding the failed offensive against Serbia was not that Habsburg training, weaponry, and tactics were inadequate, especially when fighting an experienced foe, rather that its soldiers, particularly Czechs, needed closer supervision, vigorously enforced.

Potiorek's tactless imposition of emergency martial law on the Twenty-first Division was rescinded on the personal order of Emperor Franz Joseph, who disliked anything that smacked of ethnic politics in his army, but some Czechs, including in uniform, had begun to doubt the course of the war already. The High Command's indictment of the Twenty-first Division, and by implication of Czech troops, was a poorly timed blow to the solidarity of the multinational army, and with its affront to loyal Czechs it threatened to become a self-fulfilling prophecy.

At the end of August, the Fifth Army awarded decorations to troops who had fought bravely in the ill-fated invasion of Serbia. The war's first awards for valor were bestowed on two soldiers of the Twenty-first Division: Sergeant Kulhánek of the Sixth Regiment, who blunted a Serbian cavalry charge at Petkovica, and Corporal Řiha of the divisional artillery, who defended his field gun against direct attack. They received the Silver Medal for Bravery. Both men were Czechs.[79]

6   To Warsaw!

For all his ardent desire to punish the Serbs, Conrad understood that, once the war began in earnest, Russia was the enemy that Austria-Hungary had to beat to emerge victorious. His letters regarding the mid-August debacle in the Balkans overseen by his archrival Potiorek brim with frustration, yet from early that month it was Galicia that engaged Conrad's attention almost fully. The East was where the fate of his career, his army, and his country would be determined.

As the bulk of the Austro-Hungarian Army began its slow deployment to Galicia in the first half of August, with thousands of train cars packed with men every day moving slowly to the northeast on every rail line in the Dual Monarchy, Conrad got his affairs in order and prepared to take command in the field. He settled his bills, determined which of his children would inherit what, in the event he did not return, and brooded about his personal life. Since their secret relationship began over seven years before, Conrad and Gina had never been apart for more than a few weeks, and the prospect of long-term separation brought down the general's already parlous spirits.

Conrad had his last audience with the emperor before heading to Galicia on the morning of August 15. The General Staff chief found Franz Joseph in a good mood, yet at the conclusion of the meeting the aged monarch took Conrad's hand and said with visible emotion, "God willing, all will go well, but even if it should go wrong, I will see it through." Taking leave of the emperor, Conrad said goodbye to his elderly mother. He had already seen three of his sons, all of whom were in uniform (or soon to be) and were headed to the front themselves, eventually. He did not see off his favorite son, Herbert, who was already serving in Galicia with the cavalry and who would be in action soon.

Conrad departed Vienna after midnight, in the early hours of August 16, as the High Command entourage boarded a special train headed east; it included Archduke Friedrich, the titular commander in chief, and the young Archduke Karl, only twenty-seven, who since the Sarajevo murders was the next in line for the Habsburg throne. Conrad bid adieu to a few friends at the station, including Gina. It was an emotional farewell, as she recalled: "He held my hand tight for a long time, and made me swear to him that after the war I would become his wife. Otherwise he would not leave me." A day and a half later on the afternoon of August 17, the High Command group reached the fortress city of Przemyśl in central Galicia. The great struggle against Russia was about to begin in earnest.[1]

Przemyśl was a logical place for *Armeeoberkommando* (Army High Command, or AOK) to be located for the Galician campaign, as it was a transportation and communications hub astride the San river, forty kilometers south of the Russian border and fifty-five kilometers west of Lemberg. Przemyśl was not single fortress, rather an outer ring of fortresses that fully encircled the city at a distance of five to eight kilometers out, supplemented by an inner ring of forts just outside the city. Despite its formidable appearance, Przemyśl was unready for a major siege since its guns and protection were outmoded. Given his steadfast belief in the offensive, Conrad considered fortresses to be of little value, and none of Galicia's forts—there were smaller complexes at Cracow, Lemberg, Jaroslau, Radymno, Mikołajów, Halicz, and Zaleszczyki—had been seriously updated since the late nineteenth century. A crash program to modernize Przemyśl once war began had scant effect, and despite impressive-looking fortifications, the fortress city was not ready for modern warfare.[2]

On paper, Przemyśl seemed well defended. It possessed forty-five kilometers of entrenchments and eleven fixed artillery batteries: a total of 714 cannons, 54 howitzers, 95 heavy mortars, and 72 machine guns. However, the only modern pieces were two dozen siege guns, while 299 of Przemyśl's cannons were Model 1861! The crash program to strengthen the fortress in mid-August, involving 27,000 workers, succeeded in clearing forests around the city, creating fields of fire, and laying a million meters of barbed wire in every direction, but could do nothing to change Przemyśl's fundamental unreadiness for the twentieth-century battlefield.[3]

By the time Conrad reached Przemyśl, his eastern army was mostly, if not entirely, ready to take the offensive. The First Army, on the Austro-Hungarian left flank and looking north into central Poland, was closest to the Russian frontier, with three corps and eleven divisions (nine infantry, two cavalry). Around Przemyśl the Fourth Army was marshaling with three corps and eleven divisions (nine infantry, two cavalry), facing northeast. The two corps and nine divisions (six infantry, two cavalry) of the Third Army were encamped around Lemberg, with the main body of troops lagered about fifty kilometers south of the Russian frontier. The Second Army was still fighting in Serbia and had yet to entrain for Galicia, so the right (and southern) flank of Conrad's force was held by an improvised "army group," pending the arrival of Second Army headquarters, of two corps and eight divisions (six infantry, two cavalry) headquartered at Stanislau about eighty kilometers from the border. Of the approximately forty divisions Conrad had at his disposal for his great offensive, only thirty-four were in position on time, and they faced a total of fifty-two Russian divisions.[4]

Austro-Hungarian forces were slow to deploy to their Galician staging areas for Conrad's offensive, in part due to excessively slow rail movements. Thanks to bureaucratic rules that required a number of daily halts for rest and victualing, Habsburg trains headed to war averaged a leisurely place of eighteen kilometers per hour, slower than a bicycle, and barely half the German rate, slower too than the Russian.[5] This lethargy on the rails, which had no place in wartime, nullified much of the advantage that Conrad planned to take of Russia's slower mobilization due to the vast size of the tsar's realm. By the time Austro-Hungarian forces were ready to commence their offensive after August 22, they found enemy forces were in position as well.

The High Command was well aware of the relevant geography. Galicia had ample plains, but much of the battle area was comprised of forested rolling hills with a series of major rivers, especially in Eastern Galicia, where the Bug and Dniester offered formidable obstacles. The terrain was dotted with small towns and villages; east of Lemberg stood a sea of Ukrainian peasants with islands of Poles and Jews in the few places that could be honestly termed cities. The road network was barely adequate in most areas, and the rail system served the cities and larger towns only. Divisions on the march would be forced to stay close to the few decent roads. Habsburg forces could expect problems with supply and communications, particularly once they moved into Russian territory, as the left wing of Conrad's army was ordered to do with haste.

Conrad's battle plan looked pleasing to the General Staff–trained eye, as it embraced a vigorous offensive at the start aimed at taking the war to the enemy, which seemed to be the only way to blunt the Russian steamroller before it gained momentum. However, there was considerable strategic muddling built into the plan. As Norman Stone has observed, Conrad's forces faced numerous challenges, not least "a fundamental uncertainty about what they were meant to achieve."[6] A move into central Poland offered tantalizing political objectives, not least because Vienna expected the Poles under tsarist misrule to greet Habsburg forces warmly, while advancing to the east out of Lemberg looked daunting, as any attack would face many rivers and hills, plus few concrete objectives short of Kiev, which lay fully five hundred kilometers east of Lemberg. No less, Russian deployment plans and rail lines that were known to the General Staff dictated that any Habsburg attack directly east into Volhynia would likely collide with the main

Russian force. Therefore starting the offensive with a push north toward Warsaw appeared the most attractive option, a course of action that Conrad had decided upon back in March, even though it meant he had to leave his forces around Lemberg dangerously inadequate should the Russians appear in strength in Eastern Galicia.[7] The Second Army could not arrive from the Balkans fast enough.

Making the main push into Poland also held out the promise of strategic victory, since Conrad had always wanted his German ally to meet his drive on Warsaw from the south with a Prussian move into central Poland from the north. Russian forces would be quickly encircled and annihilated. Yet this, like so many Conradian concepts, was a mirage of wishful thinking, and the General Staff knew it as it went to war. Although Conrad would later rue the lack of German offensive action against Russia that summer as he tried to pin blame on Berlin for Habsburg failure, communications between Conrad and Moltke, his Prussian counterpart, in early August include no mention of any complementary attack out of East Prussia to support the Austro-Hungarian drive into Poland. As it executed the Schlieffen Plan, Germany kept only seven divisions against Russia at the beginning of the war, to defend East Prussia; they had no offensive tasking. Not only did no coordinated war plan exist, the messages exchanged between the allied General Staffs as war began were brimming with vague Teutonic bravado and little else.

Moltke made no effort to restrain Conrad from his unsupported push into Poland; on the contrary the Prussians wanted their ally to go on the offensive as soon as possible. Russian troops of the First and Second Armies began their drive into East Prussia on August 15, before Conrad had even departed Vienna. German generals were exasperated that Habsburg forces were taking so long to get on their feet and make contact with the enemy. Moltke needed Austro-Hungarian might to tie down the bulk of the tsar's forces and thereby save East Prussia, so he seems to have averted his eyes from the reality of the situation. As he laconically told a Habsburg general that August, "You have a good army. You'll beat the Russians." This was patently untrue, as years of Prussian attaché reports from Vienna had clarified just how unprepared Austria-Hungary actually was for war against any major power. Subsequent to the disaster suffered by Conrad's forces at the hands of the Russians, top German generals found it politic to pretend that they had no idea how troubled the Habsburg military was; the reality was different. Yet as crisis turned to war, Moltke, like many senior Prussian officers, simply averted his eyes and hoped for the best: letting Austria-Hungary bear the brunt in the East for at least the first six to eight weeks of the conflict seemed the least-bad option still available.[8] Conrad was not the only senior general to succumb to wishful thinking masquerading as strategy in August 1914.

Conrad at least saw positive developments among the Galician population to encourage a degree of optimism. Although the High Command was prone to excessive vigilance about pro-Russian elements among the population, seeing spies and saboteurs beyond where they actually existed, the reality was that Galicia's peoples overwhelmingly rallied to the Habsburg cause at the beginning of the war; AOK nevertheless took no chances and at the outset placed Galicia along with Bukovina under martial law.[9] Army counterintelligence reports warned of strong pockets of "Russophiles" in East Galicia, along with sketchy reports of Ukrainians readying to greet Russian soldiers as brothers.[10] While these reports were not unsubstantiated, the overall reality was different. The province's Jews were almost uniformly behind the war against Russia, the land of the pogrom, while most Ukrainians too seemed to be rallying to Austria-Hungary's side. Fears of Ukrainian disloyalty, feared by some generals (and Galician Poles) seemed overblown. In Lemberg, the newly formed Ukrainian National Council sided firmly with the Habsburgs in a war of liberation against Russia, calling Ukrainians to battle on August 3 with the declaration, "Austria-Hungary's victory will be our victory too." Quickly a battalion of Ukrainian volunteer riflemen was formed, wearing national colors on Habsburg uniforms, calling itself a legion at the disposal of the *k.u.k. Armee*; soon there would be a full regiment's worth of volunteers seeking to liberate co-nationals from the tsarist yoke.[11]

Polish enthusiasm for war against Russia was likewise widely noted that August. Poles in Austro-Hungarian uniform appeared for duty cheerfully, brimming with desire to liberate brother Poles from tsarist rule. The Thirteenth Infantry Regiment, "Cracow's Children," departed their garrison singing Polish patriotic songs, including their national anthem.[12] Important too was the raising of the Polish Legion in early August at Cracow under Habsburg sponsorship. Led by the socialist politico and rabble-rouser Józef Piłsudski, who compensated for a lack of pro-Habsburg sentiments with a primordial loathing of anything Russian, the Legion quickly had more volunteers than it could outfit—there were 1,500 legionnaires armed and ready for action by August 10 and numbers were rising fast. They were clad in Habsburg uniform with Polish national insignia, speaking Polish as the language of command; because uniforms were in short supply, some wore a black-yellow armband with civilian attire, to indicate their loyalties.[13]

By September the Polish Legion had grown to two full infantry regiments with its own cavalry and artillery, with most recruits coming from the Polish paramilitary rifle clubs that had been discreetly supported by Austro-Hungarian intelligence before the war. Many Habsburg officers questioned the Legion's military utility, yet its political value was obvious; Conrad among others hoped the Legion, operating in small units behind enemy lines, could help deliver sorely needed intelligence on Russian troop deployments across the border.[14] The army pulled a Polish major general out of retirement, Rajmund Baczyński, a do-nothing *Kaffeehausgeneral* with little knowledge of the Legion's agenda; his main task seemed to be preventing the enthusiastic volunteers from causing too much trouble for the High Command. By the second week of August, Piłsudski's legionnaires were preparing to enter Russian territory, with or without Habsburg help.[15]

By mid-August, before battle was even joined, many Austro-Hungarian troops, especially middle-aged reservists, were weary. Since most railheads were at least dozens of kilometers from the border, units faced long marches under the hot Galician sun to reach the enemy. A *Landsturm* subaltern of III Corps recalled his long, exhausting marches in East Galicia in mid-August; like most of his men, the militia lieutenant was out of shape and had not soldiered in decades. Many *Landsturm* troops had expected home service and were surprised to be headed into battle so soon. The first-day march out of Stryj, south of the Dniester, required over sixty kilometers on foot, with a short break at midday, and "constituted a very strong test of endurance in consequence of our comparative softness and lack of training," not least because the soldiers were laden like mules:

> in addition to his heavy rifle, bayonet, ammunition, and spade, each soldier was burdened with a knapsack containing emergency provisions in the form of tinned meats, coffee extract, sugar, salt, rice, and biscuits, together with various tin cooking and eating utensils; furthermore a second pair of shoes, extra blouse, changes of underwear, etc. On top of this heavy pack a winter overcoat and part of a tent were strapped, the entire weight of the equipment being in the neighborhood of fifty pounds.

Numerous middle-aged militiamen could not keep up, with many falling on the roadside from exhaustion. Most got back on their feet after a few minutes rest, but the lieutenant heard "no murmur of complaint," even though many soldiers wondered why they were being pushed so hard, so soon, before battle had even been joined. The regiment earned a much-needed rest under the stars that night, near a monastery at the forest's edge, somewhere in East Galicia, and despite exhaustion, spirits were high from anticipation, making what the officer remembered as "an unforgettable scene of great romanticism and beauty." But the march began again shortly after six the next morning, with more than thirty kilometers to be made by midday, including fording two rivers. Many troops were simply unable to keep going by the late morning and "could hardly crawl along." Oddly, noted the lieutenant, soldiers from towns and cities seemed to be able to bear longer marches than peasants; despite generally being in worse physical shape, city folk seems to have more willpower, he noted. Slowly, the regiment reached its destination at 2:30 in the afternoon and settled down to a long rest. While many men simply collapsed and entered a deep sleep, others could faintly hear a low, dull roar off in the distance eastward. It was Russian artillery, much closer than the regiment had been told to expect. Battle would soon be joined.[16]

For many Habsburg soldiers, the warzone was an alien and unpleasant land. The rural poverty of the East Galician countryside was hardly an appealing sight to soldiers from the more developed parts of the Dual Monarchy. Many looked on the impoverished locals, Jews and Ukrainians, with equal distaste. One Austrian junior officer was shocked by the backwardness of the province as his regiment marched to battle east of Jaroslau, past village after village of poor peasants living in filth, alongside farm animals in huts: "these were the most primitive quarters I had ever seen." It was an unpleasant change from the cheerful sendoff the regiment had seen in Moravia, where at every stop civilians came to the train to give the troops gifts of bread, cakes, sausages, and eggs. In Galicia, there was nothing for them, leading the lieutenant to question in his diary Rousseau's "illusions" about noble savages![17]

This impoverished and polyglot province, which many Austro-Hungarians lamented and Russian Slavophiles romanticized as Orthodox irredenta, would be the main theater of war in the East in the summer of 1914. The die was cast on July 30, when Tsar Nicholas II ordered general mobilization.[18] Two-thirds of Russian forces would be committed against Austria-Hungary, following longstanding war plans. Russia's decision for war has recently received more attention from scholarship than it had previously been given. The idea of embarking on a crusade against Teutonic Europe, in particular to liberate Slavs from the Habsburg yoke, had currency among mystical Russian nationalists, including more than a few tsarist ministers and generals, yet there were voices counseling caution; as almost everywhere else in Europe, they were drowned out in the euphoria of the July Crisis. Sergei Witte, once one of the tsar's ablest and most favored ministers, urged that war be avoided, not least because he felt the Serbs were dangerously unsavory as allies; moreover, Witte saw no use in "liberating" Ukrainians and Poles from the Habsburgs: "Galicia? But it's full of Jews!" he told France's ambassador to St. Petersburg.[19]

An even more prescient warning had come in March 1914, when Pyotr Durnovo, a former interior minister, authored a remarkable memorandum that urged a major shift in Russian foreign policy. Predicting that war between Britain and Germany was inevitable and that a wider war could easily result that would be Russia's ruin, Durnovo foresaw radicalism and the end of the imperial system accompanying any protracted conflict. Moreover, in language Franz Ferdinand would have heartily endorsed, Durnovo believed that Russia was on the wrong side in the coming war, allied with Western states like Britain and France when its natural allies in Europe were Germany and Austria-Hungary, which were conservative monarchies like Russia herself. He likewise argued that any romantic notion of reuniting Galicia with its alleged Russian Motherland was a dangerous fantasy, since few Galicians wanted Russian rule and many would resist it actively. For all its prescience, there is no evidence Durnovo's predictions and counsel made any serious impression in St. Petersburg.[20]

As Russia mobilized its vast forces for war, the tsar appointed his cousin Grand Duke Nikolai commander-in-chief. A career cavalryman, the fifty-seven-year-old Nikolai had seen little action—he was kept at home in 1905 to shore up the bumptious domestic front, a more vital task than fighting the Japanese—but he was an experienced staffer who commanded the loyalty of most Russian officers and was generally popular with the men. Like Franz Ferdinand, he was a pious man who loved the hunt.[21] Though he had never led forces in the field, that August Grand Duke Nikolai found himself in command of the greatest army the world had ever seen, 115 infantry and 38 cavalry divisions with nearly 7,900 guns. The Grand Duke set up his Supreme Command, called Stavka (literally "tent" in archaic Russian) at Baranovichi; at the beginning of the campaign he made little effort to exercise close control, most of which stayed with front and field army commanders.

The biggest portion of the tsar's army was assigned to the Southwestern Front, opposite Austria-Hungary, under General Nikolai Ivanov. The sixty-three-year-old Ivanov, a gunner by trade, had seen considerable combat, including against Turkey in the Balkans in 1877–78, and against Japan in Manchuria in 1904–5, including commanding a corps at Liaoyang and Mukden. Ivanov's reputation in battle was lackluster, but he had commanded the Kiev Military District from late 1908 and was considered to be a loyal officer. He also understood the Habsburg enemy well, as his prewar headquarters in Kiev had focused solely on Austria-Hungary for years, and it received purloined intelligence from Redl's treachery. Ivanov's staff at the Southwestern Front went to war with a good understanding of the organization and capabilities of the foe they were soon to face in Galicia. The force at Ivanov's disposal was vast, with four field armies comprising fifteen corps—over fifty divisions—aligned by mid-August in a half-moon that stretched three hundred kilometers from the Vistula river in the northwest to the Dniester in the southeast, well over a million men in all. A fifth army, the Ninth, was established around Warsaw in early August, adding five more divisions as a strategic reserve.[22] The choice of Austria-Hungary as the main effort for the Russian Army in 1914 stemmed from many factors, including an understanding that the Habsburg military would be easier to defeat than the Prussians; no less, there were commonplace estimations that many Habsburgs Slavs would be eager to embrace the Russians as liberators, which turned out to be wishful thinking of a Conradian sort. Nevertheless this fantasy was countered by the reality that Austria-Hungary could be knocked out of the war more easily than Germany. Hence the effort by the Northwestern Front employed only eight corps, less than half the forces arrayed in the Southwest, though the attack into East Prussia began a week before Ivanov's divisions were ready to march into Galicia. That day, August 22, was the same day Conrad was finally ready to commence his own great offensive. The two armies, with some two million men between them, were set to collide all along the Galician front, in encounter battles of a size and ferocity the world had never seen.

Both armies faced the challenge of determining where the enemy actually *was*. Gaining actionable intelligence was a critical advantage, especially in meeting engagements where it was imperative to inflict quick, sharp blows against the enemy, before he could bring his full forces to bear. But the realities of intelligence in 1914 made this difficult for all armies. Agents—that is, spies behind enemy lines—were hard to come by, often of dubious credibility and reliability, frequently caught, and their information was not especially timely under wartime conditions. Cavalry had already passed its prime as the forward eyes of the army, while aircraft were unreliable, short-ranged, not always understood by field commanders, and possessed in only small numbers by both the Russians and Austro-Hungarians. The nascent discipline of signals intelligence, which would soon become a critical source of information on the battlefield, was about to come into its own, but not just yet in the summer of 1914.

Thus both armies approached the battlefield with a high degree of uncertainty about where the enemy could be found. Habsburg and tsarist forces alike grappled with ways to gain an edge in intelligence, with mixed results. Although Redl's betrayal had granted the Russians a considerable strategic advantage in understanding the *k.u.k. Armee,* including important information about plans and deployments, this proved little help in finding the enemy once battle was imminent. Alexei Brusilov, the most successful Russian general of the Great War, whose Eighth Army would inflict grave injury to Austro-Hungarian forces before Lemberg, rued this blindness as he prepared to enter Galicia:

> Our information as to the enemy's forces was somewhat sketchy, and to tell the truth our intelligence was on the whole anything but well organized. Reconnaissance by air, with the few and second-rate

machines that we had, was quite inadequate; however, what information we had was obtained in this manner. Our spy system was not extensive, and the agents we hastily recruited were of no great service. Cavalry reconnaissances could not be pushed very far because the frontier, the River Zbrucz, was held in its entire length by strong bodies of enemy infantry. All we knew was that up to date no very powerful enemy forces had been discovered facing us.[23]

This inability to develop a better-than-hazy image of the enemy's dispositions plagued Habsburg commanders just as badly in mid-August. With the war's outbreak, the *Evidenzbureau* dispatched most of its small staff to join AOK at Przemyśl, renaming itself the Intelligence Department (*Nachrichtenabteilung*—NA) upon mobilization, for the duration of the conflict. Under the command of Col. Oskar von Hranilović, a skilled Croat who had only been in the position for a few months, the intelligence staff began collecting new talent, especially polyglot reservists able to function in Russian.[24] Prewar intelligence assessments of the Russian military, which were based largely on attaché reports and open sources, were broadly accurate about orders of battle, peacetime deployments, and tactics, and portrayed a force that would be a formidable foe. Of particular interest was a special assessment of Russian artillery at the end of July that made it abundantly clear that the *k.u.k. Armee* could expect to be outgunned in Galicia. The secret report offered impressive detail about recent Russian gunnery improvements and left no doubt that late-model field guns and howitzers possessed more range and hitting power than Austro-Hungarian equivalents, while at the division level, enemy units had approximately one-third more tubes than Habsburg forces did.[25]

While NA staffers churned out reports on the Russian Army at an impressive pace, the main task before Hranilović's officers—locating the enemy's main forces in a timely fashion—proved elusive. To their credit, intelligence officers in Przemyśl from the first day of August were collating an impressive array of sources—daily reports from border guards and cavalry patrols near the frontier, supplemented by agent reports and aerial reconnaissance—but seldom did NA daily assessments provide much specificity about enemy deployments.[26] The ability to see behind enemy lines was limited by technology and Russian vigilance. Agents, mainly Poles, roamed and brought back what information they could, but enemy counterintelligence made it difficult to report information as rapidly as Conrad's staffers needed it, not to mention that overzealous Habsburg troops not infrequently detained returning agents on suspicion of being Russian! Moreover, agents operating in enemy territory provided a wealth of data about Russian fortifications and fixed defenses, such as voluminous information about the fortress complex at Ivangorod near Warsaw, which was being reinforced rapidly, but little about major troop movements closer to the border. In whole areas, for instance west of the Vistula, NA on some days had no current reporting of any kind to offer.[27]

Moreover, relations between NA staff and its Polish agents, many of whom were linked with Piłsudski's budding Legion, were touchy, and some Habsburg officers felt the Poles were delivering skewed information to bolster their agenda, particularly reports that co-nationals in Russia were ripe for rebellion. Polish agents crossing the border delivered considerable information daily and claimed they had no difficulty finding fellow Poles eager to betray Russia, but much of the genuine intelligence value of their reporting was limited, mainly vague descriptions of enemy units on the march, and rarely timely enough to matter to operational decision making.[28]

Aerial reconnaissance was by far the best source of detailed intelligence about Russian deployments, since pilots personally reported their findings immediately upon their return to base and sometimes offered detailed descriptions of enemy troop movements, but there were so few airframes on hand that coverage was limited. Slow-moving Austro-Hungarian aircraft were able to roam the skies over Poland almost at will, and the bulk of detailed and timely reporting in NA daily reports came from aerial reconnaissance. In mid-August, one pilot was able to fly all the way to Warsaw, taking notes about Russian units along the way, hand-dropping a few small bombs on Ivangorod's fortifications for good measure, a mission that lasted almost five hours and tested the endurance of man and machine.[29] But the reality was that the army had too few airframes to provide more than a sporadic look behind enemy lines. In addition, readiness was poor due to unreliable engines. Worse, troops on the ground tended to fire at any aircraft overhead, so Habsburg pilots were endangered by their own side as much as by the Russians. By August 19, even before the offensive began, three aircraft, 10 percent of the total on hand, were shot down by friendly forces. It exasperated Conrad, who stated, "the fliers perform a great service, but we have far too few and of these, 50 percent and more are shot down. They called me a fool when I recommended 1,200 airplanes for the army. Now they see I was right."[30]

By mid-August it was evident that intelligence reporting had failed to locate the bulk of the enemy's Southwestern Front. Given what Hranilović's officers knew already about Russian plans and rail lines, there had to be considerable tsarist forces marshaling about 130 to 150 kilometers east of Lemberg, south of the Pinsk marshes, but this message was unwelcome at AOK, where Conrad was readying to execute his first, major push northward, in the opposite direction, an act that would leave the Third Army dangerously vulnerable. A detailed NA report on August 10, including maps, showed the Russian XI Corps around Łuck— where it actually was—as well as five more corps gathering opposite East Galicia, another accurate assessment, but this intelligence seems to have made no impression on Conrad or his staff.[31] While some of the failures of Austro-Hungarian intelligence in the summer of 1914 can be blamed on Redl, who compromised many sources, the reality is that AOK seems to have had scant interest in intelligence that did not support Conrad's plans.

It was also important to keep the enemy blind. To protect the border and thwart minor Russian probes into Galicia that aimed at gathering intelligence, the paramilitary Gendarmerie was ordered to bolster its positions on the frontier. The Gendarmerie command for Galicia was the biggest in Austria, with thirty-five detachments, each with between ten and thirty-five posts, scattered all over the province. Those close to the border were reinforced by *Landsturm* and ordered to prevent penetrations by probing Russian units. All along the frontier, small Gendarmerie detachments fought wild battles with the enemy, some of them counting as more than skirmishes. Before dawn on August 14 at Bełżec, a hundred-man Gendarmerie detachment was struck by an enemy force ten times its size, which the defenders managed to keep at bay, even though probing attacks continued for days. Wherever the Russians crossed the border, the forces of the Gendarmerie were usually the first to fight.[32]

In Bukovina, the Austrian Gendarmerie was the bulwark of the defense, as the *k.u.k. Armee* had few forces to spare to defend the Dual Monarchy's most remote province. In the capable hands of Col. Eduard Fischer, who had served in the province for much of his career and was well informed about the Russian subversive network in Bukovina, his five detachments of gendarmes, bolstered by Ukrainian, Romanian, and Jewish volunteers, waged an economy of force campaign against far larger numbers of invaders, usually Cossacks supported by infantry in up to brigade strength. Beginning on August 6, Russian reconnaissance patrols dashed across the border and Fischer's gendarmes resisted where they could, relying on local knowledge to compensate for weakness in men and firepower. The Austrians sent patrols across the Russian border too, to keep the enemy off balance. There were a few pitched battles between the Gendarmerie and the Russians, namely at Nowoselica on August 19, followed by a three-day fight for Rarancze on August 20 that inflicted a thousand dead on the enemy. But the Russian Army could not be long resisted by gendarmes, and the order to evacuate Czernowitz, the provincial capital, came on August 31. Thereafter, Fischer's forces headed for the Carpathian foothills and conducted hit-and-run attacks on the Russians to buy time.[33]

Possessing more enthusiasm than finesse, Piłsudski's Polish Legion had no intention of waiting for orders from Przemyśl to start its war of liberation against tsarist rule. It was helping agents clandestinely transit the border on a daily basis but it was chomping at the bit for a bigger role. Beginning in the first week of August, volunteers in company-to-battalion-sized detachments, as many as 450 men, crossed the frontier in the Cracow area, seeking to stir up trouble. There was only limited coordination with Habsburg authorities. Most volunteers returned within hours, ammunition expended, with tales of derring-do and little else to show for their effort. On August 11, 2,500 Poles crossed the border with the intent of fomenting a full-fledged rebellion against the tsar; Austro-Hungarian officers were skeptical of this actually happening—properly, as it turned out. While the legionnaires were greeted by fellow Poles, few Russian subjects sought to join in the action. On August 12 and 14, legionnaires again launched raids into Russian territory, this time in coordination with the Seventh Cavalry Division, but this produced only limited intelligence. While these raids panicked Russian authorities, they delivered little actionable information and were not the hoped-for precursor to a general Polish revolt in favor of Austria-Hungary.[34]

Seeking hard information about the enemy so that he could begin his grand offensive, Conrad ordered a massive cavalry sweep by ten full mounted divisions across the entire Galician front, to begin August 15, to find the Russians. The cavalry happily obliged, since this was the kind of task its generals wished to undertake, semi-independent missions in the saddle, in front of the main force, opportunities for glory. At last they could prove their continuing relevance on the modern battlefield. How the Habsburg cavalry saw its mission was concisely explained by Gen. Oskar Wittmann, commander of the Sixth Cavalry Division, who told his assembled officers at the beginning of August, "a good cavalryman at the front uses the saber, and his carbine only in special cases of danger."[35] Such outmoded thinking, coupled with the limited firepower of Habsburg cavalry divisions, meant that Conrad's sweeping concept of reconnaissance in force across the whole Galician front by massed cavalry stood little chance of success.

There were already indications that galloping blindly toward the Russians would end badly. Two days before the cavalry sweep began, Hranilović's staff published a detailed classified assessment of what to expect from the enemy, a concise primer on Russian tactics. It was authored by Count Stanislaus Szeptycki, a Polish colonel and artillery-man who had served as an observer with the Russians in Manchuria in 1904–5, which gave him unique insights into how the Russians liked to fight. Szeptycki's report in particular noted the power and accuracy of Russian artillery, which the tsar's forces liked to deploy forward in indi-vidual batteries to support cavalry and infantry patrols that Habsburg forces could expect to meet at the start of any fight. Aggressive patrol-ling was the norm with the enemy, and Russian forward detachments, operating in front of the main force and combining horse, foot, and guns, could be expected to be a formidable foe. There is no evidence that Szeptycki's accurate assessment made any significant impression on AOK before the war for Galicia began in earnest.[36]

Cavalry action to screen the armies and provide intelligence on Rus-sian dispositions almost immediately encountered problems. The basic unsuitability of the army's standard saddle soon became obvious—it was better suited to the parade ground than mounted patroling for days and tired out the horses quickly—but Russian artillery was a greater hazard. Habsburg cavalry divisions were weak in guns, with only a battalion's worth of horse artillery at most, and in any artillery duel with the Russians, Austro-Hungarian mounted forces would emerge the loser, usually at a high cost.

Many of the cavalry divisions were assigned infantry battalions to compensate for their limited staying power in any sustained fight. Lacking intelligence, many units blundered into Russians suddenly and painfully. On August 15, the first day of the reconnaissance in force, the Sixth Cavalry Division crossed the Russian frontier as the forward eyes of the Fourth Army and promptly ran into trouble. The division encountered strong resistance and since the sabers favored by its commander, General Wittmann, were inadequate to the situation, the two battalions of infantry assigned to it, from Vienna's Fourth Regiment, were brought up to deal with the situation. The *Deutschmeister's* commander, Col. Ludwig von Holzhausen, ordered a hasty attack. At Podlesina, he personally led one battalion, arrayed in skirmish lines, in a bayonet charge at Russian entrenchments, yelling *Vorwärts!* while pointing at the enemy with his saber. Holzhausen was quickly cut down, along with much of the battalion, as the attack faltered in the face of intense Russian artillery and machine-gun fire.[37]

Patrols in the expanse of the East Galician borderland, where no one was sure where the Russians lurked, quickly turned dangerous. On August 17, the Fifth *Honvéd* Cavalry Division encountered enemy forces at Gorodok, leading its commander, Gen. Ernst von Froreich, to order a hasty charge by half of the division, eleven mounted squadrons, to catch the Russians off balance. This "brave but foolish event," in Brusilov's words, turned into a rout, not for want of *élan*, with the charging Hussars being cut down by enemy batteries they could not see that poured fire on them, shrapnel scything down horses and men. "Very soon our machine guns started to rake them from end to end," the Russian general recalled.[38] The charge broke, and panic followed, with cavalry fleeing the battlefield; the chaos soon spread to the division's trains, and the situation became uncontrollable. Before order was restored several hours later, the division had lost hundreds of men, and among the dead was General von Froreich, the first Austro-Hungarian general to die in the war. His death was played down, however, because von Froreich in fact had shot himself in despair as his division melted away around him, an embarrassment that the High Command sought to conceal from the public.[39]

On August 21 at Jaroslawice, northeast of Złoczów near the Russian frontier, the cavalries collided in the manner dreamed of by *arme blanche* traditionalists for decades. Here the Fourth Cavalry Division, led by the dashing Polish horseman Maj. Gen. Edmund von Zaremba, met the Russian Tenth Cavalry Division and, in *beau geste* fashion, the Austro-Hungarian cavalry charged headlong into battle, sabers raised amid cheers, directly toward the enemy. In the lead rode the Fifteenth Dragoons, one of whose subalterns was Herbert Conrad, son of the General Staff chief. The prestigious "White Dragoons" charged into battle in full dress uniforms as if the twentieth century had not begun, led by their commander yelling *hurrá* as Russian artillery rounds exploded above them. Enemy shelling caused the lion's share of Habsburg casualties, with few men being lost in the mounted cavalry-on-cavalry fight with sabers that was more dramatic than decisive, and losses would have been higher had the Russian artillery not misjudged the range, as many shrapnel shells exploded harmlessly, too high in the air. Casualties were nevertheless steep, with the attackers losing nearly a thousand men, including 10 officers and 165 troopers of the Fifteenth Dragoons dead or wounded. The Russians lost only one-sixth as many men.[40] The attack had no real impact, despite its color and drama, not least because Zaremba had joined in the charge and was unable to exercise command and control during the mounted melée. In the end, weary Austro-Hungarian horsemen rode back to their starting positions, thus ending the last major mounted cavalry engagement in world history.

The journalist Joseph Redlich, who arrived at AOK in Przemyśl as a liaison officer for the Foreign Ministry only a day after the Jaroslawice fight, observed that widespread talk of the battle focused more on the *Bravour* of the cavalry than on their losses, or what was actually achieved. "It sounds unbelievable but it is the case, that our lancers and hussars have made attacks against trenches and have also taken them; admittedly the losses are also great." Redlich encountered Conrad in better spirits than at their last meeting in Vienna at the beginning of August. The General Staff chief was worried about his sons in uniform, though he was pleased that Herbert was not among the casualties at Jaroslawice. Conditions at Przemyśl even for top generals were austere, with Conrad sleeping on straw in a barracks. The conversation with Conrad soon shifted to talk of Gina, as was the norm, with the lonely widower stating, "she alone is the little bit of sun that I still have in my life." Redlich noted Conrad's "pessimistic-sentimental" mood as the fight for Galicia was about to commence.[41]

Losses among Habsburg cavalry, particularly to Russian guns, continued to mount, for minimal gains. On August 23 at Buczacz in a border region of East Galicia southeast of Lemberg, the First Cavalry Division was struck by Russian artillery while patrolling and forced into a retreat that nearly turned into a rout due to aggressive pursuit by quick-moving Cossacks. The division was saved by the sacrifice of one of its horse artillery batteries that stood its ground and bought time by raking the oncoming Cossacks with shrapnel, but at the cost of all the battery's officers plus the battalion commander, as well as thirty-five gunners.[42] By then, the epic struggle against Russia had commenced in earnest, and cavalry actions had become an afterthought. The real fight now belonged to the infantry.

Conrad's August 22 order to commence his great offensive committed the army to moves that ultimately would be its undoing. It dispatched his left flank to immediate action, with a supporting offensive on the right to follow. To begin: with its left flank covered by the Vistula, the First Army would advance north toward Lublin, while a day later the neighboring Fourth Army, to its right, would advance northeast on Chełm. Soon the Third Army would march eastward out of Lemberg, supported by the Second Army when it eventually arrived from the Balkans. While the offensives on the left flank were mutually supporting and aimed at central Poland, these were coordinated with the right flank's advance only notionally. In the interest of acting quickly, Conrad was splitting his forces and sending them into two separate offensives, pointed in different directions; moreover, the drive to the east would not start for several days, as it required the arrival of the Second Army. In the meantime, the Third Army would move toward the border, its precise mission unclear.[43]

Already some generals were beginning to wonder if Conrad's plan would actually work. The rightmost flank was being held by Hermann Kövess von Kövessháza, one of the top Protestant generals in a very Catholic army, whose XII Corps had been renamed an "army group," with the addition of two more divisions, pending the arrival of the Second Army from Serbia. A German from Transylvania, like many of the troops under his command, Kövess was falling prey to doubts about the whole enterprise. August 18, Franz Joseph's birthday, was a celebratory event for the army, even in the field, with troops not already in action attending field mass, their caps adorned with the *Feldzeichen*, the sprig of oak leaves that Habsburg soldiers had worn into battle for centuries. For officers there was the obligatory dinner with toasts to his majesty. At his command's dinner at a restaurant in Stanislau, Kövess lifted a glass to the emperor and proceeded to share a dose of reality with his staff: "So, gentlemen—if many of you perhaps think that you will be home to celebrate Christmas, as you hear all over the place, I suggest you give up this great deception, because I'm afraid we will be celebrating quite a few Christmases in the field!" Kövess's mood had not been helped by the disaster that befell the Fifth *Honvéd* Cavalry Division the previous day in his sector. As recounted in a letter to Conrad, the hussars had attacked "*mit grosser Bravour*," but the operation fell apart in the face of intense Russian fire, and soon "the panic was complete. The division's trains, which were not under attack, fled . . . the commander. General Froreich, fell in this 'affair.' The division sustained needlessly high casualties."[44]

Conrad's concept would unintentionally aid the Russians. Ivanov's battleplan was based on misunderstandings of Austro-Hungarian intentions. The Southwestern Front believed that the main Habsburg push would come eastwards out of Lemberg, so Ivanov placed his stronger armies, the Third and Eighth, on his left to counter and defeat it. Those armies in fact began their slow, steady advance on Lemberg on August 18, though it would take AOK several days to understand this movement for what it was. The Russians expected a weaker push on their right, that is on Conrad's left flank, when that was in truth the main Austro-Hungarian effort. As a result, each army's weaker flank was set to collide with the opponent's stronger one.

Russian spirits were high, based on reports of a local victory at Gumbinnen in East Prussia, so Ivanov ordered his Fourth and Fifth Armies to get on their feet and march, battle-ready, toward the frontier and then into central Galicia on August 22, as Conrad was dispatching his First and Fourth Armies to meet them. They would encounter each other on the Russian side of the border, in the first major battle between Romanov and Habsburg forces in the war.

There was no good news at AOK, as word of setbacks in Serbia depressed moods, but Conrad was expecting great things from the First Army, which led his offensive, and he had confidence in its commander, fifty-nine-year-old Gen. Viktor Dankl, a cavalryman and General Staff success story. Dankl had three corps: I (Cracow), V (Pozsony), and X (Przemyśl) deployed left to right. Opposing them was the Russian Fourth Army, headquartered at Lublin under Anton von Salza, one of the many of the tsar's generals who was of German descent. Unlike Dankl, Salza had extensive combat experience, having participated in the suppression of the Polish revolt of 1863, as well as several Balkan battles against the Turks in the 1870s, and most recently had commanded a division in Manchuria against the Japanese, but his seventy-first birthday was approaching, and he was tired.

The armies were roughly evenly matched, each possessing three corps on a front of slightly less than fifty kilometers. Dankl's order of battle included nine infantry and two cavalry divisions supplemented by four *Landsturm* brigades, for a total of 144 infantry battalions and seventy-one cavalry squadrons backed by 354 cannons. Salza's army had 104 infantry battalions, 100 cavalry squadrons, and 350 cannons.[45] While both armies expected to make contact with the enemy somewhere near the border, neither headquarters had a clear picture of where the other side's forces really were or in what strength. Aerial reconnaissance had detected several Russian divisions marshaling south of

Lublin, but details were scarce. Cavalry patrols had revealed little either, since much of the area just north of the border was thickly forested, bisected by the Tanew river, a minor tributary of the San. For more than a week, Habsburg patrols, mounted and on foot, had scoured the southern end of the Tanew woods seeking the enemy and had encountered little save short, sharp ambushes. Moving through the swampy forest was tricky, and Dankl's lead battalions were cautioned to march slowly and maintain their flanks, lest they blindly stumble into the enemy.[46]

The First Army started moving on the evening of August 22, with I Corps on the left flank crossing the San, while V and X Corps, which already stood a few kilometers inside Russian territory, began cautiously making their way forward through the Tanew woods. Skirmishes with Russian pickets began immediately, and by the morning Habsburg units would be in contact with elements of Salza's main force. At the same time, the Russian Fourth Army was slowly moving south, directly toward Dankl's marching divisions. By the evening of August 22, Russian forward battalions had reached the Wyżnica river that flows into the town of Kraśnik. The next morning the battle would commence, taking its name from that town.

The terrain where the armies dueled beginning on the morning of August 23 was largely open, punctuated by hills and woods, making it ideal for the kind of maneuver warfare that generals in all European armies were seeking to achieve decision on the battlefield. There were no trenches, rather battalions moving in the open, rapidly, trying to win firefights beginning at ranges of several hundred meters, and sometimes more. Dankl's I and V Corps would see heavy fighting while X Corps, on the right, did not make sustained contact with the Russians on August 23, as Salza's left flank, the Grenadier Corps, was trailing behind the rest of his front.

Austro-Hungarian troops were tired from days of marching, but they entered battle full of fight that hot, sunny Sunday. Gen. Paul von Puhallo's V Corps, from western Hungary, had the objective of wresting

Kraśnik from the Russian XVI Corps. The Austro-Hungarian Fourteenth Division was marching up the road to the town when it encountered stiff resistance at the village of Polichna atop a rise, fourteen kilometers southeast of Kraśnik. The Seventy-sixth Regiment was ordered to clear the town shortly after noon, starting an intense brawl that lasted most of the afternoon, which the survivors remembered as "hellish." The regiment's German and Magyar troops, led energetically by their colonel, Johann (Ion) Boeriu, stormed Polichna in a frontal attack with two battalions forward, without waiting for artillery support. Soon the third battalion was thrown into the fight, as a Russian counterattack nearly pushed the first wave out of the village. Savage, seesaw fighting witnessed house-to-house combat at bayonet point for three hours. Belatedly, Habsburg artillery was brought forward to break enemy resistance, burning down much of the village in the process. The Russians ceased their counterattacks around 4:30 that afternoon, withdrawing toward Kraśnik, The Seventy-sixth Regiment took its objective, but at a frightful cost: twelve hundred casualties—more than a third of the regiment—including over five hundred dead. Thirty-five officers (eleven killed) were among the losses, including all three battalion commanders. Colonel Boeriu, a Romanian from Transylvania, wounded in the attack, was awarded the war's first Order of Maria Theresia, the highest Habsburg decoration, for taking Polichna. "Every soldier was a hero," was his recollection of the day.[47]

That afternoon, nearly twenty kilometers to the west, troops of I Corps were engaging the Russians in sharp encounter battles. Morale was high among the mostly Polish troops, with regiments cheering the customary *hurrá* as they crossed the frontier, headed for battle. The Forty-sixth *Landwehr* Division had its baptism of fire on the afternoon of August 23, when it encountered elements of the enemy's XIV Corps, in particular its artillery. The scene was remarkable, according to one of the division's brigadiers, August von Urbański, who little over a year before had been chief of the *Evidenzbureau* when the Redl scandal broke. Conrad's *Protektion* saved his tattered career, and Urbański got the field command he coveted. That afternoon he suddenly realized his own mortality, as Russian artillery and rifle fire began exploding all around him as his brigade marched forward:

> You only appreciate the seriousness of battle when you realize that death could come at any second. The constant buzzing of bullets passing overhead—left, right, in front and behind—striking the earth. I paused for a respite behind a clover patch with a staff officer. We didn't think of taking cover, it happened automatically. I have to admit, I didn't buckle with the first rifle shots, but it's a different feeling, being targeted personally, unlike what I experienced with artillery fire.

After a few minutes of this "concert from Hell," Urbański found his courage and got up from the safety of his clover patch and returned to the fight, leading his brigade, "overtaken by complete fatalism." He soon witnessed one of his company commanders being taken to the rear with grievous bullet wounds to the neck and head, streaming blood over his face and uniform that the captain could not staunch with his handkerchief. Yet his brigade's losses were relatively light overall on August 23, as the Russians withdrew before serious battle was joined. The next day would bring worse.[48]

On August 24, the full might of both Dankl's and Salza's armies were fully engaged, leading to intense fighting along a front of forty kilometers, as regiments vied for hills and villages. As Habsburg intelligence had predicted, Russian units proved adept at surprising advancing Austro-Hungarian units, who seldom had artillery support ready, but the First Army compensated with sheer grit and an eagerness to charge the enemy that astonished many officers. The heaviest fighting took place around the village of Suchodoły, less than ten kilometers west of Kraśnik. Troops of I Corps marched through dense woods late in the morning, looking for the enemy but finding hardly any Russians.

Troops of the Thirty-first *Landwehr* Regiment, part of Urbański's brigade, found the seemingly endless forest eerily quiet, encountering only a single dead Russian infantryman as they made their way toward where they expected the enemy to be. The regiment emerged from the woods at the village of Liśnik, just south of Suchodoły, where they had a brief midday rest. But at 12:45 they were ordered to get on their feet and clear the nearby Hill 282 of Russians, who thanks to their drab, mustard brown field uniforms were difficult to spot at a distance. Two of its battalions were committed to the attack, which was undertaken without artillery support, as the division's guns were far behind. The troops, a jumble of Germans, Czechs, and Poles from Silesia, were cheered onward by officers yelling "For the emperor!" in three languages, followed by cries of *Vorwärts!* which got going the customary shouts of *hurrá* as the infantry ran forward, bayonets fixed, in what ought to have been skirmish lines but, due to enthusiasm and lack of training, devolved into dense columns of infantry.

Officers were the first to fall, as they made easy targets with their shiny sabers and yellow sashes. The first lieutenant to go down yelled, "I'm hit—keep going, boys!"—and so they did. By the middle of the afternoon, Hill 282 belonged to the attackers, taking a hundred Russian prisoners, including six officers, but at the cost of hundreds of casualties. Primitive Habsburg tactics, in particular the want of finesse in the attack and the absence of any artillery support, nevertheless carried the day thanks to sheer numbers and *élan*.[49]

The Fifth Division attacked toward Suchodoły on Urbański's left flank, and it too took its objectives, but at a high cost. Cracow's Thirteenth Regiment, which had a minor baptism of fire the day before, losing only eleven wounded, was in the thick of the fight on August 24. Led into battle by officers shouting *Polacy, naprzód* (Poles, forward!), it pushed the Russians back, losing almost three hundred men, including fifty-six killed, among them nine officers. Their brigadier, Maj. Gen. Richard Kučera, led his men into battle mounted, in nineteenth century style, and was promptly blasted off his horse, dead. Again, many attacks were undertaken without artillery support, and even when Austro-Hungarian gunners were in position to shell the enemy, many were distressed to discover that they were significantly outranged by Russian batteries that shelled them with impunity. Needless casualties mounted among Habsburg artillery as many guns lacked the protective shields possessed by all Russian field pieces.[50]

Steep losses aside, August 24 was a successful day for Dankl's army. While Salza's Fourth Army was far from broken, it was reeling from harder blows than they had expected to absorb. His forces had not anticipated meeting so many Habsburg divisions along the Vistula, and by the end of the second day strains were showing. Dankl's plan for the third day was for the main push to be made on his left flank, by Gen. Karl von Kirchbach's I Corps, with its shoulder to the Vistula, which Dankl wanted to press forward toward Lublin, turning rightward to force Salza's flank. Dankl was pursuing the battle with greater energy and skill than his aged Russian counterpart, and August 25 would prove the decisive day on this front.

Due to exhaustion, I Corps did not get moving until 10:00 in the morning, but reinforced by *Landsturm* brigades that gave it a local advantage in battalions it soon was pushing the Russian XIV Corps across the Wyżnica river. By the late afternoon, Kirchbach's forward units were turning Salza's right flank as planned, and the Russians were in retreat toward Lublin. The battle for Kraśnik had been decided in Austria-Hungary's favor. In three days of heavy fighting, the First Army had defeated the Russians, even the elite grenadiers of the Guard, and pushed back Salza's oncoming army some ten kilometers, and in some places more like twenty. Six thousand Russian troops and twenty-eight cannons had been captured, as well as three regimental colors.[51] While this was a local victory that could not be construed as decisive, it was a much-needed boost to Habsburg morale, which was flagging after the unexpected setback in Serbia after Cer.

Yet victory at Kraśnik was costly. Dankl's army lost about fifteen thousand men, with Salza's numbers of dead and wounded being roughly equal. A high percentage of the losses were fatalities, due to teething pains of the army medical service adjusting to such mass casualties and to the highly lethal nature of modern bullets and shrapnel. The carnage was enough to try the nerves of the hardest men. Scenes of mass death at Kraśnik shocked many witnesses, including Jozef Tiso, who a quarter-century later would become the leader of Slovakia's fascist puppet state, but in 1914 was a Catholic priest and reserve chaplain with the Slovak Seventy-first Regiment, part of V Corps. An unskilled equestrian, Tiso rejected a mount and decided to ride across Galicia in a bumpy wagon. His regiment was in the thick of the fight for Kraśnik, losing over two hundred killed and over half its officers in the three-day battle. His diary recorded horrors such as witnessing a soldier with his hands shot off, crying, "What will my two little children do?" Tiso was shaken by the "horrible rattles and uneasy moans" of the maimed and dying men he tried to comfort. He attempted to provide "comforting and compassionate words" to the wounded while under Russian fire, terrified for his own life. After Kraśnik was taken, Tiso blessed mass graves, admitting that his "shattered nerves" were the frontline chaplain's "sacrifice."[52]

Nevertheless, such sacrifices did not dampen enthusiasm at AOK, where Conrad greeted news from Kraśnik joyously. It was only a start, but the right kind of start, to the war with Russia. His forces had managed a victory in the opening round of the sort that had just eluded Potiorek. Conrad was particularly pleased to hear reports of the courage with which Habsburg regiments had fought, displaying the dash under fire that he so prized. Russian officers taken prisoner at Kraśnik told their captors that Austro-Hungarian infantry had stormed into battle with more ferocity than even the Japanese had displayed in Manchuria, thus seeming to confirm Conrad's longstanding faith in courage and conviction against firepower.[53]

That said, some officers who fought at Kraśnik were less certain they had found the key to victory. They had achieved a local triumph over Salza's forces, helped by the fact that the Russians had not expected to be met with such might on the Southwestern Front's rightmost flank. The Fourth Army was not yet ready for the major battle in which it found itself, was led indifferently, and lost. Habsburg infantry had won the fight, showing the *Bravour* that so many of their generals prized, but many of the casualties were unnecessary, as infantry frequently attacked without waiting for artillery support. Such enthusiasm was admirable but could be successful only at a cost that could not be sustained. Moreover, Habsburg artillery was showing itself to be dangerously outgunned against the Russians. Austro-Hungarian tactics needed revision, but that would have to wait until after the struggle for Galicia ended that summer.[54]

Viktor Dankl was hailed as a much-needed national hero after his victory and was ennobled for his performance at Kraśnik. His army was showered with decorations amid adulation in the Austro-Hungarian media, with guidance from AOK. Stavka was less pleased than Conrad's staff with the verdict at Kraśnik, and placed blame on the aged Anton von Salza for not exercising energetic leadership; he was relieved by Gen. Alexei Evert on the last day of the battle, who was only two years younger. By no means was Russian command at Kraśnik flawed across the board, and some generals were praised by Stavka for their performance (among them was Baron Carl Mannerheim, commander of a Guards cavalry brigade and the future Finnish leader, who was decorated for his leadership in the battle). Once Evert was in place, Ivanov ordered the neighboring Fifth Army to join the fight to relieve some of the pressure on the Fourth Army and hopefully to turn Dankl's right flank in the process. While the fighting south of Lublin continued at a lower degree of intensity, the main weight of the battle for central Poland now shifted east, in what would be called the battle of Komarów (by Austrians) or Tomaszów (by Russians), after towns located south of the baroque city of Zamość, in the area where most of the combat took place.

The main Habsburg force here would be the Fourth Army, under Gen. Moritz von Auffenberg, a sixty-two-year-old infantryman who had last seen action as a junior officer in the 1878 occupation of Bosnia-Hercegovina. His brief tenure as war minister was cut short in 1912 by a financial scandal that generated bad press for Auffenberg and the army, but he stayed on active service and was known to be an aggressive leader. His field army included nine infantry and two cavalry divisions among four corps—Vienna's II, Northeast Hungary's VI, Bohemia's IX, plus the just-created XVII—for a total of 147 rifle battalions, seventy-four cavalry squadrons, and 438 cannons. Opposite Auffenberg was the Russian Fifth Army, led by Gen. Pavel von Plehve, a sixty-four-year-old cavalry officer of German background who had seen action against the Turks in the Balkans and against the Japanese in Manchuria. Plehve actually commanded a bigger and better-gunned force than his adversary, as the Fifth Army encompassed 4 reinforced army corps, for a total of 180 battalions of infantry, 174 mounted squadrons, plus 684 cannons. Neither army expected the grand encounter battle that developed beginning on the morning of August 26. Plehve's forces were marching southwest to strike Dankl's exposed right flank, while Auffenberg's divisions expected to encounter only about an army corps' worth of the enemy, when in fact they made contact with several times that many Russians. The result was a day of wild, savage meeting engagements along a forty-kilometer front.

Auffenberg's message to the troops breathed fire: "Soldiers of the Fourth Army! Our cause is the most just and holy in the history of warfare. God is therefore with us. . . . Our unshakeable will brings us FORWARD to victory and glory!"[55] On the opening day of the battle, Auffenberg's left flank, Vienna's II Corps, marched toward Zamość, its left shoulder on the Wieprz river, with Dankl's army on the opposite bank. Its cavalry patrols ran into the Russian XXV Corps preparing to strike the First Army in the side. Auffenberg cut this short by ordering four divisions up, two divisions each from II and IX Corps, and into the attack without delay. What followed was a series of vicious firefights that culminated in the Russians retreating in disarray into Zamość that evening. The bloodlust of Habsburg infantry surprised Auffenberg, who described the ferocious Viking-like "true Beserker courage" of the Thirteenth *Landwehr* Division that he witnessed as its regiments went forward into battle on the afternoon of August 26, amid cries of *hurrá* from thousands of voices.[56] Everywhere before Zamość, Austro-Hungarian regiments assaulted the enemy at bayonet point, with a passion to close with and kill the enemy.[57]

A remarkable scene unfolded that afternoon before II Corps, recalled a subaltern of the Ninety-ninth Regiment, for whom the first battle created indelible memories. They heard the Russians long before they saw them, listening to artillery in the distance as Habsburg battalions marched northward up the road to Zamość. The lead battalion deployed in skirmish lines by platoon as they prepared to meet the enemy. Contact was reached at about four hundred meters, with both sides exchanging rifle fire as the Habsburg soldiers slowly tried to move forward. The lieutenant took over his company when the commander fell wounded, entrusting his own platoon to his best sergeant, who was soon gravely wounded as well. Under fire, fatalism and training took over in equal measure, he recalled: "Although I found myself in this most dangerous place, it never occurred to me that I would get hit." And, miraculously, he did not, as his company gradually closed to within two hundred meters of the Russians, shouting *hurrá* all the way. He prepared his men to mount a bayonet charge across that final distance to bring the firefight to a close, when suddenly the enemy withdrew. The Russian retreat was unexpected and mystifying, since they could have continued to inflict serious losses on the exposed Austrians.

By 5 p.m. the enemy had fled toward Zamość, and two hours had elapsed since the Austro-Hungarians had first spotted the Russian positions. Exhausted and thirsty, the soldiers of the lead battalion began digging shallow entrenchments to defend their hard-won ground. The lieutenant's company had lost twenty casualties in the encounter, while the battalion altogether had suffered twenty-eight dead and sixty wounded, including nine of its seventeen officers. Once the tired soldiers were fed a hard-earned dinner, the surviving officers discussed their first taste of battle and realized that such losses were not sustainable for very long. The lieutenant later cursed the politicians in Budapest who had condemned them to fight outgunned against the Russians—who, he noted, were sitting out the war in comfort.[58]

By nightfall II Corps had pushed the Russians back to the walls of Zamość, but its casualties on August 26 were nothing short of horrific. The Thirteenth Division registered losses ranging from 340 casualties in Kremsier's Twenty-fifth *Landwehr* Regiment to the appalling case of Brünn's Fourteenth *Landwehr* Regiment, which started the day with almost three thousand riflemen and by evening had only six hundred left; both units were mostly Czech.[59] The casualties of VI Corps were just as heavy on the first day of the battle. Attacking northward from Tomaszów toward Komarów, this formation from northeast Hungary battled against the Russian XIX Corps all day long. Officer casualties in its forward battalions averaged 50 percent on August 26. The Thirty-ninth *Honvéd* Division saw its infantry run out of ammunition, so long did the fighting rage. Its Ninth *Honvéd* Regiment lost twenty-seven officers—three-quarters of those committed to battle—along with over twelve hundred men dead and wounded.[60]

The commander of VI Corps was Svetozar Boroević, the most energetic general in the Habsburg Army. A Serb from Croatia and a son of the Military Border, which had employed his family on both his father's and mother's sides for generations Boroević was passionately loyal to the Habsburgs and had made a successful career through drive and determination. Lacking connections—his father had retired as a *Grenzer* junior officer, after long service as an NCO—he worked his way up the General Staff ladder, seeing action in Bosnia in 1878 as an infantry subaltern, gaining a reputation for grit that was unsurpassed in the army's officer corps. Short of stature, the fifty-seven-year-old Boroević could be pugnaciously vain and never suffered fools lightly, but none doubted his ability to soldier effectively; he took his profession seriously, and he intended to win.[61]

Boroević's views on warfare were of a piece with the period, and he ranked among the army's strongest prewar advocates of the offensive *à l'outrance*. His related views on discipline were equally forceful. As he observed in a letter to Stjepan Sarkotić, a friend and fellow Croatian general:

> I personify the authority, the discipline and the free self-acknowledgment of the same. All my subordinates from the highest to the lowest know and feel this and can depend on it. If I had the power, I would knock the whole of mankind into the bond of discipline and force it to work within the same framework. You would see success—it would have to be a hundred times greater than now. Only authority and discipline are suitable to bind the troops to their colors, to bind them to their duty. The same is true regarding all of mankind. Unfortunately, discipline is easily undermined by senseless demands, therefore I ruthlessly get rid of all fools. These people then are afraid of me, and also create enemies for me. On the other hand, all efficient people respect me very much.[62]

On August 11, after their arrival in Galicia, Boroević sent a message to all senior officers of VI Corps about the hard fight ahead and what would be required to prevail in it, registering his unhappiness with the current situation, while noting that there was not much time left to get it right:

> I am not impressed with I have seen so far of the combat and service troops of this corps. There is a lack of serious discipline and order; the men are letting themselves go, and some of the officers too. There is a lack of focus, and concentration is not at the level that will be required in the imminent encounter with the enemy. . . . Therefore it is a duty, and a requirement of wisdom too, without a moment's delay, to bring officers and men to an understanding that the primary and most authoritative condition for success is iron discipline.[63]

Boroević's messages to his officers before and during the battle of Komarów were filled with a vigor and intensity that were rare in the Habsburg military. *Schlamperei* cut no ice with Boroević, who exuded disgust for slackness in all its forms. He exhorted his generals to move quickly and with purpose, to be alert at all times, to find and destroy the enemy without delay, and to lead by example.[64] It is tempting to write off Boroević as a martinet, and perhaps a micromanager, but he set an example that too few Austro-Hungarian generals followed in 1914. Descended from a long line of tough warriors, Boroević seemed born for war, and once his corps detrained in Galicia and began marching northward to meet the enemy, he marched with them, sleeping on straw, eating and sleeping little, and drinking nothing stronger than tea. Victory was coming into focus, and Boroević was confident he knew how to achieve it.

It is therefore not surprising that VI Corps attacked the Russians with unexampled vigor, without concern for losses, at the battle of Komarów. Its soldiers were a mix of Magyars, Slovaks, Romanians, Ukrainians, and Jews, with nothing to unite them save loyalty to the Habsburg dynasty and a willingness to follow Boroević's demanding orders. On the afternoon of August 26, as troops all along the VI Corps front enjoyed their baptism of fire in bitter fights with the Russian XIX Corps, brutal shoving matches among hills, creeks, and copses that cost many lives, soldiers of the Eighty-fifth Regiment began emerging from a dense forest near Pawłowka hill. The infantry—Ukrainians, Romanians, and Hungarians from the wooded Carpathian valleys of northeast Hungary—were hit by artillery and rifle fire as soon as they began exiting the safety of the forest, but morale was high, and the troops readied to clear the enemy from the hill. The frontal attack was undertaken without any artillery support, with two battalions abreast, bayonets fixed, with regimental colors unfurled. Although enemy fire cut down the attackers, with artillery shells taking out dozens of men a minute, the Eighty-fifth pressed on amidst shouts of *hurrá*, and within an hour the regiment had overwhelmed the defenses and taken the hill, and with it 240 Russian prisoners plus three machine guns. Cold steel had prevailed against fire, but at a frightful cost. Six officers and 450 men lay dead, while 29 officers and eight hundred more men were wounded. The casualty rate in the lead battalions well exceeded 50 percent.[65]

By nightfall on August 26, as the 400,000 troops on both sides who were engaged around Zamość and Komarów rested as best they could, the situation was developing to Habsburg advantage, though neither Auffenberg nor Plehve as yet had a clear picture of exactly how many of the enemy he was fighting in this battle. The next day would be concerned with each headquarters trying to gain local victories and turn the enemy's flanks to achieve envelopments. It began with an unexpected Habsburg setback. Early on the morning of August 27, a raid by a couple of Cossack squadrons caused a panic in the bivouacs of the Tenth Cavalry Division near Uhnów. Caught by surprise, the jumpy hussars fled rather than fight, and the division could not be regrouped until the afternoon, by which point it had retreated fifteen kilometers. Panic soon gripped the Sixth Cavalry Division too, and it was out of action most of the day as its command tried to collect its regiments after a disorderly retreat of several kilometers.[66]

On the left flank of the Fourth Army, the advance continued as II Corps took Zamość without much of a fight. The Twenty-fifth Division reached downtown by 1 p.m., finding most of the population gone, but several hundred Russian prisoners willing to surrender, including one general.[67] Boroević's VI Corps bore the brunt of the fight for the next twenty-four hours, as it pushed northward with all its might, yet finding its progress to the northwest across the Huczwa river, difficult thanks to tenacious Russian resistance. By the evening of August 27, VI Corps had managed to advance a few more kilometers near Tomaszów, with the Thirty-ninth *Honvéd* Division experiencing heavy losses during its advance, but swampy conditions around the Huczwa made movement slow. Yet morale was high, with one of the brigadiers of the lead Fifteenth Division, noting a "victory panic" among the troops, with men shouting exclamations in a half-dozen languages, as they had bested the Russians in their first effort. This was Col. Carl von Bardolff, who was Alexander von Brosch's successor as military aide to Franz

Ferdinand. With the archduke's assassination, Bardolff had requested a field command, and now, exactly two months after Sarajevo, he was in the thick of the action. Bardolff subsequently attributed the fate of his division to Russophile agents among the local population, but the more important fact was that the Fifteenth Division, in its exhaustion from days of marching and fighting, had simply walked into a trap.[68]

Approaching midnight, the bulk of the division settled down for a rest, strung out on narrow roads in a swampy area dotted with forests and a few small villages. The Habsburg forces were surrounded on three sides by most of a Russian army corps, complete with artillery. It was a shooting gallery for the enemy, and when the battle began at two in the morning, the Fifteenth Division stood little chance of escape.[69] Bottled up and unable to fight their way out, elements of the division made their stand around the village of Pukarzów, a savage ten-hour fight that ended with the annihilation of the defenders. The lone Habsburg artillery battalion that got into the fight was crushed; by noon on August 28, it had gone through all its ammunition, losing 17 officers, 486 men, and twenty-five cannons, almost everything it had. A battalion of the First Bosnian Regiment fighting alongside met the same fate, going from nearly a thousand men to just 2 officers and 133 men by the next morning.[70]

Ordered by Boroević to take action, Colonel Bardolff rushed into battle to save the division, but his efforts were largely in vain, as less than half the division was left by midday on August 28, the Russians having taken four thousand prisoners, over twenty guns, and two regimental colors. Troops who would make it out of the cauldron had done so by breakfast. Confusion had reigned before the dawn. In panic, battalions trying to find sanctuary collided with each other, walking into what the survivors recalled as "murderous fire" from three sides. Most of the division's artillery, strung out on roads, had never unlimbered. Whole battalions had been cut down by presighted Russian artillery and machine-gun fire, and could not be located.[71] Thousands of troops of the Fifteenth Division were missing and presumed dead, among them their commander, Gen. Friedrich von Wodniansky, who had blundered by marching his division into an ambush and failing to coordinate a proper defense. He would face no punishment, however, because Wodniansky was among the dead—by his own hand, it turned out, something the High Command discovered quickly but suppressed.[72]

Bardolff collected what remained of the Fifteenth Division on the morning of August 28, assembling it in a ragtag single brigade. Officer casualties were so severe that three of the division's four infantry regiments, each of which was now only a large battalion in size, were commanded by majors. To take just one example, the Fifth Regiment posted losses of forty-six officers, including six killed, thirty wounded, and ten missing, several of whom were dead; three-quarters of company commanders had been lost.[73] Nevertheless, Boroević ordered VI Corps to execute a "general attack" northward on the early afternoon of August 28, with the Fifteenth and Twenty-seventh Divisions in the lead. The remnants of the Fifteenth Division, not surprisingly, attacked with something less than full vigor that afternoon. Their hard luck continued. Tired troops managed to wrest a key hill from the Russians at Janówka, but a sudden enemy counterattack pushed them off it in disarray. Bardolff's energetic leadership, in accordance with Boroević's dictates on discipline, would win him the Order of Maria Theresia, but he could not give the Fifteenth Division the men and strength it no longer possessed.[74]

The battle raged throughout August 28 all along the Komarów front. Austro-Hungarian forces continued their slow yet steady advance, while Plehve's army was beginning to expose itself to a possible double encirclement; Auffenberg was beginning to detect the outlines of a major victory, greater than Kraśnik, emerging before him. The XVII Corps on Auffenberg's right flank was finally getting into the fight in earnest and was beginning to exert pressure on Plehve's left, where he could not afford it. There Habsburg troops took half a startled Russian division captive on August 28. But signs of weariness were not confined to the enemy on this third day of the battle. One Habsburg horse artillery battalion, in what was becoming a typical experience, found itself outranged by Russian batteries and ended a hard day of fighting near Rutzki by limbering its guns and riding back toward its own lines. Yet the gunners promptly came under fire from their own infantry, which jumpily mistook them for Cossacks. Nothing made Austro-Hungarian troops shudder more than the cry of *Kosaken kommen!* and scared riflemen, who often saw a Cossack on every horse, had already taken to the habit of shooting first on grounds of safety. This mistake cost the horse artillery battalion two dead and fourteen wounded, including a battery commander, plus most of the horses in two of its batteries.[75]

Identifying friend from foe on the battlefield was hardly the only challenge facing Habsburg forces as they engaged the enemy in late August. The critical lack of timely intelligence on Russian dispositions needed remedy if AOK wanted to win, but the army was only beginning to assemble proper channels for interrogating prisoners and disseminating their information. Russians were being taken captive by the thousands now, but local commanders were often lackadaisical about exploiting them for intelligence. On August 25, Colonel Hranilović explained in a message to all field commanders on the Eastern Front that prisoners, especially officers, needed to be made available for questioning as soon as possible: "The faster that interrogation takes place and its information can be distributed through intelligence channels, the greater its operational value will be."[76]

For all the bravado about *élan*, many commanders by late August were growing concerned about mounting casualties, especially to Russian artillery. Based on initial battlefield reports, an AOK message warned that Russian gunnery was proving even deadlier than prewar assessments had predicted, and the enemy's widespread use of presighted artillery was the leading cause of Habsburg casualties. Russian batteries, having already estimated ranges, took a deadly toll on the attacker. Commanders were exhorted to take account of Russian artillery skills in their battle plans. Moreover, an X Corps message on August 28, drawing from opening experiences of combat in the East, explained that Russian gunnery was so deadly that infantry should dig in, even shallowly, at every opportunity since staying in the open invited death at ranges the infantry could do nothing to remedy. Many of the casualties being suffered were needless, and Habsburg infantry at once needed to develop an appreciation for the lethality of enemy firepower. Worse, many regiments were advancing under fire in dense lines and battalion columns, causing "disorder and heavy losses to enemy artillery."[77] In the heat of battle, most Austro-Hungarian commanders were too overwhelmed by events to implement doctrinal change quickly. Nor was it clear that Habsburg infantry, consisting of so many reservists, could make such alterations, particularly because its officers were so quickly suffering losses in great numbers. Above all, while Conrad's forces marching northward into Poland were enjoying success, the strategic debacle set to unfold in East Galicia would have an impact far greater than any merely tactical missteps.

7 Meeting the Steamroller

While Dankl and Auffenberg were winning victories and clearing a path to Warsaw, or so Conrad hoped, the Third Army had not yet entered the fight in any real way. In Lemberg, its commander, Rudolf von Brudermann, was itching to get in the war. The fifty-six-year-old Brudermann was a cavalry general of the old school, filled with dreams of martial glory that had little to do with the modern battlefield. A general's son, Brudermann and his three brothers all pursued an officer's career; his younger brother Adolf went to war leading a cavalry division in Auffenberg's army. Before the war, Rudolf commanded cavalry at every level, from regiment to brigade to division, and served as inspector general of the cavalry, using his position to fight a successful bureaucratic campaign to keep mounted regiments in full dress uniforms while the rest of the army donned drab field outfits, and generally keeping the cavalry in a nineteenth century mindset. Brudermann would prove more adept at fighting the War Ministry than the Russians.

Since Brudermann had assumed command at Lemberg on August 11, he dispatched fiery messages to his commanders. He wanted to see aggressive moves against the enemy. Admitting "this difficult mission standing before us," Brudermann advised his officers to ensure the men did not go through their ammunition supply too quickly in the heat of battle, but even if they did, the bayonet was there to be used too.[1] The Third Army was impressive on paper, with nine infantry and four cavalry divisions on the order of battle by the third week of

August, but its forces were spread out on a vast front stretching over a hundred kilometers east and north of Lemberg, with significant gaps between units.

Conrad had ordered Brudermann to get his forces moving eastward beginning August 22, but *Armeeoberkommando* (Army High Command, or AOK) wanted a slow, cautious advance, while the Third Army commander sought a more aggressive drive directly at the Russians, not just the "brief, energetic blow northward" that the High Command had ordered. Cavalry patrols in the border region of East Galicia revealed considerable numbers of Russians, but exactly how many divisions were bearing down on Lemberg was unclear to Brudermann or Conrad. Brudermann's flanks in particular were vulnerable. On his left, north of Lemberg, the Third Army's XIV Corps was ordered to attack in support of the right flank of Auffenberg's Fourth Army, while on the right, the Second Army was only beginning to arrive in Galicia from Serbia, and was not yet ready to fight as a coherent force. On August 24, AOK ordered Second Army command to concentrate its forces, as soon as they detrained, around Stanislau, seventy kilometers south of Lemberg, so that they could push the advancing Russians back before they posed a mortal danger to Brudermann's right wing. Conrad's order to this effect was vague and optimistic, beyond some encouraging words about what Dankl and Auffenberg were achieving, revealing that Przemyśl lacked specifics about where the Russians marching into East Galicia actually were.[2]

As a result, Brudermann's forces facing the main body of the advancing Russian steamroller amounted to only two corps, while what was coming their way was most of the tsar's Third and Eighth Armies, the main strike force of the Southwestern Front, six army corps in all. The brunt of what Vienna termed the Battle of Złoczów, after the Galician town standing in the middle of the Russian advance, was borne by Nikolai Ruzskiy's Third Army, while Brusilov's Eighth Army, to the south, played a supporting role, with two of its four corps engaged against Brudermann's front. The sixty-four-year-old Ruzskiy, a veteran of the Russo-Turkish and Russo-Japanese wars, was an aggressive tactician, while the sixty-one-year-old Brusilov, a general's son who had grown up as an orphan, would cement his reputation in the fight for Galicia as the tsar's finest field commander.

Brusilov's forces crossed the Zbrucz river and entered Galicia on August 18, meeting only fleeting resistance from Habsburg gendarmes and small cavalry detachments. Yet progress was slow, as the Russian Third Army was meeting somewhat stiffer, if entirely local, resistance, as it approached Lemberg from the northeast, while Brusilov's forces were moving cautiously in the advance. The Eighth Army committed half its forces toward Halicz, where the Austro-Hungarian Second Army was marshaling upon its arrival from the Balkans, while Brusilov dispatched two of his corps, VII and XII, toward Lemberg to support Ruzskiy's main effort. Between the Russian steamroller and Lemberg lay the Gniła Lipa river, forty kilometers east of the Galician capital; as its valley was swampy and there were few bridges capable of supporting artillery and supply trains, it formed a natural defense line against any attacker coming from the east. Brusilov believed the Austrians would make their stand behind the Gniła Lipa, since it would be foolishness to fight before it, with the river at their backs.[3] Which is exactly what Brudermann proceeded to do.

The outcome of this battle was never in doubt. Besides Brudermann's basic tactical error, his forces were massively outnumbered, nearly three to one. On the morning of August 26, the Third Army, with 115 infantry battalions, 91 cavalry squadrons, and 376 cannons, advanced headlong into a Russian force of 292 battalions, 162 squadrons, and 720 guns.[4] Such numbers notwithstanding, Brudermann's message to his army on the eve of battle was vague and cliché-ridden; citing Prussian and Habsburg victories so far, which to date were more supposed than real, he concluded: "Such a remarkable army can only be victorious. Therefore—forward!"[5]

Yet coordination and synchronization proved difficult in Lemberg, and even before the fighting started in earnest, Brudermann's headquarters was having a hard time tracking the locations of divisions and regiments, as units became spread out in their slow, overextended advance into East Galicia.[6] While Kövess's XII Corps advanced on the right flank, in the direction of Tarnopol and XI Corps walked toward its own fight northeast of Lemberg largely unconnected to the main engagement, the main blow of the August 26 battle was absorbed by Graz's III Corps, which contained some of the best Habsburg regiments, hardy Alpine mountaineers from Styria, Carinthia, and the Slovene lands. Both armies had advanced slowly for days across the monotony of East Galicia—fields and forests dotted by poor, grimy villages—expecting battle at any moment. So once it was joined at last, passions burst forth. Knowing the enemy was nearby, excited infantry of III Corps marched into combat an hour ahead of schedule on the morning of August 26, so eager were they to get into the fight.[7]

In its baptism of fire, III Corps collided with the left flank of the Russian Third Army around the town of Gologóry. Its three infantry divisions—Twenty-eighth, Sixth, and Twenty-second *Landwehr*—advanced in a tight line north-to-south, and quickly encountered stiff resistance.[8] Everywhere accurate, presighted Russian artillery, which was often hiding behind the low hills that undulated across the Galician terrain, took a terrible toll on advancing Habsburg infantry, while their own batteries, stuck on clogged roads, struggled to get in the fight.

In the Sixth Division, in the middle of III Corps' line, the Eighth *Jäger* Battalion's experience was typical. Mid-morning, having sighted the enemy, it fixed bayonets and stormed through heavy Russian artillery fire, getting no support from Habsburg gunners, yet managed to shove the enemy back, taking over two hundred prisoners, but losing one-third of its men and over half its officers in its first engagement. Advancing as part of the same brigade, using identical tactics, placing Habsburg foot soldiers against Russian guns, the Seventeenth Regiment lost all its senior officers—its colonel and all four battalion commanders—dead or wounded.[9]

The fate of the Twenty-eighth Division was similar. It advanced in three columns abreast, headlong at the enemy. By the mid-afternoon had taken at least some of its objectives, but at a frightful cost. Styrians of its Forty-seventh Regiment marched into their first fight with spirits high, taking the blood-red early morning sun as a good omen. They marched into battle singing a mordant old soldier's ditty:

Morgenrot, Morgenrot, leuchtest mir zum frühen Tod! ("Morning sun, morning sun, show me an early death!")

Which was exactly what several hundred of them achieved before noon on August 26. Two Forty-seventh battalions advanced tightly packed straight into Russian fire, "practically like on a parade-ground," one of the officers present noted. The attack quickly stalled before shrapnel, and the regiment took staggering losses: 168 dead, 702 wounded, and 417 missing, most of them dead. Forty-eight officers were among the casualties. The same fate befell its sister regiment, the Eighty-seventh—which was mostly Slovenes while the Forty-seventh was mainly Germans—which also marched into combat as if on parade and lost 350 killed and 1,050 wounded, or about half the troops committed to the attack. Their brigadier, Maj. Gen. Alfred von Hinke, was among the gravely wounded.[10]

Russian artillery dominance was the prominent feature of the Third Army's failed effort to advance on August 26. For III Corps especially, where forty thousand Habsburg infantry were marching on a front of twenty-six kilometers, commanders had difficulty getting their forces off the few roads and into the fight before their attacks were shattered by Russian gunnery. Time and again, accurate artillery salvos proved able to break up III Corps attacks before Austro-Hungarian infantry could close with the enemy. In many cases, panicked infantry, raked by fire from Russian guns they could not see, broke and ran. Often units braved fire only to be pinned down within two hundred meters of the enemy after their assault faltered, unable to advance or retreat without serious losses. Their own gunnery was either silent or desultory, as batteries had trouble moving up, and the lack of communications meant forward observers seldom did their job in a timely fashion. If Habsburg infantry managed to get close enough to actually engage directly with Russian infantry, casualty rates were horrific.[11]

Prewar training had woefully prepared the infantry for taking on the Russians, as the first day of battle for the Third Army demonstrated. Infantry assaults on August 26 quickly degenerated into bunched-together masses of foot soldiers that made easy targets for enemy artillery fire, which was much more accurate and heavy than anything that Austro-Hungarian forces possessed. Even motivated infantry frequently found it impossible to make progress. Graz's III Corps, hailed as the "Iron Corps" for its ardor throughout the war just starting, found skills, not valor, wanting. Its Seventeenth Regiment, long known to Slovenes as their *Kranjski Janezi* (Carniolan Johnnies), met a typical mishap on its first day in battle at Gołogóry. It executed a hasty assault at 10 a.m., two battalions forward, which faltered before the wall of Russian artillery shells in front of it. By the early afternoon the attack was stalled, both battalion commanders were dead and the colonel was badly wounded; overall losses for the regiment were 50 percent. Only its Third Battalion, on the right flank of the main assault, escaped the battle reasonably intact.[12]

Losses were especially heavy among the reservists who had to bear so much of the fight in Galicia. *Landsturm* regiments, which were thrown into battle alongside first-line units, suffered particularly badly. Their soldiers, most in their late thirties and early forties, were exhausted even before battle was joined. Out of shape, many were dead tired from long marches before they encountered the enemy. They had no experience with modern tactics—most had last soldiered in the 1890s—and when committed to the attack they did so as if on parade, forsaking open order and skirmish lines, and making little if any use of cover. They knew no better. Unsurprisingly, successes were few, casualties were steep, and the horrors caused by accurate and deadly Russian artillery fires were wholly unexpected.[13]

The terror inflicted by those invisible Russian guns was recalled by a *Landsturm* officer of III Corps who witnessed its impact at Gołogóry. As his regiment marched toward the front line, the cannonades became louder and he saw "harmless looking round clouds, looking like ringlets of smoke from a huge cigar" exploding in the air some fifteen hundred meters in front of them. This was Russian shelling, though the novice soldiers did not yet realize what it was. Soon shrapnel shells were exploding above them, as the regiment advanced into battle. Men began to fall here and there, "with an agonizing cry," mortally wounded, but the regiment maintained its plodding advance until a Russian aircraft flew over them—this was an artillery spotter directing fire onto them—and the men ducked for cover before it got worse. They never got into the main fight on August 26, being kept in support as other regiments marched into Russian fires directly. They lost fewer than twenty men, a number that "seemed extraordinarily small when compared with the accuracy of the Russian artillery's aim," the officer noted, given that his men had been under sporadic fire for about two hours.[14]

Other regiments were less fortunate on August 26, and all along the Third Army's front, thousands of Habsburg troops fell dead and wounded. It was the same story on the northern flank, where Lemberg's XI Corps, mostly Ukrainians who were fighting on their home soil, launched dashing yet futile attacks into the right wing of the Russian Third Army. It was a "disaster," recalled a staff officer, as everywhere enemy gunnery chewed up Habsburg infantry, which went into battle with "*Hurrátaktik*"—dense columns of shouting infantry—that showed more valor than sense and had no place on the modern battlefield. Several regiments, shattered by enemy fire, having suffered "monstrous losses," particularly among officers, were in retreat by the afternoon. Survivors streamed toward Lemberg in panic and disarray.[15]

Conrad's connection to battlefield reality, never firm, was beginning to slip as troubling developments emerged from East Galicia. In its daily message to army commanders, AOK described the events of August 26 as a victory, observing that Brudermann "has thrown the enemy back," adding that Dankl and Auffenberg had achieved decisive victories that were not, in fact, decisive in any strategic sense. Perhaps in a reflection of how dire the Galician situation actually was becoming, Conrad ordered the Second Army to get on its feet at once and get in the fight.[16]

But the morning of August 27 brought more bad news that even AOK could not fully shelter itself from. III Corps, Brudermann's Alpine mailed fist, which was aimed eastward, was unable to make any progress. All day, its units battled the Russians among the hills, swamps, and creeks around Gołogóry, to no avail. Valor was not lacking. However, most attacks faltered fast, while even those that made progress did so at unsustainable cost. Heavily outnumbered, III Corps was beginning to buckle. The retreat had begun, against orders. Trieste's Ninety-seventh Regiment, raked by Russian gunnery, broke and fled westward; stragglers were still streaming into Lemberg, forty kilometers behind the front, two days later, where thousands of shaken Habsburg soldiers who had fled battle were collecting.

Conrad would hear no talk of a retreat, instead pressing for more attacks straight into the Russian steamroller. As was his wont, the General Staff chief took reports of battlefield successes at face value and wanted more; the actual condition of the faltering Third Army was not something Conrad desired to hear. Yet a telephone conversation on August 27 between Colonel Pitreich at Third Army headquarters and Colonel Metzger from the Operations staff at AOK, clarified just how grim the situation really was. Brudermann and his staff seemed overwhelmed by the rising debacle. The front line was about to collapse, and Conrad, with a heavy heart, reluctantly authorized a limited retreat by the Third Army to the Gniła Lipa line. Avoiding reality, Brudermann did not issue the order until 2:15 p.m. the next afternoon, when the tired survivors of the fight for Złoczów tried to make their way to safety behind the Gniła Lipa, where they should have been in the first place. In a report to AOK on the evening of August 28, Brudermann's staff admitted that its III and XI Corps were exhausted, its XII Corps was nearly as spent, and only one division could be considered intact and ready for battle.[17] Yet there would be no rest.

The previous day, Conrad had written a letter to Gen. Arthur von Bolfras, Franz Joseph's elderly military adjutant, explaining his viewpoint.[18] It overflowed with his customary drama, evasions, and grandeur: "In the gravest moment of my life," it began:

> The battle is proceeding which will decide the fate of the Monarchy. . . . There is not much to say about our successes compared with those of the Germans, mainly because the German victories have been gained at our expense. . . . The enormous weight of the Russian Army is thrown upon us, and moreover we have the war against Serbia and Montenegro to conduct. . . . I have nothing to do with the policy which has led to this result. Foreseeing the events which have now arisen, I advised a course of action in 1909, and again in 1912, but in vain. It is a malicious freak of Fate that it is I who now have to bear the consequences of that neglect . . . our troops are everywhere fighting just as gallantly as the Germans, who are engaged not against Russians, but only against Frenchmen.

Conrad still continued to derive hope from what good news was trickling into Przemyśl. August 28 brought limited victories even around Lemberg. To the north of the Galician capital, the elite Tyrolean XIV Corps, led by Archduke Joseph Ferdinand, launched a sharp attack that secured the important connection to Auffenberg's Fourth Army, which was engaged heavily against the Russian Fifth Army. In the lead was XIV Corps' Third Division, which entered battle against the enemy's XVII Corps with 22,000 men (15,300 of those riflemen) in four full infantry regiments and thirty-eight cannon plus two cavalry squadrons and a sapper company. One of its regiments was the Second *Kaiserjäger*, led by Col. Alexander von Brosch, who itched to exact revenge for Franz Ferdinand's murder. His regiment was four battalions strong, four thousand riflemen backed by eight machine guns and moved along by over four hundred horses for carrying supplies and officers.[19]

Brosch commanded his regiment energetically in its baptism of fire at the village of Wasylów. They had spent days marching in the hot sun through remote Galician villages where the locals, "poor, dirty people," recalled one officer, greeted them warmly. On the morning of August 28, Brosch received word that the Russians were near. At last, battle could be joined, and his murdered mentor might be avenged. His Tyroleans, colors flying, marched forward in skirmish lines beginning about nine hundred meters from the enemy. They advanced through a curtain of shrapnel and engaged Russian infantry at six hundred meters, beginning a firefight that lasted over an hour, with enemy artillery and machine-gun fire chewing up the lead companies, until an advance forward to settle the issue was ordered.[20]

Men fell by the platoon under deadly Russian gunnery, but those still in the fight pushed onward. Adrenaline flowed, buttressed by sheer aggression, and the more officers and men fell, amidst screams and flames, the more their comrades wanted to settle scores and prevail. When a standard bearer collapsed, wounded, Brosch charged forward and grabbed the colors, saber in the air, exhorting his men to follow him through the fire: "*Hurrá, Kaiserjäger!*" The men—about two-thirds Germans and one-third Italians—followed, rifles in hand, closing with and overwhelming the defenders, many of whom fled into nearby woods at the sight of hundreds of screaming Tyroleans coming at them with bayonets. The Second Regiment took a whole Russian artillery battery, seven guns and 150 men, captive, while its Second Battalion kept pushing, leading the Third Division into a significant local victory over the enemy. By nightfall, several thousand Russians were prisoners along with forty guns, a whole division's worth of artillery.

This triumph was not without cost: the Second *Kaiserjäger* lost a thousand men dead and wounded at Wasylów—in one of his lead companies, only thirty men out of the 260 who began the attack remained unscathed—but Brosch was elated by the victory. Russian prisoners called his men "flowery devils" from their edelweiss insignia—the Tyroleans liked the sound of *Blumenteufel*—while the wounded commander of the captured artillery battery, a veteran of the Russo-Japanese War, confided in Brosch, "In the attack, the Japanese are real devils, but the *Kaiserjäger* are even bigger ones." He wrote a letter to his wife, explaining why he had so recklessly exposed himself to danger, surviving miraculously unscathed: "I wanted to give the men an example of cold-bloodedness and courage on our first day of battle." Now, he felt the men, seeing he was a tough leader, would follow him anywhere.[21]

There were signs that the Russians were growing weary. The Third Division's Fourteenth Regiment, attacking on Brosch's flank on August 28, did nearly as well in its baptism of fire at Oferdów, taking two hundred Russians and four guns captive, with the loss of "only" 386 casualties, a light total by the standards prevailing in Galicia. Although the men were exhausted after eighteen hours of marching, Linz's high-spirited Fourteenth charged into action at noon, executing a frontal attack that showed that Austro-Hungarian tactics could work, as long as the troops were willing to face withering fire and the Russians were tired. If Habsburg troops braved heavy artillery and rifle fire and managed to get close to the Russians, the enemy often surrendered or simply fled in panic.[22]

All along the Third Army's front on August 28, Habsburg units attacked into the teeth of the Russian steamroller, in desperate attempts to save the increasingly hopeless situation. Most of these efforts failed, but even the successes were bought with much blood. Typical was the mid-afternoon attack by elements of the Second Bosnian Regiment, part of III Corps' Sixth Division, with its First Battalion arrayed as if on parade, led into battle with flags and the regimental band. Few units in the *k.u.k. Armee* surpassed the Second Bosnians in sheer grit; the legendary *Zweier Bosniaken* would become the most decorated Habsburg regiment in the entire war. At 3:00 that afternoon, they charged headlong at the Russians, knives and bayonets in hand, and managed to push the foe out of his positions. More than a few of the enemy broke and ran at the sight of hundreds of fez-wearing Bosnians descending upon them. But the cost of this local victory was steep, with half the battalion lost, including most of its officers dead, the battalion commander among them. Such bravery did nothing to save the overall position of the Third Army, which was dire.[23]

Yet even local victories were the exception. The pursuit of Bruder-mann's retreating forces by the advancing Russian Third and Eighth Armies was not as fast as some staff officers, envisioning a rapid rout east of Lemberg, were fearing. Habsburg forces were falling back, often in disorder, faster than the enemy, encumbered by artillery and long supply columns needing bridges over rivers, could keep up. Addition-ally, Conrad took inspiration, not from the impending debacle in East Galicia, but from the good news that continued to reach Przemyśl from the north, from Dankl's First and Auffenberg's Fourth Armies. On the left, Dankl's troops continued their march on Lublin but resistance remained strong. Here Habsburg troops showed the same *Bravour* combined with tactical ineptness that they displayed across the Gali-cian front. First Army headquarters was growing concerned about the serious losses incurred by the infantry. On August 28, its X Corps sent a withering memo to all its senior officers, admonishing them to learn modern tactics without delay, as primitiveness was causing needless deaths. Infantry was not yet digging in, resulting in serious casualties inflicted by Russia's powerful artillery. In the attack, Habsburg foot soldiers were still bunching up and advancing in straight lines that made easy targets for Russian gunners, leading to "disorder and heavy losses to enemy artillery."[24]

The story was much the same with Auffenberg's army. On his left, Vienna's II Corps by August 28 was getting tantalizingly close to envel-oping the right flank of Plehve's Fifth Army, but every advance was bought with much blood. That day, the First Bosnian Regiment received its baptism of fire, attacking past Zamość with the Twenty-fifth Divi-sion. They advanced into shrapnel and machine-gun fire "completely loyally," recalled one of the few officers in the lead battalion to survive the ordeal. Yet three-quarters of his *Bosniaken* fell dead or wounded, as well as almost every officer; the battalion was disbanded.[25] Like most

Habsburg units II Corps continued to be plagued by poor infantry-artillery coordination, and resulting losses among the foot soldiers. In a typical case, the Forty-ninth Regiment of its Fourth Division launched a hasty attack on a Russian hill position on the late afternoon of August 30, in an effort to push hard on the flanks of Plehve's forces, that were increasingly being encircled. Even though artillery was in position to support the advance, the hasty attack was ordered without any supporting fire from II Corps gunners. Through sheer grit, the Forty-ninth Regiment wrested Hill 230 from the tired Russians in a short, sharp engagement that saw the enemy fleeing into the woods behind. But within an hour, as Russian artillery came to bear, the Forty-ninth withdrew from the hill and retreated to its original position, unable to withstand the barrage. The regiment lost almost five hundred men, including 209 dead, in this needless setback.[26]

Despite such losses, Auffenberg kept pushing his troops hard, hoping for a double envelopment of Plehve's Fifth Army. While Vienna's II Corps held the left flank, the Bohemian IX Corps pushed inward, as the XVII and XVI Corps did the same from the right, with Boroevic's hard-fighting VI Corps maintaining pressure in the middle, around the town of Komarów. Intense fighting on August 29–30 at last brought a major victory within reach. While Kraśnik had been an impressive local win, what seemed almost in Auffenberg's grasp now would be the Cannae-like annihilation of Plehve's forces, equivalent to what the Prussians were achieving at Tannenberg at exactly the same time. Conrad wanted this above all.

All through August 29 IX Corps pushed hard against the Russian XIX Corps, resulting in savage fighting while trying to turn its flank. The enemy resisted this furiously, with the Twenty-sixth *Landwehr* Division receiving hammer blows all day long. Its 9th *Landwehr* Regiment was ordered to hold the village of Janówka at all costs. Their colonel, Joseph von Reyl-Hanisch, told the men that retreat was no option, they would die in place, fighting to the last man, as a Russian division bore down on them. Companies of enemy infantry, clad in mustard-brown, were cut down, yet there always seemed to be more Russians, and other companies appeared to keep the pressure on the defenders. Wounded, Reyl-Hanisch exhorted his Bohemians to keep fighting as ammunition ran low and casualties mounted. The colonel was cut down while personally manning a machine gun, alongside several hundred of his soldiers who would never leave Janówka.[27]

The savagery of the fighting continued unabated, shocking staff officers who read the daily reports. In the chaos of battle and unprecedented casualties, especially among officers, some Habsburg units failed to update their daily logbooks, an unthinkable happening in the paperwork-obsessed *k.u.k. Armee*. Losses mounted as Innsbruck's XIV Corps pushed to envelop the Russian Fifth Army from the right. On August 31 alone, its Fourteenth Regiment registered a loss of a thousand wounded and four hundred killed.[28] On the other side of the envelopment, II Corps continued to meet stiff resistance from the right wing of Plehve's forces. Even when exhausted, Russian troops, terrified of encirclement, launched counterattacks to take back ground they had recently lost. In a typical example, on August 30 near Zamość, the Eighty-first Regiment resisted twelve hours of fierce enemy assaults, with orders to hold what II Corps had taken, no matter the cost. As ammunition ran low, the Czech and German riflemen pleaded for reinforcements. Every available man—sergeants, bandsmen, officers' manservants—ferried ammunition forward from supply wagons, under intense fire, while the wounded kept shooting at the enemy from where they lay. When the order to get up and charge the Russians came, heralded by bugle calls, hundreds of men stood, bayonets fixed, and ran toward the enemy, frightening them into a temporary retreat. Like clockwork, a Russian counterattack soon emerged from nearby woods, only to be cut down by well-sighted Eighty-first machine guns. By nightfall the ordeal was over.[29]

A disproportionate role in Auffenberg's budding success was played by Svetozar Boroević and his hard-fighting troops from northwest Hungary. On August 29, as his VI Corps shoved the Russian V Corps back all along its front, Boroević committed two brigades of replacement (*Marsch*) troops to battle, to make up for the missing Fifteenth Division, which was still recovering from its near destruction on August 28. Hungarians, Slovaks, and German fought with unexampled vigor under Boroević's leadership on August 29, the fourth and decisive day of Auffenberg's offensive, with the Twenty-seventh Division bearing the brunt of the fight. They charged straight at the enemy, bayonets fixed, without regard for enemy fire or steep casualties. The following day the Fifteenth Division reentered battle, bolstered by seven *Marsch* battalions to replenish its shattered regiments. Boroević was determined to push the Russians back and win a decisive victory.[30]

While Auffenberg pushed for a grand encirclement, giving rise to hopes by Conrad and his staff that a decisive victory was approaching, Brudermann's forces were barely holding on and starting to lose any grip. III Corps made its stand on the northernmost reaches of the Gniła Lipa, around the town of Przemyślany, where most of the Russian X Corps struck the Twenty-second *Landwehr* Division. Forty-eight hours of savage combat followed through August 29–30, including house-to-house fighting up and down the burning streets of Przemyślany. One Austrian battery that supported the infantry through the battle eventually had to disengage as it had gone through so many rounds that the barrels of their 100 mm howitzers grew too hot to keep firing.[31]

Despite such valiant resistance by many Habsburg units, August 29 was the day that the Russians achieved major breakthroughs all along Brudermann's front. Fighting raged in a half-moon east of Lemberg—in some places, the defenders were close enough to make out the city's spires with the naked eye—but it was unclear how or where the Russian onslaught could be halted. The enemy's superior numbers rendered resistance temporary. By late on August 30, it was evident even to AOK that the outnumbered and defeated Third Army was on the verge of complete collapse and the Gniła Lipa line had fully crumbled before the Russian Southwestern Front. On Brudermann's northern flank, XI Corps was in dissolution, with regiments fleeing to sanctuary in—and even past—Lemberg at speed, while things were not much better to the south. The Third Army stood little chance on August 30, being hit by the full force of fifteen Russian infantry divisions and five of cavalry. Sensing that Habsburg forces were close to collapse, the Russians pushed harder than ever.

By that evening, III Corps was in the suburbs of Lemberg, while south of the city XII Corps, which until now had shown less inclination to retreat, had devolved into panic, with scared regiments fleeing westward. Fearing Cossacks, many units were running as fast as they could, leaving behind wagons, supplies, even artillery. Before the morning, it was clear to attentive staff officers in Lemberg that the city could not be held, that the only defensible position for the remnants of the Third Army now was the Wereszyca River, twenty-five kilometers west of the Galician capital. Conrad would hear none of this, understanding the steep political cost of losing Lemberg to the Russians. Regardless, at 10:45 p.m. on August 30, Brudermann's staff gave the increasingly shambolic III Corps, holding the center of the front, the order to begin movement westward, to save its remnants from the advancing steamroller.[32]

The failure of the Transylvanian XII Corps to stem the Russian tide south of Lemberg bears examination, as Hermann von Kövess, its commander, was an astute tactician and energetic officer possessing a healthy respect for the enemy, and until now his troops had held up to the strains of battle better than Brudermann's other army corps. On August 30, his slowly retreating troops tried to stiffen the buckling line around the village of Świrz, and in the chaos of fluid fighting late that afternoon, Kövess and his staff found themselves in the middle of the action, buffeted by shrapnel, the general nearly being killed. Although he avoided wounds from the enemy by taking cover as shells exploded above, he was nearly stomped to death by a mounted squadron of hussars that—men and horses—panicked under fire, running amok. It was, he confided to Conrad, "the most terrifying day of my life."

Kövess wound up in the front line thanks to contradictory orders from Brudermann's confused staff, which changed constantly. "You wouldn't believe the rank stupidity that was coming out of Third Army command," he informed Conrad. By ordering one of his brigades out of action, without consulting Kövess, Brudermann's staff caused XII Corps' front to give way on August 30, leading to an unforced and disorderly retreat. Worse, the Cossack-panicked Eleventh Division then fled and abandoned most of its artillery.[33] Such *Schlamperei* emanating from Lemberg, where senior officers were losing their heads, unraveled the already parlous condition of his front, reported Kövess, who denounced the senselessness of the situation. Once panic set in, there was no stopping it, even when Cossacks were not on their heels. At Bóbrka, panicky railroad personnel abandoned a train filled with two hundred badly wounded men, leaving them to the Russians. It all drove Kövess to exasperation.[34]

Proper leadership could not give ailing Habsburg units men and firepower they did not possess, nor could it calm shattered nerves, and it was clear by that evening to savvy leaders like Kövess that Lemberg was lost. Some generals, however, were approaching a state of panic, just like the men, a fact that Kövess frankly acknowledged privately: "Some generals are already morally shattered and have abandoned the army," as he wrote to his wife. One of his divisional commanders, Franz Paukert, was relieved of command shortly after the debacle of August 30, complaining of stomach maladies and stress. A few days later the general threw himself under a train.[35]

As the Third Army buckled, it was imperative that Eduard von Böhm-Ermolli's Second Army, still arriving from Serbia, get into the fight immediately. Conrad and his staff fired off reams of orders demanding energy from Böhm-Ermolli's staff in Stryj, which they turned around as orders to corps headquarters. But movement was sluggish, so Second Army command sent out a senior staffer to investigate and shake things up. Lieutenant Colonel Kapretz arrived at the headquarters of

VII Corps at the town of Chodorów at two in the morning on August 30, finding disorder, even chaos. Officers, tired from long train rides and forced marches, seemed listless, and Kapretz realized it would be a challenge to shake VII Corps out of its torpor. The root problem, he learned, was transport and supply, compounded by a dearth of leadership. Traffic jams impeded movements; tired and frustrated troops stood around aimlessly. Everywhere he witnessed Hungarian soldiers meandering in exhaustion. In the main square of Chodorów, Kapretz encountered an artillery battalion that had been marching for five days to reach the front, the last three days without any food; the troops were too tired to move, as were the broken horses. It was the same story with the infantry: five days on foot, the last three without any rations. The logistical and transport system had broken down. Total exhaustion had set in.

Speaking for Second Army headquarters, Kapretz told the senior officers of VII Corps, including their commander, Gen. Otto von Meixner, that they must get on their feet at once, as the fate of Galicia depended on it. They complied, and by the dawn troops were headed to the front, slowly. Yet Kapretz painted a grim picture to his superiors. There was chaos stewing, with panic close behind. As he headed back to Stryj, he came across three battalions of infantry replacements "without any order among them." Officers were absent or ignored, while men were sleeping on the roads and in fields nearby, where they had dropped their packs from sheer exhaustion. Those who were awake seemed to be ignoring orders, and officers were not taking charge. So Kapretz did, demanding food be brought forward and requiring military police to pick up stragglers and send them to the front immediately. Even then, not all the infantry listened.[36]

Disorder was spreading beyond the tired Second Army. Reports were reaching AOK of hungry Habsburg units plundering and vandalizing, taking time off from battle to forage for food, which was hardly surprising, given the parlous state of supply.[37] Nevertheless, there was no time to waste, and that day, August 30, the battle for Rohatyn was

VII Corps' introduction to the Eastern Front. They had departed Serbia on August 23, and a week later they were at war again. Its Sixty-first Regiment, which was in better shape than the units Kapretz visited, had the rare pleasure of transiting their home city of Temesvár en route to Galicia; the "whole city" came out to greet them with music and bands. They received gifts of food, which would prove vital as the army's supply system crashed. For many it was a final farewell, as the Sixty-first entered the fight at Rohatyn on the Gniła Lipa on August 30 with gusto, amidst shouts of *hurrá*, with its lead battalions taking almost two hundred Russian prisoners but at the cost of over half their own men.[38] Yet this was the exception, as most attacks by VII Corps that daily failed, some dissolving quickly in the face of Russian artillery fire, which far surpassed anything these troops had seen in Serbia.

The Russians incurred steep losses in this fight too, and most of the troops opposite VII Corps, Brusilov's Eighth Army, were new to battle themselves. The "stern and terrible engagement" of August 30–31 that crushed Habsburg forces east of Lemberg, however, gave the Russians vigor and confidence, their commander noted: "The previous engagements, which had been increasing in importance, had been a very good school for troops which had not hitherto been under fire. Their successes had raised their morale, convinced them that the Austro-Hungarians were their inferiors at all points, and inspired them with confidence in their leaders."[39]

Conrad did have some understanding of the desperate situation around Lemberg, and, like Kövess, he too remembered August 30 as "the most fearful day of my life," though he was nowhere near the battlefield.[40] Despite the impending collapse of the Third Army, he averted his eyes from Lemberg and looked north, continuing to hope that the encirclement of Plehve's Fifth Army might change the strategic equation. He pushed the Fourth Army to fight harder than ever to complete the rout of the enemy. Thus was August 31, the day of renewed offensive by Auffenberg's forces, the turning point of the Battle of Komarów. Here Boroević's VI Corps played a pivotal role in Habsburg success. His years of serious study of tactics paid off. The tough Serb pushed his men as hard as he pushed himself. There would be no excuses for failure or for anything less than vigor and ardor about crushing the enemy. Never prone to false modesty, Boroević confided to a friend: "The Battle for Komarów would have been lost without me. Had the Fourth Army been unable to shift its forces, thanks to my corps, the renewed offensive (August 31) would have been impossible, and the war would have been lost." Here he only exaggerated modestly, and Boroević was especially pleased to have shown Prussian liaison officers how much *Bravour* his soldiers of VI Corps demonstrated against the Russians that day, clearing the wooded hills south of Komarów of the last pockets of enemy resistance.[41]

While VI Corps pushed forward with all its might, Auffenberg's left and right flanks maneuvered under fire to close the trap on most of three Russian corps—XIX, V, and XVII—some 100,000 men in all. Yet, in a fashion typical of the chaos of battle, all went wrong on the afternoon of August 31; or, as Churchill preferred to style it, "Fortune was now to play a mischievous trick" on the Fourth Army.[42] On the left, Vienna's II Corps was moving to shut the door on the Russian XIX and V Corps, an action that would pin them against the Huczwa river, where Boroević's advancing troops, full of fight, could crush them to pieces. But intelligence from cavalry patrols indicated that the northern flank of II Corps was about to be turned by a surging Russian cavalry division, imperiling the enterprise. In fact, the "threat" was a few mounted squadrons, no more, but in the fog of battle a retreat ten kilometers back to Zamość, to preserve flanks, was ordered.

Virtually an identical misunderstanding befell Archduke Joseph Ferdinand's XIV Corps, surging on the right side of Auffenberg's trap, that day. Aerial spotters located Russian troops—they reckoned a division—massing to the right and rear of Austrian positions, while Habsburg troops were advancing in the opposite direction, shutting the door on the Russian XVII Corps as it tried to retreat northward.

This was a valid concern, as a yawning gap had emerged between the right wing of XIV Corps and the north end of the ailing Third Army. Habsburg staff officers had little idea where the Russians lurked, or in what numbers; one of the distressing aspects of the campaign for Austro-Hungarian planners was how large numbers of the enemy had the knack of appearing unexpectedly, often as if from nowhere. Although this report too overestimated the extent of the threat, Joseph Ferdinand, fearing his own envelopment, ordered his cavalry and parts of two infantry divisions pulled out of the main advance to defend the Sołokija River line, some ten kilometers to the rear. That flank was indeed secured, but it was not until the next morning that the full extent of these errors became plain to see.[43] Here, hopes for a Cannae around Komarów evaporated. Plehve's Fifth Army, while beaten, narrowly escaped encirclement thanks to Habsburg mistakes, namely the unnecessary pullback of both of Auffenberg's flanks. Conrad's grand plan to annihilate the Russians south of Warsaw had come to naught. Although the Fourth Army would keep its advance going for two more days, pushing Russian forces deeper into Poland, taking prisoners all the way, the strategic value of that victory dropped precipitously in the last hours of August.

Frustrations were mounting as casualties increased and decisive victory grew more elusive. The war was growing brutal. Jumpy Habsburg troops saw Russian spies at work among the Ukrainian population, a fear that intelligence assessments warning of secret cadres of "Russophiles" in Galicia indeed had emphasized. While they did exist, authorities exaggerated their reach, and—as with Potiorek's Serbian fifth column in Bosnia—many soldiers saw spies and saboteurs lurking everywhere, in every village and Orthodox church. The hunt for traitors, real and imagined, was energized by battlefield reverses, while evidence mounted of atrocities perpetrated by Russians and their sympathizers. On August 30, near Zamość, troops of II Corps came across the corpses of fifty Habsburg soldiers who had been mutilated, many of them bayoneted repeatedly. "Here I had my first impression of the cruelty of war," recalled one junior officer, who noted that he was one of the lucky 30 percent of his regiment's officers not yet killed or seriously wounded.[44] Word of such atrocities spread like wildfire among Habsburg troops in the field, seeding more violence.

The casual brutality of it all dismayed Joseph Tiso, serving as a Catholic chaplain with V Corps. At the end of August, his Seventy-first Regiment was fired upon by snipers in a village, killing a corporal. Furious, the Slovak troops sought revenge. Although villagers pleaded that the snipers were Russian *agents provocateurs*, which Tiso felt was likely, the troops nevertheless surrounded the village, shot it up, then burned it down in a fifteen-minute frenzy. "In war," he noted, "there is no legal relief." Villagers who tried to flee the flames were shot. Tiso decried this "thoughtless" justice "that does not care how many innocents suffer," but he reluctantly accepted that "extraordinary circumstances do not admit a more precise investigation. . . . We pity these poor ones but we cannot do anything else." Tiso confided the horrors to his diary:

> We avert our eyes in disgust, but everywhere we turn it is the same picture—houses standing in flames, here and there the scorched corpse of a shot-down man, not far from him the sooty, burnt remains of a piglet that couldn't get away or a penned-up hen! . . . Crying, the trembling people come out of the village and kneel before us, imploring us to mercy and compassion. We look on them with impotent sympathy.[45]

Casualties had begun to mount so seriously, beyond anything that had been anticipated, that the High Command was unable to process their vast numbers administratively. Delays in notifying next of kin had grown so serious that, even before the end of August, Conrad's staff at AOK was warning, "the public is losing its confidence" in the army, and casualty notification had to be improved at once. Archduke Friedrich admonished staffers that more care had to be given to casualty reporting, since families were being told loved ones were dead when, in fact, they were only wounded, and vice versa: "more rigor" was needed immediately.[46]

That an unprecedented disaster was unfolding was impossible to hide as thousands of families across the Dual Monarchy daily received notice of the deaths of husbands, fathers, and sons, but AOK was eager to keep the full extent of the debacle in Galicia from the public. While censors and intelligence officers did their best, soldiers too were cautioned to keep quiet. Following the High Command's lead, a September 1 order by III Corps command, issued as it and the whole Third Army were in jeopardy, explained:

> When officers and military officials criticize our war leadership, and the public hears this, the consequences can be most unfavorable. Regarding this completely unmilitary and undisciplined conduct, in wartime this must be countered in a manner appropriate to the seriousness of the situation. Therefore all military personnel (including the wounded) are instructed to urgently refrain from any unauthorized disclosure of their combat experiences and also of their personal accounts from the battlefield, and to remain vigilant regarding the dissemination of information about military matters during wartime. Violations of this order will be punished in the most severe manner.[47]

As August ended, though the public in the Dual Monarchy had no idea what was really happening, Conrad faced a daunting situation of his own making that promised strategic disaster and defeat. Although Dankl's First Army continued its successful drive toward Lublin, and perhaps Warsaw beyond, that was devoid of strategic meaning without the hoped-for German push southward out of East Prussia, which by now no staff officers in Przemyśl really thought was coming. While Auffenberg's victory at Komarów appeared hopeful, without a successful encirclement to cut off Plehve's forces it would remain an indecisive win. More seriously, an alarming gap was growing between the Fourth Army and the retreating Third Army, which appeared on the cusp of losing Lemberg, something that the arrival of the Second Army at the front, at last, could do little to remedy, so mighty were the Russian forces bearing down on East Galicia now. How Conrad reacted to this rapidly deteriorating situation, which would tax the most gifted strategist, would determine the fate of his army and his country.

8   Lemberg–Rawa Ruska

Tuesday, September 1, brought the first rainfall of the Galician campaign, breaking the summer heat that scourged the infantry around midday. Otherwise there was no good news for Austro-Hungarian forces fighting in the East that day. While Rudolf von Brudermann's Third Army had fallen back on Lemberg, it could not form a coherent defensive line. Its headquarters had nearly ceased to function. In Przemyśl, the High Command suspected that Brudermann was having a nervous breakdown. Panic was taking over in Lemberg as Russian troops approached the city. Daily *Armeeoberkommando* (Army High Command, or AOK) inquiries about what was going on in East Galicia were met with evasions that betrayed confusion. Nobody seemed to be in control of the disaster unfolding. Brudermann had never gotten along well with his staff chief, Maj. Gen. Rudolf Pfeffer, indeed the men seemed to bicker rather than collaborate, but Pfeffer's sacking at the end of August did nothing to improve the functionality of Third Army command.[1]

Not having a clear picture of what was happening in East Galicia only magnified Franz Conrad von Hötzendorf's ability to avoid topics he did not wish to contemplate. Late on the afternoon of September 1, Conrad again ordered the Third Army to hold Lemberg, with support from the Second Army; his message, with its encouraging optimism about stemming the Russian tide, described a situation that did not actually exist.[2] To make matters worse for Austria-Hungary's General Staff chief, while major victory eluded him, his Prussian partners, whom he disliked and envied, were finding success. By the end of August, German forces in East Prussia under General Paul Hindenburg had delivered a crushing defeat to the Russian Second Army, encircling it and taking a hundred thousand prisoners—exactly the sort of grand victory that eluded Auffenberg.

By September 1, German armies in the West were marching on Paris while French divisions fled before them; a truly decisive win seemed within Berlin's grasp. But word of Habsburg difficulties was causing worry among Prussian generals, who saw through Conradian obfuscations and blame-shifting, and feared that Russia was on the cusp of defeating the *k.u.k. Armee* in East Galicia in detail, a development that would undermine German grand strategy immediately. How could Germany achieve victory in France if Austria-Hungary failed to hold off the Russians for several more weeks? Helmuth von Moltke, Germany's General Staff chief, confided his concern to his diary on September 2: "In Austria it's going badly. The army is not moving forward. I see it coming, they will be defeated." He came to this conclusion thanks to detailed reports sent by Gen. Hugo von Freytag-Loringhoven, Berlin's representative to AOK, who explained just how bad things really were in Galicia. Conrad's forces did not meet Prussian standards: "This Austria is already a half-Balkan state," he observed when seeing Lemberg. The Habsburg military, he noted, was hardly more than a militia, and while the Russians were really no better, there were a lot more of them. Freytag-Loringhoven's reports cited poor generalship, inept tactics, eroding morale, and shoddy supply overtaking Habsburg forces in Galicia. As for a successful offensive against Russia, Conrad's unready and ill-equipped army could not make the transition from "wanting" to "achieving."[3]

Chaos and panic were submerging the whole Third Army now, as the Russians continued to advance in overwhelming numbers. Brudermann was far from the only general in East Galicia who was losing his head, while countless lower-ranking soldiers were fearful and suffering from stresses heretofore never imagined. The bloody ruckus of the machine-dominated battlefield reduced some soldiers to speechless panic. Many regiments reported troops suffering from what would later be termed "shell shock" after meeting Russian artillery. Hospitals were flooded not just with tens of thousands of casualties daily, but with men clearly experiencing profound shock; some troops—doctors noted peasants were more prone than city-dwellers—simply could not cope with the stresses and were rendered speechless, unable to function.

For the Habsburg Army's medical corps, the Galician campaign was like nothing ever before seen or even imagined by most doctors and nurses in their worst prewar nightmares. Although reports from the Russo-Japanese and Balkan Wars had revealed that modern bullets and artillery gave terrible wounds, with a high percentage of injured dying of shock, the scale of the bloodbath in Galicia overwhelmed all efforts to deal with it properly. A nurse at one casualty collection station in East Galicia noted that on just one day in the first week of September, her unit processed 8,600 wounded. All over East Galicia, wounded men overfilled hospitals, schools, churches, barracks—anywhere space could be found. Thousands died from wounds that there were no doctors or nurses to treat, as the overwhelmed medical corps was no more ready than the rest of the army for this much bloodletting. Medical staff, mainly reservists, did their best in impossible situations, working for days nonstop. They noted a high percentage of lethal head wounds, especially among officers, whom the Russian snipers were picking off—they were easy to spot with their yellow sashes and shiny sabers— while a worryingly large number of the casualties apparently had been hit by their own artillery and infantry. In the heat of battle, panicky Habsburg troops were taking too little care about marking the right targets. Discouragingly, cholera and typhus were beginning to appear in significant numbers too, as the troops, living rough without decent supplies, lacked clean water or sanitary conditions. The impending retreat only made matters worse, as the overflowing roads made any movement difficult, to say nothing about the panic that gripped many transport units, who tended to see Cossacks lurking behind every hill and copse.[4]

A moving reminder of these late summer horrors was left by Georg Trakl, a twenty-seven-year-old pharmacist from Salzburg who was at the front with the Third Army. Trakl had served as a one-year volunteer in the medical corps before the war yet found civilian life difficult, so he returned to the forces, which gave him much-needed structure. A promising poet prone to binges of drug and alcohol abuse, Trakl found the strains of his job in Galicia unbearable as gravely wounded men cried out for hours, without succor. One night in early September at an overflowing field hospital at Gródek, west of Lemberg, he was required to care for ninety wounded men jam-packed in a barn, lacking proper medical supplies. The agony overwhelmed him, and he had to be dissuaded from shooting himself by comrades. The experience inspired him to write a poem, simply titled "Grodek":[5]

At evening the autumn woods are full of the sound
Of deadly weapons, golden fields
And blue lakes, over which the darkening sun
Rolls down; night gathers around
Dying warriors, the animal cries
Of their shattered mouths.
And the grazing fields fall silent
A red cloud, in which a furious god,
The spilled blood itself, has its silent home
All roads end in death-black putrefaction.
Under the gold branches of the night and stars
The sister's shadow falters through the silent grove,
To greet the ghosts of the heroes, bleeding heads;
And from the reeds the sound of the dark flutes of
    autumn rises.
Oh prouder grief! you bronze altars,
The hot flame of the spirit is fed today by a more violent agony,
The unborn grandchildren.

Reality was slowly intruding at the High Command that Lemberg was lost and the Third Army was about to collapse, as demonstrated by an order from AOK to discreetly prepare for the blowing of all bridges in East Galicia, to hinder enemy pursuit, but the actual order to commence demolition had to come directly from Przemyśl.[6] As a result, most bridges around Lemberg fell into Russian hands intact. The High Command tried to inject toughness into its retreating forces in East Galicia, without much success. A message from Archduke Friedrich on September 3, to be read to the troops in their own languages, captured the AOK spirit, which increasingly had little to do with battlefield events:

> I expect all generals, staff, and senior officers to set an example of loyalty to duty and dedication to their subordinates, to demonstrate manly ruthlessness, particularly in moments of crisis, keeping cool under pressure and showing courageous stoicism.[7]

Brudermann's efforts to exert control over his dissolving army were without effect. He, too, sent out fiery message to the troops, which were ignored. One of his last such dispatches, on September 3, bemoaned the condition of the Third Army, insisting the troops had to get on their feet and fight harder. Reports from the field showed that the Russians in places outnumbered Habsburg forces around Lemberg six-to-one and that the front could not be held. These messages were ignored.[8] Instead, Brudermann exhorted his soldiers to hold the Wereszyca line at all costs—everything else was secondary.[9]

Yet forming any coherent defense proved elusive for the battered Third Army in the first days of September. Frontline units were short of men, guns, ammunition, and supplies—everything. In a typical case, the mostly Ukrainian Eleventh Division, which had suffered serious reverses around Lemberg, reported to Brudermann on September 2 that it had under half its allotted infantry—its four foot regiments were down to 2,033, 1,700, 1,554, and 830 (less than a battalion) riflemen each—and many of those were replacements, while the division hardly had any artillery left, most of its guns having been abandoned to the enemy. To make matters worse, all divisions in the Third Army were having serious supply problems. The chaos of retreat combined with poor discipline among logistical units meant that fighting troops were running low on everything, most critically ammunition. Shell shortages in artillery batteries were commonplace by early September.[10]

On the eve of Lemberg's fall to the Russians, as the Third Army prepared to march westward with what remained of its shattered divisions and regiments, Brudermann continued to send dispatches exhorting the troops to fight on against all odds, but it no longer mattered. His headquarters had ceased to function, and the staff, Brudermann's bottle-green boys who had tried and failed to run the fight for East Galicia from Lemberg, increasingly saw that its orders carried no weight with commanders trying desperately to hold back the Russian steamroller. In one of his last messages to his generals, on September 2, Brudermann admitted shortcomings, allowing a degree of resignation, noting, "the exceptionally difficult condition which the Third Army has found itself in, in difficult battles against a superior enemy, taking into account particularly the sacrificial actions of its senior officers to get our brave troops completely back into the fight as soon as possible." But such talk from could not deliver action from Brudermann's tired officers and panicked troops. The message included the usual threats about harsh discipline for shirkers and cowards, but it no longer mattered. In a few days of terror, defeat had gone from battlefield reality to a state of mind throughout the Third Army.[11]

Exhausted troops were turning into sand running through the fingers of all but the most dedicated officers, whose efforts to instill discipline were ailing. By the last hours of September 1, retreating units of the Third Army north of Lemberg, belonging to the fleeing XI Corps, devolved into a full panic. Tired and scared, the troops succumbed to Cossack panic and fled the battlefield by the thousands. At Kulików, twenty-five kilometers north of Lemberg, Hungarians of the Ninety-seventh Militia Brigade and the Twenty-third *Honvéd* Division, the latter freshly arrived from the Balkans, were struck by forward elements of the Russian XXI Corps and broke. In the darkness of the predawn hours of September 2, all efforts to restore order failed, and whole battalions ran headlong toward Lemberg. By the morning, what was left of them gathered in the northern outskirts of the city. The collapse of the Twenty-third *Honvéd* Division, opening the north gate to Lemberg, caused a panic on Brudermann's staff and illustrated how dire things had actually become.[12]

By sunrise on September 2, it was evident to even the most optimistic Third Army staffers that the only hope left to stem the Russian advance was abandoning Lemberg and trying to hold the Wereszyca line. Lacking modern fortifications, the city gave the defenders few advantages, and by now Russian numbers were unstoppably vast. The relieving of Gen. Heinrich Daempf, commander of the all-but-dissolved Twenty-third *Honvéd* Division, *pour encourager les autres*, had no discernible effect. The inevitable, awkward call to AOK at Przemyśl was placed at 7:00 a.m., informing Conrad's staff of the grim news that Lemberg was being abandoned to the enemy, as the Third Army was no longer intact and capable of resistance without trading space for time. Reestablishing defenses on the Wereszyca, twenty-five kilometers westward, was the only option left to stave off complete defeat at the hands of the surging Russian Third and Eighth Armies.[13]

Conrad's confidence in Brudermann, which had been waning ever since the fighting began in earnest in East Galicia, was now shattered. AOK was aware that panic had infected the whole Third Army, beginning from the top, and this now endangered Austria-Hungary's war against Russia, to say nothing of the political cost of giving up Lemberg without a fight. Nevertheless, it was apparent to staffers in Przemyśl that Brudermann had suffered a collapse of will and confidence, and probably needed to be relieved, but the extent of the debacle made even that difficult; moreover, firing Brudermann would be another political setback, so Conrad optimistically decided to wait a bit longer to see if new defenses might be established west of Lemberg.

Even aggressive censorship could not obscure such a defeat from the public for long. AOK was already getting worrying reports from cities across the Dual Monarchy, where, thanks to the vast casualty rolls, the home front was starting to sense the extent of the debacle unfolding in Galicia. In Trieste, wounded soldiers began arriving home on September 2 after their Ninety-seventh Regiment was ripped to pieces before Lemberg, with only four hundred men of the three thousand committed to battle surviving unscathed. Survivors described unimaginable horrors that sounded different from what the army was telling the public—"it was a hurricane, a cloud of death," recounted one mutilated infantryman—that shocked listeners and depressed civilian morale.[14]

Holding the Wereszyca line, AOK's last hope in East Galicia, was placed in the hands of Hermann von Kövess, the Third Army's best corps commander, but his forces were in a lamentable state. His XII Corps had managed to form coherent defenses on the Wereszyca by midday on September 3, thanks to energetic leadership, but Kövess was on his own, as Third Army headquarters had ceased to function, and he wondered whether his orders to hold the new line at any cost could actually be executed by his depleted and weary Transylvanian troops. His three divisions came to barely twenty thousand men, only 40 percent of authorized strength, and they were tired and short of everything. The chaos of the retreat, amidst the realization that Lemberg was lost needlessly, dragged morale down further, even among senior officers. Kövess let out his frustrations in a letter to Conrad, noting that the much-needed supplies he had managed to procure for his hungry troops were burned on the orders of Third Army, which wanted to deny the Russians anything as they advanced. "It makes you want to pull your hair out," Kövess explained: "Thus was Lemberg thoughtlessly evacuated." Worse, he elaborated, Brudermann and his staff slipped out of Lemberg on the sly, issuing no real orders down the chain of command, while abandoning thousands of rifles to the Russians, leaving the troops in the lurch. It all drove Kövess to distraction. As he told

Conrad, "Above all we need men. These old ladies and head-cases in uniform are killing us!"[15]

The Second Army was committed to battle all along the southern flank of East Galicia, but it too was barely holding on. The collapse of the Third Army to its north rendered a general retreat necessary in any event. Confusion reigned. A *Honvéd* regiment of mostly Romanians arrived at Halicz, on the right flank of Habsburg forces, on September 2 just in time to witness tons of stores being blown up, to prevent their fall into Russian hands. The rail bridge over the Dniester was blasted by sappers, to the amusement of the watching *Honvéd* troops. Defeat was taking its toll on morale, observed a Romanian junior officer, who seethed with resentment at the Hungarians:

> The officers were angrily ashamed of our defeats and used no measured language. The great mistake we had made was in underestimating our enemy and making our attacks according to books and theories. Each unit, as it arrived in Galicia, was hastily thrown into action, and the men attacked as at maneuvers, advancing all together in open formation. The Russians, usually entrenched at the edge of a wood, let us approach within three or four hundred paces and, just as we yelled our "*Hurrá!*" for the "final assault" with the bayonet, opened rapid fire with rifles and machine guns which decimated our ranks in a few seconds. The few who survived wandered panic-stricken all over Galicia and soon lost any military identity they ever had.[16]

In the face of such chaos among Austro-Hungarian forces, the victorious Russian entry into Lemberg proved as ad hoc as the Habsburg retreat. Alexei Brusilov, commander of the surging Eighth Army, learned on September 2 from aerial reconnaissance that enemy units had begun a mass rail-borne evacuation westward out of Lemberg, while cavalry patrols reported that Austro-Hungarian forces surrounding the city were pulling back, as if preparing a general retreat. He quickly consulted with Nikolai Ruzskiy, commander of the neighboring Third Army and his senior, to devise a coordinated plan to take Lemberg. They expected to have to lay siege to the city, which they could not believe Habsburg forces would relinquish without a fight. However, forward Russian patrols were finding the suburbs empty of troops and their fortifications unoccupied. General Ruzskiy did not consider that Austria-Hungary would give up Galicia's capital so easily, so he took time to be convinced that a reconnaissance-in-force into the city would be wise. Eventually he relented, and on September 3, squadrons of the Twelfth Cavalry Division advanced cautiously into the city, expecting ambushes. They met none, and the Russian mounted troops trotted into downtown, finding no Habsburg troops there. They seized Lemberg without firing a shot. The Southwestern Front's official communiqué hailing this triumph credited Ruzskiy, even though the troops who took Lemberg were Brusilov's. "I made no protest, for I did not seek glory but only desired the success of our arms," he recalled.[17]

The capture of Lemberg was hailed across the Russian Empire with great fanfare as a serious, perhaps fatal blow to Habsburg power and prestige. For Slavophiles, this was an especially joyous event with spiritual implications, as it heralded the unification of "brother" Ukrainians with the Motherland. However, the tsar's generals knew that the taking of Lemberg, while important, was not the end of the Galician campaign. Austro-Hungarian forces, though pushed back, were not yet defeated strategically. Victory in Galicia would not be complete until they were pushed across the San river, some ninety kilometers to the west. Not until the San was reached, with the Russian tricolor flying above the fortress of Przemyśl on its banks, would the Ukrainian lands of Galicia be fully in Russian hands.

How to achieve that was the question before the Southwestern Front after the capture of Lemberg. While Brusilov favored a headlong push toward the San, steamrollering the defeated Third Army before it had a chance to establish firm defenses, he was overruled, and the Southwestern Front ordered a northwest push by the Third Army, toward

Rawa Ruska, with the addition of Brusilov's XII Corps. Although this made some strategic sense, as it would block the flanking move of the Habsburg Fourth Army, which imperiled the right shoulder of the Russian advance, it also meant that a hell-for-leather push to the San was out of the question. Ruzskiy, the senior officer, won out. The Eighth Army was ordered to keep advancing west of Lemberg, in support of the Third Army, pushing past the Wereszyca line and taking Gródek. Brusilov was disappointed but September 4 brought good news to his headquarters, namely the fall of Halicz to his XXIV Corps almost without a fight, while his Second Cossack Division had seized the city of Stanisławów. His left flank was meeting little resistance as it marched toward the Carpathian foothills; the fragile state of Austro-Hungarian morale was becoming clear. Brusilov moved his staff into the comfier surroundings of the former Habsburg governor's palace in Lemberg and prepared to crack Austro-Hungarian positions around Gródek, opening the path to the San. By that evening, elements of the Third Army, including troops of Kövess's XII Corps, had begun to dig in around Gródek, but their positions were shaky, their artillery was short of shells, and they had little confidence they could stop the Russians on the Wereszyca.[18]

Having failed to accomplish Conrad's hoped-for Cannae on the plains of southern Poland, Auffenberg's Fourth Army, fresh from victory at Komarów, was ordered to wheel dramatically southward toward Lemberg to stave off the full collapse of the Eastern Front. A more sensible approach, which would have taxed tired regiments less, would have been to order a general retreat to the San line, where the ramparts of Przemyśl could bolster defenses, but Conrad continued to hold out hope for a reversal in his fortunes. The loss of Lemberg could be an opportunity rather than merely a disaster, he felt, particularly if he could turn the Russians' flanks north of the city. On September 2, Vienna's II and Innsbruck's XIV Corps, in a composite group under Archduke Joseph Ferdinand, were ordered to keep a northeastern focus and maintain pressure on Plehve's Fifth Army around Zamość, while the bulk of Auffenberg's forces—the Bohemians of IX Corps, Boroević's hard-fighting VI Corps, plus XVII Corps—began their shift to the southeast, toward Rawa Ruska, a town with a key rail junction located nearly fifty kilometers northwest of Lemberg. This would put them on a collision course with the bulk of Ruzskiy's Third Army, which was marching toward Rawa Ruska too. Yet again, Conrad dispatched his forces into an unequal fight.

The direst matter was the impending collapse of the Third Army, which was faltering west of Lemberg as Brusilov's pursuit began to get on its feet. Brudermann was now wholly ineffective, the word *Panik* being increasingly heard in AOK circles when his name came up, and the failed cavalry general's court connections could no longer protect him. On September 4, Conrad made the difficult decision and informed Vienna that the Third Army's commander was being relieved. In truth, he ought to have been fired considerably earlier, but political considerations combined with Conrad's well-honed ability to push out of mind things he did not wish to deal with, meant that Brudermann's fall came only after Lemberg was lost, along with most of the Third Army. Conrad's private views were scathing; he despised Brudermann as a representative of the backward-thinking, horse-obsessed senior officers who gave his prewar army reform efforts so much grief. As he wrote regretfully to Kövess on September 7, "your wonderful corps found itself placed in such a sad situation due to the weakness, stupidity, and even disobedience of the Third Army command."[19] Brudermann was dispatched back to Vienna without fanfare and his retirement papers were processed as soon as possible.

The faint good news for AOK was that Conrad felt that he knew just the officer to take over the shattered, retreating Third Army, a general who possessed seemingly limitless reserves of vigor and unshakable force of will. Brudermann's antithesis would be Svetozar Boroević, who got the call at 4:30 on the afternoon of September 4 to relinquish command of VI Corps and head for the Wereszyca line with all haste. Boroević relished this seemingly thankless job. Never short of drive or vanity, he was confident that he had earned this promotion and that he, alone, could get the panicked Third Army under firm control and on its feet, thereby saving the Dual Monarchy from total defeat. Although he confided to a friend that he was "very sad" to leave VI Corps, feeling that his troops' fiery performance at Komarów ranked among the greatest achievements in the annals of Habsburg arms, he was honored by his new assignment. "Without me the battle of Komarów would have been lost," he stated, taking the greatest pride in the fact that Freytag-Loringhoven and Kageneck, Berlin's representatives to AOK, "couldn't grasp it fully when I described the *Bravour* of my troops."[20]

Though widely respected among General Staff officers, and popular with the troops for his toughness and willingness to live as rough as they did, the not infrequently abrasive Boroević was far from universally popular with his peers. There was often more toughness than tact. A perennial outsider—a man without connections, the son of a junior officer commissioned from the ranks, the product of a cadet school rather than the Theresian Military Academy, a South Slav Orthodox in an officer corps heavily German and overwhelmingly Catholic—Boroević had risen to the top through talent and sheer grit. He had little use for fellow officers who lacked his drive and skill and made few efforts to hide his contempt, particularly now that war had started, and badly for Austria-Hungary at that. His vanity was much noted on the General Staff, while a fellow general who admitted Boroević's soldierly acumen nevertheless noted the "boundless mistrust" in others that constituted his major character flaw.[21]

Boroević arrived at the Third Army's shambolic headquarters at the town of Mościska on the morning of September 5 in a modest, two-car convoy, one of which kept breaking down, nevertheless confident in his mission: "My old soldier's luck brought me to this position," as he explained. He had Conrad's gratitude for taking on the seemingly hopeless task of restoring order and discipline in East Galicia. "You will be doing me an invaluable service," by getting the Third Army back on his feet, the General Staff chief told Boroević, describing what

Brudermann left in his wake as, "simply a rout, they've all lost their heads." Immediately upon arrival, the new commander began restoring the order and discipline he prized above all other martial virtues. A special force of sixteen hundred military policemen was established at once to get the Third Army's shirkers and malingerers back to the front where they were needed. Henceforth, units would enter battle with military police behind them, wearing white armbands so the troops could see them easily, to discourage malingering and cowardice, not least because so many soldiers became casualties during disorderly retreats. Above all, officers were ordered to set a good example to the men, keeping a cool head even when things went wrong.[22]

Boroević's message to the defeated Third Army, only hours after his arrival to take Brudermann's place, exuded a brash confidence, declaring himself "the victor of a murderous seven-day battle," ready to get his new command back in the fight at once. "A victorious army is in a hurry to annihilate the enemy," he stated, "and I am certain that the Third Army will soon exact a hefty price from the Russians."[23] The reality was less encouraging. Panic engendered at the front by defeats and mauling by Russian artillery had spread to the rear, causing disorder, amidst rumors that enemy spies were masquerading as Habsburg officers to foment further chaos. This situation, with the resulting spy mania, grew serious enough that AOK ordered military police to routinely check the identity tags of all unwounded personnel found in the rear. Galician civilians suspected of espionage were to be handed over to the military justice system—summarily, if dictated by circumstances; Boroević ordered the Third Army that "in cases where treason is suspected, to proceed with the most severe punishments under emergency decree, without concern for scruples."[24] Indiscipline in noncombat units was becoming a serious concern for the High Command. Reports proliferated of shirking and worse, while the first mutiny to come to Przemyśl's attention occurred when troops of a militia labor detachment in the Carpathians, far behind the front, refused to follow orders. A reserve lieutenant wasted no time and shot nine "mutineers" before the situation got out of hand, ordering the military police to deal with the rest of the unwilling soldiers, an action that won the praise of AOK for quick thinking and ruthlessness.[25]

Shortages of trained men were growing serious already, due to unexpectedly heavy casualties. Upon taking command, Boroević immediately ordered the Third Army to break up its replacement (*Marsch*) brigades, which so far had been used as fighting units, often without success, and to distribute the men as replacements, since line infantry battalions were growing desperately short of troops. On September 4, the War Ministry called the conscript classes of 1892 through 1894 to the colors, with few exemptions. The army lacked modern uniforms and rifles for the newly conscripted, but the voracious war machine demanded men.[26]

Intelligence brought at least some good news to AOK. Debriefings of Russian prisoners and deserters portrayed an enemy force that was nearly as weary and struggling as the *k.u.k. Armee*. High casualties were eroding Russian morale, they explained, with the supply system breaking down the deeper they advanced into Galicia, while many non-Russian troops were unenthusiastic, to the point they needed to be kept in the line with bayonets, with some—especially Poles—deserting in large numbers.[27] The most important intelligence source, however, was radio intercepts, what intelligence professionals would later term signals intelligence (SIGINT). Here Conrad's prewar enthusiasm for wireless telegraphy paid huge dividends, as Habsburg Army radio stations at Cracow and Przemyśl, supplemented by eleven mobile radio units serving in the East, began listening to Russian military communications even before battle was joined. To confuse any Russians who might listening to Habsburg communications, beginning on September 4, the High Command followed the advice of their intelligence experts and ordered its field army headquarters to send false messages, unencrypted, to deceive the enemy.[28]

At AOK in Przemyśl, a radio intelligence cell under Captain Hermann Pokorny, the *Evidenzbureau's* best Russian linguist, began intercepting and analyzing Russian military communications beginning on

August 13, and within a week they had established a basic system of intercepting, transcribing, then translating the intercepts: thus was Austria-Hungary's SIGINT effort against Russia born. It soon became, in the words of Max Ronge, who shepherded the growth of Pokorny's small cell, an intelligence source "like the world had never seen." Russian communications indiscipline helped. In the first place, they used radio more than Habsburg forces did, who had been trained to limit usage of radios, due to their vulnerability to interception. Moreover, a high percentage of Russian traffic was *en clair*, lacking encryption except for high-level communications, and even when ciphers were used they were sometimes applied imperfectly; Pokorny's staff could scarcely believe this Russian carelessness. In Galicia, as at Tannenberg, Russian use of open radio caused them setbacks from the outset of the campaign. AOK was only beginning its SIGINT efforts, which in time would become a vast enterprise and a huge force-multiplier. In the opening weeks of war on the Eastern Front, its role was less pronounced, thanks mostly to a lack of linguists, and of senior officers who understood SIGINT's potential impact, but already by early September, AOK was receiving a high percentage of unencrypted Russian messages at the same time as their intended recipients were. Cracking Russian ciphers, the next step, would take a little longer, but was already being examined by Pokorny's cell, which was expanding rapidly as he put out the call for trustworthy soldiers with skills in mathematics and Russian.[29]

After only twenty-four hours at Mościska, surveying his new command, Boroević issued a blistering assessment-cum-order to all the generals of the Third Army. This eyes-only document was vintage Boroević, sparing no feelings and demanding loyalty and service above all, unto death.[30] It began:

My impressions of the troops and units of this army, in the short period of time since I assumed command, do not satisfy me. The grave shortcomings of prewar training have become obvious and must be dealt with seriously, through all possible means.

There is a serious lack of discipline and order; drive has disappeared; apathy and a lack of self-confidence are tearing things apart. Yesterday I witnessed a whole battalion, nearly all stragglers, which had to be escorted back to the front by military police. You could see soldiers, many of them NCOs, unembarrassed by this disgrace.

Units were complaining about exhaustion, which in my eyes means nothing other than their commanders are tired because they missed the opportunity in peacetime to prepare for war. In 28 days in the field, I have slept on straw 25 nights, living only on tea during battle, not changing my clothes or even sleeping for days on end, and I have never succumbed to exhaustion, even though I am in my 43rd year of military service. When a unit fails that means: the commander has failed.

He further cautioned officers that the consequences of failure would be severe, and he paid no attention to rank: "From now on, commanders who demonstrate unreliability will be relieved and replaced without delay, as I can always find enough men in this army who will follow my orders scrupulously. Rank is irrelevant to me, I care about the man behind it." He continued vigorously, holding up his victorious VI Corps as the example to follow:

Whining about the depressive effects of heavy casualties shows that those affected have a fully mistaken impression of war. On its 1st day of battle, the 39th *Honvéd* Division lost roughly 40% of its strength, yet kept fighting bravely for six more days, as if nothing had happened. Due to a mistake by its commander, the 15th Division was attacked at night on the 3rd day of battle and fell apart. It lost 40% of its combat strength, but just 24 hours later, I was able to lead these brave troops into battle again, and they would play a decisive role on the 7th day of the fight. My corps lost 15,000 men in seven days of fighting, facing unprecedented stresses, and not once did I ponder reporting they were tired or depressed about casualties. The 85th Regiment lost 33 officers and 1,900 men in battle, and was still attacking on the 7th day of the fight. At this point I am not comfortable comparing the 3rd Army to my brave VI Corps.

Having shamed his new subordinates, Boroević continued, detailing many of the problems he had witnessed after just one day at his new command. Supply and transport units, in particular, were rife with indiscipline and slovenliness, and must cease looking like "a wandering band of gypsies." He then offered the Third Army—and its generals— the chance to redeem themselves under his firm command:

> Every unit—even the best ones—can suffer misfortune. But that only becomes a setback for an entire army when it cannot get back on its feet and look forward with confidence. Should this occur, there is only one solution: relieving commanders who have failed . . . I am determined that the 3rd Army will do better, and I order all its generals to support me in this effort with all their strength, sharing the burden of this sad necessity, sacrificing in the interests of all things holy. I offer myself in cold blood, if needed.

Failed generals who did not opt for a pistol or throwing themselves under trains had the option of "falling ill," which several did promptly. One of Boroević's top commanders, the Hungarian cavalryman Desiderius Kolossváry de Kolozsvár of XI Corps, soon decided he was too ill to stay in the field and was replaced. In the neighboring Fourth Army, Count Karl Georg Huyn, leading XVII Corps, similarly cited medical reasons for why he needed to leave the front, though his *Kosakenangst* was frequently cited among his peers and subordinates alike. The commander of Vienna's II Corps, General Blasius Schemua, who had briefly served as General Staff chief, was dispatched to a rear area command after falling victim to what II Corps' chief surgeon vaguely termed "anxiety and circulatory problems." Several of Boroević's divisional and brigade commanders in the Third Army similarly found it convenient to promptly discover serious illnesses. General Alois von Pokorny, who had lost control of his Eleventh Division before Lemberg, requested sick leave during battle, prompting one of his brigadiers to note tact-fully, "it's the same whether you take a bullet or die from illness for the Fatherland." The test of war reduced even some of the most promising Habsburg generals to shame. Heinrich von Krauss-Elislago, considered a "water-walker" in the army, being hailed as "the shining example of a General Staff officer" by the late Archduke Franz Ferdinand, failed as commander of III Corps' Twenty-second *Landwehr* Division and had to be relieved.[31]

Troops at the front quickly detected a change in tone within the Third Army once Boroević arrived and began reshaping the command in his image. Although it would take time to fix vast problems with doctrine, tactics, and supply, a new spirit was apparent almost at once. His September 6 message to the fighting men was admirably clear: "Russian newspapers have reported gleefully that our Third Army has been completely annihilated and rendered wholly unfit for battle. . . . Our mission now, in the battles that stand before us, is to provide proof to our enemy of just how wrong they are."[32]

How this all looked to infantrymen trying vainly to hold the line west of Lemberg, as the Southwestern Front bore down on them, was described by the violinist-turned-*Landsturm* subaltern Fritz Kreisler, whose III Corps battalion of mostly middle-aged Styrians was com-mitted to battle near Gródek on September 6.[33] Supply of food and ammunition was intermittent, due in part to the constant threat of Cos-sacks appearing behind the lines, which terrified the transport corps. The men had not bathed or had proper food in days, leading Kreisler to note, "centuries drop from one, and one becomes a primeval man, nearing the cave-dweller in an incredibly short time." Retreating was not good for morale, he observed, and the men, "looking like shaggy, lean wolves, from the necessity of subsisting on next to nothing," had resorted to licking dew from grass in the morning to get water. They cared about nothing anymore except fighting and surviving.

The battle for Gródek, the linchpin of the Wereszyca line, found the militiamen in the novel position of defending, since their experience of battle to date had been offensive. Holding a position astride the main enemy avenue of advance, one of the few available due to the swampy terrain, Kreisler's battalion came under heavy Russian artillery fire that silenced Habsburg batteries. Then the infantry came, supported by Cossacks, but the Styrians held off the frontal attack with rifle fire, forcing the Russians to dig in about five hundred meters away. This was the first time they had gotten close enough to the enemy for any period of time to get a good look at them—until now, death had come mainly from invisible Russian artillery—and the struggle settled into a standoff for the next four days. There was little mutual hatred, Kreisler noted, despite the regular potshots taken at each other, and both sides clearly found it curious to be able to watch the other through binoculars.

But by the evening of the third day, it was obvious that the Austrian positions could not be held much longer, as the number of enemy troops was increasing. The defenders' shallow trenches became waterlogged thanks to the surrounding swamps; food and water had run out, while ammunition stores were getting dangerously low. Every night, brave soldiers tried to bring supplies forward, dodging Russian fires, but it was not enough to sustain the battalion. They were in no condition to resist a major enemy push. By that third night, Kreisler recounted, men expected the worst and wrote goodbye letters to their loved ones, leading him "to admire the wonderful power of endurance and stoicism of our soldiers," whose spirits stayed high despite it all.

The fourth day brought rain, making the soupy trenches even more intolerable, and at 10:00 a.m. one of the militiamen jumped out of his trench, stripped off all his clothes and ran amok, dancing naked before the enemy. The Russians, perhaps in awe, fired no shots at the crazed soldier, or at the two comrades who ventured out to rescue him by dragging him back into the trench. At 5:00 that afternoon, the battalion at last received word that it was to evacuate the trenches that night, under cover of darkness. As many officers feared, the Russians attacked while they tried to pull back and inflicted serious losses on the battalion. Fritz Kreisler was among them, slashed by a Cossack's saber as his platoon struggled to find safety. He was invalided home, his war over. He was fortunate, however, as the savagery of the fighting around Gródek, against surging elements of Brusilov's Eighth Army trying to breach the Wereszyca line, took a frightful toll on the III Corps. In just four days of that seesaw fighting, September 6–10, Styria's Forty-seventh Regiment reported a loss of fifteen hundred troops killed and wounded, with their colonel counting among the dead.[34]

Christened the "Iron Corps" for its heroic performance, III Corps bought time but could do no more to save the deteriorating situation. On September 8, its Sixth Division's Second Bosnian Regiment, weakened by previous engagements and led by a major, executed an attack aimed directly at strong Russian positions near Gródek, commencing a fierce battle that raged for hours. Two battalions of *Bosniaken* charged at the enemy, almost two kilometers away, and managed to overwhelm the defenders, despite steep losses among officers and men. Most companies were reduced to fifty men, yet the Bosnians held out in the face of repeated Russian counterattacks. In the lead company, Sergeant Osman Alagić, seeing that all his officers had fallen, took charge and manned a machine gun, mowing down most of a Russian battalion that was bearing down on the Bosnians. The position held until the morning and Alagić received the first of the forty-two Gold Medals for Bravery (the highest decoration bestowed on Austro-Hungarian enlisted men) that the *Zweier Bosniaken* would win in the war.[35]

Brusilov's failure to break the Wereszyca line in these engagements can be largely attributed to the difficulties with supply his advancing forces encountered after the capture of Lemberg. It took days for transport units to make their way forward in unfamiliar territory, over roads clogged with troops, wagons, prisoners, and wounded. Neither was Habsburg intelligence wide of the mark when it reported discipline and cohesion problems in some Russian units that had taken heavy losses in the fight for East Galicia. The Russian Eighth Army would not be able to make a major, sustained push past Lemberg until September 10, restricting itself to more localized attacks before then, which gave

Boroević several vital days to pull the Third Army away from the brink of collapse. In the meantime, Ruzskiy's Third Army drove on Rawa Ruska, where Auffenberg's Fourth Army stood in their path.

By September 6, once Auffenberg had completed his shift to the southeast, the Austro-Hungarian Fourth, Third, and Second Armies at last stood in a reasonably coherent line west of Lemberg, stretching north to south from the Sołokija river down to the Dniester, a distance of over ninety kilometers. Although these forces were seriously depleted and in places the gaps between Habsburg units were big enough to drive whole Cossack brigades through, they nevertheless formed a strong enough defense that the Southwestern Front could not penetrate with ease. Over the next four days, Austro-Hungarian and Russian divisions battled each other all along this line, at a cost of tens of thousands of casualties on each side, yet neither army achieved more than tactical victories, thanks largely to their tired condition and depleted supplies.

The severity of these combats ought not be underestimated. Though weary from fighting and marching, both armies remained capable of inflicting grievous losses on each other, though rarely achieving more than tactical advantage. North of Auffenberg's left shoulder, across the Sołokija, an ad hoc group of Habsburg forces under Archduke Joseph Ferdinand, consisting of II and XIV Corps, faced Plehve's Fifth Army. Sharp engagements ensued east of Komarów, and no Austro-Hungarian regiments suffered more in these battles than the four elite regiments of Tyrolean *Kaiserjäger*.[36] Three of them were serving with the Eighth Division, which was struck on September 7 by two divisions of the Russian XXI Corps at the town of Radostów. Fighting raged throughout the day around a hill where a windmill, an ideal observation post, was perched. Outnumbered and outgunned, the *Kaiserjäger* ran low on ammunition. Runners trying to bring supplies forward were largely cut down, and the Tyroleans were savaged by the crossfire of the two divisions facing them. The First *Kaiserjäger* Regiment alone lost over a thousand men, dead and wounded, including over twenty officers, while casualties across the Eighth Division were equally bad at Radostów.

The fate of the Second *Kaiserjäger* Regiment, serving with the neighboring Third Division, was grimmer still. On the evening of September 6, its commander, Alexander Brosch von Aarenau, led his Second and Third Battalions into a marshy area near the village of Hujcze. Neither side had a real understanding of where the front line was as darkness fell. The possibility for heroism and disaster, in equal parts, was obvious. "My dear Brosch, you're sure to get the Order of Maria Theresia," were his brigade commander's last words to the colonel as he dispatched him into the darkness. Having seen his regiment take enormous casualties already, Brosch accepted that his own death was imminent, and he stood ready to "live and die with honor" like the model Habsburg officer he was.

The nocturnal engagement began splendidly for his *Kaiserjäger* when a forward company stumbled upon and captured the headquarters of the Russian Eleventh Division, almost without a shot, including its commander, the artillery brigadier, four of his gun batteries, plus numerous staff officers. In the darkness, it was obvious to Brosch and his officers that a large number of troops lurked in the woods nearby—but whose? The rest of the Third Division was in the vicinity, but Brosch could not be certain where; he dispatched runners to get reinforcements while he pushed on, into the dark swamp, with his Fifth Company and parts of the Second and Third Battalions. They never returned.

They marched into the middle of the enemy's Eleventh Division, where a savage, confused fight raged until the morning. Although troops of the nearby Fifty-ninth Regiment, along with many *Kaiserjäger*, tried to rescue Brosch and his men, once it became apparent to divisional headquarters that they had walked into a trap, it was a hopeless task: there were too many Russians, and in the darkness it was impossible to tell friend from foe except at hazardously close ranges, plus nobody could be certain exactly where Brosch had led his doomed contingent. Mid-morning, the Third Division encountered stragglers, including a twenty-five-man group of *Kaiserjäger* that had escaped the nocturnal melée, but of Brosch and much of his Second and Third Battalions, there was no trace. The High Command had its worst fears confirmed when the Russian press showed off the captured Imperial colors of the Second *Kaiserjäger* in Kiev. Of Brosch and his men, however, there was no sign.

Their fate remained unknown for several years, until some of the survivors emerged from Russian captivity. Brosch and his men met their end at the village of Zaborze, four kilometers northwest of Hujcze, across the large swamp from where troops of the Third Division tried to find them. They were surrounded on all sides by Russian infantry and artillery that poured fire onto them through the night. Their numbers dwindled as men fell dead or wounded, and ammunition ran low. By the dawn it was evident that they would not be rescued in time, and Brosch, given his prominence as Franz Ferdinand's former factotum, decided he should not fall into Russian hands. He died around 8:00 a.m. on September 7, alongside most of his command group, next to the *Kaiserjäger* who tried vainly to keep their colors from being captured. He exhorted his men to hold out to the bitter end, and they did. As the enemy closed in, a corporal jumped in front of his colonel, taking a Russian bullet for him, but Brosch was soon cut down too, his last words being, "greet my wife for me." He was one of 14 officers and 158 men killed at Zaborze, while 160 *Kaiserjäger* were captured, most of them wounded. Brosch had sought a heroic death after the murder of Franz Ferdinand, and he found it in a Polish swamp.

The ordeal of his regiment continued. Without their colonel, the remainder of the Second *Kaiserjäger* fought on, and by September 9, only 260 men—equivalent to a rifle company with a single officer left—remained of the more than four thousand troops that Colonel Brosch had led into Galicia only three weeks before. The other *Kaiserjäger* regiments serving with the Eighth Division suffered nearly as badly at Machnów on September 8–9, which witnessed the First, Third, and Fourth Regiments advancing abreast, in a line, against the Russians, with dismal results.[37] The Tyroleans, the Dual Monarchy's most loyal troops, were gutted by these futile engagements.

The fluid fighting that raged across East Galicia involved countless minor skirmishes between patrols, mounted or on foot, that encountered the enemy, often unexpectedly, leading to short, sharp combats that usually mattered little except to those killed or maimed in them. Cavalry units, trying to screen the hard-pressed infantry, bore much of this burden as Habsburg forces attacked and retreated in equal measure. On the eve of his death in one such early September skirmish, Count Alberti, a subaltern of the Fifteenth Dragoons, one of the army's poshest regiments, known colloquially as the White Dragoons from the facing color of their blue tunics, wrote prophetically:[38]

Three White Dragoons ride along
Through Russia's endless forests,
Riding with spring in their hearts,
But winter—winter—is coming soon.

When spring finally comes,
You will find three lonely crosses
In a windy birch grove,
Standing utterly alone.

In a September 9 attack, on a hill located five kilometers northeast of Rawa Ruska, three subalterns of the Fifteenth Dragoons, all from its First Squadron, were killed. This would have been of little note except that one of the three fallen lieutenants was Herbert Conrad von Hötzendorf, the twenty-three-year-old favorite son of the General Staff chief.

On the morning of September 9, Budapest's IV Corps, the last element of the Second Army to reach Galicia, was committed to battle against the Russians for the first time. In an effort to hold the shaky southern end of the Wereszyca line, two of its divisions, the Thirty-first and Thirty-second, which had been bloodied by the Serbs at Šabac, launched frontal attacks against the Russian XXIV Corps, in the style of the IV Corps commander, the cavalryman Karl von Tersztyánsky, who valued courage over tactical finesse. The morale of the troops was high, the commander of the Thirty-first Division, the Magyarophile Archduke Joseph, recalled. He observed Budapest's storied Thirty-second Regiment, which bore the name of the eighteenth-century Empress-Queen Maria Theresia, beloved by Hungarians, in perpetuity, enter its first fight in Galicia with spirits high. Artillery support was limited, but the infantry charged straight at the Russians amid thousands of voices shouting of *hurrá* and *rajta magyar* ("come on, Hungarians," a revolutionary paean from 1848 by the national bard Sándor Petőfi: perhaps fittingly, Petőfi not long after fell in battle against an invading Russian Army). Hundreds of Hungarians died side by side when the dense columns encountered shrapnel and bullets, and the Budapest boys got a rough baptism of fire in the East as their attack, like so many others, faltered under intense fire.[39]

A similar fate befell the Sixth Regiment, part of the neighboring Thirty-second Division. The troops had only reached the front on September 7, following the long journey from the Balkans, and after a day to get ready they were up at 5:00 a.m. on September 9 to do battle. Mostly Germans and Serbs from southern Hungary, the regiment had seen action against the Serbs, but that had prepared them little for what awaited them at the village of Rumno. They entered battle at 10:00 a.m. and fought until the late afternoon under the hot summer sun, vying for control of the village, which was burned down altogether by artillery fire. Despite ample *Bravour*, the regimental history admitted that Rumno brought *Massentod* (mass death) to the Sixth that day, as nightmarish Russian artillery and machine-gun fire, far worse than anything the Serbs had proffered, created a wall of steel that Habsburg troops could not penetrate, though hundreds died trying. They gained nothing that day but an appreciation that the Russians knew how to fight.[40]

Not all IV Corps efforts on September 9 were failures. In Archduke Joseph's Thirty-first Division, the Third Bosnian Regiment, a Balkan island in a sea of Magyar troops from central Hungary (whom the Bosnians affectionately referred to as *naše šogori*—"our brothers-in-law") managed to inflict serious losses on the Russians, taking six hundred prisoners plus six machine guns and a dozen artillery pieces as booty. The fez-wearing *Bosniaken* charged the enemy with trademark gusto, howling and brandishing fighting knives as they closed in, and in a panic the defenders broke and ran. Although their losses were serious, including the maiming of their commander, Lt. Col. Ferdinand Breith—a replacement, as their initial colonel was lost in the brief campaign against Serbia—the Bosnians managed to best the Russians in their inaugural fight in Galicia. But this was the exception for IV Corps that day.[41]

As Auffenberg's Fourth Army shifted toward Rawa Ruska and was fully committed in East Galicia, a gap developed between his left flank and Viktor Dankl's First Army, which continued to battle against the Russian Fourth Army south of Lublin. Before long, this gap grew to nearly two dozen kilometers. The Fourth Army was in the capable hands of Gen. Aleksei Evert, Baron von Salza having been replaced by Stavka for his failures at Kraśnik. The more energetic Evert launched a counteroffensive southward in early September, and by the beginning of the second week of the month, once the Russian Ninth Army had arrived to tilt the odds, the numerical imbalance began to weigh against Habsburg forces. Soon seven Russian army corps faced four Austro-Hungarian ones, and Dankl had to begin giving ground.

Dankl's forces remained tenacious as they withstood repeated Russian assaults, with second-line militia units playing an important part in the fighting. A major Russian attack on September 2 at the town of Chodel, on an important seam between two of Dankl's corps, was blunted by troops of the Hundredth *Landsturm* Brigade from western Hungary, its lead battalion withstanding hours of assaults. Despite being badly outnumbered, the militia battalion held onto Hill 229, north of the town, depriving the Russians of a victory and guaranteeing the integrity of the First Army's front, at least for another day. Its commander, Maj. Anton Lehár—the younger brother of Franz, the former army bandmaster and noted composer, best known for his operetta *The Merry Widow*—received the Order of Maria Theresia for his heroic defense of Chodel. On September 5–6, Cracow's I Corps managed to shatter Russian attacks on its sector that aimed at pushing Habsburg troops back to the San. Its Twelfth Division, Poles now fighting close to their home, massed its guns on the night of September 5 and poured fire onto enemy attacks, breaking them so badly that sixteen hundred panicked prisoners were taken. This rare case of Habsburg artillery dominating the Russians received special praise from the High Command.[42] Despite these successes, it was evident by September 9 that the growing gap between Dankl's and Auffenberg's forces represented a strategic vulnerability that could unravel the integrity of the San river line and, if the Russians proved audacious, might imperil the High Command at Przemyśl itself. There were few Austro-Hungarian forces on hand to plug the gap, and Conrad knew he eventually would have to order the First Army to pull back to secure the San line, but he preferred to delay that decision as long as Dankl's forces seemed to be keeping the Russians in check.

In addition, AOK had to worry about the Balkans again too. Festering in Sarajevo, Potiorek sought another invasion of Serbia, to accomplish what his first offensive had so signally failed to achieve. Nothing less than a decisive victory over the hated Serbs could now repair his shattered reputation at court. By early September, replacements had filled the ranks of his depleted Fifth and Sixth Armies, and at least on paper they looked ready to try again to subdue Serbia. The renewed offensive, which posited coordinated attacks across the Drina and Sava rivers, assumed that the Serbian Army was in worse condition than Potiorek's forces.[43] But Belgrade had other ideas. Potiorek was obsessed with the alleged Serbian fifth column inside Austria-Hungary, and his fears, though overblown, had basis in fact. A network of Habsburg subjects serving as Serbian agents and sympathizers indeed had enabled the Sarajevo assassination, while propaganda from Belgrade openly called upon Serbs in Croatia, Bosnia-Hercegovina, and southern Hungary to rise up against the Dual Monarchy. Potiorek particularly worried about the loyalty of Habsburg Serbs should Belgrade's forces attempt an invasion of Austro-Hungarian territory. In that case, a military operation of only modest size might bring substantial political dividends for the enemy, particularly if Habsburg subjects greeted Belgrade's forces as liberators.

Serbia's forces indeed had been weakened by their successful defense of their country in mid-August, but they remained full of fight and, moreover, their leadership wanted to inflict further pain on the Habsburgs wherever they could. Invading the Dual Monarchy, in the expectation that his soldiers would be greeted warmly by fellow Serbs, was exactly what *Vojvoda* Putnik had in mind. Such an offensive might also delay the movement of the Habsburg Second Army to Galicia, which would assist Serbia's "big brother" Russia. Forces would be sent northward, across the Sava, and if that went well, a general offensive westward, across the Drina, would follow; additionally, troops in the Užice area were ordered to infiltrate Bosnia, with support from Montenegrin forces who would do the same in eastern Hercegovina and in the strategically vital Cattaro area, where the Habsburg Navy concentrated much of its fleet. All these areas had substantial Serbian populations.

The Serbian invasion of Austria-Hungary commenced at 7:00 on the morning of September 6, a Sunday, when lead elements of the Timok I Division crossed the Sava river near the town of Mitrovica in the easternmost region of Croatia known as Syrmia. Covered by their own artillery, the Serbian troops had no great difficulty making the crossing in small boats, as the opposite shore was lightly defended by *Landsturm* troops. Word of the invasion reached Sarajevo quickly, as did alarming reports that the locals around Mitrovica, most of them Serbs, had greeted the invader warmly, just as Potiorek had feared.[44] Fortunately for him, although the Sava line was weakly held, there were forces nearby available for a counterattack, which Potiorek ordered as quickly as possible, before a full-fledged revolt against Habsburg rule could materialize.

The Timok Division's advance got held up in the late morning at the village of Šašinci, about three kilometers inland from the Sava and some five kilometers due east of Mitrovica, where Habsburg infantry put up stiff resistance, buying time for reinforcements to arrive. At the town of Ruma, only a few kilometers northeast of Šašinci, was bivouacked the Twenty-ninth Division, a hard-fighting outfit of mostly Germans from northern Bohemia, veterans of the recent battle for Šabac. Their commander, Gen. Alfred Krauss, the former War College commander, was an avid tactician who itched to exact revenge upon the hated Serbs, and this was his chance. His division had received a contingent of fresh replacements only the day before, and was ready for combat. If they expected a walkover, the Serbs had invaded at exactly the wrong place. Krauss ordered his troops to throw the invader back across the Sava without delay.[45]

By the early afternoon, the Serbian Thirteenth and Fifteenth Infantry Regiments were firmly stalled around Šašinci, while the Timok Division's Twentieth Regiment was having difficulty making headway in the direction of Mitrovica. Krauss's well-planned counterattack commenced at 3:00 p.m. with coordinated artillery fires that shocked the Serbs, who had grown overconfident in their dealings with the detested *švabe* ("Swabians," the Serbian derogatory term for anything vaguely Germanic). Once the gunners had done their work, the Bohemian regiments surged forward—the Ninety-second and Ninety-fourth were mostly Germans while the Seventy-fourth was largely Czech—with vigor, and before long they pushed the Serbs out of Šašinci at bayonet point. The invader's attempts to form a coherent defense south of the village crumbled under hammer blows. By nightfall it was a rout, with the remnants of the Timok Division trying to escape back across the Sava under fire. The Twenty-ninth Division kept up the pressure, and by midnight no Serbian forces remained around Mitrovica. Krauss did not exaggerate when he reported to Potiorek about the "destruction" of the Timok Division. Total losses among the invader came to 6,300, including 62 officers and 4,880 men taken prisoner, along with four artillery pieces and ten machine guns. The disaster at Cer had been avenged. Most of the Serbian forces that crossed into Habsburg territory on the morning of September 6 stayed there. What Krauss and his Bohemians achieved at Šašinci represented the first Habsburg victory over the Serbs, bringing elation in Sarajevo.[46]

The much-needed triumph at Šašinci was not the only indication that the Serbs had overreached. Their occupation of Semlin, the Habsburg town opposite Belgrade, proved short-lived, while their invasion of eastern Bosnia-Hercegovina via Užice, by forty battalions backed by thousands of irregulars, initially caused panic, not least because here again local Serbs had sometimes greeted the invaders warmly, but Austro-Hungarian forces proved more tenacious in the defense than the Serbs had expected. This odd invasion, which featured irregulars swarming the Bosnian countryside, took most of September to fully eradicate, thanks largely to the vast mountainous territory with few roads that the Sixth Army had to defend. At one point, marauding Serbian troops came within twenty kilometers of Sarajevo, causing worry at the Konak, but the uprising against Habsburg rule that Belgrade expected their invasion would engender failed to materialize. Potiorek's oppressive measures to combat espionage and subversion worked, while some Habsburg Serbs proved more loyal than either Vienna or Belgrade had anticipated. In one celebrated case, during battles in the Drina valley on September 8–9 by elements of the Eighteenth Division to push back the invaders, Serbs in Habsburg uniform defeated their co-nationals handily. Two battalions of the Dalmatian Twenty-second Regiment assaulted hill positions above the Drina in an effort to clear out the invader. The attack was led by Capt. Stanko Turudija, an energetic officer who was himself a Serb. As the Dalmatians closed in for the kill, braving enemy fires, the defenders realized that their attackers were ethnic kin. "You're Serbs too, don't fight against us," came the cry, leading Turudija to redouble his attack, which carried the position, taking many prisoners.[47] Such incidents served to illustrate that the root problems of the Habsburg military were not ethnic in nature, rather military and financial, and that too many generals had questioned the loyalty of Slavic troops too easily.

9 From Defeat to Catastrophe

By the evening of September 9, Conrad knew that the time left to him to seek a reverse decision in East Galicia was waning rapidly. His grand scheme to win a quick, decisive victory against Russia had collapsed, and his efforts to save Lemberg had failed; thus it was imperative that the Galician capital be retaken, for political more than for military reasons. A renewed Russian push to the San could be expected soon, probably in the morning, but at last Conrad faced the tsar's Southwestern Front on something like even odds. Or so it seemed on paper. Auffenberg's Fourth Army was holding the line around Rawa Ruska against Ruzskiy's Third Army, while Brusilov's Eighth Army faced Boroević's Third and Böhm-Ermolli's Second Armies, down to the Dniester. Eight Russian army corps confronted an equal number of Austro-Hungarian corps on a front of roughly eighty kilometers. If he could take on the Russians at something like equal odds, at last, he might find success, Conrad believed. The encouraging outcomes at Kraśnik and Komarów, where roughly even odds had delivered impressive Habsburg victories, offered hope. Yet, notwithstanding the fact that Russian army corps were better armed and equipped than his own, Conrad's assessment, as always, took too little account of the actual condition of his forces, which were exhausted and depleted, particularly around Lemberg.

That said, Alexei Brusilov had his own worries that night. The occupation of East Galicia was proving trickier than Stavka had anticipated. Fewer Ukrainians had greeted their "liberators" warmly than the Russians had counted on, while the bulk of the province's Poles and Jews were nearly openly hostile. What goodwill the Russians encountered evaporated rapidly once it became apparent that even peaceful opposition to tsarist rule would not be tolerated. From his palace in Lemberg, Brusilov issued orders that property was to be respected, civilians who obeyed military orders would be left in peace, and touchy ethnic and religious matters were to be left alone while the fighting raged.[1] However, the sincerity of these orders was never taken seriously by Galicians who saw the Russians as foreign occupiers. Before long, Brusilov had the head of the Greek Catholic Church, Metropolitan Archbishop Andrey Sheptytsky, who was the de facto leader of the Ukrainian cause in Galicia, arrested and sent to Russia, where he would remain, confined for nearly four years.[2] Soon Count Vladimir Bobrinskiy, a nationalist member of the Duma of strongly Slavophil views, was appointed Galicia's governor-general, determined to bring the province's "brother Slavs" into full union—political, economic, and spiritual—with Mother Russia with all haste. The Greek Catholic Church was repressed in favor of Orthodoxy; and Russian ways in faith, language, and culture were pronounced standard. The clock tower of Lemberg's city hall was changed to St. Petersburg time to reflect the new order. It did not take long for the Russians to wear out their welcome among all but the most ardent Russophiles in Galicia.[3] For Galicia's Jews, many of whom were strongly loyal to the Habsburgs as well as fearful of pogroms, the arrival of the Russians was a source of deep concern, even terror. Almost immediately upon his installation in Lemberg, Bobrinskiy had over four hundred Jews rounded up and taken hostage by the military, he explained, "as an insurance against Jewish denunciation and spying." By the following spring, the number of Jewish hostages had reached almost five thousand, while the total number of Jews taken forcibly by the Russian military in the war zone on the Eastern Front would eventually reach at least a half-million and perhaps twice that number, making it one of the largest cases of forced migration before the Second World War.[4]

As Conrad feared, Brusilov planned a major push by his Eighth Army against the Gródek-Wereszyca line on September 10. While Ruzskiy's Third Army would renew its efforts in the Rawa Ruska sector, Brusilov wanted to at last resume his drive toward the San. He feared a Habsburg counteroffensive, which hasty repairs to bridges over the Wereszyca by Austrian pioneers indicated, not least because Brusilov worried that the combined Second and Third Armies outnumbered his own forces (in fact they were close to evenly matched, considering the weak condition of Habsburg field units). To make matters worse, the Eighth Army was having serious supply problems, thanks to the different gauge used by Habsburg rail; to keep their forces supplied with food and munitions, the Russians had to employ captured rail stock and engines, as there was no time to lay new track. Brusilov pushed his logisticians hard to ensure the Eighth Army was ready for a major battle on the morning of September 10.[5] Like Robert E. Lee at Chancellorsville, he was too weak to defend, so he attacked. Conrad was thinking along identical lines, and the result was a ferocious encounter battle west of Lemberg that would decide the fate of the entire campaign.

Conrad's orders for September 10 included the retreat of Dankl's First Army behind the San line, as there was no need for those forces to be defending north of the river, in what amounted to a private war south of Lublin that had become disconnected from the main effort around Lemberg. Meanwhile, the bulk of Conrad's forces, the Fourth, Third, and Second Armies, were ordered to assault the Russian positions before them with maximum energy and violence. The actual condition of those forces left a great deal to be desired, no matter how intact they may have appeared on staff maps at *Armeeoberkommando* (Army High Command, or AOK). They were exhausted, their rifle battalions filled with unskilled replacements, short of trained officers and NCOs, and although astute generals knew that ineffective prewar tactics had to be unlearned in favor of more modern methods, there was no time to do so. As had become the custom, they went into battle expecting to be outgunned by Russian artillery. There was little confidence remaining in victory. The orders emanating from headquarters encouraged sacrifice, informing the troops that passivity was to be eradicated from the ranks, while officers unwilling to lead the men forward were asked to step aside.[6] But strong words alone could not vanquish cold steel.

Even fire-breathers like Boroević could only ask so much of men who were tired and short of weapons and shells. Reserves of artillery munitions, which were only two-thirds of Russian level, were inadequate to the needs of combat, and in the first weeks of the war, Habsburg factories produced only 7,400 artillery shells a day, less than three rounds per gun. On paper, the Third Army, charged with retaking Lemberg, looked impressive: six-and-a-half infantry divisions, three cavalry divisions, plus three militia brigades, but its artillery was under strength and short of munitions, while the condition of the infantry, which would bear the brunt of the battle, was lamentable. Most rifle companies were at half strength or less, with many units reporting rolls as low as fifty or sixty men, versus an authorized strength of 250 riflemen.[7]

Despite all this, many Habsburg regiments went forward into battle on the morning of September 10 with a desire to defeat the enemy and avenge previous defeats. The soldiers knew that the culminating point of the campaign, indeed the entire war against Russia, had been reached. Weight of shell and tactical finesse were found more wanting than courage. That day, for the first time in the war, Conrad visited the front. Sallying forth from Przemyśl by automobile with Archdukes Friedrich and Karl among his retinue, the latter being the youthful new heir to the throne, the General Staff chief paid a visit to Boroević's forces fighting in the Gródek sector. They did not get particularly close to the front, and the round trip only lasted six-and-a-half-hours.[8]

The tactical shortcomings that had plagued Habsburg forces from the war's beginning were fully in evidence on September 10. Austro-Hungarian artillery was outranged and outgunned by their Russian counterparts, leaving the infantry vulnerable, while Habsburg rifle units displayed weaknesses in basic tactics that proved fatal for many soldiers, particularly green replacements. Combat in the forests around

Janów, west of Lemberg, was decided in the enemy's favor that day, mainly thanks to poor infantry-artillery coordination. In the woods, artillery forward observers found it almost impossible to mark their targets, while the gunners' reliance on shrapnel, rather than high explosive shells, meant that their fires, even when accurate, had little effect, because the shrapnel bounced off trees rather than harming the Russians. Austro-Hungarian infantry was left in the lurch by the artillery and defeated at Janów largely by superior enemy gunnery.[9] Casualties were especially heavy in militia units that had never been trained in modern infantry tactics, yet found themselves in the front line. An attack on September 10 in the Gródek sector by a regiment of middle-aged Tyrolean *Landsturm* showed what could, and often did, go wrong. Tactical improvisation was widespread, as commanders realized the corpse-producing effects of much their prewar doctrine, but in the heat of battle panicked troops reverted to old habits. The Tyroleans advanced on Russian positions—primitive trenches a few hundred meters beyond—in skirmish lines, not dense columns, to minimize casualties, especially to enemy artillery, but they were stalled at a forest's edge by intense rifle and machine-gun fire. Without supporting artillery, there was little the militiamen could do except pull back into the forest, away from the worst effects of Russian bullets. But they had never been trained in executing retrograde actions under enemy fire, and the attempted retreat fell apart in chaos, with whole platoons being ripped apart by accurate Russian shooting. The survivors rued that they had never been trained in digging proper entrenchments, as the enemy clearly had been. In just three days in the Gródek sector, the *Landsturm* regiment dropped from three thousand effectives to barely seven hundred.[10]

September 10 proved very costly for both sides, the Russians being astonished at the ferocity of the Austro-Hungarian attacks, and casualties mounted all along the front, without decision. Brusilov was seriously concerned about his front cracking at Gródek, so intense was Habsburg pressure on the Eighth Army, and by the afternoon his forces were digging in, rather than continue launching futile attacks into the teeth of the enemy. He was particularly worried that if Boroević's Third Army managed to break through, there was no obvious rallying point for a defense before Lemberg, and he might wind up having to do what the enemy had done only a few days before, but in reverse; losing the Galician capital so soon after its capture was something Brusilov desperately wanted to avoid, so he requested all possible reserves from Stavka to hold the line. He obtained a few thousand troops, including a Cossack division, but no more. By nightfall on September 10, particularly in light of warnings from the Southwestern Front to conserve artillery ammunition, which was running low, Brusilov wondered if the next day would bring disaster.[11]

September 11 began like the previous day, with Habsburg and Russian forces exchanging blows all along the East Galician front. Artillery and infantry pummeled each other through the morning, with freewheeling cavalry squadrons trying to locate gaps that might be exploited by infantry. Boroević was pushing his weary forces hard, and the Third Army made important local gains on the Gródek front, including shattering the Russian Forty-eighth Division, capturing twenty-six guns, over half its artillery, abandoned as the enemy retreated. The Habsburg breakthrough toward Lemberg that Brusilov feared and Boroević expected was slowly coming into focus. However, the important developments that morning were all to the north, where Auffenberg's Fourth Army was holding its own in tough combats around Rawa Ruska, yet was suddenly imperiled by encirclement.

The vast gap between the Fourth Army's left flank and the right shoulder of Dankl's First Army, nearly fifty kilometers wide, had caused concern at AOK, but not enough for the ever-hopeful Conrad to do anything substantial about it. In fairness, he had no forces to plug the gap anyway, so there was nothing to be done except to pull his front back to the San, thereby abandoning any chance of retaking Lemberg. That he had been unwilling to do. Sketchy reports of considerable numbers of Russian cavalry moving into the gap had been received in Przemyśl for days, and it was evident that something had to be done before a crisis made an appearance. Nevertheless, AOK persisted in its hopeful belief that Plehve's Fifth Army was still licking wounds from its defeat at Komarów and therefore was unable to seriously threaten Auffenberg's forces with envelopment. Conrad and his staff were wrong.

Just how wrong they were was made plain on the morning of September 11, when Hermann Pokorny's radio intelligence section at Przemyśl intercepted Russian orders, *en clair*, indicating that Auffenberg's army was in mortal danger. Specifically, two of Plehve's corps were preparing to turn the left flank of the Fourth Army, while a full corps of cavalry under Dragomirov threatened to wreak havoc in Auffenberg's rear and cut off its avenue of retreat to the San. If the Russian V Corps reached Cieszanów and the XVII Corps seized Brusno, as they had been ordered to do, thereby turning Auffenberg's left flank, his whole army risked encirclement and annihilation. As was his wont, Conrad fierily ordered Auffenberg to counterattack, but his subordinate knew this was impossible. His best troops, the Tyrolean XIV Corps, had barely ten thousand infantry on hand, having lost forty thousand soldiers in the last two weeks. In a typical case, one of its infantry regiments, the First *Landesschützen* (the *Landwehr*'s equivalent of the elite *Kaiserjäger*), suffered "monstrous losses" of more than 65 percent of its strength over just four days, September 8–11, and could not be pushed any harder.[12]

Wasting no time, Auffenberg ordered the Fourth Army to disengage at Rawa Ruska and begin an orderly withdrawal to the southwest, toward the San. Pokorny's SIGINT provided Auffenberg with accurate updates on enemy plans and dispositions, allowing the Fourth Army to extricate itself from the Russian trap just in time. Similarly, Conrad's order to the Second Army "to attack without halting, with energy and regardless of loss," was ignored by Böhm-Ermolli, who understood that his tired divisions were at the breaking point. By the afternoon, even Boroević's forces stalled from sheer exhaustion. Lemberg would not be retaken. Conrad could avoid the awful reality no longer, and the inevitable order for a general retreat to the San river was issued by AOK at 5:30 that afternoon.[13]

It was the misfortune of the Central Powers that Conrad's decision to retreat to the San coincided almost exactly with the German decision to pull back at the Marne, their effort to knock France out of the war in six weeks having failed. Based partly on the downbeat field assessment of a gifted staff officer, Lt. Col. Richard Hentch, that was submitted September 10, Moltke reluctantly concluded that a withdrawal by his exhausted forces away from Paris was necessary, to establish more defensible positions. It was a momentous decision that ensured that the war on the Western Front would become protracted. Even the vaunted Prussians had failed to bring a quick, decisive victory.[14] Whatever *Schadenfreude* Conrad may have savored from Moltke's misfortune at the Marne was undercut by the realization that, having failed to subdue France in six weeks, Berlin would have little help to offer Austria-Hungary in her hour of need in Galicia.

The Russians were initially unaware of the Austro-Hungarian withdrawal. Although the pullback of the Fourth Army to secure its flanks had been noted by the Southwestern Front, the Russians detected no general retreat as yet. Based on aerial reconnaissance, Brusilov anticipated that Boroević would attempt to crack Russian defenses around Gródek again on September 12, which the wily Russian planned to cut short with a sharp attack of his own. However, the expected Habsburg offensive failed to materialize, with Third Army attacks that day seeming half-hearted: "a demonstration rather than a real effort," as Brusilov termed it. He surmised that enemy forces were preparing to retreat, as they did after nightfall, blowing the Wereszyca bridges before they withdrew.[15]

On September 12, Conrad decided that AOK needed to be moved away from Przemyśl, which would soon be in the thick of the fighting. The High Command began its move to the safety of Neu Sandez (Nowy Sącz), at the edge of the Carpathians, not far from Cracow and a full

150 kilometers behind the front. Upon his arrival there, Conrad learned of the death of his son Herbert at Rawa Ruska, news that devastated him. His dark premonitions had come true, and he was not even able to visit his son's grave, which was now deep behind enemy lines; he had only Herbert's last photograph to console him. As he wrote to his beloved Gina, "This shadow will always hang over my life."[16]

The retreat to the San was a rollercoaster affair. Heavy rains covered the withdrawal of several hundred thousand Habsburg troops, making the roads muddy, which slowed the retreat, but also the Russian pursuit. In places, columns of Austro-Hungarian troops fell prey to marauding Cossacks, while elsewhere, the vanquished were scrambling to the safety of the San faster than the victors could pursue them. While some regiments maintained good march discipline, others bled men every mile of the march—deserters and those too exhausted to keep going. Effective commanders kept the men marching, while ineffective ones lost control of frightened, exhausted, and hungry masses. Tens of thousands wound up in Russian captivity, while thousands more fell to Cossacks. The great retreat came as a heavy blow to many Habsburg officers, particularly those in the Second and Third Armies facing Lemberg, who felt that they had been close to cracking Brusilov's defenses when the order to pull back was received. There were harsh words for Auffenberg, in particular, whom some generals felt had carelessly let his army be outflanked. After suffering grievous losses, the Russian line on the Wereszyca was finally wavering, observed Hermann von Kövess, whose XII Corps was ready, indeed eager, to make one last attack toward Lemberg, which he was confident would have pushed the Russians past their breaking point. It was not to be.[17]

It was impossible to mask the full extent of the debacle. Some Habsburg troops made it across the San as early as September 12, while other units took three more days to reach the safety of its left bank. From the approximately 900,000 Austro-Hungarian troops committed to battle against Russia in late August, only slightly over half of them reached the safety of the San in mid-September. In three weeks of fighting, Conrad had lost approximately 420,000 men, including over 100,000 killed, about 100,000 in Russian captivity, and some 220,000 wounded.[18] The overall loss was equal to the size of Austria-Hungary's prewar standing army. This was a disaster without precedent in military history. In three weeks, Conrad had destroyed his country's army, losing half of Galicia in the process. Russian casualties surely exceeded 250,000—figures are even sketchier than for Habsburg forces—but the tsar's huge empire, with its vast manpower reserves and far larger standing army, could absorb such losses better than the Dual Monarchy could.

Examination of infantry casualties reveals how steep losses were in Habsburg combat units in Galicia. When it crossed the San on September 12, having abandoned its wagons to accelerate the withdrawal, the men marching with what they could carry, Salzburg's Fifty-ninth Regiment had 62 officers left, compared to 123 at mobilization in August. There were 2,082 men on strength, compared to well over 4,000 riflemen alone, from a total strength approaching 5,000 counting support personnel across four battalions, when the campaign began. This, however, is a deceptive figure, as the regiment had received an infusion of replacements while in combat, a *Marsch* battalion over a thousand strong, so the actual loss rate from three weeks of fighting was roughly two-thirds. Of the regiment's sixteen company commanders who had gone to war, just three crossed the San: three were dead, seven were wounded (three of those were taken prisoner), while three had been invalided seriously ill.[19]

When it crossed the San, the much-blooded Twenty-seventh Division from northeast Hungary, part of VI Corps, had about 8,700 riflemen, about two-thirds of the authorized figure, thanks to having received two infusions of replacements in the field. But one of its regiments, the Eighty-fifth, which had attacked Pawłowka hill with great *Bravour* on August 26, at the beginning of the Komarów offensive, losing almost 1,300 men in a single, successful attack, was down to less than a thousand rifles. It had lost over four thousand infantrymen in Galicia, a casualty rate exceeding 80 percent.[20] The four regiments of elite Tyrolean *Kaiserjäger* lost 9,700 riflemen in the three-week war for Galicia, a casualty rate of nearly two-thirds.[21]

Losses were severe across the army, not just in first-line infantry units. Austria's Second *Landsturm* Regiment, whose middle-aged militia shipped out of Linz in mid-August 3,875 strong, a month later had only 1,675 men left, a casualty rate approaching 60 percent.[22] Fresh riflemen could be had; however, the staggering losses in Galicia of junior officers and NCOs, the trained prewar cadres who formed the backbone of the army, could not be made good and, in a tactical sense, doomed the Habsburg Army at the outset. Analysis of field reports tells the sorry tale. Once it crossed the San, VI Corps concluded that, on average, its field units were missing 60 percent of their men and 70 percent of their officers. At the company level, trained officers barely existed anymore, with reserve lieutenants or officer cadets, even NCOs, leading rifle companies, while battalions were commanded by captains, sometimes senior lieutenants. Moreover, the quality of replacements left much to be desired; in the rush to get men to the front, training was cut down to the point that recruits barely knew how to fire their weapons and knew nothing of tactics.[23]

To make matters worse, disease was rife among the troops who made it to the San. Weeks of living off the land, eating and drinking what they could scrounge as the army's supply system had let them down, made many soldiers ill. In particular, cholera swept through the forces on the San, and in the two weeks after the retreat IV Corps reported two thousand men infected, of whom a shocking two-thirds died. Strict orders to the troops never to drink unboiled water while in the field came too late to save thousands who survived the fighting only to succumb to cholera.[24]

Those lucky enough to escape East Galicia without grave wounds were often changed men. Some sought escape in wine and women, as soldiers have done as long as there has been soldiering, while others took to more placid pursuits. Many carried little books with them, often poetry, and after they reached the safety of the San, there was finally time to enjoy some solitude. Officers were intrigued by men, savages living off the land just days before, becoming bookworms with the appearance of a little leisure time. A lieutenant of a Moravian regiment that had seen fierce combat with the First Army was surprised to see one infantryman, not noted for intellectual pursuits, reading a book intently. It was poetry, the man explained, a gift from his wife upon his departure for the front. "If I'd gotten the book earlier, before the war, I never would have read it. Now I like it so much that I'm really happy to have it," he confided. When the officer asked what it was he liked so much about it, the soldier replied: "I can't really say, but when I read it I feel like a completely different person." The lieutenant, a career officer, suspected exactly what the man wanted to forget.[25]

Forgetting the carnage was impossible for some veterans. The mental cost of Conrad's catastrophic three-week war for Galicia is an issue that has never received proper research, but there are hints that the number of soldiers suffering from serious mental trauma was large. Only in the second half of the war did militaries begin to seriously address the issue of psychiatric casualties, and, befitting its status as the world leader in psychoanalysis, Austria-Hungary made some noteworthy efforts toward understanding what the British termed "shell shock." As early as September 1914, Habsburg army doctors noticed that some men simply could not cope with the stresses of battle, with a certain minority rendered speechless or otherwise nonfunctional, sometimes permanently; it was termed "nerve shock" or sometimes simply hysteria, and it defied conventional treatments.[26] Suicide rates spiked among veterans of the Galician nightmare, but information is anecdotal. One soldier who killed himself was Georg Trakl, the pharmacist and poet who was traumatized by the battle for Lemberg and the horrendous casualties it caused. He repeatedly talked of suicide and wanted to go to the front as an infantryman, for which he was clearly temperamentally unsuitable. He never returned to normal, falling into a deep depression after the retreat across the San, taking his own life on November 4 with a cocaine overdose.[27]

The trauma of battle combined with the shock of defeat frayed the bonds of an already hazardously diverse army. Incidents of ethnic bad feelings, which had been undetectable in August when euphoria and patriotism submerged them temporarily, began to make an ugly appearance in mid-September. Matters were not helped by the fact that the desperate need to get replacements into the line quickly often jumbled troops of different ethnicities together, leading to miscommunication and bad feelings.[28] The rot, however, first took hold in the rear, not at the front. In perhaps the worst case, on September 16 a column of suspected "Russophiles" being marched through Przemyśl under armed guard was spontaneously set upon by a crowd of angry soldiers, mostly Magyars, armed with clubs and knives. Magyar troops in the garrison had been causing mayhem in Przemyśl for weeks, stealing from locals whom they considered "foreigners," and indiscipline was mounting, culminating in the rampage of September 16. Bloodlust against the traitorous "foreigners" exploded in rage. By the time the military police restored order, forty-five of the suspects were dead, among them the daughter of a Greek Catholic priest; none of the suspects, it turned out, were actually Russian spies.[29]

Senior officer worries about the loyalty of Slavic troops, pervasive before the war, reemerged in defeat, with AOK receiving numerous reports indicating concerns about desertion and worse. On September 20, the commander of Cracow's fortress reported that four battalions of Czech *Landsturm* in his garrison were so unreliable that they might mutiny at any moment. (They did not.) These second-line units, from the Prague area, had been severely bloodied in Galicia, and their morale was indeed fragile, but here the officer corps was reverting to its ingrained habit of ascribing to nationalism a discontentment that was at least as much rooted in post-combat stress and anger over bad leadership. Nor did Czech troops appreciate being singled out as troublemakers by many generals. It is hardly surprising that by early October some Czech units did indeed display rising signs of discontentment about the war itself.[30]

To rebuild the shattered field army, the War Ministry ordered the establishment of two new replacement (*Marsch*) battalions per infantry regiment (these were the fourth and fifth per regiment raised so far in the war), each of roughly a thousand men. Men previously exempted from conscription were being called to the colors with haste. Raw conscripts needed considerable training, but there was no time for that, as the Dual Monarchy was in a desperate struggle for survival, and men would be dispatched to the front as soon as possible.[31]

The causes for the enormous casualties suffered by the *k.u.k. Armee* in Galicia in the late summer of 1914 were many and varied. At root, Conrad's army was not ready for the modern battlefield. That said, the most basic reason was that Russian artillery proved superior in skill, range, and weight of shell to Austro-Hungarian gunnery. Simply put, the Habsburg Army was blasted off the battlefield by Russian artillery. The First World War was a war of artillery *par excellence*, with gunnery being responsible for something like 70 percent of casualties overall, and the figure appears to have been even higher in Galicia, where Russian gunnery likely claimed as many as three-quarters of Austro-Hungarian dead and wounded. The psychological effect of shelling was widely noted by Habsburg units on the receiving end of deadly Russian artillery, where the inability to see, much less strike back at, the enemy was agonizing. Many troops who considered themselves "bullet-proof" were felled by shrapnel, the invisible foe.[32]

The central role of being outgunned by Russian artillery in the Galician defeat, both tactically and psychologically, was explained succinctly in a report to the High Command:

> The inferiority of our field artillery materiel, especially the field and heavy howitzers and the ammunition of the field gun, to the first-class enemy artillery materiel and ammunition has not only

caused greater losses among our infantry than necessary in the recent hard fighting, but has made the latter nervous in the face of overwhelming enemy artillery fire.[33]

Artillery doctrine was rapidly revamped, while orders for more modern guns and howitzers—designed before the war but never produced for want of funds—were placed immediately by the War Ministry. The Galician campaign made plain that the Austro-Hungarian Army had overvalued cavalry in its prewar planning. While mounted regiments still had some function on the modern battlefield, principally in scouting and covering actions, there was no need for the vast formations of mounted troops—eleven divisions—that the army had on the order of battle, which were expensive to raise and maintain, and of limited utility on the machine-dominated battlefield. As soon as possible, cavalry regiments were issued drab field uniforms, the same that they had resisted before the war, as their gaudy garb had led to needless deaths in Galicia. As early as the autumn of 1914, cavalry regiments began to dismount and henceforth would fight as infantry units in all but name. Although a limited number of cavalry squadrons were kept mounted for scouting missions, by 1916 the large majority of Austro-Hungarian cavalry units had become foot soldiers, dismounted units with dashing titles.[34]

In many ways, the Habsburg cavalry in the summer of 1914 represented a microcosm of the myriad shortcomings of the army at a unit level: conservative if not outright reactionary in its thinking about warfare, inadequately trained, tactically primitive, not to mention plagued by class-derived prejudices that hindered military effectiveness. In the aftermath of the Galician defeat, a Hungarian officer of the Tenth Hussars elaborated the errors of his regiment's prewar training that had contributed to defeat, compiling what modern militaries might term a "lessons learned" list. His regiment spent too little time in training for reconnaissance, its real mission. There had been too much emphasis on mounted charges, not enough on aggressive patrolling by small units. The men needed more training in the use of the carbine, less with the sword—marksmanship was unacceptably poor—while there was a pressing need for more effective use of terrain while in the field, to mask movements. Drab field uniforms, like those issued to the rest of the army, were required in the cavalry immediately. The issue of discipline needed to be revisited, since there had been too much value given to "barracks discipline" over "battlefield discipline": curiously, he noted, reservists who had served with the regiment when it was garrisoned in Bukovina from 1901 to 1908, close to the Russian border, were better prepared for the rigors of combat than active duty troops, who went to war from their spit-and-polish barracks in Budapest. NCOs had frequently underperformed, often because they lacked status and were too friendly with the rank-and-file. In contrast, the distance between officers and men was too great and did not promote cohesion or effectiveness. Senior officers needed to spend more time with the troops, while all officers needed to demonstrate more concern for the welfare of the men. Field uniforms should be identical for officers and rankers; officers should never eat before their men did, neither should they bed down before the rank-and-file were able to. Last, the endemically lackadaisical attitude toward many important issues, including supply and security in the field, required urgent repair. In short, the cavalry needed to get serious about war without delay, which was good advice for the rest of the Habsburg Army to boot.[35]

Similar themes were echoed in a harsh after-action report by the Second Division, whose commander, Gen. Anton Lipoščak, was a hard-charging Croat. Flawed prewar training and a lack of leadership meant that the troops did not handle enemy barrages well and were prone to panic under fire, he observed, resulting in a "tendency to retreat" when not needed. Worse, he witnessed "enormous carelessness" resulting in unnecessary casualties in battle, leading to broken battalions fleeing combat against orders. For this, Lipoščak, argued, officers needed to be held accountable; otherwise they would not regain the trust of the men. "There is no dogma that your manservant must bring you coffee before you get moving in the morning, "he scathingly informed officers: "First comes the punctual adherence to orders regarding the hour of departure. Coffee can be 'served' to you somewhat later."[36]

Never one to mince words, Boroević held the officers of his Third Army accountable for what had gone wrong in Galicia. His criticism of prewar tactics was detailed, providing a roadmap for rapid reforms. Officers were responsible for teaching the men better methods, without delay, above all how to dig in to escape enemy shelling; carelessness here had cost thousands of lives. When defending, units needed to dig in quickly, taking care to create enfilading fires, particularly with camouflaged machine guns, which formed the basis of infantry defenses. Terrain needed to be used better, while flanks needed to be guarded properly; above all, the artillery must take more care to coordinate its fires with the infantry, who needed their protection and support.[37] For this sorry state of affairs, the men bore no blame, Boroević insisted, rather their officers did. Leaders were not leading, which was the core of the problem, and in many units "officers have lost control of their men," he insisted in a September 19 order that was issued to all officers of the Third Army. "The men do not salute, they dress however they like, and they do not follow orders unconditionally, as is imperative IN WARTIME."

To make matters worse, Boroević continued, officers were using heavy losses as an excuse for not doing their jobs and letting the men slack off. "I have seen officers drunk on duty, guards drunk at their posts, I have experienced things that have made me blush with shame." The bottom line, he explained, was simple: "A unit is only as good as its officers. No more, no less! There are no good units with bad officers." The Third Army was in a sorry state when he inherited it, Boroević conceded, but that was no excuse any longer, particularly because hard days were ahead. Officers had allowed some units to retreat to the San in a disorderly fashion, with men doing as they pleased, even sleeping in the streets, which could not be repeated. The war had only just begun, and if officers did not take responsibility soon, disaster would result. "Sharp discipline" alone would get the Third Army back on track, and officers needed to start by dressing and acting in accordance with their rank and responsibility, showing concern for the welfare of their men while enforcing rules strictly. This was nothing less than a "matter of honor" for every officer.[38]

Berlin realized, painfully, in mid-September that their ailing ally was at risk of strategic collapse. The Prussians doubted whether Conrad's tattered forces could hold the San line against the surging Russians. Austria-Hungary's polyglot army, as Kageneck warned would happen, had been defeated and needed an injection of seriousness and order. Thus did Gen. Erich Ludendorff, the man of the hour as the architect of the recent victory at Tannenberg, arrive at Neu Sandez on September 18 to discuss strategy with AOK. His advice to Conrad was to keep retreating to more defensible positions; there would be time to retake lost territory later, once order had been reestablished and the army rebuilt. AOK decided to pull back 150 kilometers more, surrendering nearly all of Galicia. Within ten days, the Second and Third Armies would be guarding the vital Carpathian mountain passes, while the First and Fourth Armies would block any Russian advance into Silesia, with their backs to Cracow. Fatefully, Conrad decided to leave more than 120,000 troops at Przemyśl, that vast but rather dilapidated fortress on the San, to serve as a thorn in the enemy's side that might slow down the Russian advance while his forces established firm defenses to the west.[39]

Perhaps the sole bright spot for the *k.u.k. Armee* in the aftermath of the Galician debacle was its superlative intelligence, which prevented the retreat from becoming a total rout. Hermann Pokorny's efforts to crack Russian codes bore fruit beginning on September 19, when he rendered his first intercepted encrypted message into plaintext. AOK now had access to high-level Russian communications and used this secret information to guide its forces as they withdrew deep into Habsburg territory, avoiding enemy traps along the way. Pokorny's staff quickly grew proficient at decrypting Russian messages, analyzing, translating, and reporting them to senior officers within only a few hours, while enemy efforts at cipher changes proved no match for Habsburg code breakers. A new Russian cipher introduced at the end of September was broken by Pokorny "in a few minutes," and it happened again in October. Much of this success can be attributed to the rare genius of Pokorny, the son of a Moravian postmaster, who possessed mathematical and linguistic ability in equal measure as well as, critically, the ability to spot talent in others. His boss, Max Ronge, did not exaggerate when he termed Pokorny's work "a triumph over the Russian steamroller"—in truth, it was the only one Austria-Hungary had.[40]

The loss of his son placed Conrad in a melancholy mood. In this he was hardly alone: given the tendency of sons in the Dual Monarchy to follow their fathers into the army, many senior officers were grieving in the aftermath of the defeat in Galicia. One such was Conrad's friend Gen. Hermann von Kövess, who mourned the death of his son Béla, one of the many subalterns of the First *Kaiserjäger* Regiment to fall near Rawa Ruska. The loss of a favored son was so painful that Kövess, like Conrad, never fully got over it, his letters revealing private agony.[41] Yet the General Staff chief also had to contend with the reality that he had been defeated in battle; he had lost the grand campaign that he had so long sought as the crowning glory of his career. Condemnations of the Germans as faithless friends who had doomed Austria-Hungary to defeat were commonplace in the hallways of the High Command. Despite the encouraging news for the public emanating from AOK, consisting largely of paeans to "heroic sacrifice" amidst vague assurances of victories to come, Conrad was well aware that he had been defeated. He noted to several confidants that, had Franz Ferdinand not been murdered at Sarajevo, the heir to the throne would have had him shot for his performance in Galicia.

Conrad's mood veered from melancholy toward depression, not helped by the fact that the stresses of defeat had given him, a normally robust man, a persistent case of influenza. Perhaps most painfully for him, he had failed to secure the great victory that he hoped would convince his married lover to leave her husband for him. A distressing amount of Conrad's concerns in September revolved around Gina, including spending hours every day writing long, tortured letters to his beloved, instead of running the war. "I am amazed that the good Conrad finds the time during a campaign for such extensive private correspondence," explained his friend Joseph Redlich, a journalist and regular visitor to AOK. "He is not senile," added Redlich, but others were less certain. Col. Max von Hoen, head of press matters at AOK, considered that Conrad's "relations with Frau von Reininghaus are a sign of his senility" and believed he should retire. Even a staunch backer like Redlich concluded that his friend "does not believe in his own historical calling to be the generalissimo of Austria against Russia." It was no wonder that Vienna had lost confidence in Conrad, as Redlich realized in the aftermath of the Galician catastrophe.[42]

The search for scapegoats commenced without delay. Some pointed a finger at Alfred Redl, "the hangman of the army," whose treachery supposedly led to the High Command undercounting Russia's might by seventy-five divisions, greater than the strength of the whole Habsburg Army. Count Adalbert Sternberg, a friend of Conrad's, claimed that Redl had prospered under the *Protektion* of a clandestine gay cabal on the General Staff, what he termed "the homosexual organization."[43] With Redl dead, this conspiracy theory was difficult to discredit, but in fact there was no serious prewar undercounting of the tsar's forces by the *Evidenzbureau*. The General Staff had a decent idea of the size and strength of Russia's military, and pursued a strategy that was doomed to fail regardless.

The highest-ranking scapegoat for the defeat was Gen. Moritz von Auffenberg, who took the fall for the retreat from Rawa Ruska, not altogether fairly. Brudermann had already been relieved, so another general needed to be blamed for what went wrong after the loss of Lemberg. Notwithstanding that he was ennobled for his victory at Komarów, Auffenberg was relieved of command at the end of September, ostensibly on grounds of ill health, and soon retired, with the Fourth Army being given to Archduke Joseph Ferdinand. Conrad did not personally blame his old friend for the defeat; indeed he seemed far angrier with the Prussians for their alleged disloyalty than at anyone wearing a Habsburg uniform, but someone had to be sacrificed, and such was Auffenberg's fate.

That Conrad's madcap plan to defeat Russia alone, without German assistance, had ended disastrously ought to have been no surprise, given the condition of Habsburg forces in the summer of 1914. Always prone to wishful, and sometimes magical, thinking, Conrad sent his outnumbered and unready army to war with an impossible task: to defeat both Serbia and Russia in a month of fighting. It was a mission that would have pushed even the finest army to the breaking point, and it was simply beyond the capabilities of the Austro-Hungarian Army that actually existed in 1914. While it is proper to point out the responsibility of the Dual Monarchy's diplomats and politicians for creating the conditions that led to the Galician debacle, blame must fall primarily on the General Staff chief for the three-week catastrophe that destroyed Austria-Hungary as an independent great power.

There is palpable irony in this, as the Dual Monarchy went to war in the summer of 1914 to shore up its flagging status as a great power. Six weeks after that declaration, Vienna found its field army destroyed, Serbia far from cowed, with the Russians occupying most of Galicia while threatening Cracow and even Hungary. Perhaps most painfully, the Habsburg military, shattered in Galicia, was increasingly dependent on Germany for its survival. The purely military causes of this disaster can be summarized—and were, by Gen. Alfred Krauss, Conrad's old nemesis, after the war. Chronic underfunding had created an army that was adequate for internal security and war against minor powers, but far from prepared to take on Russia. While he did not spare politicians in Budapest their share of the blame for their "suicidal" antics in the Hungarian parliament that made adequate funding before 1914 an impossibility, he was just as withering in his critique of the General

Staff chief. Krauss considered Conrad to be a fine line infantry officer, yet anything but a competent strategist; he was really "in his element" at the battalion level of command and "saw everything as tactics," and could not grasp strategy in any systematic fashion. Worse, Conrad paid little attention to logistics, leading to supply problems of vast proportions in 1914, while the General Staff chief was content to view the war on maps at AOK, not how it actually was. Unavoidably, such weaknesses—above all the lack of modern artillery—led to Austria-Hungary's regiments being blasted apart by the Russians in Galicia, causing the loss of all the army's best troops at the outset. Creating a new army schooled in modern tactics while holding off the Russian steamroller was a supremely difficult task that cost countless lives, Krauss explained.[44]

In fairness to Conrad, his tactical reforms before 1914 had made the Habsburg military more ready for war than when he became General Staff chief in 1906. His emphasis on morale and combat motivation, which were of a piece with European trends of the period, no doubt helped Austro-Hungarian forces achieve some noteworthy victories at the outset of the war. It is a telling fact that, whenever fresh divisions encountered the Russians on something like equal terms, as at Kraśnik and Komarów, Habsburg forces prevailed in battle. The courage of Austro-Hungarian troops at the beginning of the Great War shocked the enemy and their own generals in equal measure. Yet Conrad, a military man, could not overcome Hungarian obstructionism and the dysfunctional nature of Viennese politics, so his army went to war with too few divisions and far too little modern artillery, with deadly consequences. Of this basic reality, Conrad took grossly inadequate account. Bravery and ardor in battle, combined with modern weapons, might have defeated the Russians in 1914 in detail, but the famous Habsburg *Hurrátaktik* by itself led to tens of thousands of needless deaths in Galicia and ultimately the undermining of the Dual Monarchy itself.

In 1931, Churchill provided a fitting epitaph for the prewar *k.u.k.* *Armee*, that remarkable multinational institution that Conrad sent to its doom in Galicia:

> This mutilation of the Austro-Hungarian Army in the terrible battle of two nations called Lemberg ranks with the turn at the Marne as the most important and irrevocable result of the war in 1914. It is the supreme condemnation of Conrad's narrow military creed, tense, sincere, lion-hearted as it was. His finest qualities were the cause of his country's undoing. Of all the campaigns that were ever fought the Austro-Hungarian campaign in Galicia required most of all the use of Time. Of all the armies that have ever existed since Hannibal marched into Italy, the Austro-Hungarian Army needed the most careful handling. Conrad broke their hearts and used them up in three weeks.[45]

The Austro-Hungarian Army, the ultimate bulwark of the Habsburg dynasty, was indeed destroyed in Galicia in the summer of 1914. What replaced it was a war-raised force, essentially a militia, led by inadequately trained junior officers. With the collapse of traditional discipline that Boroević so castigated, it would not be long before the national animosities, which the prewar army effectively kept in check, reemerged to undermine the war effort and the cohesion of the Dual Monarchy itself. Indeed, this war-raised and battle-scarred army was barely recognizable to the career officers and NCOs who managed to survive the Galician catastrophe. A young officer cadet, pressed into service to make good the losses of that summer, was bluntly informed by an old sergeant in his battery, "on the first of August 1914, the real army disappeared."[46]

10 Aftermaths

Defeat in Galicia represented the end of Austria-Hungary's prewar standing army, but it was only the beginning of a vast conflict that would last over four more years, culminating in the dissolution of the Habsburg realm and its military. By early October 1914, Conrad's new defensive positions in western Galicia, up against the Carpathians, had attained some strength. The situation was bolstered by good intelligence plus a few German divisions and helped by the fact that the Russians too had sustained serious losses of men and materiel and had difficulty restarting their offensive. This had something to do with Przemyśl, which the Russian Third Army was charged with investing. Expectations were that conquest would be quick. As Brusilov explained, "after such a succession of defeats and heavy losses, the Austrian Army was so demoralized and Przemyśl so little prepared to stand a siege (for its garrison, composed of beaten troops, was far from steady), that I was absolutely convinced that by the middle of October the place could have been taken by assault without any serious artillery preparation."[1]

Although Przemyśl's defenses were not particularly formidable—Redl had given the Russians the detailed plans to the fortress in any event—and its garrison indeed was demoralized, it was a fortress all the same, and uninspired Russian tactics meant that the siege lasted far longer than either side expected. The garrison left behind during the great retreat in mid-September came to 131,000 men under Gen. Hermann von Kusmanek, but aside from the Twenty-third *Honvéd*

Division most of the troops were *Landsturm*, including forty labor battalions that were far from ready for battle, much less a protracted siege. Morale was low inside the fortress from the start, with ethnic resentments much in evidence, particularly among third-line Habsburg troops. Without relief, Przemyśl stood little chance of holding out under sustained Russian pressure.[2]

Throughout the autumn, the Polish lands witnessed extensive combat, and the Germans succeeded in pushing the Russians into central Poland, safely away from the Silesian industrial heartland. Seesaw fighting raged across central Galicia throughout the autumn, including offensives and counteroffensives by both sides, with the siege of Przemyśl being briefly lifted by Boroević's Third Army, causing a temporary Russian withdrawal. However, by the end of 1914, the Galician front was pretty much where it had been in late September: close to Cracow, with Habsburg forces defending the vital Carpathian mountain passes, the gates to Hungary, while Przemyśl was besieged over a hundred kilometers behind Russian lines.

The war against Serbia had gone no better. Despite the success in early September defeating the Serbian offensive into Austria-Hungary, Potiorek proved incapable of bringing "Dog Serbia" to heel. Elated by defensive success in Syrmia, he ordered the Fifth and Sixth Armies to launch major attacks into Serbia.[3] While the Sixth Army, in particular, made progress into hilly central Serbia, the Fifth Army again stalled across the Drina in the face of stiff enemy resistance. Trench warfare set in that taxed the morale and staying powers of both armies, and by the end of September, Potiorek's second invasion of Serbia had run its course without knocking the Serbs out of the war.[4]

His next effort, launched in mid-November, initially pushed the tired Serbs back toward Belgrade, which was occupied by Habsburg troops, and victory at last seemed within Potiorek's grasp. Yet *Vojvoda* Putnik cut short any celebrations in Sarajevo with a sharp counteroffensive on the Kolubara River in early December. Fighting was intense, and both sides showed impressive tenacity, but Austro-Hungarian troops began to give way. They abandoned Belgrade on December 15 in defeat, leaving behind vast quantities of equipment and tens of thousands of prisoners. The sting of a third major defeat inside five months at the hands of a Balkan peasant kingdom was too much for many Habsburg patriots to bear, and even Potiorek's excellent court connections could not save him now. He was relieved on December 22, along with the Fifth Army commander von Frank; his career ended in disgrace. Deeply depressed, Potiorek retired into obscurity.

Potiorek's failed campaigns against Serbia cost Austria-Hungary a staggering total of 273,000 soldiers, including 30,000 killed and over 70,000 prisoners in Serbian hands. Belgrade's losses of 132,000 men, including 22,000 dead and 19,000 captured, were crippling, and Serbia's military was exhausted at the end of 1914, rendered incapable of any offensive action.[5] But there was no mistaking that Vienna had signally failed to crush Serbia. Tough talk in the summer had been shown to be just that, no more. Franz Ferdinand had not been avenged, with the Dual Monarchy losing twice as many men as the Serbs had. The blow to Habsburg prestige was incalculable.

Yet even Potiorek's terrible losses represented only a fraction of the casualties the Austro-Hungarian Army incurred by the end of 1914. In all, the army lost 1,269,000 soldiers to all causes in little more than four months of fighting in 1914; some 995,000 of those casualties had been incurred against Russia. The butcher's bill included 155,000 dead (representing more than 12 percent of the army), 480,000 wounded, 285,000 seriously ill, and 348,000 missing, some of whom were actually dead. The army lost an average of over eight thousand men every day during the 1914 campaigns.[6] Of the 50,000 active and reserve officers mobilized in August 1914, 22,000 had become casualties by the end of the year; the loss rate among junior officers in the infantry exceeded 80 percent. Even though the Eastern Front had received 1,340,000 fresh soldiers as replacements by the end of December, at the turn of the year the average strength of infantry divisions battling the Russians was only 5,000 riflemen, equivalent to a strong regiment.[7]

The beginnings of ethnic problems were already visible by late September. High Command warnings about the questionable reliability of Czech troops grew louder, amidst reports that some regiments were not fighting as hard as they should; the all-Czech Thirty-sixth Regiment, which had some prewar problems with nationalism in the ranks, was frequently cited. The hard-luck Twenty-first *Landwehr* Division also continued to be a source of concern to *Armeeoberkommando* (Army High Command, or AOK). Committed to Potiorek's second invasion of Serbia, the division quickly became bogged down on the Parašnica peninsula, a narrow finger at the confluence of the Sava and Drina Rivers. The division was repeatedly ordered to execute futile frontal assaults on Serbian trenches cutting across the peninsula, which was little more than a kilometer wide. Maneuver was impossible, and thousands of *Landwehr* troops fell in the hopeless attacks, and the division's morale plummeted. On September 23, a replacement battalion of the division's Eighth *Landwehr* Regiment departed Prague carrying Czech national flags and signs stating, "shipment of Czech meat to Serbia." An investigation determined that the problem revolved around having too many troops—the double-strength battalion had 2,500 recruits—supervised by too few officers, only four regulars to be precise, while most of the reserve officers were German. The departure of replacements for Prague's Twenty-eighth Regiment, headed to Galicia, included identical scenes of overt Czech nationalism amid barely concealed antiwar and anti-Habsburg sentiments. Rather than deal with these issues, the High Command determined that the solution was more discipline and greater supervision of its Czech troops.[8]

AOK's hunt for subversives spread, and by the end of 1914, over seven hundred Czechs, mostly civilians, had been remanded to military courts to face political charges, while the army shut down forty-six newspapers and thirty-two private clubs in Bohemia and Moravia that were judged by the military to hold subversive or antiwar views. While there were Russophiles in certain segments of Bohemian society, principally among intellectuals, their numbers were not large. The army inserted itself deeply into Czech society in its effort to raise morale and stamp out dissent, including supervision of schoolbooks and curricula.[9] The impact of such measures on Czech morale can be easily imagined. In Bohemia, what remained of the patriotic euphoria of August 1914 that was not quashed by the debacle in Galicia was undone by the military's heavy hand in dealing with civilian views it did not approve of. While Czechs got special attention from AOK, other ethnic groups were also viewed suspiciously after the defeat in Galicia. Italians in uniform judged by the army to be potentially unreliable were taken out of combat units and collected in unarmed labor battalions, as were Serbs, particularly if they came from regions close to the Serbian border, where enemy propaganda was judged to have had a cancerous impact.[10]

In effect, Austria-Hungary created an entire second army after the Galician defeat, because the prewar army was gone. It had to learn how to fight while fighting. Its junior officers, the men who bore the brunt of war at the company level, received just six weeks' training and were expected to show a good example to the men by dying bravely. In a fateful decision, the army maintained its one-year volunteer system, albeit at an accelerated pace, rather than commissioning battle-proven NCOs from the ranks, as many armies would do during the Great War, as class barriers fell due to unprecedented casualties. The officer's sash and saber remained limited to the educated classes, becoming a source of resentment in the ranks, where even the highest valor decorations did not make a soldier worthy of a commission. (A very rare exception was Sergeant Josef Kiss, a celebrity pilot and the highest-scoring Hungarian ace, who was commissioned a reserve lieutenant in 1918—posthumously.) Moreover, this had a particularly negative impact in the Habsburg Army, where the better educated rarely spoke the languages of the peasantry who made up the bulk of the infantry. Communication problems coupled with class resentment was no recipe for cohesion under fire.[11]

Conrad was not relieved at the end of 1914, like Potiorek, in part because there was no obvious replacement (though the firing of lesser generals continued, a total of four army commanders, eight corps commanders, and twenty division or brigade commanders by the war's first Christmas). Nevertheless, the General Staff chief was eager to avoid more bad headlines, which at the beginning of 1915 meant that Przemyśl, which had become a rallying cry across Austria-Hungary, must not fall to the Russians. To prevent such, that winter Conrad launched three major offensives, between late January and late March, to lift the siege.[12] This horror, little understood beyond specialist historians yet known to Austro-Hungarian troops as the *Karpathenwinter*, must rank among the cruelest follies of the Great War. Despite good intelligence indicating the Russians were tired and overstretched, the offensives rapidly devolved into disaster. It was impossible for the troops to make headway in the frozen mountain passes, particularly without adequate artillery support, while the infantry, lacking proper winter gear, succumbed in the hundreds of thousands to frostbite and disease. Even Boroević and his Third Army could make little progress, so severe were the conditions. In the end it made no difference, and the starving garrison of Przemyśl surrendered on March 22, 1915, with nine generals, 2,300 officers, and 110,000 men entering Russian captivity. Conrad's winter offensives to lift the siege cost the Dual Monarchy as many as 800,000 troops: in the chaos, as whole battalions disappeared in the snow, the army lost effective count of its losses.[13] The best that could be said of this unprecedented disaster is that the Russians lost nearly as many men in the appalling Carpathian battles.

How the army stayed in the war at all under such horrifying stresses must be considered. In the first place, Austro-Hungarian infantry was largely comprised of peasants, tough and uncomplaining, most of whom were willing to do their duty, particularly if offered marginally competent leadership. Most were men of simple faith who were willing to keep fighting unto the end, confident in their salvation by serving in a just cause, though the frozen horrors of the Carpathians pushed many soldiers past their breaking point. Intelligence mattered too, however, and the role of SIGINT in particular must be acknowledged.

Pokorny's successes against Russian ciphers continued, and by 1915 Austria-Hungary had the most impressive code-breaking effort of any belligerent. It was so effective that intelligence was a rare area where the Prussians sought to learn from Habsburg forces. It was kept strictly confidential during the war, but SIGINT proved a major force-multiplier for Conrad and AOK, who often had foreknowledge of Russian moves in Galicia. Edmund Glaise-Horstenau, the wartime General Staff officer who oversaw the writing of Vienna's Official History in the 1930s, admitted that, without code-breaking, Austria-Hungary would have lost the war during that first terrible winter. Not for nothing did Max Ronge, the last chief of intelligence for the *k.u.k. Armee*, term his service's wartime SIGINT effort "the great secret of the Imperial-and-Royal Army."[14]

All the same, it was in the Carpathians in the winter of 1915 where the army's touchy intertwined issues of ethnicity and reliability came to the fore. In the frozen mountains, troops were captured by the thousands, often after being wounded (one of the many was Josip Broz—known in the next war as Tito—a decorated NCO with Zagreb's Twenty-fifth *Domobran* Regiment, captured after being badly wounded). But in some cases *en masse*, even by the battalion. AOK believed that some of this conduct amounted to disloyalty, perhaps treason, and could be attributed to the unwillingness of Slavic troops, Czechs especially, to do their duty. By the spring of 1915, there was superficial evidence to make this case, as many generals were eager to do. Advocates honed in on the collapse of Prague's Twenty-eighth Regiment at the beginning of April at the Dukla Pass, where most of two battalions, some eighteen hundred men, wound up in Russian captivity. This came only a week after a similar Carpathian mishap in the Czech Thirty-sixth Regiment, a unit with a bad reputation for indiscipline at AOK, whereby two battalions were lost, 1,543 men and 31 officers, most of them captured.[15] Some accounts of the Twenty-eighth Regiment's ignominy, which were soon the rage in Prague café circles, claimed that the Czechs went over to their "brother Slavs," bands playing and flags waving: Czech nationalists and Habsburg generals told a remarkably similar tale, albeit with different motivations. The scandal that followed led to the disbanding of the ancient regiment, to save the army's honor.

The reality was less dramatic. The Twenty-eighth Regiment, which had performed well in Galicia in 1914, found itself caught up in the Carpathian horrors the following winter. On the eve of the Dukla Pass battle, it received a considerable draft of reinforcements, who had received only five weeks of training, and many of the men did not even know how to fire their rifles. Worse, these urbanites had been treated like peasants by the army, which had relocated them to a "safe" garrison in Hungary, away from the nationalist temptations of Prague, which led to regular brawls with locals. Morale was low before the replacements got near the front, and there were far too few trained officers on hand to restore discipline. When thrown into the frozen hell at Dukla, many men simply gave up. While it is impossible to rule out nationalism as a cause, it is clear that the scared, unready replacements wanted out of the war more than anything else.[16] Moreover, collapses and mass surrenders by non-Slavic units, which happened in the Carpathians, never raised questions among officers about the loyalty of those ethnic groups. The poisoned political debate about Czech troops, which burst into the media, only worsened the already parlous relations between Slavs and Germans in the Dual Monarchy.[17]

The Carpathian disaster exposed numerous weaknesses in the army, not least that many soldiers did not understand what their officers were saying. The peacetime "regimental language" system, which ensured that officers could communicate with the rank-and-file in their own languages, broke down during wartime. Newly commissioned officers, drawn largely from towns and cities, spoke few "minority" languages and had no time to learn them even if they wanted to. The case of the Seventeenth Division, which fought through the *Karpathenwinter*, losing over ten thousand men in Conrad's futile offensives, is illustrative. Although this Transylvanian division included a high percentage of Romanians, practically no officers could speak their language. Nobody in the Seventeenth Division's senior leadership did, including none of the four infantry regimental commanders, while less than one-quarter of the division's battalion commanders were functional in Romanian. In some units, not a single officer could speak to the men, while most of the newly commissioned lieutenants were urban Magyars with no inclination to learn Romanian, a despised "peasant tongue." The divisional command reported ominously about "chauvinist-nationalist and other pernicious influences" among junior officers, which was *k.u.k.* code-speak for subalterns looking down on the men; the ethnic disputes that so polarized the Dual Monarchy had been mobilized into the army—and among no groups were the divisions sharper than those between Magyars and Romanians, whose mutual hatreds ran deep. Perhaps surprisingly, the Seventeenth Division's desertion rate was no higher than average, which can perhaps be attributed to the fact that, however much Romanians loathed Magyars, neither did they have any love for Russians.[18]

While the troops froze in the Carpathians, Conrad was entertaining Gina at Teschen in Silesia, safely behind the front, where the High Command had established more permanent, and far more comfortable, surroundings than they had enjoyed in Galicia. The General Staff chief was lovesick without her, and he practically begged her to visit him, which she did in January. Senior officers had "comfortable villas" at Teschen where mistresses were entertained discreetly, and the top general was no exception. Conrad had lost touch with the troops, and possibly with reality altogether. Some AOK staffers moved their wives to Teschen, where the daily schedule was far from arduous, between tennis and parties, and social life continued as if the war barely existed. Gina made regular visits until the summer of 1915, at which point she was living with her paramour effectively full-time, while the couple's active social calendar was the subject of much gossip in Vienna and Berlin, none of it flattering to Conrad. He seemed not to care, however, and Gina took up a great deal of his time and energy. Although he had not won any war, Gina eventually agreed to separate herself from her husband. Conrad's dream came true in October 1915, when, against the advice of his children, he married his longtime mistress, who had become a Protestant through her adoption by a Hungarian general who offered to discreetly facilitate Conrad's remarriage by dodging the Catholic Church–inspired marriage laws.[19]

More successful at love than war, Conrad had failed embarrassingly in the Carpathians, despite the contribution of a few Prussian divisions and a Prussian field army headquarters, a defeat that brought AOK's relations with the Germans to low ebb. The General Staff chief blamed the Prussians, the hated *Piefkes*, for the Galician disaster of the previous summer and made inadequate efforts to hide this view. In January 1915, he startled General Josef Stürgkh, the AOK liaison officer to Berlin, by asking, "Well, what are our secret enemies the Germans up to, and what is that comedian the Kaiser doing?"[20] This was more than dynastic puffery: Conrad understood that, in the wake of his failure in Galicia, the Dual Monarchy was deeply dependent on Germany's military and economic assistance to stay in the war, and Austria-Hungary had irrevocably lost its independence to Berlin. Misunderstandings abounded, with Habsburg officers viewing Prussian allies as overbearing and tactless, unable to understand the complexities of Austria-Hungary's multinational forces, while the Germans considered their partners to be soft, careless, riddled with *Schlamperei*, fundamentally unserious about the war.[21] Hence the famous wartime joke. In Berlin the situation was serious but not desperate, while in Vienna it was desperate but not serious.

Berlin had its resentments too, yet in the spring of 1915, with the Western Front now fully static, it assented to a major offensive in the East, with the purpose of staving off a complete Austro-Hungarian collapse, which appeared likely by April, as Conrad's forces bled to death in the Carpathians. Vienna's second, militia army, raised the previous autumn to replaced what was lost in Galicia, itself had been sacrificed. For the Germans, there was no choice, as the only thing more terrifying to Berlin than fighting the war with Austria-Hungary, its only real ally, was continuing without the Habsburgs. Thus resulted in the Gorlice-Tarnów offensive, launched at the beginning of May. Although Austria-Hungary's whole Eastern Front (*Ostfront*) participated, the spear point of the attack was the German Eleventh Army, equipped with modern artillery and schooled in the latest tactics: the Western Front was a hard school, particularly for gunnery. The Prussians, guided by Pokorny's SIGINT, blasted a hole in Russian defenses east of Cracow, and soon the enemy crumbled; the Russians were nearly as spent by the Carpathian campaign as the Austro-Hungarians were. The result was what became known as the Great Retreat, the Russian withdrawal along nearly the whole Eastern Front. By the time they stopped retreating in the late summer, the Russians had lost a million men as prisoners alone, and the front line stood deep in enemy territory. Przemyśl was recaptured in early June, and by the end of the month Lemberg was again under the Habsburg double eagle. Only a small slice of easternmost Galicia remained in Russian hands.

While this was fundamentally a Prussian triumph, there was nevertheless elation in Vienna and Teschen. Russia was not defeated, yet she was surely humbled, and the threat to Hungary had evaporated. For Conrad, however, this was not enough. He wanted to prove himself and his army as first-rate fighters, independently of the Prussians. This required a major push, grandly termed the *Schwarz-Gelbe Offensive* to honor the dynasty. By the time it commenced at the end of August, Conrad has assembled a third army, including hundreds of thousands of teenaged conscripts, to make good his enormous losses of over 2.5 million soldiers in a year. Despite continuing resistance from Budapest over manpower issues, as Hungary felt it had already supplied too many soldiers to the war effort, field units were again at full strength. New artillery was arriving, and shell reserves had increased, while infantry-artillery coordination had improved considerably. Conrad intended to punish the Russians and show Berlin that he and Vienna still mattered strategically, while avenging his humiliating defeat in Galicia the previous summer.

The offensive, launched in what is today western Ukraine and Belarus, on some of the same East Galician battlefields where Brudermann had been defeated exactly one year before, made some progress initially, but the Russians did not give ground easily, and the terrain, swampy and short of roads, made advancing slow. Conrad ignored Frederick the Great's warning that it is not enough to beat the Russians, you must beat them dead.[22] The tide turned when Brusilov launched a counter-offensive, and soon Habsburg forces began showing serious problems. As the Prussians had feared, Conrad's offensive bogged down, and his fragile army was choking under pressure. Just as in the Carpathians, companies, then battalions began surrendering without offering much resistance, and Habsburg generals seemed to have lost control of the situation. The troops were sand in their hands. It was apparent to AOK that something had gone dreadfully wrong, and the campaign, officially termed the Battle of Rowno, became known as Conrad's "autumn swin-ery" (*Herbstsau*) among cynical staff officers who saw that the army was simply incapable of generating sufficient combat power against the Rus-sians to win. In the end, the offensive did not significantly alter the front line. Yet by the time it sputtered out at the beginning of October, almost 231,000 Austro-Hungarian troops had been lost, including a shocking 109,000 listed as missing, of whom about a hundred thousand were in Russian captivity. In some divisions, well over half the casualties had "gone missing," including a shocking number of junior officers, and it was impossible to ignore that, per the High Command's self-fulfilling prophecy, many of the regiments with the highest rates of "missing" were Slavic, particularly Czech. In one particularly embarrassing incident, the heavily Czech Nineteenth Division, whose troops, many of them diffident replacements, had protested at being reinforced by Prussian troops with shouts of "Our blood is cheaper!" fell apart during a Rus-sian attack on September 10, losing 4,800 men and 67 officers, most of them taken prisoner without offering much of a fight.[23] The enemy captured so much Habsburg equipment that two Russian army corps were outfitted entirely with Austro-Hungarian weaponry.[24]

Conrad's dream of avenging his defeat in Galicia died with his "autumn swinery," alongside tens of thousands of his soldiers, and Berlin took the firm lesson that the Austro-Hungarians could not stand on their own against the Russians. AOK would not be permitted to execute independent operations of any size in the East. Henceforth, Prussian staff officers were injected into Habsburg headquarters on the Eastern Front to supply some much-needed rigor and discipline. To Conrad, this was an affront to pride, dynastic and personal, yet as the weaker partner in the alliance, he had no choice but to accept it. Besides, he now had other fronts to worry about, particularly the Italian, which opened up in late May 1915 with a "felonious" attack on Austria-Hungary's vulnerable rear by her faithless ally in Rome, just as Conrad had predicted. In an effort to gain "unredeemed Italy" (*Italia irredenta*) on the cheap, the Italian Army attacked Tyrol, while its major push came on the Isonzo River, at the mountainous edge of the Slovene lands. Luigi Cadorna, the Italian generalissimo, believed he could reach Ljubljana and perhaps even Vienna once he crossed the Isonzo and the mountains behind. But he was a callous incompetent who made Conrad look like Napoleon, and Cadorna's four major offensives on the Isonzo in 1915 made hardly any progress, at the cost of hundreds of thousands of casualties. Although Habsburg troops on the Isonzo were outnumbered and outgunned by the Italians, the enemy's tactical primitiveness helped, as did the fact that, everywhere along the front, the defenders held the critical high ground. Importantly, Austro-Hungarian forces on the Isonzo were commanded by Svetozar Boroević, whose toughness and acumen in defensive tactics made him an ideal choice. The gallant stand of his Fifth (later Isonzo) Army against the hated invader made him a national hero and celebrity, just as he craved.[25]

Additionally, the war against Italy was genuinely popular with the Austro-Hungarian public, which viewed the struggle against a faithless ally who attacked the Dual Monarchy in her hour of desperation as just and righteous. South Slavs in particular viewed this as their war, as they knew Italy craved their land, and even Serbs were perfectly willing to fight in Habsburg uniform against Italians. The army sent divisions with shaky reputations in the East to the Isonzo, where they performed creditably. Czechs too battled on the Italian front with gusto, and Prague's Twenty-eighth Regiment, which had failed so ignominiously in the Carpathians, redeemed itself on the Isonzo when its replacement battalion earned plaudits from Boroević.

Serbia finally got her comeuppance in October 1915, when her army, still weak from the previous autumn's fighting, was crushed by the combined forces of Germany, Austria-Hungary, and Bulgaria. *Vojvoda* Putnik never had a chance against such odds, but his army fought bravely until the year's end, when it was pushed out of Serbia into Albania to be rescued by sea by the Allies. Defeating and occupying the country that, in Habsburg eyes, caused the war, was satisfying, but the reality was, despite the considerable role played in the campaign by Hermann von Kövess's Third Army, the defeat of Serbia was principally a Prussian enterprise, under the command of FM August von Mackensen. The defeat of little Montenegro at the beginning of January 1916 by Austro-Hungarian troops under General Stjepan Sarkotić, without German assistance, was a sop to Habsburg pride.[26]

Conrad perennially sought to restore the tattered reputation of himself, the army, and the dynasty through success on the battlefield. Italy offered that chance. The Italians had always been Conrad's bugbear, while the Germans had little interest in that front, seeing it as a distraction from the real war, east and west. In the southern Tyrol, where he had once commanded a division and knew every mountain, Conrad envisioned his great victory. He planned a sharp strike out of the high mountains by crack Habsburg mountain divisions into the plains beyond. If it succeeded, the offensive—termed *Strafexpedition* (Punitive Expedition) by the Italophobe Conrad—might knock Italy out of the war altogether.

Yet it did not succeed. Launched in mid-May, behind schedule due to unusually late snowfalls in the Dolomites, the attack exhibited effective infantry-artillery coordination and pushed the Italians back with heavy losses, setting the Asiago plateau ablaze, but the high mountains made any advance difficult, even for specialist alpine troops. As usual, Conrad's plans exceeded the capabilities of his forces and took too little account of terrain and logistics. While the offensive was a tactical victory, in never became a strategic one. Most importantly, it had to be suspended in early June, short of a decisive win, when another disaster befell the Austro-Hungarian Army in Galicia.

June 4, 1916, was the beginning of what was subsequently termed the Brusilov Offensive, after its commander, while for the Habsburg Army it was the death knell of its war against Russia. Employing innovative tactics, particularly in artillery, Alexei Brusilov's Southwestern Front launched a major offensive, with the intent of taking pressure off France, which was bleeding out at Verdun. It succeeded beyond expectations, and within two weeks the Russians had inflicted a serious defeat on Austro-Hungarian forces. The Fourth Army, led by the incompetent playboy Archduke Joseph Ferdinand, buckled under Russian blows and essentially evaporated, losing 82,000 of its 110,000 infantry in six days, most as prisoners. Tens of thousands of Habsburg troops were captured, frequently by the battalion. In more than one Habsburg division, panicked artillerymen had abandoned their guns and left the doomed infantry to their fate. While AOK, as ever, sought to attribute this disaster to Slavic troops giving up too easily, the reality was that Habsburg regiments of all nationalities failed to resist the Russian offensive with adequate fervor. Units considered thoroughly reliable— Croats, Magyars, even Germans—had fallen apart too. This represented a systemic failure of an extraordinary kind.[27]

Intelligence had given the generals multiple warnings of an impending Russian attack, but these were ignored. The prevailing view at AOK was that the Russians had been so thoroughly defeated the previous year that any offensive could be stopped without great difficulty. Defensive positions in East Galicia, including extensive trench networks, were deemed sturdy by commanders, who assessed them capable of withstanding heavy enemy blows. Moreover, the army believed that after the embarrassing failures of the previous year on the Eastern Front, it had solved much of its ethnic problem by moving the training depots of suspect regiments to "safe" areas, far from home. Moreover, the troops were regularly indoctrinated by commanders and chaplains in their duty to emperor and God, and command assessments of even Czech units in Galicia in the spring of 1916 were mostly positive; few reports to the High Command indicated problems lurking, rather the contrary.

The Germans, however, were less confident in their ally's battle-worthiness. They had their concerns about Czech troops especially, but Prussian officers were more disturbed by the slack nature of the whole Habsburg military, which even two years into the war had yet to shed peacetime habits. A trenchant critique was offered by Col. Hans von Seeckt, a Prussian staff officer (and future architect of the *Reichswehr*) who served in the East long enough to get a clear impression of Austro-Hungarian ways of war.[28] The soldiery was mostly "excellent," he observed, tough peasants, "physically strong and humble, as well as accustomed to work and subordination." Training, however, was "poorly organized" and inadequate to the needs of the front. The problem was the officer corps: most of the war-commissioned junior officers were "unsuitable for a military career," and even the regulars were "clumsy" and "too schematic," prone to sluggish, by-the-book solutions to battlefield problems. Energy was lacking, while *Schlamperei* abounded, and army maintenance, supply, and administration all needed work: again, officers, not men, were to blame. While probably no army but his own would have met Seeckt's Prussian high standards, it is painfully clear that his assessment, which echoed those of many Austro-Hungarian senior officers, particularly Boroević, was accurate about the deep-seated problems of the Habsburg military.

These were exposed, harshly, by Brusilov's grand offensive. By the time the fighting wound down in mid-September, Russia's losses were vast as well, thanks to the usual cycle of offensives and counteroffensives, but Austria-Hungary's *Ostfront* had been shattered for good.

Losses came to three-quarters of a million men, half of them taken prisoner. The self-confidence of the army, at least when fighting Russians, was broken, never to recover. German assessments of what had gone wrong elaborated a tale of woe that centered on poor leadership and outdated tactics; significantly, they did not cite morale problems or Slav defeatism as causes. Henceforth, Prussian staff officers would be inserted throughout Habsburg commands in the East, to ensure a modicum of competence, and Prussian officers and even NCOs were introduced into Austro-Hungarian tactical units to provide know-how and determination, while shaky Habsburg regiments on the Eastern Front saw themselves brigaded with German ones, acting as stiffeners. A modest illusion of Habsburg independence was preserved, with Austro-Hungarian generals leading their own corps and field armies, but it was fiction, as they had Prussian staff officers at their side, while all the major commands were in Berlin's hands. Conrad's Galician debacle in the summer of 1914 ended his country's status as an independent great power, but by September 1916, after the third Habsburg summertime defeat in Galicia in three years, the Dual Monarchy was reduced to Germany's satellite. For the rest of the war, Austria-Hungary would be wholly dependent on Prussian leadership, military assistance, and increasingly weaponry and even food, to survive.

This was a blow from which Conrad's reputation, in Vienna or Berlin, could not recover. He had lasted as General Staff chief for so long for want of a plausible alternative, but that changed with the death of Emperor Franz Joseph on November 21, 1916, at the age of eighty-six. For years, he had left military matters to professionals, but his young successor, Karl, had different ideas. Only twenty-nine when he acceded the throne, Karl did not have much military background, having served as a subaltern with the cavalry, but this did not deter him from possessing strongly held views on military matters. A devout Catholic, Karl hated the war and desperately wanted to extricate his kingdom from it, seeming not to understand that Austria-Hungary was now so intertwined with Germany that abandoning the war unilaterally was functionally impossible. Karl infuriated conservatives with his liberal policies, including letting political prisoners free, some of whom began agitation against the Dual Monarchy with Allied help, while his humanitarian meddling in military affairs, including ordering an end to field punishments and forbidding the use of poison gas without his permission, infuriated the generals, none more than Conrad. Karl had wanted to replace him for some time, seeing the hotheaded Conrad as a failure as well as an obstacle to his peace plans, while viewing his personal life with distaste. Once the new emperor took command of the war effort himself, pushing aside Archduke Friedrich, there was no reason for Conrad to remain on duty, although he was made a field marshal for services rendered.

He requested retirement, which Karl refused, and effective March 1, 1917, Conrad was appointed commander of an army group in his beloved Tyrol. But his role was much reduced, his place as General Staff chief taken by Arthur Arz von Straussenburg, a Transylvanian German who was more pliant to the young emperor's wishes. Not a strong personality like his predecessor, Arz served as a military advisor to Karl, the commander-in-chief, and was willing to back the emperor's strategies, which aimed at ending the war, with or without German approval. Karl's first year on the throne brought good news, namely the collapse of Russia into revolt and revolution, which ended the Eastern Front victoriously for the Central Powers, but the underlying weakness of the Dual Monarchy contradicted the outward appearance of strength. The army was running out of men, while, as in Germany, the Allied blockade was strangling the war economy and bringing famine to the civilian population. The purely military situation appeared formidable. The Balkan Front was quiet at last, and 1917 ended with the epic victory at Caporetto, the great joint offensive with Germany that shattered the Italian Army, almost knocking Italy out of the war; it was an even bigger triumph than what Brusilov had achieved in Galicia. But Italy did stay in the war, thanks to help from Britain and France, and 1918 would bring disaster to the Dual Monarchy.

The year began with strikes across the Dual Monarchy caused by massive civilian discontent over hunger and inflation. Thanks to Hungarian obstructionism, Austria's cities were starving, while the entire economy was creaking to a halt from a shortage of raw materials and the collapse of the transportation system.[29] Troops were employed in the cities to restore order, and a military dictatorship was considered, but even some army bases were briefly in revolt, in sympathy with the civilian protestors. Karl continued to seek avenues to end the war, including secret discussions of a separate peace with the Allies, which were conducted through his wife's family. Unfortunately for him, the Germans learned of this parley, which they viewed as treachery, and to atone for his disloyalty, Karl promised his allies an offensive against Italy, to support Berlin's last attempt to win the war in the West that spring. The army was unready for any offensive, as the troops were starving and short of shells and supplies, and the outcome of the attack, launched on the Piave River in mid-June, was a foregone conclusion. It accomplished nothing save the destruction of the last Austro-Hungarian field army. Conrad was finally sent into retirement, a broken man, while Arz, the General Staff chief, bluntly informed the Germans that Austria-Hungary needed to leave the war imminently, since by the end of the year, the troops would be needed to restore order on the home front, which was spiraling into chaos.

They would not have that long to wait. In late September, the Balkan front began to collapse when an Allied offensive, led by Serbian troops, broke through Bulgarian defenses and exposed the Dual Monarchy's defenseless southern flank. Neither Vienna nor Berlin had forces to plug the gap, and the Central Powers began their retreat toward Central Europe. By the end of October, Germany was pulling back in the West, while the long-awaited Italian "victory offensive" was finally launched to avenge Caporetto. The Austro-Hungarian Army gradually collapsed before it. Emperor Karl, continuing his well-intended yet inept ways to the end, issued a manifesto in mid-October, granting self-determination to Austria's peoples. It was too little and too late to satisfy nationalists who were already looking beyond the Habsburgs, yet it did produce deep confusion in the military, not to mention in Hungary, which was not included in the manifesto. Budapest, seeing the Allies advancing up the Balkans straight toward Hungary, recalled its troops fighting in Italy, thereby unraveling Habsburg defenses on the Italian front.

It made little difference in the end, as Germany's imminent defeat was bringing Austria-Hungary down with it, which Karl could not comprehend until it was too late. Here his willful escapism exceeded even Conrad's. The dependency on Berlin created by the defeat in Galicia in the summer of 1914, and cemented by Conrad's subsequent disasters in the East, meant that the fate of Germany unavoidably would be shared with the Habsburg realm too. Prussian generals had griped throughout the war about their weak-willed ally, complaining about being "shackled to a corpse," but in the end the reverse turned out to be true.

The collapse of the Habsburg military was neither sudden nor total, and into early November there was a considerable body of troops under Boroević in Italy, hardened combat veterans who were willing to keep fighting under "our Sveto." Now a field marshal, he remained deeply loyal to the dynasty, and he repeatedly cabled Vienna asking for orders to march on the imperial capital, to restore order and secure the Habsburg patrimony. But Karl, never strong-willed, lacked the stomach for a fight to keep his throne, and never responded. No Radetzky, Boroević was unwilling to disobey his emperor to save him, and after a few days without any response from Vienna the old soldier told the troops to go home.

Boroević himself had no home to go to. Denied entry into the newly proclaimed Yugoslavia, as Belgrade considered him a traitor for serving the Habsburgs—they turned down his offer to help fight against the Italians, who after the armistice were occupying South Slav land—he settled in Carinthia, living in a tiny cottage. He was a broken man, depressed over the loss of everything he valued, including the death of his son, an only child and a teenaged army cadet, in a freak accident in the war's last month. Vienna denied Boroević's pension request, since he had been living in Croatia, not Austria, at the war's outbreak, and he lived in penury off the charity of fellow officers. He died in May 1920 after suffering a stroke.

Karl purchased his most loyal field marshal an impressive tomb in Vienna's main cemetery, but he did not long outlive Boroević. After having Hermann von Kövess sign the armistice document proffered by the Allies, to spare any Habsburg the dishonor, on November 11, 1918, Karl issued a not-quite-abdication document and promptly went into exile. He devoted his energies to a restoration, including two attempts in Hungary that fell short of causing a likely civil war, dying of pneumonia on Madeira in May 1922, before his thirty-fifth birthday. He was unpopular with many generals, who considered him a naïve dilettante, whose bumbling helped along defeat, but the Catholic Church felt differently, beatifying him in 2004 for his efforts on behalf of peace.

Conrad did not mourn his emperor's passing. After the war, with Gina by his side, he devoted himself to writing his memoirs, which appeared in five volumes between 1921 and 1925, selling well.[30] An apology for his service, Conrad blamed myriad others—the Prussians and Hungarian politicians, preeminently—for the disasters incurred by the *k.u.k. Armee* under his leadership, taking no responsibility himself. He portrayed himself as the Austro-Hungarian Cassandra who had warned vividly of the doom ahead that might have been avoided by the military action he had repeatedly counseled before 1914. While Conrad had his detractors, most veterans considered him a heroic figure who had tried to avert the Habsburg collapse that tore apart Central Europe after 1918. This became the consensus view in the Austrian military and held sway for a half-century among most Austrian historians.

It helped that Conrad was not tarred with National Socialism since, despite having some German nationalist views that became evident after 1918, including a tendency, like many former generals, to place blame on "traitorous Slavs" rather than his own incompetence, he died long before the Anschluss. An increasingly unwell man, Conrad succumbed while taking the cure in southern Germany in August 1925. His Viennese funeral drew 100,000 mourners as well as much praise for his alleged military accomplishments. His reputation was not significantly tarred by Gina's subsequent publication of a slightly tawdry memoir that illuminated just how lovesick the general had been.[31] After the Second World War and Allied occupation, Austria's re-created military needed heroes untainted by Hitler, and Conrad nicely fit the bill. Thus did the Conradian cult, whose portrayal of the field marshal avoided the painful realities of his leadership, remain in effect in Vienna until the 1960s, when a younger generation of historians began to ask questions about the genuine nature of Conrad's long tenure as chief of the General Staff.

The most telling epitaph for Conrad's generalship is that more than a million Habsburg soldiers died under his command. Of the eight million troops who wore Austro-Hungarian uniform during the Great War, the men experienced the hopeless struggle that Conrad predicted at the very outset: some 90 percent became casualties of some kind, the highest loss rate of any major belligerent. Tragically, the hundred thousand Habsburg troops killed in Galicia in the first three weeks of the war represented barely a tenth of those who would make the ultimate sacrifice for the doomed Dual Monarchy in the Habsburgs' last war.

Death was not equally distributed, however, and the safest place to serve in the Habsburg Army during the war was on the General Staff. The officers whose flawed planning did so much to undermine the war from the outset seldom paid the price for their mistakes with their lives, as so many frontline soldiers did. In the War College's class of 1898, which graduated ninety-nine officers, only five were killed in action, four of those in 1914. Only thirty-six "bottle-green boys" fell in the entire war.[32]

Col. Alexander von Brosch's body was found in a shallow grave near Hujcze in the summer of 1915, after the Russian Great Retreat, and he and the *Kaiserjäger* who died with him were given a proper burial. Before his departure for the front a year before, he had written emotionally in what might be considered a prophecy for himself, his army, and his country:

> This is the end for me. Our fate approaches with brutal inevitability. The enormous dance that will annihilate us all is coming ever closer and even super-human powers will not suffice to stop it.[33]

Gavrilo Princip achieved his dream of evicting the Habsburgs from Bosnia and creating Yugoslavia on Serbia's terms, though he did not live to see it. Convicted of murder, he had been less than a month shy of his twentieth birthday when he killed Franz Ferdinand and Sophie; thus he was not eligible for the death penalty under lenient Austrian laws that forbade the execution of teenagers. Instead, he was sent to a military prison in Bohemia, where he gradually succumbed to tuberculosis, dying only a few months before the end of the war, and of Austria-Hungary. The War Ministry in Vienna received a terse message: "Commander, Military Prison, Theresienstadt, reports that Gavrilo Princip, Sarajevo assassin, died on 28 April at 6:30 p.m."[34]

NOTES

INTRODUCTION

1. Herwig, *The Marne, 1914*; Showalter, *Tannenberg: Clash of Empires*.
2. Churchill, *The Unknown War*.
3. Boterbloem, *"Chto delat'?*, 408. There is growing popular interest in Russia, however: Christian Neef, "Russia Revisits Pivotal Role in World War I," *Der Spiegel*, January 13, 2014.
4. Lein, *Pflichterfüllung oder Hochverrat?*
5. For instance Uyar, "Ottoman Arab Officers."
6. When asked in 1940 about a fellow wartime officer, Jan Masaryk replied, "I served with him in the old army. . . . Those were good times." About the defunct empire's legacy and the peoples of Central Europe, he responded, "it was far better than anything they've had since." *The Tablet* (London), September 12, 1951, 12.
7. Kranjc, "The Neglected War."
8. For instance, Ferrell, *Collapse at Meuse-Argonne*.
9. For a balanced assessment, see Broucek, "Österreichische Militärgeschichtsschreibung."
10. Tunstall, "The Habsburg Command Conspiracy."
11. *Österreich-Ungarns letzter Krieg* (Austria-Hungary's Last War): Glaise-Horstenau became a general in Hitler's Wehrmacht and committed suicide in 1946 while in Allied detention.
12. There is but one English-language biography, which is academic, revisionist, and scathing: Sondhaus, *Franz Conrad von Hötzendorf*.
13. Broucek and Peball, "Strömungen und Ziele seit 1945."
14. These are *Lemberg 1914* and *1914: Die militärische Probleme unseres Kriegsbeginnes*.
15. Drummond and Lubecki, "Reconstructing Galicia." It should be noted that narratives of Galicia's once large Jewish minority are now entirely historical due to that community's almost total annihilation under German auspices during the Second World War.

16. In the United States, the leading scholarly proponent of the Habsburg countermyth has been the Hungarian émigré István Deák, while the standard bearer of portrayals of the Habsburgs and their military as malevolent fools is Geoffrey Wawro.

17. As one regiment noted frankly of its 1914 ordeal, "there is no unit diary before October 8th": *Feuerbereit!*, 16.

18. Bator, *Wojna galicyjska*, 311.

1. AEIOU

1. Jobst, *Führer durch die k.u.k. Theresianische Militärakademie*, 5–9.

2. See Wheatcroft, *The Habsburgs*. The "Habsburg myth" was defined by the Triestine literary scholar Claudio Magris in his groundbreaking 1963 work *Il mito asburgico: Umanità e stile del mondo austroungarico nella letteratura austriaca moderna*.

3. Deák, *Lawful Revolution*.

4. Höbelt, *Franz Joseph I*, 43–62.

5. Deák, *From Habsburg Neo-Absolutism*.

6. Tihany, "Austro-Hungarian Compromise."

7. Marácz, "Multilingualism," 275–84.

8. On the political mechanics, Gerő, *Hungarian Parliament*.

9. *Hof-und Staatshandbuch der Österreichisch-Ungarischen Monarchie für das Jahr 1915*, 361.

10. Judson, *Guardians of the Nation*.

11. Austroslavism's unfulfilled possibilities are explored in this collection: Moritsch, *Austroslavismus*.

12. Svoboda, "Political struggles."

13. Popovici, *Die Vereinigten Staaten*.

14. Kronenbitter, "Haus ohne Macht?," 169–70, 208.

15. Jeřábek, *Potiorek*, 52.

16. Frank, *Oil Empire*.

17. Wandycz, "The Poles in the Habsburg Monarchy."

18. Himka, "The Greek Catholic Church."

19. Wendland, "Die Rückkehr der Russophilen." See also Bihl, "Die Ruthenen."

20. Baczkowski, *Pod czarno-żołtymi sztandarmi*, 109–82, 320–21, 382–99.

21. Bachmann, *Ein Herd der Feindschaft*, 196–232.

22. Bachmann, *Ein Herd der Feindschaft*, 65–75. See also Gaul, "Legiony Polskie."

23. David F. Good, "Stagnation and 'Take-Off.'" See also Mokyr, "And Thou, Happy Austria."

2. THE MOST POWERFUL PILLAR

1. Jászi, *Dissolution of the Habsburg Monarchy*, 141.

2. Rothenberg, *Napoleon's Great Adversaries*.

3. Sked, *Radetzky*.

4. Wawro, *Austro-Prussian War*.

5. Schindler, "Defeating Balkan Insurgency."

6. Rothenberg, *Army of Francis Joseph*, 162.

7. Allmayer-Beck, "Das Heerwesen," 75.

8. Jászi, *Dissolution*, 141.

9. Rothenberg, "Toward a Hungarian National Army."

10. Papp, "Die königliche ungarische Landwehr."

11. Barcy, *Királyért és hazáért*, 91–101.

12. Rothenberg, "Toward a Hungarian National Army," 814.

13. Horel, *Soldaten zwischen nationalen Fronten*, 203–25.

14. Rothenberg, "Struggle over Dissolution."

15. Pojić, "Ustroj austrougarske vojske na ozemlju Hrvatske 1868–1914," 154–60. In Istria and Dalmatia, Croatian regions that were part of Austria, the second-line forces belonged to the *Landwehr*.

16. Papp, "Die königliche ungarische Landwehr," 653. See also Somogyi, "The Hungarian *Honvéd* Army."

17. Rothenberg, *Army of Francis Joseph*, 148.

18. Stone, "Constitutional Crises in Hungary," 167–69.

19. Peball and Rothenberg, "Der Fall 'U.'"

20. Péter, "Army Question in Hungarian Politics," 97–100.

21. Berkó, *A magyar királyi honvédség története 1868–1918*, 97–100; Kronenbitter, "*Krieg im Frieden*," 155–59.

22. Franek, "Probleme der Organization im ersten Kriegsjahre," 18.

23. Rothenberg, *Army of Francis Joseph*, 148.

24. Rothenberg, *Army of Francis Joseph*, 160.

25. Wagner, "Die k.(u.)k. Armee—Gliederung und Aufgabestellung," 591; Rothenberg, "Austro-Hungarian Campaign against Serbia in 1914," 128.

26. Stone, "Army and Society, 107.

27. Allmayer-Beck, "Die bewaffnete Macht in Staat und Gesellschaft," 138.

28. Rothenberg, *Army of Francis Joseph*, 165–72.

29. Ehnl, "Die öst.-ung," 5.

30. Kiszling, "Die Entwicklung der österreichisch-ungarischen Wehrmacht," 801.

31. Rothenberg, *Army of Francis Joseph*, 172.

32. Stone, "Army and Society," 103.

33. Sked, *Decline and Fall*, 258.

34. Winkler, *Anteil der nichtdeutschen Volksstämme*, 1–2.

35. Allmayer-Beck, "Die bewaffnete Macht," 97–98; Ehnl, "Die öst.-ung. Landmacht," 14.

36. Maior, *Habsburgi și Români*, 105–14.

37. Jones, "Imperial Russia's Forces at War," 281.

38. Deák, *Beyond Nationalism*, 102.

39. Jászi, *Dissolution*, 143.

40. Pauschenwein, *Feuer!*, 19.

41. Broucek, *General im Zwielicht*, 143.

42. Šehić, *U smrt za cara i domovinu!*, 56–64.

43. Deák, *Beyond Nationalism*, 105.

44. Allmayer-Beck, "Die bewaffnete Macht," 93–94.

45. Wagner, "Die k.(u.).k. Armee," 534.

46. This could get rather long: Budapest's own *k.u.k.* infantry regiment was formally titled "Imperial-and-Royal Infantry Regiment Empress-Queen Maria Theresia No. 32."

47. Rothenberg, *Napoleon's Great Adversaries*, 22.

48. Hämmerle, "Die k.(u.)k. Armee," 183–84.

49. Leidinger, "Suizid und Militär."

50. Cole, "Military Veterans."

51. Stergar, "National Indifference," 45–46.

52. Stergar, "National Indifference," 49–51. For more see Stergar and Polajnar, *Slovenci in vojska*.

53. Fučík, *Osmadvacátníci*, 23–38. Martin Zückert, "Antimilitarismus," 199–209.

54. Kriegsarchiv Wien (KA), Nachlass B/726 Robert Nowak, "Die Klammer des Reichs," Nr 1/I, 191–94.

55. Kriegsarchiv Wien (KA), Nachlass B/726 Robert Nowak, "Die Klammer des Reichs," Nr 1/I, 205–27.

56. Stone, "Army and Society," 101.

57. Kronenbitter, "*Krieg im Frieden*," 123–24.

58. Cole, "Der Radetzky-Kult."

59. Stone, "Army and Society," 99.

60. Deák, *Beyond Nationalism*, 98.

61. Thümmler, "Nationalismus."

62. Schmidl, *Juden in der k.(u.)k. Armee*, 68.

63. Wagner, "Die k.(u.)k. Armee," 494–524.

64. Godsey, "Quarterings and Kinship."

65. Kann, "Social Prestige," 159–64.

66. Rothenberg, "Nobility and Military Careers," 184.

67. Kann, "Social Prestige," 130–33.

68. Kann, "Social Prestige," 122.

69. Zehetbauer, "Die 'E.F.,'" 8–12.

70. Kreisler, *Four Weeks*, 10.

71. Rothenberg, *Army of Francis Joseph*, 127; Allmayer-Beck, "Die bewaffnete Macht," 99.

72. *Jahresbericht der k.u.k. Theresianischen Militärakademie*, 75–78.

73. Schmidl, *Juden*, 133. Deák, "Pacesetters of Integration," 24, 31.

74. Deák, "Pacesetters of Integration," 23. The Bavarian and Württemberg Armies, however, did commission some Jews in the reserve before 1914.

75. Deák, *Beyond Nationalism*, 70.

76. Deák, *Beyond Nationalism*, 128–35. See the same author's "Chivalry."

77. Zeinar, *Geschichte des österreichischen Generalstabes*, 512.

78. Zeinar, *Geschichte des österreichischen Generalstabes*, 516–43; Kronenbitter, *"Krieg im Frieden,"* 34–57.

79. Hubka, *Jahrgang 1896/98*, 4–7.

80. Fahey, "Secret Poison Plot."

81. Kronenbitter, *"Krieg im Frieden,"* 21–22.

82. Jeřábek, *Potiorek*, 12–20.

83. Jeřábek, *Potiorek*, 29, 39.

84. Jeřábek, *Potiorek*, 43–45.

85. There is one English-language biography: Sondhaus, *Conrad*.

86. Sondhaus, *Conrad*, 27–30.

87. Sondhaus, *Conrad*, 78–80.

88. Williamson, "Influence, Power, and the Policy Process," 420–21.

89. Kronenbitter, "Haus ohne Macht?," 196–208.

90. Wittich, "Zur Weltanschauung Conrads von Hötzendorf," 9–14.

91. Scheer, *Die Ringstrassenfront*, 19.

92. Sitte, "Alexander von Brosch," 5–13, 120–22.

93. Sondhaus, *Conrad*, 117.

94. Krauss, *Ursachen unserer Niederlage*, 101–2.

3. WAR PLANS

1. Oršolić, "Vojnateritorijalna podjela i reorganizacija austrougarske vojske 1867.–1890."

2. Dragoni, "Die Organization der österreichisch-ungarischen Wehrmacht."

3. Franek, "Probleme der Organization," 978–79.

4. Kiszling, "Die Entwicklung der österreichisch-ungarischen Wehrmacht," 801.

5. The best synopsis of Habsburg thinking in the period is Kronenbitter, "Austria-Hungary."

6. Zeinar, *Geschichte des österreichischen Generalstabes*, 471–73.

7. Kronenbitter, "Generalstabsmässig in die Katastrophe."

8. Sondhaus, "The Strategic Culture of the Habsburg Army."

9. Hannig, "Die Balkanpolitik," 36.

10. Tunstall, *Planning for War against Russia and Serbia*, 55–135.

11. Kronenbitter, *"Krieg im Frieden,"* 357–67.

12. Kronenbitter, *"Krieg im Frieden,"* 369–414; Pitreich, *1914*, 121–22.

13. Stone, "Moltke and Conrad," 223–24, 229.

14. Kronenbitter, "Falsch verbunden?"
15. Herwig, "Disjointed Allies," 267.
16. Kronenbitter, "Austria-Hungary," 38.
17. Cramon, *Unser österreichisch-ungarischer Bundesgenosse im Weltkriege*, 200.
18. Hadley, "Military Diplomacy in the Dual Alliance."
19. Rothenberg, *Army of Francis Joseph*, 148.
20. Sondhaus, *Conrad*, 41–42.
21. Broucek, "Taktische Erkentnisse," 194.
22. Sondhaus, *Conrad*, 90–93.
23. DiNardo, "First Modern Tank."
24. Bernhard, "Die österreichisch-ungarische Kavallerie."
25. Eder, "General der k.u.k. Armee," 204–17.
26. Sondhaus, *Conrad*, 74–77; Broucek, "Taktische Erkentnisse," 197–201.
27. Ortner, "Soldatsein," 174.
28. Ortner, "Soldatsein," 175, 187–88.
29. Ortner, "Soldatsein," 198; Broucek, "Taktische Erkentnisse," 203.
30. Zell, "Der Kampf."
31. Tomši, "Vorschrift."
32. Krauss, "Infanterie-Geschütze?," 635.
33. Rudel, "Die neue Exerzierreglement," 413–15.
34. Herrmann, *Arming of Europe*, 99–100.
35. Hadley, "Military Diplomacy," 303, 307–8.
36. Kiszling, "Enwicklung," 791. Infantry battalions serving in Bosnia and Herce-govina were authorized 520 soldiers in peacetime. See also *Programm für die achtwöchentliche Ausbildung*.
37. Rothenberg, *Army of Francis Joseph*, 174.
38. *Österreich-Ungarns letzter Krieg* (henceforth ÖULK), 34; Krauss, *Ursachen unserer Niederlage*, 97.
39. Schmidl, "From Paardeberg to Przemysl," 257.
40. Kann, "Social Prestige," 124.
41. Franek, "Probleme der Organization," 984.
42. Czegka, "Die Wandlungen," 3–5; Balla; *A magyar királyi honvéd lovasság*, 131–34.
43. Hadley, "Military Diplomacy," 305.
44. Ortner, *Austro-Hungarian Artillery*, 300–305.
45. ÖULK, 1.31.
46. Kiszling, "Entwicklung," 801.
47. Wagner, "Die k.(u.)k. Armee," 452. See also *Generalstabshandbuch*, 246. For technical details on the M.5/8 see Ortner, *Austro-Hungarian Artillery*, 192–205.
48. *Generalstabshandbuch*, 247; Wagner, "Die k.(u.)k. Armee," 452.

49. Mountain artillery batteries performed much more effectively than the field artillery during the invasion of Bosnia-Hercegovina in 1878, the last major Habsburg campaign—see this author's "Defeating Balkan Insurgency."

50. Ortner, *Austro-Hungarian Artillery*, 214–33.

51. Franek, "Probleme der Organization," 987.

52. ÖULK, 1.79. Rothenberg, *Army of Francis Joseph*, 149–50, 164.

53. On the modern gun designs not put into prewar production see Ortner, *Austro-Hungarian Artillery*, 306–43.

54. Franz Andele, "Entwicklung der Radiotelegraphie."

55. Reinhard Desoye, "Die k.u.k. Luftfahrtruppe," 37–39; Madárasz, "Die k.u.k. Luftfahrtruppen," 544.

56. Kronenbitter, *"Krieg im Frieden,"* 233–47; Reifberger, "Entwicklung des militärischen Nachrichtenwesens."

57. Walzel, *Kundschaftsdienst oder Spionage?*, 9–24.

58. KA, Gst(Evb), Fasz. 1104, "Jahresbericht über die russische Wehrmacht 1913," k.u.k. C. des GS., Evb.Nr. 250.

59. KA, Gst(Evb), Fasz. 1104, Evidenzbureau des k.u.k. Generalstabes, Evb.Nr. zu 2942 Res, 31 Jul 1914.

60. Moll, "Austro-Hungarian Counterintelligence."

61. KA, Qualifikationsliste, Kart. 2695, Alfred Redl.

62. Sondhaus, *Conrad*, 148.

63. The standard scholarly work on the case is this author's "Redl—Spy of the Century?"

64. See the recent cover story of one of Austria's lead newsmagazines: "Oberst Redl: Spion aus Leidenschaft," *profil* (Vienna), October 13, 2012.

65. This fact has led one author to posit, on the basis of no evidence, that Redl was Hitler's mentor and case officer! Bryukhanov. *Uchitel' i Uchenik.*

66. Schindler, "Redl," 495–97.

67. KA, Qualifikationsliste, Kart. 3589, August Urbański von Ostyrmiecz

68. Pethö, *Agenten für den Doppeladler*, 231–32.

69. Camillo Caleffi, "Un romanzesco caso di spionaggio," *Corriere della Sera* (Milan), August 20, 1957.

70. Mikhail Alekseev, "Agent No. 25." See the same author's *Voyennaya razvedka Rossii*, 186–92.

71. Pethö, *Agenten*, 236–37; Pokorny, *Emlékeim*, 52–65.

72. Rauchensteiner, *Tod des Doppeladlers*, 363. Mil'shtein, "Delo polkovnika Redlya," 48. The only officer with a similar name in the whole army was Josef Jandriszak, a reserve chaplain in Galicia, who could not have been the suspect that Mil'shtein described.

73. Schindler, "Redl," 500.

4. JULY CRISIS

1. Jeřábek, *Potiorek*, 78.
2. Jeřábek, *Potiorek*, 19, 55, 70–71.
3. Broucek, *Ein österreichischer*, 201, 225–26.
4. Jeřábek, *Potiorek*, 68–72.
5. Williamson, "Influence, Power, and the Policy Process," 426–31.
6. Jeřábek, *Potiorek*, 52.
7. Sondhaus, *Conrad*, 132–34, 137.
8. Jeřábek, *Potiorek*, 76–82.
9. See *Instruktion für den militärischen Kundschaftsdienst*.
10. For background on Apis and his violently conspiratorial milieu see MacKenzie, "Officer Conspirators and Nationalism."
11. The most comprehensive assessment is Würthle, *Die Spur führt nach Belgrad*, though it lacks rigorous historical analysis. It should be read with the supplementary information found in Würthle's collection of court files: *Dokumente zum Sarajevoprozess*.
12. For a recent review see Williamson and May, "Identity of Opinion," 350–53.
13. Much detail on Apis can be found in David MacKenzie's alarmingly sympathetic biography: *Apis: The Congenial Conspirator*. See also Drašković, *Pretorijanske težnje u Srbiji*. On Apis's admission of guilt see Gavrilović, "New Evidence."
14. McMeekin, *Russian Origins*, 46–47.
15. Jeřábek, *Potiorek*, 83–87. See also Clark, *Sleepwalkers*, 367–76, for the assassination.
16. Sondhaus, *Conrad*, 139.
17. Gina Conrad, *Mein Leben*, 113–14.
18. Kronenbitter, "'Nur los lassen,'" 175.
19. "*Dann ist eben Krieg*"; Hans Werner Scheidl, "1914: Franz Joseph wollte den Krieg," *Die Presse* (Vienna), September 20, 2013.
20. On the "blank check" see Kronenbitter, "Bundesgenossen?," 164–65.
21. Sondhaus, *Conrad*, 141; Rauchensteiner, *Der Tod des Doppeladlers*, 67–85.
22. Sondhaus, *Conrad*, 142–43.
23. Kronenbitter, "Nur los lassen," 164–66, 178–80, Jeřábek, *Potiorek*, 88.
24. Kronenbitter, "Nur los lassen," 186–87.
25. Sitte, "Alexander von Brosch," 120–26.
26. Sondhaus, *Conrad*, 143–44.
27. Williamson, "Aggressive and Defensive Aims," 71–72.
28. Stone, "Hungary and the Crisis," 167.
29. Kronenbitter, "Nur los lassen," 159–60.
30. Rauchensteiner, *Tod des Doppeladlers*, 92–93.
31. Williamson and May, "Identity of Opinion," 358.
32. Churchill, *World Crisis*, 133.

33. Stone, "Mobilmachung," 69–71.
34. Tunstall, "Habsburg Command Conspiracy."
35. Tunstall, "Habsburg Command Conspiracy," 186.
36. Tunstall, "Habsburg Command Conspiracy," 195–96.
37. Sondhaus, *Conrad*, 108–15, 171–81. See also Harmat, "Divorce and Remarriage."
38. Cited in Clark, *Sleepwalkers*, 470.
39. Kreisler, *Four Weeks*, 3–7.
40. On the complexity of the staff work e.g., KAW/NFA, Kart. 220, k.u.k. X. Korpskommando, Weisungen für das Beziehen der Aufmarschgruppierung, 5. Aug 1914.
41. Kriegsarchiv Wien (KAW)/Neue Feld Akten (NFA), Kart. 3, k.u.k. Armeeoberkommando, Etappenkmdo, Res.Nr. 44, 2. Aug 1914.
42. Moll, "Austro-Hungarian Counterintelligence."
43. Rendulić, 44–45.
44. KAW, Nachlass B/726 Robert Nowak: "Die Klammer des Reichs: Das Verhalten der elf Nationalitäten Österreich-Ungarns in der k.u.k. Wehrmacht 1914-1918": Nr. 1/I, 253.
45. Auffenberg von Komarów, *Aus Österreich-Ungarns Teilnahme*, 97–100.
46. Ranchi, "'La luna vista a girarsi,'" 285–86.
47. Hoen et al., *Deutschmeister*, 40–42, 51.
48. Baxa, *Geschichte*, 329–30.
49. Hubka, *Geschichte*, 28–29.
50. KA/NFA, Fasz. 909, k.u.k. VI. KorpsKmdo., Korpskmdobefehl Nr. 34, Kassa, 5. Aug 1914.
51. Oberklofer and Rabovsky, "Tiroler Kaiserjäger," 510–11.
52. Mobilization data are taken from Dragoni, "Die Organization." See also Kiszling, "Entwicklung," 801; Hecht, "Fragen," 48–49.
53. In the Austro-Hungarian cavalry and artillery, the "division" (*Division*) was a battalion-sized unit of two to three batteries or squadrons, not to be confused with the all-arms division (also *Division*).
54. Franek, "K. und k. Truppen."
55. Desoye, "Die k.u.k. Luftfahrtruppe," 55, 103, 108.
56. *Heldenweg*, 16–17.
57. Stolz, *Tiroler Landsturmregiment Nr. II*, 149–53
58. Binder, "Truppenbetreuung," 7.
59. Scheer, *Ringstrassenfront*, 28–38, 42–51.

5. DISASTER ON THE DRINA
1. Jeřábek, *Potiorek*, 118.
2. For the order of battle see *Österreich-Ungarns letzter Krieg* (henceforth ÖULK): vol. 1, *Das Kriegsjahr 1914*, 63–69.

3. Rothenberg, "Austro-Hungarian Campaign," 131–34.

4. Pitreich, *1914: Die militärische Probleme*, 94–95; Jeřábek, *Potiorek*, 111.

5. Jeřábek, *Potiorek*, 24–26.

6. Krauss, *Ursachen*, 106, 122–27.

7. Pitreich, *1914*, 92.

8. Jeřábek, *Potiorek*, 108.

9. Radenković, *Cerska operacija*, 381. For full order of battle see Pavlović, *Bitka na Jadru*, 80–98.

10. Kriegsarchiv Wien (KAW)/Neue Feld Akten (NFA), Fasz.1188, "Kriegsordre de bataille der serbischen Armee Juli 1914."

11. KAW/NFA, Fasz.1188, "Über Wesen, Ausrüstung und Kampfesart der Komitadschis."

12. Peball, "Der Feldzug," 21.

13. On the shortcomings of Belgrade's forces see Lyon, "'Peasant Mob.'"

14. KAW/Generalstab(EB), Fasz.1104 (1913), Evb.Nr.1274, Mai 1913.

15. KAW/Generalstab(EB), Fasz.1104, "Resumé über die serbische Armee im Feldzüge 1912/13," 6 Jun 1913.

16. Jeřábek, *Potiorek*, 123.

17. Djordjević, "*Vojvoda* Putnik," 70–71.

18. Rothenberg, "Austro-Hungarian Campaign," 135–37.

19. Ehnl, "Die öst.-ung. Landmacht," 75, 79.

20. Ehnl, "Die öst.-ung. Landmacht," 53, 81, 83. KAW/NFA, Fasz.1188, 21.LITD Kmdo., "Trainorganization," 10. Aug 1914.

21. KAW, Qualifikationsliste, Kart.2629, Arthur Przyborski; Jeřábek, *Potiorek*, 121.

22. KAW/NFA, Fasz.1188, k.k. Landwehr Kmdo. in Prag, Pras.Nr.1064, 28 Jul 1914; k.k. Landwehr Kmdo. in Prag, Pras.Nr.80, 31 Jul 1914; k.k. LIR Prag Nr.8, Res. Nr.215 Mob.,1. Aug 1914.

23. KAW/NFA, Fasz. 1188, k.k. 21.LITD Kmdo., Nächtigung vom 9. auf den 10. August.

24. The front page of the *Sarajevoer Tageblatt* for August 8 included no less than a half-dozen reports of Bosnian Serb disloyalty, including armed uprisings; as this newspaper had a close relationship with Potiorek's staff, none of the reports can be considered fully credible.

25. KAW/NFA, Kart. 3, k.u.k. Gendarmeriekorps für Bosnien und die Hercegovina, KNr.295, Situationsmeldung, 4. Aug 1914.

26. KAW/NFA, Kart. 3, k.u.k. Gendarmeriekorps für Bosnien und die Hercegovina, Res.Nr.233/I, 8. Aug 1914; k.u.k. Gendarmeriekorps für Bosnien und die Hercegovina, KNr. 317. 10. Aug 1914.

27. KAW/NFA, Fasz.1187, k.k. 21.LITD Kmdo., Abfertigung, 8. Aug 1914; Fasz.1188, k.u.k.5.ArmeeKmdo., Op.Nr.77, 10. Aug 1914.

28. Gumz, *Resurrection*, 39.

29. Spence, *"Die Bosniaken kommen!,"* 304–5.
30. KAW/NFA, Kart. 3, FZM Potiorek, Op.Nr.149, an GdI Frank, 9. Aug 1914.
31. Zanantoni, *Geschichte*, 20.
32. KAW/NFA, Kart. 3, Gstabt. des k.u.k. Mil.Kmdos. in Budapest, KNr.70, Nachrichten aus Serbien, 3. Aug 1914.
33. KAW/NFA, Fasz. 1668, k.u.k. 5.AKmdo., Op.Nr.261, 13. Aug 1914.
34. Kun, *A cs. és kir. 23. gyalogezred hadialbuma*, 35–36.
35. Gumz, *Resurrection*, 47.
36. Schön, *Šabac!*, 108–18.
37. KAW, Sammlung Balaban 10, k.k. 21.LITD Kmdo., Frührapporte, 12 Aug 1914. Gefechts-Berichte, k.k. 41.LIBrig. Kmdo., 13. Aug 1914
38. KAW/NFA, Kart. 882, k.k. 21.LITD Kmdo., Op.Nr.77/1, "Operationen der 21.LITD in der Zeit 12.-21.8.1914," 23. Aug 1914
39. KAW/NFA, Kart. 3, k.u.k. XV.KorpsKmdo., Telegramm an 6. ArmeeKmdo., 18. Aug, 6.40 pm
40. Rothenberg, "Austro-Hungarian Campaign," 137.
41. KAW, Nachlass Robert Nowak, B/726, Nr.1/I, "Die Klammer des Reichs: Das Verhalten der elf Nationalitäten Österreich-Ungarns in der k.u.k. Wehrmacht 1914–1918," 261–63. Pitreich, *Lemberg 1914*, 103–4.
42. Skoko and Opačić, *Vojvoda Stepa Stepanović u ratovima Srbije 1876–1918.*
43. Djordjević, "*Vojvoda* Putnik," 573.
44. KAW, Gefechts-Berichte 17, k.k. 21.LITD Kmdo., Op.Nr.84/5, 31. Aug 1914. Nachlass Robert Nowak, Nr.I/1, 263.
45. Radenković, *Cerska operacija*, 146–47. KAW, Gefechts-Berichte 17, k.k. 21.LID Kmdo., Op.Nr.84/5, 3. Aug 1914.
46. Schön, *Šabac*, 166–68. KAW, Gefechts-Berichte 17, k.k. 21.LID Kmdo., Op.Nr.84/5, 31. Aug 1914.
47. Wagner, *Geschichte*, 75–78.
48. Martinek, *Kriegstagebuch eines Artillerie-Offiziers*, 13; Radenković, *Cerska operacija*, 160–63.
49. Djordjević, "*Vojvoda* Putnik," 577.
50. KAW, Gefechts-Berichte 17, k.k. 21.LITD Kmdo., Op.Nr.75/4, 22. Aug 1914. *Geschichte des k.u.k. Dragoner-Regiment Fürst zu Windischgrätz Nr.14*, 31–33.
51. KAW/NFA, Fasz. 1188, k.k. 21.LID Kmdo., Op.Nr.77/1, 23. Aug 1914. Wagner, *Geschichte*, 80.
52. KAW/NFA, Fasz. 1188, k.k. 42.LIBrig. Kmdo., Nr.1, an das 21.LITD Kmdo., 18. Aug 1914; Hoen, *Geschichte*, 27–29.
53. KAW/NFA, Fasz. 882, k.u.k. 5.Op.AKmdo., Op.Nr.403/44, 24. Aug 1914.
54. KAW/NFA, Fasz. 1188, k.k. 21.LITD Kmdo., Op.Nr.76/6, 22. Aug 1914. Fasz.1191, k.k. 21.LITD Kmdo., Op.Nr.80/5, Verlust-Ausweise, 25. Aug 1914. k.k. LIR Pisek Nr.28, Frührapporte, 23. Aug 1914.

55. Kisch, *"Schreib das auf,"* 12, 59–63.

56. Hoen, *Geschichte*, 37.

57. KAW/NFA, Fasz. 1668, k.u.k. 42.LITD Kmdo., Verlustliste, 23 Aug 1914. That Marshal Tito fought against "brother Serbs" was considered a state secret in Communist Yugoslavia, where the official story was that Sgt. Broz spent the latter half of 1914 in a military jail for "political agitation" against the war.

58. *Ratni dnevnik C.K. varaždinske pješačke pukovnije br. 16*, 23; KAW/NFA, Fasz.1668, k.u.k 36.ITD Kmdo., Res.Nr.200/30, Verlustliste, 30. Aug 1914.

59. *ÖULK:* vol. 1, 141–45.

60. Schön, *Šabac*, 234–38, 294.

61. Schön, *Šabac*, 211–12, 301.

62. Zanantoni, *Geschichte*, 53–70; Schön, *Šabac*, 359–66, 401–9.

63. *ÖULK:* vol. 1, 152; Jeřábek, *Potiorek*, 131.

64. Schön, *Šabac*, 175; Conrad, *Dienstzeit*, vol. 4, 522.

65. Kalvoda, "Podhajský," 305–6.

66. KAW, Nachlass Robert Nowak, I/1, 268–269; Jeřábek, *Potiorek*, 121–24, 141.

67. KAW/NFA, Fasz. 1188, k.u.k. 5.Armee-Etappenkmdo., Res.Nr.120, 22. Aug 1914. k.u.k. 8.KorpsKmdo., Op.Nr. 108, 22. Aug 1914.

68. KAW/NFA, Fasz. 1188, k.u.k. 5.ArmeeKmdo., Op.Nr.402/15, 22 Aug. 1914 (emphasis in original).

69. *ÖULK:* vol. 1, 151. KA, Nachlass Robert Nowak, I/1, 268–69.

70. KAW, Nachlass Robert Nowak, I/1, 269–71.

71. Schön, *Šabac*, 175–81.

72. Schön, *Šabac*, 336–38.

73. KAW/NFA, Fasz. 1188, k.u.k. 5.Armee-Etappenkmdo., Res.Nr.120, 22. Aug 1914. k.u.k. 8.KorpsKmdo., Op.Nr.108, 22. Aug 1914.

74. KAW/NFA, Kart. 882, k.u.k. 8.KorpsKmdo., "Wahrnehmungen während der letzten Gefechte," 24. Aug 1914.

75. KAW/NFA, Kart. 1668, k.u.k. 5.A.Kmdo., Op.Nr.403/20 zu I, 25. Aug 1914.

76. Gumz, *Resurrection*, 58–59; Anton Holzer, "Mit allen Mitteln," *Die Presse* (Vienna), 19 September 2008.

77. Krauss, *Ursachen*, 99.

78. KAW/NFA, Kart. 882, k.k.21.LITD Kmdo., Op.Nr.76/2, Retabilierung, 22. Aug 1914.

79. KAW/NFA, Fasz. 1188, k.u.k. 5.ArmeeKmdo., zu Res.Nr.35/72, 27. Aug 1914.

6. TO WARSAW!

1. Sondhaus, *Conrad*, 150–51.

2. Bodganowski, *Fortyfikacije*.

3. Forster, *Przemyśl*, 148–49.

4. For order of battle details see the Official History: *Österreich-Ungarns letzter Krieg* (henceforth *ÖULK*): vol. 1, *Kriegsjahr 1914*, 69–79.

5. Norman Stone, "Mobilmachung," 83.

6. Stone, *Eastern Front*, 80.

7. Pitreich, *1914: Die militärische Probleme*, 121–22.

8. Craig, "World War I Alliance," 338–40; Hadley, "Military Diplomacy," 312.

9. Peball, "Um das Erbe," 31–32.

10. Kriegsarchiv Wien (KAW), Neue Feld Akten (NFA), Fasz. 1721, k.u.k. 11. Korps-Kmdo., Res. Nr. 84, Res. Nr. 89, 19. Aug 1914.

11. Monolatii, *Ukrains'ki Lehionery*.

12. Kwaśny, *"Krakowskie dzieci,"* 30.

13. Kriegsarchiv Wien (KAW), Neue Feld Akten (NFA), Kart. 220, Delegierter GSoffz. des k.u.k. AOK, K/Nr. 15/9, 9. Aug 1914.

14. Plaschka, "Die polnische Legion," 176–78.

15. Tych, "Victor Adler," 414.

16. Kreisler, *Four Weeks in the Trenches*, 12–17.

17. Rendulić, *Soldat*, 48–50

18. Turner, "Russian Mobilization in 1914."

19. Prusin, *Nationalizing*, 13.

20. The Durnovo Memorandum has generated interest from historians for nearly a century; for a more skeptical view see MacDonald, "Durnovo Memorandum."

21. Robinson, "Grand Duke Nikolai Nikolaevich."

22. Golovin, "Russian War Plan of 1914," 73–76.

23. Brusilov, *Soldier's Notebook*, 43–44.

24. Walzel, *Kundschaftsdienst*, 41–42, 129–33.

25. KAW, Gs-Evidenzbureau, Fasz. 1104, Evb.Nr. zu 2942, 31. Jul 1914.

26. KAW/NFA, Kart. 220, k.u.k. AOK, Evidenzgruppe "R" bis 1. Aug 1914, 1200.

27. KAW/NFA, Kart. 111, k.u.k 4. ITD.Kmdo., Op.Nr. 53, 15. Aug 1914. Kart. 220, k.u.k. GSAbt. des Festung Krakau, KNr. 2279, Bericht von 12. Aug 1914. k.u.k. AOK, Evidenzgruppe "R," Resumé bis der 15. Aug 1914.

28. KAW/NFA, Kart. 220, k.u.k. 4. Op.ArmeeKmdo., Kundschaftabteilung, KNr. 49, Resume der Nachrichten bis 18. Aug 1914. See also Jerzy Gaul, "Służby informacyjne."

29. KAW/NFA, Kart. 220, Op.Nr. 70/2, Fliegermeldung aus Nisko, 14. Aug 1914. k.u.k. 1. Op.Kmdo., Op.Nr. 234/1, Fliegermeldung, 20. Aug 1914.

30. Sondhaus, *Conrad*, 153.

31. KAW/NFA, Kart. 220, k.u.k. 1. Op.ArmeeKmdo., Op.Nr. 3/5, EvGruppe, 10. Aug 1914.

32. Jung, "Feldverwendung," 92–93, 149.

33. Fischer, *Krieg ohne Heer*.

34. KAW/NFA, Kart. 220, Delegierter GSoffz. des k.u.k. AOK, KNr. 16/9, 11. Aug 1914. k.u.k. 4. Op.ArmeeKmdo., Kundschaftabteilung, KNr. 19, Nachrichten bis 18. Aug 1914.

35. Scheff, "Aufklärungsgefecht," 657.

36. KAW/NFA, Kart. 5, k.u.k. AOK EvGruppe "R," Kurze Andeutungen über Kampfweise der Russen nach den Erfahrungen aus dem russ.-jap. Krieg, 13. Aug 1914. Colonel Szeptycki was the brother of Andrzej, the primate of the Ukrainian Greek Catholic Church from 1900 to 1944.

37. Kuderna, "Das erste Gefecht."

38. Brusilov, *Soldier's Notebook*, 44–45.

39. Pitreich, *Lemberg 1914*, 13–14. In the tactful words of the Official History, written sixteen years after the event, Froreich's suicide "has not been established." *ÖULK:* vol. 1, 165.

40. Winzor, *Weisse Dragoner*, 36–56.

41. Sondhaus, *Conrad*, 153–54.

42. Pfannenstiel, "Todeskampf."

43. Pitreich, *Lemberg 1914*, 159–61.

44. Reichlin-Meldegg, *Des Kaisers Prinz Eugen?*, 96–97.

45. *ÖULK:* vol. 1, 184.

46. KAW/NFA, Fasz. 106, k.u.k. 2.ITD.Kmdo., Op.Nr. 35, 16. Aug 1914.

47. Mascher, *Die 76er*, 19–24; KAW, Sammlung Balaban, Kart. 1903, k.u.k. 14.ITD. Kmdo., Ordre de bataille, 21. Aug 1914.

48. Urbański, Russian batteries, having already estimated ranges, took a deadly toll on the attacker. *Geschichte*, 24.

49. Boleslawski, *Das k.k. LIR 31*, 19–25.

50. *Vormarsch*, 15–23.

51. KAW/NFA, Fasz. 106, k.u.k. 1. Op.ArmeeKmdo., Armeekommandobefehl Nr. 6, 26. Aug 1914.

52. Ward, *Priest, Politician, Collaborator*, 31.

53. Sondhaus, *Conrad*, 154.

54. Urbański, *Geschichte*, 34–35.

55. KAW/NFA, Kart. 3, k.u.k. 4.Op.ArmeeKmdo., Op.Nr. 14, ArmeeKmdo., Befehl Nr. 1, 11. Aug 1914.

56. Auffenberg, *Teilnahme am Weltkrieg*, 156–57.

57. See Izdebski, *Bitwa pod Zamościem 26–27 sierpnia 1914 r.*

58. Rendulić, *Soldat*, 54–61.

59. Leppa, *Schlacht bei Komarów*, 39–43.

60. Leppa, *Schlacht bei Komarów*, 34, 57–58.

61. On Boroević's background see Roksandić, *Lav ili lisica sa Soče?*, 17–24. Boroević has usually been considered a Serb by virtue of his religion, but he customarily declared himself "a Croat of the Orthodox faith"; he certainly had no sympathy with Great Serbian viewpoints.

62. Hoffmann, "Boroević von Bojna," 14–19. He added to Sarkotić: "Thank God, the natural mentality of our people"—meaning Croats—"is so powerfully

developed that I can allow myself to be more pleasant than I have to be unpleasant."

63. KAW/NFA, Fasz. 470, k.u.k. 6. KorpsKmdo., Res.Nr. 15 an das 15.ITD.Kmdo., 11. Aug 1914.

64. KAW/NFA, Fasz. 909, k.u.k. 6. KorpsKmdo., Nr. 98 an 15.ITD.Kmdo., 24. Aug 1914.

65. Mátyás, *A cs. és kir. 85, Számu Gaudernak Báró gyalogezred története*, 13–17.

66. ÖULK, vol. 1, 198.

67. KAW/NFA, Kart. 111, k.u.k. 2.KorpsKmdo., Op.Nr. 167/25, 27. Aug 1914. Leppa, *Komarów*, 87–94.

68. Bardolff, *Soldat i*, 197–99.

69. Gebert, *A kassai VI. hadtest harcai 1914 Aug. 25.–30.*, 37–44.

70. Ruppert, "Untergang."

71. Auffenberg, *Teilnahme*, 177–78.

72. Rauchensteiner, "Tod des Generals Wodniansky," 67–69.

73. KAW/NFA, Fasz. 909, k.u.k. 15.ITD.Kmdo., Abfertigung für 28. Aug 1914. Op.Nr. 471.1, 31. Aug 1914. Ordre de bataille, 29. Aug 1914. IR 5, Op.Nr. 15/2, Verlustliste, 2. Sep 1914.

74. Auffenberg, *Teilnahme*, 214–15. KAW/NFA, Fasz. 909, k.u.k. 6. KorpsKmdo., Op.Nr. 96/30, 28. Aug 1914.

75. *Die k.u.k. Reitende Artillerie-Division Nr. 5*, 20–21.

76. KAW/NFA, Kart. 220, k.u.k. AOK NAbt, Kr.Nr. 319, 25. Aug 1914.

77. KAW/NFA, Fasz. 1271, k.u.k. AOK, Op.Nr. 1084, Eigenheiten der russ. Kampfweise, 24. Aug 1914. K.u.k. 10. KorpsKmdo., Op.Nr. 231, 28. Aug 1914.

7. MEETING THE STEAMROLLER

1. Kriegsarchiv Wien (KAW), Neue Feld Akten (NFA), Fasz. 1721, k.u.k. 3. Armee-Komdo., Armeebefehl Nr. 1, 11. Aug 1914. Op.Nr. 71, 15. Aug 1914.

2. KAW/NFA, Kart. 5, k.u.k. AOK, Op.Nr. 1117, An das 2. ArmeeKmdo., 24. Aug 1914.

3. Brusilov, *Soldier's Notebook*, 46–48.

4. *Österreich-Ungarns letzter Krieg* (henceforth ÖULK), vol. 1 (Vienna, 1930), 204–9.

5. KAW/NFA, Fasz. 1544, k.u.k. 3. ArmeeKmdo., Op.Nr. 207, 25. Aug 1914.

6. KAW/NFA, Fasz. 1721, k.u.k. 3.ArmeeKmdo., Op.Nr. 35, Verbindungsdienst, 24. Aug 1914.

7. For details see KA/NFA, Fasz. 1271, 3. Korps, Tagebuch Nr. 1, 26–28. Aug 1914.

8. For an overview, see Fabini, "Feuertaufe."

9. Baxa, *Geschichte*, 333.

10. Vogelsang, *Infanterieregiment Nr. 47*, 35–46; Berndt, *Die 5er Dragoner*, 42–43.

11. Pitreich, *Lemberg 1914*, 59, 131–33; Ortner, "Soldatensein," 22–23.

12. Kiesewetter, *Mit den Siebzehnern*, 5.

13. Stolz, *Tiroler Landsturmregiment*, 154–55, 164.

14. Kreisler, *Four Weeks*, 19–29.

15. KAW/Archiv der Truppenkörper (AdTK), Kart. 1906, Ms/1.Wkg/Rus/1914: Joly, "Kämpfe der 3. Armee östlich Lemberg bis zum Rückzug an die Wereszczya," 18–19.

16. KAW/NFA, Kart. 5, k.u.k. AOK, Op.Nr. 1172, An das 2. ArmeeKmdo., 26. Aug 1914.

17. KAW/AdTK, Fasz. 1906, Joly, 22–34.

18. Quoted in Churchill, *Unknown War*, 162–63.

19. KA/NFA, Fasz. 152, 3.ITD, Frührapport, 21. Aug 1914. K.u.k. 2. Regt. TKR, Frührapport, 19. Aug 1914.

20. Oberklofer and Rabofsky, "Tiroler Kaiserjäger," 506–8.

21. Jakoncig, *Tiroler Kaiserjäger*, 13; Witzhaupt, *Tiroler Kaiserjäger*, 46–54.

22. *Linzer Hessen*, 91–93.

23. Gandini, *Das bosnisch-herzegovinische Infanterie-Regiment Nr. 2*, 13–14.

24. KAW/NFA, Kart. 1271, k.u.k. 10. KorpsKmdo., Op.Nr. 231, 28. Aug 1914.

25. KAW, Nachlass Twerdy (B/1338), "Feuertaufe und Ende der Wiener Bosniaken (Aug 1914)."

26. Auffenberg, *Österreich-Ungarns Teilnahme*, 219–20.

27. Beh, *Die Neunerschützen*, 4–5.

28. *Linzer Hessen*, 96–97.

29. Altrichter, *Falkenhahnen*, 5–6.

30. Leppa, *Schlacht bei Komarów*, 224–33, 281–90.

31. Pauschenwein, "Feuer!," 35.

32. KAW/AdTK, Joly, "Kämpfe der 3. Armee," 37–41.

33. Although the Official History is frank about this debacle (see vol. 1, 244), the Eleventh Division's artillery brigadier self-published a rejoinder, claiming that he and his gunners were maligned: Dieterich, *Berichtigung*. The official records of the Eleventh Division are so spotty, due to the panic and losses of late August, that it is impossible to verify General Dieterich's claims.

34. Reichlin-Meldegg, *Kaisers Prinz Eugen?*, 97–98, 100–102.

35. Rauchensteiner, "Tod Generals Wodniansky," 69–70.

36. KAW/NFA, Kart. 5, 2. Armee, "Bericht über meine Tätigkeit gelegentlich der Entsendung zum 7. KorpsKmdo., am 30. Aug 1914."

37. KAW/NFA, Kart. 3, k.u.k. 4. Armee-Etappenkmdo., Op. Nr. 641, 28. Aug 1914.

38. *61 in Waffen: Kriegsalbum*, 116–21.

39. Brusilov, *Soldier's Notebook*, 49.

40. Sondhaus, *Conrad*, 155.

41. KAW, Nachlass Boroević, B/4, "Brief an Huber," 8. Sep 1914.

42. Churchill, *Unknown War*, 165.

43. Leppa, *Die Kämpfe*, 337–45.

44. Rendulić, *Soldat*, 61–62.

45. Ward. *Priest, Politician, Collaborator*, 31–32.

46. KAW/NFA, Fasz. 106, k.u.k. AOK Etappenkmdo., Nr. 877, Verlustlisten, 29. Aug 1914. Fasz. 909, k.u.k. AOK, Res.Nr. 189, 30. Aug 1914.

47. Baxa, *Geschichte des k.u.k FJB 8*, 335–36. Emphasis in the original.

8. LEMBERG–RAWA RUSKA

1. Rauchensteiner, "Tod Generals Wodniansky," 70–72.

2. Kriegsarchiv Wien (KAW)/Neue Feld Akten (NFA), Kart. 5, k.u.k. AOK, Op. Nr. 1452, 1. Sep 1914.

3. Hadley, "Military Diplomacy," 295.

4. Biwald, *Von Helden und Krüppeln*, 343–46.

5. Wright and Bly, *Twenty Poems of Georg Trakl*, 27. Translation by the author.

6. KAW/NFA, Kart. 220, k.u.k. AOK Etappenkmdo., Op. 2041, 30. Aug 1914.

7. KAW/NFA, Kart. 5, k.u.k. AOK, Op. Nr. 1523, 3. Sep 1914.

8. KAW/NFA, Kart. 1544, k.k. 105. Ldst.I.Brig., Op. Nr. 88/10, 4. Sep 1914.

9. KAW/NFA, Kart. 1544, k.u.k. 3. ArmeeKmdo., Op.Nr. 385, 3. Sep 1914.

10. KAW/NFA, Kart. 1544, k.u.k. 11. ITDKmdo., Op.Nr. 105/4, 2. Sep 1914. k.u.k. 12. KorpsKmdo., Op.Nr. 106/30p, 3. Sep 1914.

11. KAW/NFA, Kart. 1544, k.u.k. 3. ArmeeKmdo., Nr. 3740p, 2. Sep 1914.

12. KAW/Archiv der Truppenkörper (AdTK), Kart. 1906, Ms/1.Wkg/Rus/1914: Joly, "Kämpfe der 3. Armee östlich Lemberg bis zum Rückzug an die Wereszczya," 44–49. This event, like most of the debacle of the Third Army, is glossed over in the Austro-Hungarian Official History, making only a passing appearance.

13. "Armee östlich Lemberg bis zum Rückzug an die Wereszczya," 49–51.

14. Todero, *Dalla Galizia all'Isonzo*, 59–60.

15. Reichlin-Meldegg, *Des Kaisers Prinz Eugen?*, 103–4. Emphasis in original.

16. Tăslăuanu, *Austrian Army in Galicia*, 57–59.

17. Brusilov, *Soldier's Notebook*, 53–55.

18. Brusilov, *Soldier's Notebook*, 55–57. KAW/NFA, Kart. 1544, k.u.k. 12. Korps-Kmdo., Op.Nr. 109/25, 4. Sep 1914.

19. Reichlin-Meldegg, *Des Kaisers Prinz Eugen?*, 104.

20. KAW, Nachlass Boroević, B/4: 3, Brief an Huber, 8. Sep 1914.

21. Hoffmann, "Svetozar Boroević von Bojna," 351–52.

22. Hoffmann, "Svetozar Boroević von Bojna," 20–22; KAW, Nachlass Boroević, B/4: 13, k.u.k. 3. ArmeeKmdo., ENr. 163, 6. Sep 1914. Res. Nr. 134, 5. Sep 1914.

23. KAW, Nachlass Boroević, B/4:13, k.u.k. 3. Armeekmdobefehl Nr. 3, 5. Sep 1914.

24. KAW, Nachlass Boroević, B/4: 12, k.u.k. 3. ArmeeKmdo., Res.Nr. 162, Feindl.-Spionage-Verhinderung, 9. Sep 1914.

25. KAW/NFA, Kart. 5, k.u.k. AOK Etappenkmdo., Op.Nr. 2503, 4. Sep 1914. Kart. 3, AOK Etappenkmdo., Op.Nr. 2535ad., 7. Sep 1914.

26. Hecht, "Fragen zur Heeresergänzung," 115–16; KAW/NFA, Kart. 1544, k.u.k. 3. ArmeeKmdo., Op.Nr. 442, 5. Sep 1914.

27. KAW/NFA, Kart. 1544, k.u.k. 12. KorpsKmdo., Op.Nr. 110/5, 5. Sep 1914.

28. KAW/NFA, Kart. 5, k.u.k. AOK, Op.Nr. 2455, 4. Sep 1914.

29. Podrazil, "Entwicklung," 65–66, 72. See also Pokorny, Emlékeim, 66–68.

30. KAW, Nachlass Boroević, B/4:12, k.u.k. 3. ArmeeKmdo., Res.Gstbs.No.3, Reservatbefehl an alle Generale der 3. Armee, 6. Sep 1914.

31. Rauchensteiner, "Tod Generals Wodniansky," 72–73.

32. Baxa, Geschichte, 337.

33. This account is taken from his memoir, Four Weeks in the Trenches, 60–82.

34. Vogelsang, Das steirische Infanterieregiment Nr. 47, 94–102.

35. Gandini, Das bosnisch-herzegowinische Infanterie-Regiment Nr. 2, 15.

36. This account is taken largely from Witzhaupt, Tiroler Kaiserjäger, 100–10. See also Murrer, Hujcze.

37. KAW/NFA, Fasz. 470, 8.ITD, Tagebuch, 4.VIII.1914–31.I.1915: 8. Sep 1914.

38. Winzor, Weisse Dragoner, 139–40. Translation by the author.

39. Tábornagy, Budapest, 148–53.

40. Tumlirz, Waffengänge, 19–22.

41. Blašković, B.H. 3, 13–14.

42. Here the Twelfth Division's artillery commander, Maj. Gen. Tadeusz Jordan-Rozwadowski, a future chief of the Polish General Staff, received the Order of Maria Theresia. Österreich-Ungarns letzter Krieg (ÖULK), vol. 1, Das Kriegsjahr 1914, 265–68

43. KAW/NFA, Kart. 882, Kmdo. der Balkanstreitkräfte, Op. Nr. 517, 5. Sep 1914.

44. KAW, Nachlass Nowak, B/726: "Die Klammer des Reichs: Das Verhalten der elf Nationalitäten Österreich-Ungarns in der k.u.k. Wehrmacht 1914–1918," Nr. 1/I, 336–37.

45. Zanantoni, Geschichte, 71–81.

46. KAW/NFA, Kart. 882, k.u.k. 5. Op.ArmeeKmdo., Op.Nr. 418/26, 7. Sep 1914. See also Leppa, Gefecht bei Schaschintzi.

47. Broucek, Ein österreichischer General, 239–40.

9. FROM DEFEAT TO CATASTROPHE

1. Brusilov, A Soldier's Notebook, 57–59.

2. Born Andrzej Szeptycki into a family of Polonized Ukrainian nobility, the archbishop had done military service as a one-year volunteer in the Austro-Hungarian cavalry before taking holy orders, while his brother Stanisław was a colonel in the k.u.k. Armee and after 1918 became a top Polish general.

3. Prusin, Nationalizing a Borderland, 32–47.

4. Lohr, "Russian Army and the Jews."

5. Brusilov, *A Soldier's Notebook*, 60–63.

6. Kriegsarchiv Wien (KAW)/Neue Feld Akten (NFA), Kart. 5, k.u.k. 2. Armee-Kmdo., Op.Nr. 307, 9. Sep 1914.

7. KAW/NFA, Nachlass Boroević, B/4: 13, k.u.k. 3. ArmeeKmdo., Res. Nr. 163, 9. Sep 1914. Fritz Franek, "Probleme der Organization im ersten Kriegsjahren," *Militärwissenschatftliche Mitteilungen*, Heft 11/12, 987.

8. Sondhaus, *Conrad*, 155.

9. Hoen, *Deutschmeister*, 101.

10. Stolz, *Tiroler Landsturmregiment Nr. II*, 155–60.

11. Brusilov, *A Soldier's Notebook*, 61–64.

12. *Geschichte des k.k. Kaiserschützenregimentes Nr. I*, 36.

13. Churchill, *Unknown War*, 171–72; *Österreich-Ungarns letzter Krieg (ÖULK)*, vol. 1, *Kriegsjahr 1914*, 308–12.

14. Herwig, *The Marne*, 266–85.

15. Brusilov, *A Soldier's Notebook*, 67–70.

16. Sondhaus, *Conrad*, 156.

17. Reichlin-Meldegg, *Des Kaisers Prinz Eugen?*, 105.

18. The Official History claims a loss of not less than 350,000 men, but this is a face-saving underestimate. *ÖULK*, vol. 1, 320–21.

19. Hoen, *Geschichte des salzburgisch-oberösterreichischen k.u.k. Infanterie-Regiments*, 81–82.

20. KAW/NFA, Kart. 649, k.u.k. 27. ITD Kmdo., Ausweis, 17. Sep 1914.

21. Oberklofer and Rabofsky, "Tiroler Kaiserjäger," 506–7.

22. *Der Heldenweg des Zweier-Landsturm*, 28.

23. KAW/NFA, Kart. 649, k.u.k. 6. KorpsKmdo., Op.Nr. 116/12, 16. Sep 1914.

24. Biwald, *Von Helden und Krüppeln*, 346; KAW/NFA, Kart. 1271, k.u.k. 1. Armee-Kmdo., Op.Nr. 1287, 29. Sep 1914.

25. Rendulić, *Soldat*, 69–70.

26. Biwald, *Von Helden und Krüppeln*, 580–89.

27. Stupp, "Neues über Georg Trakls Lazarettaufenhalte."

28. KAW/AdTK, Kart. 1906, Sammlung Balaban, k.u.k. 30. ITDKmdo., Frührapport, 19. Sep 1914.

29. Wolfgang, *Przemyśl 1914/15*; Forster, *Przemyśl*, 159.

30. KAW, Nachlass Nowak, B/726: "Die Klammer des Reichs: Das Verhalten der elf Nationalitäten Österreich-Ungarns in der k.u.k. Wehrmacht 1914–1918" Nr. 1/I, 291–300, 335.

31. Hecht, "Fragen zur Heeresergänzung," 129–30, 137.

32. *Das Vierundachtzigerbuch* (Vienna, 1919), 29–31.

33. Ortner, *Austro-Hungarian Artillery*, 362.

34. Czegka, "Die Wandlungen," 8–15.

35. Kozma, *Mackensens ungarische Husaren*, 37–38.

36. KAW/NFA, Fasz. 106, k.u.k. 2.ITDKmdo., Resumée der bisher gemachten takt. Wahrnehmungen, 22. Sep 1914. Emphasis in original.

37. KAW, Nachlass Boroević, B/4: 12: k.u.k. 3. ArmeeKmdo., E.Nr. 256, 21. Sep 1914.

38. KAW, Nachlass Boroević, B/4: 12, k.u.k. 3. ArmeeKmdo., Res.Nr. 223: Armee-befehl Nr. 9, 19 Sep 1914. Emphasis in original. See also k.u.k. 3. ArmeeKmdo., Op.Nr. 724, 20. Sep 1914.

39. Sondhaus, *Conrad*, 156.

40. Podrazil, "Entwicklung," 68–73; Walzel, *Kundschaftdienst oder Spionage?*, 62–63.

41. Reichlin-Meldegg, *Des Kaisers Prinz Eugen?*, 105–6.

42. Sondhaus, *Conrad*, 158–59.

43. For the extended version, see Sternberg, *Warum Österreich zugrunde gehen musste*, 117–29.

44. Krauss, *Ursachen*, 63, 99–101.

45. Churchill, *Unknown War*, 230–31.

46. Nowak, "Die Klammer des Reichs," Nr. I/1, 7.

10. AFTERMATHS

1. Brusilov, *A Soldier's Notebook*, 76.

2. Forstner, *Przemyśl*, 152.

3. Kriegsarchiv Wien (KAW)/Neue Feld Akten (NFA), k.u.k. 5. Op.ArmeeKmdo., Op.Nr. 410/5, 30. Aug 1914.

4. Nemeth, "Aus den Kämpfen."

5. Peball, "Feldzug," 30.

6. Franek, "Probleme der Organization," 20.

7. ÖULK, vol. 2: *Das Kriegsjahr 1915/I*, Appendix 1, Table 1, 3.

8. KAW/NFA, Fasz. 1191, k.u.k. Militärkmdo. in Prag, Pras.Nr. 2197, 27. Sep 1914. See also Plaschka. "Prag September 1914," 360–62.

9. KAW, Nachlass Nowak, B/726: "Die Klammer des Reichs: Das Verhalten der elf Nationalitäten Österreich-Ungarns in der k.u.k. Wehrmacht 1914–1918" Nr. 1/I, 300–19; Führ, *Das k.u.k. Armeeoberkommando*, 30–31.

10. Ongari, *Guerra in Galizia*, 28–29.

11. Zehetbauer, "Die 'EF.'" For instance, Ukrainians made up 8 percent of the army's rank and file, but in 1914 only one career officer in eight hundred was a Ukrainian, and even among reserve officers there was but one in two hundred: Bihl, "Die Ruthenen," 572–73.

12. Tunstall, *Blood on the Snow*.

13. Ratzenhofer, "Verlustkalkül," 31–39.

14. Pethö, *Agenten für den Doppeladler*, 134–44. See also Ronge, *Meister der Spionage*.

15. KAW, Nachlass Nowak, B/726: "Die Klammer des Reichs," Nr 1/II, 448–49.

16. The initial investigation that debunked many contemporary claims is Plaschka, "Zur Vorgeschichte." For a more recent English version see Lein, "The 'Betrayal.'"

17. Recent research indicates that, contrary to widespread myth, Slavic troops, even Czechs, were not taken prisoner in substantially greater percentages than other nationalities in the army: Rachamimov, *POWs and the Great War*, 31–34, 146–47.

18. KAW/NFA, Fasz. 1041, k.u.k. 17.ITD Kmdo., Op.Nr. 345/8, 6. Apr 1915. Fasz. 1020, 17.ITD Kmdo., "Fragen," 2. Jan 1915. Op.Nr. 218/8, 17. Feb 1915. Revealingly, the High Command's 1915 assessment of the army's Romanian troops was, "loyal, contrary to expectations."

19. Sondhaus, *Conrad*, 165–66, 180–82. See also Harmat, "Divorce and Remarriage."

20. Craig, "World War I Alliance," 341.

21. Kronenbitter, "Von 'Schweinehunden' und 'Waffenbrüdern,'" 126–35.

22. Kerchnawe, "Feldzug von Rowno," 232.

23. KAW, Nachlass Nowak, B/726: "Die Klammer des Reichs," Nr. 1/II, 475–76, 479, 496.

24. For an overview of the campaign: Rauchensteiner, *Tod des Doppeladlers*, 287–96. For the official version, see ÖULK, vol. 3, *Das Kriegsjahr 1915/II*, 51–185.

25. The extended version is Schindler, *Isonzo*.

26. Bauer, *Der letzte Paladin*, 77–90.

27. Schindler, "Steamrollered in Galicia."

28. Peball, "Führungsfragen," 420–21.

29. Wargelin, "Economic Collapse."

30. *Aus meiner Dienstzeit 1906–1918*, vols. 1–5.

31. *Mein Leben mit Conrad von Hötzendorf.*

32. Hubka, *Jahrgang 1896/98*, 506.

33. Sitte, "Alexander von Brosch," 127.

34. Plaschka, "Aus dem Haft-Akten," 489.

BIBLIOGRAPHY

ARCHIVAL COLLECTIONS

KAW: Kriegsarchiv Vienna

   Archiv der Truppenkörper

      Kart. 1906, Ms/1.Wkg/Rus/1914: Joly, "Kämpfe der 3. Armee östlich Lemberg bis zum Rückzug an die Wereszczya."

   Gefechts-Berichte

      Kart. 17, k.k. 21.LITD Kmdo.

   Generalstab (Evidenzbureau)

      Fasz. 1104, k.u.k. Evb 1913.

   Nachlässe

      Nachlass B/4 Boroević.

      Nachlass B/726 Robert Nowak, "Die Klammer des Reichs: Das Verhalten der elf Nationalitäten Österreich-Ungarns in der k.u.k. Wehrmacht 1914–1918."

      Nachlass B/1338 Twerdy, "Feuertaufe und Ende der Wiener Bosniaken (Aug 1914)."

NFA: Neue Feld Akten

      Fasz. 106, k.u.k. 1. Armeekommando.

      Fasz. 152, k.u.k. 3. ITD Kmdo.

      Fasz. 470, k.u.k. VI. Korpskommando.

      Fasz. 882, k.u.k. 5. Armeekommando.

      Fasz. 909, k.u.k. VI. Korpskommando.

      Fasz. 1021, k.u.k. 17. ITD Kmdo.

      Fasz. 1040, k.u.k. 17. ITD Kmdo.

      Fasz. 1187, k.k. 21. LITD Kmdo.

      Fasz. 1188, k.k. 21. LITD Kmdo.

      Fasz. 1191, k.k. 21. LITD Kmdo.

      Fasz. 1271, k.u.k. III. Korpskommando.

      Fasz. 1544, k.u.k. 3. Armeekommando.

Fasz. 1271, k.u.k. X. Korpskommando.

Fasz. 1721, k.u.k. XI. Korpskommando.

Fasz. 1668, k.u.k. 5. Armeekommando.

Kart. 3, k.u.k. Armeeoberkommando.

Kart. 5, k.u.k. Armeeoberkommando.

Kart. 111, k.u.k. II. Korpskommando.

Kart. 220, k.u.k. 1. Armeekommando.

Kart. 649, k.u.k. 27. ITD Kmdo.

Kart. 882, k.k. 21. LITD Kmdo.

Qualifikationsliste

Kart. 2629, Arthur Przyborski.

Kart. 2695, Alfred Redl.

Kart. 3589, August Urbański von Ostyrmiecz.

Sammlung Balaban

Kart. 10, k.k. 21. LITD Kmdo.

Kart. 1903, k.u.k. 14. ITD Kmdo.

Kart. 1906, k.u.k. 30. ITD Kmdo.

PUBLISHED SOURCES

61 in Waffen: Kriegsalbum des k.u.k. Infanterieregiments Nr. 61 1914–1917. Budapest: Self-published, 1918.

Alekseev, Mikhail. "Agent No. 25," *Sovershenno Sektretno*, no. 8 (1993).

———. *Voyennaya razvedka Rossii—Ot Ryurika do Nikolaya II: Kniga II.* 2 vols. Moscow: Russkaya Razvedka, 1998.

Allmayer-Beck, Johann-Christoph. "Die bewaffnete Macht in Staat und Gesellschaft" in Adam Wandruszka, Peter Urbanitsch (Hrsg.), *Die Habsburgermonarchie 1848–1918: Die bewaffnete Macht* (Die Habsburgermonarchie 1848–1918), vol. 5 Vienna: Österreichische Akademie der Wissenschaften, 1987.

———. "Das Heerwesen." In *Probleme der franzisko-josephinischen Zeit 1848–1916.* Edited by F. Engel-Janosi and H. Rumpler. Munich: Oldenbourg, 1967.

Altrichter, Alton. *Die Falkenhahnen im Weltkriege.* Iglau: Self-published, 1918.

Andele, Franz. "Die Entwicklung der Radiotelegraphie im k.u.k. Heere." Special issue. *Militärwissenschaftliche Mitteilungen*, nos. 9–10 (1931).

Auffenberg von Komarów, Moritz. *Aus Österreich-Ungarns Teilnahme am Weltkriege.* Berlin: Ullstein, 1920.

Bachmann, Klaus. *Ein Herd der Feindschaft gegen Russland: Galizien als Kreisenherd in der Beziehungen der Donaumonarchie mit Russland (1907–1914).* Vienna: Oldenbourg, 2001.

Baczkowski, Michał. *Pod czarno-żółtymi sztandarmi: Galicija i jej mieszkańcy wobec austro-węgierskich struktur militarnych 1868–1914.* Cracow: Towarzystwo Wydawn, 2003.

Balla, Tibor. *A magyar királyi honvéd lovasság 1868–1914*. Budapest: Balassi Kiadó, 2000.

Barcy, Zoltán. *Királyért és hazáért: A m. kir. Honvédség szervezete, egyenruhái és fegyverzete 1868–1918*. Budapest: Corvina, 1990.

Bardolff, Carl von. *Soldat im alten Österreich: Erinnerungen aus meinem Leben*. Jena: Diederichs, 1938.

Bator, Juliusz. *Wojna galicyjska: Działania armii austro-węgierskiej na froncie północnym (galicyjskim) w latach 1914–1915*. Cracow: Libron, 2005.

Bauer, Ernst. *Der letzte Paladin des Reiches: Generaloberst Stefan Freiherr Sarkotić von Lovćen*. Graz: Styria, 1988.

Baxa, Jakob. *Geschichte des k.u.k. Feldjägerbatallions Nr. 8: 1808–1918*. Klagenfurt: Self-published, 1974.

Beh, Robert. *Die Neunerschützen im Weltkrieg*. Leitmeritz: Self-published, 1918.

Berkó, István. *A magyar királyi honvédség története 1868–1918*. Budapest: M. Kir. Hadtörténelmi Levéltár, 1928.

Berndt, Otto. *Die 5er Dragoner im Weltkrieg 1914–1918*. Vienna: Kaltschmid, 1940.

Bernhard, Alphons. "Die österreichisch-ungarische Kavallerie." *Militärwissenschaftliche Mitteilungen*, nos. 7–8 (1931).

Bihl, Wolfdieter. "Die Ruthenen." In *Die Habsburgermonarchie 1848–1918*, vol. 3, pt. 1, *Die Völker des Reiches*. Edited by A. Wandruszka and P. Urbanitsch. Vienna: Österreichischischen Akademie der Wissenschaften, 1980.

Binder, Peter. "Zur Truppenbetreuung der k.u.k. Armee von 1914–1918: Versuch einer Annäherung." Master's thesis, University of Vienna, 1999.

Biwald, Brigitte. *Von Helden und Krüppeln: Das österreichisch-ungarische Militärsanitätswesen im Ersten Weltkrieg*. Pt. 2. Vienna: Öbv & Hpt, 2002.

Blašković, Pero. *B.H. 3*. Budapest: Self-published, 1917.

Bodganowski, Janusz. *Fortyfikacje austriackie na terenie Galicji w latach 1850–1914*. Cracow: Krakowski Oddział Towarzystwa Polsko-Austriackiego, 1993.

Boleslawski, Karl. *Das k.k. LIR 31: Lesebuch der ostschlesischen Landwehr im Weltkriege*. Teschen: Self-published, 1917.

Boterbloem, Kees. "*Chto delat*'? World War I in Russian Historiography after Communism." *Journal of Slavic Military Studies* 25, no. 3 (July 2012): 393–408.

Broucek, Peter. "Österreichische Militärgeschichtsschreibung 1918 bis 1938 und Militärgeschichtsschreibung in Österreich 1938 bis 1945." In *Geschichte der österreichischen Militärhistoriographie*. Edited by P. Broucek and K. Peball. Vienna: Böhlau, 2000.

——. "Taktische Erkentnisse aus dem russisch-japanischen Krieg und deren Beachtung in Österreich-Ungarn." *Mitteilungen des österreichischen Staatsarchivs* 30 (1977).

——, ed. *Ein General im Zwielicht: Die Erinnerungen Edmund Glaises von Horstenau*, vol. 1. Vienna, 1980.

————, ed. *Ein österreichischer General gegen Hitler: FML Alfred Jansa: Erinnerungen.* Vienna, 2011.

Broucek, Peter, and Kurt Peball. "Strömungen und Ziele seit 1945." In *Geschichte der österreichischen Militärhistoriographie.* Edited by P. Broucek and K. Peball. Vienna, 2000.

Brusilov, Alexei A. *A Soldier's Notebook 1914–1918.* London: Macmillan, 1930.

Bryukhanov, V. A. *Uchitel' i Uchenik: superagenty Al'fred Redl' i Adolf Gitler.* Moscow: Intellektualnaya kniga, 2010.

Caleffi, Camillo. "Un romanzesco caso di spionaggio," *Corriere della Sera* (Milan), August 20, 1957.

Churchill, Winston S. *The Unknown War: The Eastern Front.* New York: Charles Scribner's Sons, 1931.

————. *The World Crisis: The Eastern Front.* London: Butterworth, 1931.

Clark, Christopher. *The Sleepwalkers: How Europe Went to War in 1914.* New York: Harper Perennial, 2012.

Cole, Laurence. "Military Veterans and Popular Patriotism in Imperial Austria, 1870–1914." In *The Limits of Loyalty: Imperial Symbolism, Popular Allegiances, and State Patriotism in the Late Habsburg Monarchy.* Edited by L. Cole and D. Unowsky. New York: Berghahn Books, 2007.

————. "Der Radetzky-Kult in Zisteithanien 1848–1914." In *Glanz—Gewalt—Gehorsam: Militär und Gesellschaft in der Habsburger-monarchie (1800 bis 1918).* Edited by L. Cole et al. Essen, 2011.

Conrad von Hötzendorf, Franz. *Aus meiner Dienstzeit 1906–1918,* vols. 1–5. Vienna: Rikola, 1921–25.

Conrad von Hötzendorf, Gina. *Mein Leben mit Conrad von Hötzendorf: Sein geistiges Vermächtnis.* Leipzig: Grethlein, 1935.

Craig, Gordon A. "The World War I Alliance of the Central Powers in Retrospect: The Military Cohesion of the Alliance." *Journal of Modern History* 37, no. 3 (September 1965).

Cramon, August von. *Unser österreichisch-ungarischer Bundesgenosse im Weltkriege.* Berlin: Rittler, 1920.

Czegka, Eduard. "Die Wandlungen in der Verwendung und Organization der Kavallerie-Division während des Weltkrieges." *Militärwissenschatfliche und Technische Mitteilungen* (1928).

Deák, Agnes. *From Habsburg Neo-Absolutism to the Compromise: 1849–1867.* New York: Columbia University Press, 2009.

Deák, István. *Beyond Nationalism: A Social and Political History of the Habsburg Officer Corps, 1848–1918.* New York: Oxford University Press, 1990.

————. "Chivalry, Gentlemanly Honor, and Virtuous Ladies in Austria-Hungary." *Austrian History Yearbook* 25 (1994).

———. *The Lawful Revolution: Louis Kossuth and the Hungarians 1848–1849*. New York: Columbia University Press, 1979.

———. "Pacesetters of Integration: Jewish Officers in the Habsburg Monarchy." *Eastern European Politics and Societies* 3, no. 1 (December 1988): 22–50.

Desoye, Richard. "Die k.u.k. Luftfahrtruppe: Die Entstehung, der Aufbau und die Organzation der öst.-ung. Heeresluftwaffe 1912–1918: I. Teil." Master's thesis, University of Vienna, 1994.

Dieterich, Rudolf von. *Berichtigung zu Österreich-Ungarns letzter Krieg 1914–1918: Erste Schlacht bei Lemberg am 29.–31. August 1914*. Felixdorf: Self-published, 1933.

DiNardo, R. L. "The First Modern Tank: Gunther Burstyn and His Motorgeschutz." *Military Affairs* 50, no. 1 (January 1986).

Djordjević, Dimitrije. "*Vojvoda* Putnik, the Serbian High Command, and Strategy in 1914." In *War and Society in East Central Europe*, vol. 19, *East Central European Society in World War I*. Edited by B. Király, N. Dreisziger, and A. Nofi. New York: Columbia University Press, 1985.

Dragoni, Alfred von. "Die Organization der österreichisch-ungarischen Wehrmacht in ihren letzten Friedensjahren." *Militärwissenschaftlichen Mitteilungen*, nos. 5–6 (1932).

Drašković, Radovan. *Pretorijanske težnje u Srbiji: Apis i "Crna ruka."* Belgrade: Žagor, 2006.

Drummond, Andrew J., and Jacek Lubecki. "Reconstructing Galicia: Mapping the Cultural and Civic Traditions of the Former Austrian Galicia in Poland and Ukraine." *Europe-Asia Studies* 62, no. 8 (October 2010).

Eder, Hans. "Der General der k.u.k. Armee und Geheime Rat Maximilian Csicserics von Bacsány." PhD diss., University of Vienna, 2010.

Ehnl, Maximilian. "Die öst.-ung. Landmacht nach Aufbau, Gliederung, Friedensgarnison, Einteilung und nationaler Zusammensetzung im Sommer 1914." In *Ergänzungsheft 9 zum Werke Österreich-Ungarns letzter Krieg*. Vienna: Militärwissenschaftlichen Mitteilungen, 1934.

Fabini, Ludwig von. "Die Feuertaufe des Eisernen Korps: Der erste Tag der Schlacht von Złoczów am 26. August 1914." *Militärwissenschafliche Mitteilungen*, Nos. 9/10 (1930).

Fahey, John E. "The Secret Poison Plot: Adolf Hofrichter and the Austro-Hungarian General Staff." *Journal on European History of Law* 1 (2011).

Ferrell, Robert H. *Collapse at Meuse-Argonne: The Failure of the Missouri-Kansas Division*. Columbia: University of Missouri Press, 2004.

Feuerbereit! Kriegsalbum des Feldartillerie-Regiments Nr. 104 Wien 1914–1918. Vienna: Halm & Goldmann, 1919.

Fischer, Eduard. *Krieg ohne Heer: Meine Verteidigung der Bukowina gegen die Russen*. Vienna: Franz Schubert, 1935.

Forstner, Franz. *Przemyśl: Österreich-Ungarns bedeutendste Festung.* Vienna: Militärgeschichtliche Dissertationen österreichischer Universitäten, 1987.

Franek, Fritz. "K. und k. Truppen im Westen: I." *Militärwissenschaftliche Mitteilungen,* nos. 3–4 (1931).

———. "Probleme der Organization im ersten Kriegsjahre." In *Ergänzungsheft 1 zum Werke Österreich-Ungarns letzter Krieg.* Vienna, 1930.

———. "Probleme der Organization im ersten Kriegsjahren." *Militärwissenschaftlichen Mitteilungen,* nos. 11–12 (1935).

Frank, Alison Fleig. *Oil Empire: Visions of Prosperity in Austrian Galicia.* Cambridge MA: Harvard University Press, 2005.

Fučík, Josef. *Osmadvacátníci: Spor o českého vojáka Velké války 1914–1918.* Prague: Mladá fronta, 2006.

Führ, Christoph. *Das k.u.k. Armeeoberkommando und die Innenpolitik von Österreich.* Graz: H. Böhlaus Nachf, 1968.

Gandini, Sigmund. *Das bosnisch-herzegovinische Infanterie-Regiment Nr. 2 im Weltkrieg 1914 bis 1918.* Vienna: Austrian Defense Ministry, 1971.

Gaul, Jerzy. "Legiony Polskie w orbicie zainteresowań służb wywiadowczych (1914–1916)." *Kwartalnik Historyczny: organ Towarzystwa Historycznego* 101, no. 2 (1994).

———. "Służby informacyjne Austro-Węgier wobec sprawy polskiej w latach I wojny światowej." *Studia Historyczne* 53, no. 1 (2010).

Gavrilović, Stojan. "New Evidence on the Sarajevo Assassination." *Journal of Modern History* 27, no. 4 (December 1955).

Gebert, Károly. *A kassai VI. hadtest harcai 1914 Aug. 25.–30.* Budapest: M. kir. Hadtörtenelmi Levéltár, 1929.

Generalstabshandbuch. Vienna: Austro-Hungarian War Ministry, 1912.

Gerő, András. *The Hungarian Parliament, 1867–1918: A Mirage of Power.* New York: Columbia University Press, 1997.

Geschichte des k.u.k. Dragoner-Regiment Fürst zu Windischgrätz Nr.14 im Weltkrieg. Vienna: Self-published, 1922.

Geschichte des k.k. Kaiserschützenregimentes Nr. I. Unpub., n.d.

Godsey, William D., Jr. "Quarterings and Kinship: The Social Composition of the Habsburg Aristocracy in the Dualist Era." *Journal of Modern History* 71, no. 1 (March 1999).

Golovin, Nicholas. "The Russian War Plan of 1914: II: The Execution of the Plan." *Slavonic and East European Review* 15, no. 43 (July 1936).

Good, David F. "Stagnation and 'Take-Off' in Austria, 1873–1913." *Economic History Review* 27, no. 1 (February 1974).

Gumz, Jonathan E. *The Resurrection and Collapse of Empire in Habsburg Serbia, 1914–1918.* Cambridge: Cambridge University Press, 2009.

Habsburg, József Főherceg Tábornagy. *Budapest volt házi ezredének a cs. és kir. 32. gyalogezred története.* Budapest, n.d.

Hadley, Tim. "Military Diplomacy in the Dual Alliance: German Military Attaché Reporting from Vienna, 1906–1914." *War in History* 17, no. 3 (2010).

Hämmerle, Christa. "Die k.(u.)k. Armee als 'Schule des Volkes'? Zur Geschichte des Allgemeinen Wehrpflicht in der multinationalen Habsburgermonarchie (1866–1914/18)." In *Der Bürger als Soldat: Die Militarisierung europäischer Gesellschaften im 19. Jahrhundert: ein internationaler Vergleich.* Edited by C. Hansen. Essen: Klartext, 2004.

Hannig, Alma. "Die Balkanpolitik Österreich-Ungarns vor 1914." In *Der Erste Weltkrieg auf dem Balkan: Perspektiven der Forschung.* Edited by J. Angelow. Berlin: Be-Bra Wissenschafts-Verlag, 2011.

Harmat, Ulrike. "Divorce and Remarriage in Austria-Hungary: The Second Marriage of Franz Conrad von Hötzendorf." *Austrian History Yearbook* 32 (2001).

Hecht, Rudolf. "Fragen zur Heeresergänzung der gesamten bewaffneten Macht Österreich-Ungarns während des Ersten Weltkrieges." PhD diss., University of Vienna, 1969.

Der Heldenweg des Zweier-Landsturm 1914–1918. Linz: Self-published, 1934.

Herrmann, David G. *The Arming of Europe and the Making of the First World War.* Princeton: Princeton University Press, 1996.

Herwig, Holger. "Disjointed Allies: Coalition Warfare in Berlin and Vienna, 1914." *Journal of Military History* 54, no. 3 (July 1990).

———. *The Marne, 1914: The Opening of World War I and the Battle That Changed the World.* New York: Random House, 2009.

Himka, John-Paul. "The Greek Catholic Church and Nation-Building in Galicia, 1772–1918." *Harvard Ukrainian Studies* 8, nos. 3–4 (December 1984).

Höbelt, Lothar. *Franz Joseph I.—Der Kaiser und sein Reich: Eine politische Geschichte.* Vienna: Böhlau, 2009, 43–62.

Hoen, Max von, ed. *Geschichte des ehemaligen Egerländer Infanterie-Regiments Nr. 73.* Vienna: Self-published, 1939.

———, ed. *Geschichte des salzburgisch-oberösterreichischen k.u.k. Infanterie-Regiments Erzherzog Rainer Nr. 59 für den Zeitraum des Weltkriegs.* Salzburg: Self-published, 1931.

Hoen, Max von, et al. *Die Deutschmeister: Taten und Schicksale des IR. Hoch-und Deutschmeister Nr. 4 insbesondere im Weltkriege.* Vienna: Self-published, 1928.

Hoffmann, Eduard F. "FM. Svetozar Boroević von Bojna: Österreich-Ungarns Kriegsfront an den Flüssen Isonzo u. Piave." PhD diss., University of Vienna, 1985.

Hof-und Staatshandbuch der Österreichisch-Ungarischen Monarchie für das Jahr 1915. Vienna: 1915, 361.

Horel, Catherine. *Soldaten zwischen nationalen Fronten: Die Auflösung der Militärgrenze und die Enwicklung der kgl.-ungarischen Landwehr (Honvéd) in Kroatien-Slavonien 1868–1914.* Vienna: Österreichische Akademie der Wissenschaften, 2009.

Hubka, Gustav von. *Geschichte des k.u.k. Infanterieregiments Graf von Lacy Nr. 22 vom Jahre 1902 bis zu seiner Auflösung*, vol. 1. Vienna: Self-published, 1938.

———. *Der Jahrgang 1896/98 der k.u.k. Kriegsschule in Wien*. Vienna: Reisser, 1947.

Instruktion für den militärischen Kundschaftsdienst und zur Verhinderung der Spionage in Bosnien und der Hercegovina. Sarajevo: Austro-Hungarian War Ministry, 1912.

Izdebski, Edward. *Bitwa pod Zamościem 26–27 sierpnia 1914 r.* Warsaw: Wojsk in-t nayk-wyd, 1929.

Jahresbericht der k.u.k. Theresianischen Militärakademie, Schuljahr 1912/13. Wiener Neustadt: k.u.k. Armee, 1913.

Jakoncig, Guido. *Tiroler Kaiserjäger im Weltkrieg*. Innsbruck: Verlag Wagner, 1931.

Jászi, Oscar. *The Dissolution of the Habsburg Monarchy*. Chicago: University of Chicago Press, 1929.

Jeřábek, Rudolf. *Potiorek: General im Schatten von Sarajevo*. Graz: Verlag Styria, 1991.

Jobst, Johann. *Führer durch die k.u.k. Theresianische Militärakademie in Wiener Neustadt*. Vienna: Self-published, 1913.

Jones, David. "Imperial Russia's Forces at War." In *Military Effectiveness*, vol. 1, *The First World War*. Edited by A. Millett and W. Murray. Boston: Allen & Unwin, 1988.

Judson, Pieter M. *Guardians of the Nation: Activists on the Language Frontiers of Imperial Austria*. Cambridge MA: Harvard University Press, 2006.

Jung, Peter. "Die Feldverwendung der österreichisch-ungarischen Gendarmerie 1914–1918." In *Geschichte der Gendarmerie in Österreich-Ungarn*. Vienna: Stöhr, 2000.

Kalvoda, Jozef. "General Alois Podhajský: Czechoslovak War Leader." In *War and Society in East Central Europe*, vol. 25, *East Central European War Leaders*. Edited by B. Király and A. Nofi. New York: East European Monographs, 1988.

Kann, Robert A. "The Social Prestige of the Officer Corps in the Habsburg Empire from the Eighteenth Century to 1918." In *War and Society in East Central Europe*, vol. 1. Edited by B. Király and G. Rothenberg. New York: Brooklyn College Press, 1979.

Kerchnawe, Hugo. "Der Feldzug von Rowno." *Militärwissenschaftliche Mitteilungen*, nos. 1–2 (1932).

Kiesewetter, Otto von. *Mit den Siebzehnern im Weltkrieg*. Graz: Self-published, 1934.

Kisch, Egon Erwin. *"Schreib das auf, Kisch!": Das Kriegstagebuch von Egon Erwin Kisch*. Berlin: Reiss, 1930.

Kiszling, Rudolf. "Die Entwicklung der österreichisch-ungarischen Wehrmacht seit der Annexionskrise 1908." *Militärwissenschaftliche Mitteilungen*, no. 10 (1934).

Kozma, Miklós v. *Mackensens ungarische Husaren: Tagebuch eines Frontoffiziers 1914–1918*. Berlin: Verlag f. Kulturpolitik, 1933.

Kranjc, Gregory J. "The Neglected War: The Memory of World War I in Slovenia." *Journal of Slavic Military Studies* 22, no. 2 (April 2009).

Krauss, Alfred. "Infanterie-Geschütze?" *Mitteilungen über Gegenstände des Artillerie- und Geniewesens* 44, no. 8 (1913).

———. *Die Ursachen unserer Niederlage: Erinnerungen und Urteile aus dem Weltkrieg.* Munich: Lehmanns, 1923.

Kreisler, Fritz. *Four Weeks in the Trenches.* Boston: Houghton Mifflin, 1917.

Kronenbitter, Günther. "Bundesgenossen? Zur militärpolitischen Kooperation zwischen Berlin und Wien 1912 bis 1914." In *Deutschland in den internationalen Beziehungen des 19. und 20. Jahrhunderts.* Edited by W. Bernecker and V. Dotterweich. Munich: Vogel, 1996.

———. "Falsch verbunden? Die Militärallianz zwichen Österreich-Ungarn und Deutschland 1906–1914." *Österreichische Militärische Zeitschrift* 38 (2000).

———. "Generalstabsmässig in die Katastrophe? Zur Kriegsführung der Landstreitkräfte 1914." *Historicum* (Spring 2001).

———. "Haus ohne Macht? Erzherzog Franz Ferdinand und die Krise der Habsburgermonarchie." In *Der Fürst: Ideen und Wirklichkeiten in der europäischen Geschichte.* Edited by W. Weber. Cologne: Böhlau, 1998.

———. *"Krieg im Frieden": Die Führung der k.u.k. Armee und die Grossmachtpolitik Österreich-Ungarns 1906–1914.* Oldenbourg, 2003.

———. "'Nur los lassen': Österreich-Ungarn und der Wille zum Krieg." In *Lange und kurze Wege in den Ersten Weltkrieg.* Edited by Johannes Burkhardt et al. Munich: Vogel, 1996.

———. "Von 'Schweinehunden' und 'Waffenbrüdern': Der Koalitionskrieg der Mittelmächte 1914/15 zwischen Sachzwang und Ressentiment." In *Der vergessene Front: Der Osten 1914–15: Ereignis, Wirkung, Nachwirkung.* Edited by G. Gross. Paderborn: Schöningh, 2006.

Kuderna, Wolfgang. "Das erste Gefecht des k.u.k. Infanterie-Regiments Nr. 4 im Jahr 1914." In *300 Jahre Regiment Hoch-und Deutschmeister.* Vienna: Self-published, 1996.

Die k.u.k. Reitende Artillerie-Division Nr. 5 (2) im Weltkriege 1914–1918. Vienna: Self-published, 1927.

Kun, Josef Eugen. *A cs. és kir. 23. gyalogezred hadialbuma.* Budapest: Self-published, 1916.

Kwaśny, Emil. *"Krakowskie dzieci": na polu chwały.* Cracow: Self-published, 1917.

Leidinger, Hannes. "Suizid und Militär: Debatten—Ursachenforschung—Reichsratinterpellationen 1907–1914." In *Glanz—Gewalt—Gehorsam: Militär und Gesellschaft in der Habsburger-monarchie (1800 bis 1918).* Edited by L. Cole et al. Essen: Klartext, 2011.

Lein, Richard. "The 'Betrayal' of the k.u.k. Infantry Regiment 28: Truth of Legend." In *Prague Papers on the History of International Relations.* Edited by A. Skřivan and A. Suppan. Prague: Institute of World History, 2009.

———. *Pflichterfüllung oder Hochverrat? Die tschechischen Soldaten Österreich-Ungarns im Ersten Weltkrieg.* Vienna: LIT, 2011.

Leppa, Konrad. *Das Gefecht bei Schaschintzi am 6. September 1914.* Reichenberg: Der Heimat Söhne im Weltkrieg, 1932.

———. *Die Schlacht bei Komarów: Die Kämpfe der k.u.k. 4. Armee und der russischen 5. Armee von 26. August bis 2. September 1914.* Karlsbad: Verlag Kraft, 1932.

Linzer Hessen (1733–1936): Geschichte des k.u.k. Infanterie-Regiments Ernst Ludwig Grossherzog von Hessen Nr. 14. Linz: Self-published, 1937.

Lohr, Eric. "The Russian Army and the Jews: Mass Deportation, Hostages, and Violence during World War I." *Russian Review* 60 (July 2001).

Lyon, James. "'A Peasant Mob': The Serbian Army on the Eve of the Great War." *Journal of Military History* 61 (July 1997).

MacDonald, David M. "The Durnovo Memorandum in Context: Official Conservatism and the Crisis of Autocracy." *Jahrbücher für Geschichte Osteuropas,* n.s., 44, no. 4 (1996): 485–502.

MacKenzie, David. *Apis: The Congenial Conspirator, The Life of Colonel Dragutin T. Dimitrijevic.* New York: East European Monographs, 1989.

———. "Officer Conspirators and Nationalism in Serbia, 1901–1914." In *Essays on War and Society in East Central Europe, 1740–1920.* Edited by S. Fischer-Galati and B. Király. New York: East European Monographs, 1987.

Madárasz, Ladislaus. "Die k.u.k. Luftfahrtruppen im Weltkriege." *Militärwissenschatfliche und Technische Mitteilungen,* nos. 7–10 (1928).

Magris, Claudio. *Il mito asburgico: Umanità e stile del mondo austroungarico nella letteratura austriaca moderna.* Torino: Einaudi, 1963.

Maior, Liviu. *Habsburgi şi Români: De la loialitateta dinastică la identitate naţională.* Bucharest: Ed. Enciclopedică, 2006.

Marácz, László. "Multilingualism in the Transleithanian part of the AustroHungarian Empire (1867–1918): Policy and Practice." *Linguistics (Jezikoslovlje)* 13, no. 2 (2012): 275–84.

Martinek, Robert. *Kriegstagebuch eines Artillerie-Offiziers.* Vienna: Berdach, 1975.

Mascher, Matthias. *Die 76er—Einst und Jetzt.* Vienna: Fasching, 1936.

Mátyás, Alexander v. *A cs. és kir. 85, Számu Gaudernak Báró gyalogezred története,* vol. 1, *Rész.* Budapest: Self-published, 1916.

McMeekin, Sean. *The Russian Origins of the First World War.* Cambridge MA: Harvard University Press, 2011.

Mil'shtein, Mikhail. "Delo polkovnika Redlya." *Voenno-istoricheskiy zhurnal,* no. 1 (1966).

Mokyr, Joel. "And Thou, Happy Austria." *Journal of Economic History* 44, no. 4 (December 1984).

Moll, Martin. "Austro-Hungarian Counterintelligence Activities Prior to World War I: The Local Level." *Journal of Intelligence History* 5, no. 1 (Summer 2005): 1–14.

Monolatii, Ivan. *Ukrains'ki Lehionery: Formuvannya ta boiovii shlyakh Ukrains'kikh Sichovykh Stril'tsiv*. Kiev: Tempora 2008.

Moritsch, Andreas, ed. *Der Austroslavismus: Ein verfrühtes Konzept zur politischen Neugestaltung Mitteleuropas*. Vienna: Böhlau, 1996.

Murrer, Ernst G. F. *Hujcze (September 1914): Zur Geschichte des 2. Regiments der Tiroler Kaiserjäger*. Cremona: Persico, 1996.

Nemeth, Josef. "Aus den Kämpfen der 2. Gebirgsbrigade 9–16. September 1914." *Militärwissenschaftlische Mitteilungen*, nos. 1–2 (1930).

Oberklofer, Gerhard, and Eduard Rabovsky. "Tiroler Kaiserjäger in Galizien." In *Historische Blinkpunkte: Festschrift für Johann Rainer*. Edited by Sabine Weiss. Innsbruck: Institut für Sprachwissenschaft der Universität, 1988.

Ongari, Dante. *La Guerra in Galizia e sui Carpati 1914–1918: La partecipazione del Trentino*. Calliano: Manfrini, 1983.

Oršolić, Tado. "Vojnateritorijalna podjela i reorganizacija austrougarske vojske 1867.–1890." *Rodovi HAZU* 2, no. 12 (2003).

Ortner, M. Christian. *The Austro-Hungarian Artillery from 1867 to 1918: Technology, Organization and Tactics*. Vienna: Militaria, 2007.

———. "Soldatsein im Ersten Weltkrieg: Studie zur Entwicklung der österreichisch-ungarischen Kampfverfahrens 1914–1918." Master's thesis, University of Vienna, 1994.

Österreich-Ungarns letzter Krieg, vols. 1–7. Vienna: Austrian Defense Ministry, 1930–38.

Papp, Tibor. "Die königliche ungarische Landwehr (Honvéd)." In *Die Habsburgermonarchie 1848–1918*, vol. 5, *Die bewaffnete Macht*. Edited by A. Wandruszka and Urbanitsch, vol. 5 Vienna: Österreichische Akademie der Wissenschaften, 1987.

Pauschenwein, Andreas. *Feuer! Österreichs Feldartillerie im Einsatz 1909–1918*. Vienna: Stöhr, 2007.

Pavlović, Živko. *Bitka na Jadru: Avgusta 1914 god*. Belgrade: Grafički zavod "Makarije," 1924.

Peball, Kurt. "Der Feldzug gegen Serbien und Montenegro im Jahre 1914." Special issue. *Österreichische Militärische Zeitschrift* (1965).

———. "Führungsfragen der österreichisch-ungarischen Südtiroloffensive in Jahre 1916." *Mitteilungen des Österreichichen Staatsarchivs* 31 (1978).

———. "Um das Erbe: Zur Nationalitätenpolitik des k.u.k. Armeeoberkommandos während der Jahre 1914 bis 1917." Special issue. *Österreichische Militärische Zeitschrift* (1967).

Peball, Kurt, and Gunther Rothenberg. "Der Fall 'U': Die geplannte Besetzung Ungarns durch die k.u.k. Armee im Herbst 1905." *Schriften des Heeresgeschichtlichen Museums in Wien* (1969).

Péter, László. "The Army Question in Hungarian Politics 1867–1918." *Central Europe* 4, no. 2 (November 2006).

Pethö, Adalbert. *Agenten für den Doppeladler: Österreich-Ungarns geheimer Dienst im Weltkrieg*. Graz: L. Stocker, 1998.

Pfannenstiel, [Oberst]. "Der Todeskampf der reitenden Batterie 1/7 im Kavalleriegefecht bei Buczacz am 23. August 1914." *Militärwissenschaftliche Technische Mitteilungen*, Nos. 5–6 (1929).

Pitreich, Maximilian von. *Lemberg 1914*. Vienna: Adolf Holzhausen, 1929.

——. *1914: Die militärische Probleme unseres Kriegsbeginnes*. Vienna: Adolf Holzhausen, 1934.

Plaschka, Richard Georg. "Aus dem Haft-Akten der Sarajevo-Attentäter." *Balcanica* 8 (1977).

——. "Die polnische Legion in der Beurteilung der österreichisch-ungarischen militärischen Führung am Beginn des Ersten Weltkrieges." *Zeszyty naukowe Uniwersytetu Jagiellońskiego* 57, no. 482 (1978).

——. "Prag September 1914: Nationale Impulse unter dem Eindruck der ersten Krigswochen." In *Politik und Gesellschaft im alten und neuen Österreich: Festschrift für Rudolf Neck zum 60. Geburtstag*, vol. 1. Edited by Isabella Ackerl et al. Vienna: Verlag für Geschichte und Politik, 1981.

——. "Zur Vorgeschichte des Übergangs von Einheiten des Infanterieregiments Nr. 28 an der russischen Front 1915." In *Österreich und Europa: Festgabe für Hugo Hantsch zum 70. Geburtstag*. Edited by Hugo Hantsch. Vienna: Verlag Styria, 1970.

Podrazil, Franz. "Die Entwicklung der Fernmelde-und elektronischen Aufklärung, ihr Anteil anmilitärischen Erfolgen und Misserfolgen." Master's thesis, National Defense Academy, Vienna, 1969.

Pojić, Milan. "Ustroj austrougarske vojske na ozemlju Hrvatske 1868–1914." *Arhivski vjesnik* god. 43 (2000).

Pokorny, Herrmann. *Emlékeim: A láthatatlan hírszerző*. Budapest: Petit Real, 2000.

Popovici, Aurel C. *Die Vereinigten Staaten von Gross-Österreich*. Leipzig: Elischer Nachf, 1906.

Programm für die achtwöchentliche Ausbildung der Rekruten und die zehnwöchentliche der Ersatzreservisten. Vienna: Austro-Hungarian War Ministry, 1913.

Prusin, Alexander Victor. *Nationalizing a Borderland: War, Ethnicity, and Anti-Jewish Violence in East Galicia, 1914–1920*. Tuscaloosa: University of Alabama Press, 2005.

Rachamimov, Alon. *POWs and the Great War: Captivity on the Eastern Front*. New York: Bloomsbury Academic Press, 2002.

Radenković, Milan. *Cerska operacija*. Belgrade: Vojno delo, 1953.

Ranchi, Sergio. "'La luna vista a girarsi': L'avventura galiziana negli scritti e nelle memorie degli infanteristi del Litorale." In *Sui campi di Galizia (1914–1917): Gli italiani d'Austria e il fronte orientale*. Edited by Gianluigi Fait. Rovereto: Museo storico italiano della Guerra, 1997.

Ratni dnevnik C.K. varaždinske pješačke pukovnije br. 16: 26. srpnja 1914–29. siječnja 1915. Bjelovar: Državni arhiv u Bjelovaru, 2004.

Ratzenhofer, Emil. "Verlustkalkül für den Karpathenwinter 1915." *Ergänzungsheft I zum Werke Österreich-Ungarns letzter Krieg.* Vienna, 1930.

Rauchensteiner, Manfried. *Der Tod des Doppeladlers: Österreich-Ungarn und der Erste Weltkrieg.* Vienna: Styria 1994.

———. "Der Tod des Generals Wodniansky." In *Österreichisch-polnische militärisch Beziehungen im 20. Jahrhundert.* Vienna: Austrian Defense Ministry, 2010.

Reichlin-Meldegg, Georg. *Des Kaisers Prinz Eugen? Feldmarschall Hermann Baron Kövess von Kövessháza: Der letzte Oberkommandant der k.u.k. Armee im Ersten Weltkrieg.* Graz: Ares-Verlag, 2010.

Reifberger, Josef. "Die Entwicklung des militärischen Nachrichtenwesens in der k.u.k. Armee." *Österreichische Militärische Zeitschrift,* no. 3 (1976).

Rendulić, Lothar. *Soldat in stürtzenden Reichen.* Munich: Damm, 1965.

Robinson, Paul. "A Study of Grand Duke Nikolai Nikolaevich as Supreme Commander of the Russian Army, 1914–1915." *The Historian* 75, no. 3 (Fall 2013).

Roksandić, Drago. *Lav ili lisica sa Soče?.* Zagreb: Vjeće srpske nacionalne manjine grada Zagreba, 2006.

Ronge, Maximilian. *Meister der Spionage.* Vienna: Johannes Günther, 1935.

Rothenberg, Gunther E. *Army of Francis Joseph.* West Lafayette IN: Purdue University Press, 1976.

———. "The Austro-Hungarian Campaign Against Serbia in 1914." *Journal of Military History* 53 (April 1989).

———. *Napoleon's Great Adversaries: The Archduke Charles and Austrian Army, 1792–1814.* Bloomington: Indiana University Press, 1982.

———. "Nobility and Military Careers: The Habsburg Officer Corps, 1740–1914." *Military Affairs* 40, no. 4 (December 1976).

———. "The Struggle over the Dissolution of the Croatian Military Border, 1850–1871." *Slavic Review* 23, no. 1 (March 1964).

———. "Toward a Hungarian National Army: The Military Compromise of 1868 and Its Consequences." *Slavic Review* 31, no. 4 (December 1972).

Rudel, Rudolf. "Die neue Exerzierreglement für die k.u.k. Fusstruppen." *Streffleurs militärische Zeitschrift* 1 (1912).

Ruppert, Karl Hans. "Der Untergang des Feldkanonenregiments Nr. 17 (Miskolc) bei Pukarzów." In *Ehrenbuch unserer Artillerie.* Edited by Hugo Kerchnawe. Vienna: Self-published, 1935.

Scheer, Tamara. *Die Ringstrassenfront: Österreich-Ungarn, das Kriegsüberwachungsamt und Ausnahmezustand während des Ersten Weltrkrieges.* Vienna: Bundesminister für Landesverteidigung, 2010.

Scheff, Karl. "Das Aufklärungsgefecht bei Posadów." *Militärwissenschaftliche Mitteilungen,* nos. 7–8 (1931).

Scheidl, Hans Werner. "1914: Franz Joseph wollte den Krieg," *Die Presse* (Vienna), September 20, 2013.

Schindler, John R. "Defeating Balkan Insurgency: The Austro-Hungarian Army in Bosnia-Hercegovina, 1878–1882." *Journal of Strategic Studies* 27, no. 3 (September 2004).

———. "Disaster on the Drina." *War in History* 9, no. 2 (April 2002).

———. *Isonzo: The Forgotten Sacrifice of the Great War*. Westport CT: Praeger Publishers, 2001.

———. "Redl—Spy of the Century?" *International Journal of Intelligence and Counterintelligence* 18, no. 3 (Fall 2005).

———. "Steamrollered in Galicia: The Austro-Hungarian Army and the Brusilov Offensive, 1916." *War in History* 10, no. 1 (January 2003).

Schmidl, Erwin. "From Paardeberg to Przemysl: Austrian-Hungary and the Lessons of the Anglo-Boer War, 1899–1902." In *The Boer War and Military Reforms*. Edited by J. Stone and E. Schmidl. Lanham MD: University Press of America, 1988.

———. *Juden in der k.(u.)k. Armee 1788–1918*. Eisenstadt: Österreichisches Jüdisches Museum, 1989.

Schön, Josef. *Šabac! Der Kampf der Deutschböhmischen 29. Inf.-Div., des Prager VIII. Korps, und des Budapester IV. Korps im August 1914 in Nordwest Serbien*. Reichenberg: Heimatsöhne im Weltkrieg, 1928.

Šehić, Zijad. *U smrt za cara i domovinu! Bosanci i Hercegovini u vojnoj organizacije Habsburške monarhije 1878–1918*. Sarajevo: Sarajevo Publishing, 2007.

Showalter, Dennis E. *Tannenberg: Clash of Empires*. Hamden CT: Archon Books, 1991.

Sitte, Martha. "Alexander von Brosch, der Flügeladjutant und Vorstand der Militärkanzlei des Thronfolgers Franz Ferdinand." PhD diss., University of Vienna, 1961.

Sked, Alan. *The Decline and Fall of the Habsburg Empire, 1815–1918*. London: Longman, 1989.

———. *Radetzky: Imperial Victor and Military Genius*. London: I. B. Tauris, 2011.

Skoko, Savo, and Petar Opačić. *Vojvoda Stepa Stepanović u ratovima Srbije 1876–1918*. Belgrade: Beogradski izdavačko-grafički zavod, 1985.

Somogyi, Éva. "The Hungarian *Honvéd* Army and the Unity of the Habsburg Empire: The *Honvéd* Reform of 1904." In *East Central Europe during World War One*, vol. 19. Edited by B. Király and N. Dreisziger. New York: East European Monographs, 1985.

Sondhaus, Lawrence. *Franz Conrad von Hötzendorf: Architect of the Apocalypse*. Boston: Brill Academic Publishers, 2000.

———. "The Strategic Culture of the Habsburg Army." *Austrian History Yearbook* 32 (2001).

Spence, Richard B. "*Die Bosniaken kommen*!: The Bosnian-Hercegovinian Formations of the Austro-Hungarian Army, 1914–1918." In *Scholar, Patriot, Mentor:*

Historical Essays in Honor of Dimitrije Djordjević. Edited by R. Spence and L. Nelson. New York: East European Monographs, 1992.

Stergar, Rok. "National Indifference in the Heyday of Nationalist Mobilization? Ljubljana Military Veterans and the Language of Command." *Austrian History Yearbook* 43 (2012).

Stergar, Rok, and Janez Polajnar. *Slovenci in vojska, 1867–1914: slovenski odnos do vojaških vprašanj od uvedbe dualizma do začetka 1. svetovne vojne.* Ljubljana: Filozofske fakultete 2004.

Sternberg, Adalbert. *Warum Österreich zugrunde gehen musste: Die österreichischen Hofwürdenträger.* Vienna: Verlag Tagesfragen, 1927.

Stolz, Otto. *Das Tiroler Landsturmregiment Nr. II im Kriege 1914–1915 in Galizien.* Innsbruck: Self-published, 1938.

Stone, Norman. "Army and Society in the Habsburg Monarchy, 1900–1914." *Past & Present,* no. 33 (1966).

———. "Constitutional Crises in Hungary, 1903–1906." *Slavonic and East European Review* 45, no. 104 (January 1967).

———. *The Eastern Front 1914–1917.* London: Charles Scribner's Sons, 1975.

———. "Hungary and the Crisis of July 1914." *Journal of Contemporary History* 1, no. 3 (July 1966).

———. "Die Mobilmachung der öst.-ung. Armee 1914." *Militärgeschichtliche Mitteilungen* 2, no. 16 (1974).

———. "Moltke and Conrad: Relations between the Austro-Hungarian and German General Staffs, 1909–1914." In *The War Plans of the Great Powers, 1880–1914.* Edited by Paul Kennedy. Boston: Allen & Unwin, 1979.

Stupp, Johann Adam. "Neues über Georg Trakls Lazarettaufenhalte und Tod in Galizien." *Südostdeutsche Semesterblätter.* Munich, 1967.

Svoboda, George J. "The Political Struggles in Bohemia and František Palacký (1860–70)," *Nationalities Papers* 12, no. 1 (1984).

Tăslăuanu, Octavian C. *With the Austrian Army in Galicia.* London: Skeffington & Son, 1918.

Thümmler, L.-H. "Nationalismus im österreichischen Berufsoffizierskorps in der Zeit von 1848/49 bis 1914." *Zeitschrift für Heereskunde* 59, no. 37 (1995).

Tihany, Lesley C. "The Austro-Hungarian Compromise, 1867–1918: A Half Century of Diagnosis; Fifty Years of Post-Mortem." *Central European History* 2, no. 2 (June 1969).

Todero, Roberto. *Dalla Galizia all'Isonzo: Storia e storie dei soldati triestini nella Grande Guerra.* Udine: Gaspari, 2006.

Tomši, Josef. "Vorschrift für die Tätigkeit der russischen Feldartillerie im Kampfe." *Mitteilungen über Gegenstände des Artillerie-und Geniewesens* 43, no. 9 (1912).

Tumlirz, Otto. *Waffengänge des IR.6: Skizzen aus dem grossen Kriege.* Self-published, 1917.

Tunstall, Graydon A. *Blood on the Snow: The Carpathian Winter War of 1915*. Lawrence: University Press of Kansas, 2012.

———. "The Habsburg Command Conspiracy: The Austrian Falsification of the Historiography on the Outbreak of World War I." *Austrian History Yearbook* 27 (1996).

———. *Planning for War Against Russia and Serbia: Austro-Hungarian and German Military Strategies, 1871–1914*. New York: East European Monographs, 1993.

Turner, L. C. F. "The Russian Mobilization in 1914." *Journal of Contemporary History* 3, no. 1 (January 1968).

Tych, Feliks. "Victor Adler, Ignaz Daszyński und die Polnischen Legionen." In *Politik und Gesellschaft im alten und neuen Österreich: Festschrift für Rudolf Neck zum 60. Geburtstag*, vol. 1. Edited by Isabella Ackerl et al. Vienna: Verlag für Geschichte und Politik, 1981.

Urbański, August von. *Die Geschichte der k.k. 46. Schützendivision*. Berlin: Bernard & Graefe, 1942.

Uyar, Mesut. "Ottoman Arab Officers between Nationalism and Loyalty during the First World War," *War in History* 20, no. 4 (2013).

Das Vierundachtzigerbuch. Vienna: Holzhausen, 1919.

Vogelsang, Ludwig von, ed. *Das steirische Infanterieregiment Nr. 47 im Weltkrieg*. Graz: Self-published, 1932.

Vormarsch des k.u.k. Infanterie-Regiments Nr. 13 gegen Lublin im Sommerfeldzug 1914. Olmütz: Druck J. Groák, 1918.

Wagner, Richard. *Geschichte des ehemaligen Schützen-Regiments Nr. 6*. Karlsbad, 1932.

Wagner, Walter. "Die k.(u.)k. Armee–Gliederung und Aufgabestellung." In *Die Habsburgermonarchie 1848–1918*, vol. 1, *Die bewaffnete Macht*. Edited by A. Wandruszka and Urbanitsch. Die Habsburgermonarchie (1848–1918), vol. 5. Vienna: Österreichische Akademie der Wissenschaften, 1987.

Walzel, Clemens von. *Kundschaftsdienst oder Spionage? Erinnerungen eines alten Nachrichtenoffiziers*. Vienna: "Johs" Günther, 1934.

Wandycz, Piotr S. "The Poles in the Habsburg Monarchy." *Austrian History Yearbook* 3, no. 2 (1967).

Ward, James Mace. *Priest, Politician, Collaborator: Jozef Tiso and the Making of Fascist Slovakia*. Ithaca NY: Cornell University Press, 2013.

Wargelin, Clifford F. "The Economic Collapse of Austro-Hungarian Dualism, 1914–1918." *East European Quarterly* 34, no. 3 (September 2000).

Wawro, Geoffrey. *The Austro-Prussian War: Austria's War with Prussia and Italy in 1866*. Cambridge: Cambridge University Press, 1997.

Wendland, Anna Veronika. "Die Rückkehr der Russophilen in die ukrainischen Geschichte: Neue Aspekte der ukrainischen Nationsbildung in Galizien, 1848–1914." *Jahrbücher für die Geschichte Osteuropas* 49, no. 2 (2001): 178–99.

Wheatcroft, Andrew. *The Habsburgs: Embodying Empire.* New York: Penguin, 1997.

Williamson, Samuel R., Jr. "Aggressive and Defensive Aims of Political Elites? Austro-Hungarian Policy in 1914." In *An Improbable War?: The Outbreak of World War I and European Political Culture before 1914.* Edited by H. Afflerbach and D. Stevenson. New York: Berghahn Books, 2007.

———. "Influence, Power, and the Policy Process: The Case of Franz Ferdinand, 1906–1914." *Historical Journal* 17, no. 2 (June 1974).

Williamson, Samuel R., Jr., and Ernest R. May. "An Identity of Opinion: Historians and July 1914." *Journal of Modern History* 79, no.2 (June 2007).

Winkler, Wilhelm. *Der Anteil der nichtdeutschen Volksstämme der öst.-ung. Wehrmacht.* Vienna: Seidel, 1919.

Winzor, Alfred von. *Weisse Dragoner im Weltkrieg: Die Geschichte des k.u.k. Dragoner-Regiments Nr. 15 1891–1918.* Vienna: Im Selbstverlag, 1935.

Wittich, Alfred von. "Zur Weltanschauung Conrads von Hötzendorf." *Militärwissenschaftliche Mitteilungen* 75 (January 1944).

Witzhaupt, Ernst, ed. *Die Tiroler Kaiserjäger im Weltkriege 1914–1918.* Vienna: Goeth, 1935.

Wolfgang, Bruno. *Przemyśl 1914/15.* Vienna: Payer, 1935.

Würthle, Friedrich. *Dokumente zum Sarajevoprozess: Ein Quellenbericht.* Vienna: Generaldirektion des Österreichischen Staatsarchivs, 1978.

———. *Die Spur führt nach Belgrad: Die Hintergründe des Dramas von Sarajevo 1914.* Vienna: Molden-Taschenbuch-Verlag, 1975.

Zanantoni, Eduard. *Geschichte der 29. Infanterie-Division im Weltkrieg 1914–1918,* vol. 1, *Juli 1914 bis Juni 1915.* Reichenberg: Heimatsöhne im Weltkrieg, 1929.

Zehetbauer, Ernst. "Die 'E.F.' und das Ende der alten Armee: Der Krieg der Reserveoffiziere Österreich-Ungarns 1914–1918." Master's thesis, University of Vienna, 2000.

Zeinar, Herbert. *Geschichte des österreichischen Generalstabes.* Vienna: Böhlau, 2006.

Zell, August. "Der Kampf um die Landenge von Kintschou." *Mitteilungen über Gegenstände des Artillerie-und Geniewesens* 53, no. 5 (1912).

Zückert, Martin. "Antimilitarismus und der soldatische Resistenz: Politischer Protest und armeefeindliches Verhalten in der tschechischen Gesellschaft bis 1918." In *Glanz—Gewalt—Gehorsam: Militär und Gesellschaft in der Habsburgermonarchie (1800 bis 1918).* Edited by L. Cole, et al. Essen: Klartext, 2011.

INDEX

A-Group, 68
aircraft, 73, 82, 130, 162–63
Alagić, Osman, 233
Alberti, Count, 237
Alles Erdreich ist Österreich Untertan (AEIOU), 13
Anglo-Boer War (1899–1902), 73, 78
antiwar sentiment, 11; anti-Habsburg and, 271; of Franz Ferdinand, 95–96, 100; Karl's wishful peace-seeking, 286–87
Antwerp, 116
AOK. See *Armeeoberkommando*
Apis. *See* Dimitrijević, Dragutin
Appel, Michael von, 91, 101–2, 104
Apponyi, Albert, 109
ärarisch deutsch (language of Habsburg bureaucracy), 50
Armeeoberkommando (AOK) (Army High Command), 110; Bohemia and Moravia impacted by, 271–72; Boroević given Third Army command, 224–28; Conrad, F., preeminent in, 163, 166; Czech troops singled out by, 257, 271–72, 274, 282; Dankl ennobled by, 177–78; Galicia and Bukovina under martial law by, 154; Galicia

debacle kept quiet by, 210–11, 213, 217, 220, 263; on Galicians suspected of espionage, 226–27; ignoring intelligence, 282–83; Neu Sandez relocation of, 252; panic among Third Army known to, 219, 224; Przemyśl selected by, 150–51; on questioning of prisoners, 187; radio intelligence of, 160, 227–28, 251, 262–63, 273–74, 278; receives Lemberg grim news, 219; Redlich's observations of, 168; sheltering itself from Galician debacle, 195–96; surrendering Galicia to Russia, 262; Szeptycki's assessment ignored by, 166; troop conditions reported to, 203, 206; vague orders to Brudermann from, 190; warned of Russian artillery, 187–88. See also *Evidenzbureau*
armored car, 73
Army Slavic (pidgin), 43
Artamonov, Viktor, 96
Arz von Straussenburg, Arthur, 285, 286
Asiago plateau, 282
Auffenberg, Moritz von, 53, 169, 178–86, 197, 251; blamed for

Auffenberg, Moritz von (*cont.*)
    Rawa Ruska defeat, 264; every
    advance bought with blood,
    200–203; mischievous trick played
    on Fourth Army of, 208–14; at
    Przemyśl, 151, 167
Ausgleich (Compromise of
    Austria-Hungary)(1867), 16–20,
    28, 34, 40
Austria, 12–15, 17–18; oil exports,
    25; as "other" German state, 16;
    relations between Germans,
    minority groups, Magyars in, 19
Austria-Hungary (Dual Monarchy):
    Achilles' heel of, 34; Bosnia-
    Hercegovina annexed by, 23–24;
    deadlock between Vienna and
    Budapest, 35–36, 66, 266, 286;
    enduring legacy of, 12; foreign and
    domestic problems interwoven,
    23; Germany's alliance with,
    69–70; institutionalized escapism
    of, 10–11, 69–72, 105–8; military
    conscription and funding, 36–39,
    72; official birth of, 16–17; Serbia's
    invasion of, 124–25, 132–33, 241,
    269–70, 281; suicide rate, 46
Austro-Hungarian Army: casualties
    in Serbia, 270; Eastern Front total
    casualties, 270; flawed mobilization
    and deployment of, 5–6, 66–67,
    105–8, 115–16, 118–27, 151–71;
    friendly-fire incidents in Serbia,
    145; furloughed for harvest leave,
    101; organization and size of,
    65–66; *Schwarz-Gelbe Offensive*,
    278–80; sergeant ethnicity same
    as rank and file, 43; tactful
    handling of ethnicity, 43, 44;
    total mobilization numbers,
    115–16; unreadiness for major war,

102. See also *Honvéd; kaiserlich
    und königliche Armee; Landwehr*
Austroslavism, 20
autumn swinery (battle of Rowno),
    278–80

Bach, Alexander, 15
Bach system, 15
Baczyński, Rajmunc, 155
Balkans: Allied offensive in, 286–87;
    Austria-Hungary's position
    prior to, 23–24, 66–69; Austro-
    Hungarian disaster in, 142–47;
    battle of Cer, 133–38, 143–47;
    Cer as first Entente victory, 138;
    Conrad, F., cavalier attitude toward,
    120–22; Conrad, F., War Plan "B"
    for, 68–69, 106–7, 114–16; conscripts
    to, 45; culling of potential Serbian
    fifth column, 125; Danube Flotilla
    deployed to, 105, 119, 141; decreased
    stability in, 63; Potiorek's failed
    campaigns in, 240–70; quiet at
    last, 285
Balkanstreitkräfte: readiness of,
    118–19, 122; Serbian defeat of, 142,
    147; stronger on propaganda than
    information, 130, 142
Balkan Wars (1912–13), 23–24, 39, 48,
    90; create enlarged and aggressive
    Serbian military, 39; modern
    bullets and artillery used in, 215;
    seasoned veterans of, 122–25
Baranovichi, 159
Bardolff, Carl von, 184–86
battle of Caporetto, 285, 286
battle of Cer, 133–38, 143–47
battle of Drina, 125, 130–31, 240–42,
    271; *Balkanstreitkräfte* crossing
    Drina river, 118–19
battle of Dukla Pass, 274–75

Cer, 133–37, 143–47; as first Entente victory, 138

Cerska planina, 133–44

Chlopy edict, 37

Chlumecký, Johann von, 99

Chodel, 239–40

Chodorów, 206

cholera, 215, 255

Churchill, Winston, 2, 106, 208

Cisleithania, 19

class: of career officers, 53–54; Communist emphasis on, 3–4; -derived prejudices hindering military, 259; lower-, women for pleasure of officers, 85; sergeant ethnicity same as rank and file, 43; war as great leveler of, 109, 272

Combined and Šumadija I Divisions, Serbian Army, 134

Communism, 3; historiography under, 4

Compromise of Austria-Hungary (*Ausgleich*) (1867), 16–20, 28, 34, 40

Compromise of Croatia-Slavonia (*Nagodba*) (1868), 17, 34–35

Conradian cult, avoiding painful realities, 289

Conrad von Hötzendorf, Franz: on army's budgetary predicament, 38; Austro-Hungarian defeat and, 5–6, 265; Balkans plan of, 68–69, 106–7, 114–16, 120–22; blames Berlin for failure, 153; defects and talents of, 64; "Diary of my Woes" by, 62; dodges marriage laws, 277; Eighth Division in Tyrol, 60; establishes organizations to manage press, 117; *in Evidenzbureau*, 72; Ferdinand unhappy with, 90, 92; firepower underestimated by, 72, 75, 177,

188; Franz Ferdinand and, 90, 92; Franz Joseph I and, 149; Galicia flawed plan, mobilization, and deployment, 151–59, 169–71; Germany blamed by, 277; Gródek battle visited by, 248; institutionalized escapism of, 10–11, 69–72, 105–8; Krauss's criticism of, 146–47, 266; modern weaponry unappreciated by, 72, 75, 177, 178; Potiorek and, 60–62; Redl disaster impacting, 84–89; Redlich's visit to, 168–69; Reininghaus and, 62–63, 93, 99, 101, 108, 149–50, 169, 264, 276–78; *Schwarz-Gelbe Offensive* organized by, 278–80; Serbia flawed plan, mobilization, and deployment, 66–67, 105–8, 115–16, 118–27; *Strafexpedition* of, 281–82; strategic blindness of, 103–6; "Summation of the Situation" report from, 93; War Plan "B" of, 68–69, 106–7, 114–16; War Plan "I" of, 68; War Plan "R" of, 67–68; wishful thinking of, 163, 166

Conrad von Hötzendorf, Herbert, 150, 168, 237, 253

Conrad von Hötzendorf, Kurt, 85, 93

conscription, 36, 38, 39, 72, 267

Cossacks, 250, 253; Austro-Hungarian soldiers mistaken for, 187; panic and terror of, 204–5, 218, 231–32; quick-moving, 164, 169, 184; Stanisławów seized by, 223

Cracow, 26, 265, 269; German Eleventh Army in, 278; I Corps, 28, 240; as Piłsudski's base of operations, 28; Polish Legion from, 155, 165; radio stations at, 272; Thirteenth Infantry Regiment, 155

Cramon, August von, 71

Croatia/Croatian troops, 21,
    282; *Domobranstvo* of, 35, 42;
    easternmost region of, 129, 241,
    269; *graničari*, 34–35; Sarajevo
    assassination causing riots in,
    98–99; Sixteenth Regiment, 140;
    -Slavonia, 17; Thirty-sixth Division,
    140; XIII Corps, 126
Csicserics von Bacsány, Maximilian, 73
Custoza, 16
Czechoslovakia, 3, 4
Czechs, 20; in Austria, 19; parlous
    relations between Germans and,
    274–75; in Prague's Twenty-eighth,
    126; special AOK attention on,
    271–72
Czech troops: Nineteenth Division,
    279; as patriotic and loyal, 111–12;
    Prague's Twenty-eighth earns
    plaudits, 281; rising nationalism
    among, 48–49, 271–72; singled
    out as troublemakers, 257, 271–72,
    274, 282; Twenty-first *Landwehr*
    as scapegoat, 143, 271, 274–75;
    VIII Corps, 126
Czernowitz, 164

Dalmatia/Dalmatians, 19, 113
Dankl, Viktor, 171, 176–78, 190, 196,
    239
Danube Flotilla, 105, 119, 141
Deák, Ferenc, 16
Deutschmeister. See *Hoch-und*
    Deutschmeister
"Diary of my Woes" (Conrad, F.), 62
Dienstsprache (language of service), 42
Dimitrijević, Dragutin ("Apis"), 95–96
Dniester River, 152, 159
Domobranstvo (Croatia's Home
    Guard), 35, 42
double eagle emblem, 31

Drina, 125, 130–31, 240–42, 271;
    Balkanstreitkräfte crossing of, 118–19
Dual Monarchy. *See* Austria-Hungary
dueling, 56
Dukla Pass, 274–75
Dunant, Henri, 16
Durnovo, Pyotr, 158
dynastic ideology, 14, 18, 31–32, 50,
    55–56

Eighth *Jäger* Battalion, 112–13, 192
Eighth *Landwehr* Regiment, 271
entrenchment. *See* trench warfare
escapism, institutionalized, 10–11,
    69–72, 92, 105–8
ethnicity: army dynastic ideology
    replacing ties of, 31–32; of Austro-
    Hungarian Army sergeants, 43;
    Austro-Hungarian Army tactful
    handling of, 43, 44; bad blood
    among Army units of mixed, 46;
    as excuse for Cer debacle, 143–44;
    as factor in skills and combat
    readiness, 76; as foremost issue
    in Carpathian mishaps, 274–75;
    German language dominance
    in officer corps, 50; identity by
    dynasty not, 50, 55–56; Slavs used
    as scapegoats, 3–4, 143, 244, 271,
    274–75, 282; vererans' groups
    imperial loyalty regardless of,
    47
ethno-states, 19–20
Eugene of Savoy (prince), 120
Evert, Aleksei, 178, 239
Evidenzbureau, 82–85; 1913 report
    on Serbian military, 123–24;
    Conrad, F., experience in, 72;
    Pokorny's brilliance at, 88, 227–28,
    251, 262–63, 274, 278; Przemyśl
    location for, 161, 190, 200

gerrymandering, in Hungary, 17
Giesl von Gieslingen, Arthur, 126
Gina. *See* Reininghaus, Gina von
Glaise-Horstenau, Edmunc, 5
Gniła Lipa, 191, 203, 207
Gołogóry, 192, 195, 196
Good Soldier Švejk, The (Hašek), 3
Gorlice-Tarnów offensive, 277–78
Gorodok, 167
graničari (forces of Croatian Military
    Border defense), 34–35
Graz's III Corps battalion, 192, 194
Great Patriotic War, 3
Great Retreat, Russian, 278–79, 289
Greek Catholic Church, 25–26;
    repressed in favor of Orthodoxy,
    246
"Grodek" (Trakl), 216. *See also* battle
    of Gródek
Gródek-Wereszyca line: Brudermann
    to hold, 213–20; Brusilov's major
    push against, 247–52; Kövess to
    hold, 220–21, 224, 253
Gumbinnen, 171

Habsburg army. *See* Austro-
    Hungarian Army; *hurrá*
Habsburg Command Conspiracy, 107
Habsburg monarchy: Achilles' heel
    of, 34; AEIOU motto of, 13; antiwar
    and anti-Habsburg sentiment, 271;
    ärarisch deutsch of, 50; deadlock
    between Budapest and Vienna,
    35–36, 66, 266, 286; enduring
    legacy of, 11–12; ethnic and
    religious tolerance of, 8, 43; fall
    of former lands to Communism,
    3; first major battle between
    Romanov and, 171; foreign and
    domestic problems interwoven,
    23; Galicia as critical outcome for,

1–2; institutionalized escapism
    of, 10–11, 69–72, 105–8; military
    conscription and funding, 36–39,
    72; Prussian alliance with, 69–70;
    Schlamperei trademark case, 86;
    territorial losses suffered by, 15–16;
    Ukrainian loyal to, 25–26; veterans'
    groups, 46–47, 99
Hague Disarmament Conference, The
    (1907), 38
Halicz, 150, 191, 221
Hartwig, Nikolai, 104
harvest leave time, 101
Hašek, Jaroslav, 3
Hausmacht (family firm), 13
Hinke, Alfred von, 193
historiography, of Eastern Front, 2–4;
    American revisionist, 7; to hide
    flawed generalship, 5–6; nostalgia
    versus rigorous, 8
historiography, of Galicia, 3–8;
    author's own career path and, 9–10
Hitler, Adolf, 85–86
Hoch-und Deutschmeister (Vienna's
    Fourth Infantry Regiment), 41, 112
Hoen, Max von, 117
Hohenzollern dynasty, 13, 16
Holy Roman Empire, 14, 16
Holzhausen, Ludwig von, 167
Honvéd (Hungarian Home Guard),
    33–34; Fifth Cavalry Division,
    167, 170; monolingual policy of,
    42; Ninth *Honvéd* Regiment, 181;
    political gamesmanship impacting,
    35–37, 40; Thirty-ninth *Honvéd*
    Division, 181; Twenty-third *Honvéd*
    Division, 218–19, 268
house of Savoy, 15
Hoyos, Alexander, 100
Hranilović, Oskar von, 131, 161, 163, 187,
    223; assesses Russian capability, 166

Huczwa River, 184
Hundredth *Landsturm* Brigade, 239
Hungarian obstructionism, 35–36, 66,
    266, 286
Hungary: deadlock between Vienna
    and Budapest, 35–36, 66, 266,
    286; ethnic minorities in, 17–18;
    fall of coalition government, 37;
    Germans in, 17; gerrymandering
    in, 17; obstructionism impacting
    food supplies, 286; revolt of,
    14; Romanians in, 17; Slovaks
    in, 17, 19–20; South Slavs in, 17;
    Ukrainians in, 18. See also *Honvéd*;
    Magyars
hurrá (Habsburg battle cry), 266;
    charging forward shouting, 168,
    173, 175, 180, 183, 198, 207; showing
    more valor than sense, 195;
    shrapnel and bullets greeting, 238;
    troop decimation seconds after, 221
Huyn, Karl Georg, 230

Infantry Regulations: on military
    budget, 36–38, 72; on superior
    morale, 74–76
Iron Corps, Graz's III Corps
    battalion, 192, 194
Iron Corps, Kreisler's III Corps
    battalion, 231–33
irregulars, Serbian, 122, 128–29,
    130–33, 136–38, 146, 243
Isonzo, 280–81
Italian Army: battle of Caporetto,
    285, 286; battle of Isonzo, 280–81;
    Boroević's acumen against, 280–81;
    Conrad, F., War Plan against, 68;
    conscription, 38; mobilization, 66
Italians/Italy: rising nationalism in,
    49; special AOK attention on, 272;
    Strafexpedition in, 281–82

Ivangorod fortress, 162
Ivanov, Nikolai, 159, 170–71, 178
IV Army Corps: cholera among, 255;
    in Galicia, 237–39; in Šabac, 131–32,
    140–41

Jandrić, Čedomil, 85, 93
Jandršek, Colonel, 85–89
Janówka, 186, 201–2
Jaroslawice, 167–68
Jászi, Oscar, 30
Jews: among Fischer's gendarmes,
    164; forced to migrate, 246; in
    Galicia, 158; in *k.u.k.*, 55–56
Joseph (archduke), 238
Joseph Ferdinand (archduke), 197,
    223, 282
July Crisis (1914), 100–104

Kageneck, Carl von, 71, 76
Kailer, Karl, 100
Kaiserjäger, 114–15; Brosch's Second,
    197–99, 235–36, 289; gutted
    by futile engagements, 289; at
    Machnów, 236; at Radostów, 234;
    Tyrol origin of, 44; at Wasylów,
    198–99; at Zaborze, 236
*kaiserlich und königliche (k.u.k.)
    Armee*, 32–33; B-Group as swing
    force of, 68–69, 106–7; *Bosniaken*
    regiments, 44, 129, 199–200, 233,
    238–39; cavalry division losses
    of, 78–79, 122, 165–70; Churchill's
    epitaph for prewar, 267; collapse
    of, 286–87; Conrad, F., flawed
    plans, 66–67, 105–8, 115–16; Czechs
    and Italians reporting for duty,
    111–12; division of labor within,
    44–45; ethnic diversity of, 41–42;
    in Galicia, 26, 65, 151–59, 169–71;
    Gendarmeriekorps, 94, 128–29,

of, 126; Forty-sixth Division,
173; Fourteenth Regiment, 181;
Kisch's first-hand reporting
about, 139; Kremsier's Fourteenth
Regiment, 181; Podhajský's
evaluation of, 143, 145; political
gamesmanship impacting, 35–37,
40; Twenty-eighth Regiment,
143; Twenty-second Division, 231.
See also Twenty-first *Landwehr*
Division of VIII Corps
language of command
(*Kommandosprache*), 42
language of service (*Dienstsprache*),
42
lanterns, as location give-away, 145
Lehár, Anton, 239–40
Lemberg. *See* battle of Lemberg
Lexa von Aehrenthal, Alois, 63
Line corps, I through XIV, 65. *See also*
Austro-Hungarian Army
Liśnik, 175
Lissa, 16
Lombardy, 15–16
Lublin, 169, 171–78, 211, 239
Ludovika military academy, 33

machine guns, 72; abandoned to
Serbs, 142; camouflaged, 261;
entrenchment to escape, 74;
infantry decimated in seconds
by, 76, 141, 185, 197–98, 200, 202,
221; *Landsturm* unfamiliar with,
116–17; limited number of, 78, 112,
116; Maxim and Hotchkiss, 123;
nightmarish "raking" with, 167, 238,
249; at Przemyśl, 151; Serbs better
equipped with, 122–23, 136–38
Machnów, 236
Magyars, 15–16, 282; *Ausgleich*
favoring of, 17; bloodlust rampage

in Przemyśl, 257; efforts to
Magyarize minority groups, 17–18;
minority groups and, 19
Mannerheim, Carl, 178
Maria Theresia (empress-queen), 238
Marne, 1
martial law (*Standrecht*): in field
operation zones, 110; Galicia and
Bukovina placed under, 154; for
Twenty-first Division's Czech
infantry units, 143, 148
Masaryk, Jan, 4
Masaryk, Tomáš, 4
Massentod (mass death), 238
Maubeuge, 116
McMeekin, Sean, 96
medical corps, 214–15
Merizzi, Erik von, 91–92, 97
Metternich, Klemens Wenzel von, 14
Metzger, Joseph, 69, 196
Mitrovica, 241
mobilization and deployment, *k.u.k.*:
Conrad, F., flawed, 66–67, 105–8,
115–16, 118–27; Czech and Italian
reporting for duty, 111–12; in
Galicia, 151–59, 169–71; *Hoch-und
Deutschmeister* example of, 112;
popular reaction to, 110–11; in
Serbia, 66, 105–8, 115–16
Moltke, Helmuth von, 70, 153–54, 214,
252
Montenegro, 88, 94, 121, 129, 197, 241,
281
Moravia, 29, 271–72
Moravian Compromise (1905), 29
Mościska, 225, 228–29
mountain artillery, 80
mythmaking, historiography versus, 8

Nachrichtenabteilung (Intelligence
Department), 161

277–78; Habsburg alliance with, 69–70; Hohenzollern dynasty, 13, 16; Russia's invasion of, 1

Przemyśl, 26, 278; AOK established at, 150–51; Auffenberg's Fourth Army at, 151, 167; as demarcation for Galician campaign end, 222–23; *Evidenzbureau* relocated to, 161, 190, 200; *Landsturm* troops left at, 262, 269; Magyars' bloodlust rampage in, 257; in peril, 240, 252; Redlich's visit to, 168–69. See also *Armeeoberkommando*

Przemyślany, 203

Przyborski, Arthur, 127, 134–38, 143–45

Puhallo, Paul von, 172–73

Purtscher, Lt. Col., 124

Putin, Vladimir, 3, 11

Putnik, Radomir, 124–25, 132–33; invasion of Austria-Hungary by, 241, 269–70, 281

race pure (*reinrassig*), 42

Radetzky von Radetz, Josef Graf, 31, 49

radio: intelligence, 160, 227–28, 251, 262–63, 273–74, 278; permanent stations, 82; Russian radio intelligence, 96

Radostów, 234

rapid-fire artillery, 72. *See also* machine guns

Rarancze, 164

Rašić, Mihailo, 135–36

Ratzenhofer, Emil, 107

Rauchensteiner, Manfried, 6, 99

Rawa Ruska, 223–24, 234–39, 245–53, 247, 263, 264

Red Cross, 16

Redl, Alfred, 84–89

Redlich, Joseph, 168–69

regimental ideology, 45

Regimentssprache (regimental language), 42

Reich (mystical union of dynastic family and its subjects), 14, 18

Reininghaus, Gina von, 62–63, 99, 101; Conrad, F., obsession with, 93, 108, 149–50, 169, 264; dodges Catholic marriage laws, 277; at Teschen, 276, 278

reinrassig (race pure), 42

religious overtones, war mania with, 113–15, 179, 283

repeating rifles, 116–17

Reyl-Hanisch, Joseph von, 201–2

rifle (*Jäger*) battalions, 41, 112–13, 192. See also *Kaiserjäger*

Riflemen's Association (*Związek Strzelecki*), 28

Řiha, Corporal, 148

Romania/Romanians, 17, 164; independence from Turks, 23

Romanov dynasty, 13

Ronge, Max, 86, 228, 263, 274

Rothenberg, Gunther, 34

Rowno ("autumn swinery"), 278–80

Rudolph (crown prince of Austria), 21

Rumno, 238

Russia: Conrad, F., War Plan against, 67–68; Durnovo on natural allies of, 158; espionage and covert action in Galicia, 26–28; Galician border of, 24–25; inevitability of intervention by, 103–4; military conscription in, 38; military mobilization in 1914, 66; Redl as spy for, 84–89; Serbia allied with, 24

Russian Army: AOK warned about artillery of, 187–88; Eastern Front casualties, 270; Eighth Army, 160, 190–91, 207, 221–23, 233,

Russian Army (*cont.*)
245–50; Fourth Army, 171–72, 239;
mobilization of, 66; NA secret
report details about, 161; prisoners
of war from Great Retreat of, 278;
radio intelligence, 96; Russian
Great Retreat, 278–79, 289;
V Corps, 202–3; XIX Corps, 181,
201; XXI Corps, 219, 223, 234, 237;
XXIV Corps, 223, 237
Russian Revolution, 285
Russians, scant interest in Galician
campaign, 2–3
Russo-Japanese War (1904-1905):
assessment of Russian forces after,
83; observers of, 73–74, 75, 78–79,
81, 166; participants in, 159, 171,
177, 179
Ruzskiy, Nikolai, 190–91, 219, 223–24;
inaccurately credited, 222; at Rawa
Ruska, 234, 245, 247

Šabac, 130; Austro-Hungarian Army
atrocities at, 146; intense fighting
in, 130–31, 140–41, 237, 242
Salza, Anton von, 171–75, 178, 239;
forces defeated, 176–77
San River, 67, 247, 250–57, 261–62;
as demarcation line of Galician
campaign, 222–23
Sarajevo assassination: failed
intelligence analysis leading to,
95–96; Franz Joseph's reaction to,
99–100; interpreted as declaration
of war, 99; July Crisis precipitated
by, 100–104; network of Serbian
sympathizers enabling, 95–96,
240; possible Russian involvement
in, 96–97; rioting in Bosnia and
Croatia after, 98–99; war euphoria
following, 101–2

Šašinci, 242–43
Sava River, 105, 119–20, 125, 130–31,
141, 240–42, 271
Schadenfreude (satisfaction or
pleasure), 252
Schemua, Blasius von, 64, 230
Die Schlacht (Csicserics), 73
Schlamperei (slackness; carelessness),
8, 30, 283; Boroević on, 182;
emanating from Lemberg, 205;
German joke about, 277; Habsburg
trademark case of, 86; Kafkaesque,
108
Schlieffen, Alfred von, 70
Schlieffen Plan, 116, 153
schwarzgelb (black-yellow), 47
Schwarz-Gelbe Offensive, 278–80
Second Army, 105–7, 118–19
Second Bosnian Regiment, 199,
233–35
Second *Kaiserjäger* Regiment, 197–98,
235–36, 289
Seeckt, Hans von, 283
Seine River, 70
Serbia, 21, 23; Austro-Hungarian
friendly-fire incidents in, 145;
Conrad, F., flawed war plans for,
66–67, 105–8, 115–16, 118–27; defeat
and occupation of, 281; German
blank check for war on, 100; *k.u.k.*
casualties in, 134–39, 270; *k.u.k.* in,
66, 105–8, 115–16; Potiorek's failed
campaigns in, 118–27, 269–70;
Redl's information shared with,
88; Russia allied with, 24; Sarajevo
plot foreknowledge by, 95–96, 240;
second Austro-Hungarian invasion
of, 269; third Austro-Hungarian
invasion of, 269–70; three *k.u.k.*
Army Corps bordering, 26, 101. *See
also* Balkans

Serbian Army: 1914 military
mobilization of, 66;
Balkanstreitkräfte defeated by, 142,
147; casualties incurred by 1914,
270; Combined and Šumadija
I Divisions, 134; enlarged from
Balkan Wars, 39; *Evidenzbureau*
1913 report on, 123–24; *komitadji*
assisting, 122, 128–29, 131–33,
136–38, 146, 243; Putnik's invasion
of Austria-Hungary, 124–25, 132–33,
241, 269–70, 281; readiness of,
122–25

Serbs: rising nationalism among, 49;
special AOK attention on, 272

Sereth River, 67

Seventeenth Regiment, 192, 194

shell shock, 215

Shinto, 74

SIGINT. *See* signals intelligence

signals intelligence (SIGINT), 160,
227–28, 251, 262–63, 273–74, 278

Silesian industrial heartland, 269

sixteen corps, of Austro-Hungarian
Army, 65

Sixth Cavalry Division, 165

Sixty-first Regiment, Temesvár's, 41

Six Weeks War, 16

Skakalište village, 134

Škoda Works, Bohemia, 81

Slavs: Army Slavic, 43; Austroslavism,
20; Compromise of Croatia-
Slavonia, 17, 34–35; Germans and,
274–75; Panslav congress, 20; as
scapegoats, 3–4, 143, 244, 271,
274–75, 282; Slavonia, 17, 34–35;
Slovaks in Hungary, 17, 19–20;
South, 17, 280–81; as "traitorous,"
288; Yugoslavia, 290

Slovenes, 194

smokeless gunpowder, 72

social Darwinism, 22, 61

Solferino, 15–16

Sołokija, 234

Sophie, Duchess of Hohenberg, 98

South Slavs, 17, 280–81

Southwestern Front, 159–78, 190,
203–34, 245–83

spy wars: aerial reconnaissance, 130,
162–63; AOK ignores intelligence,
282–83; after Bosnian Crisis, 84;
failed intelligence analysis leads
to Sarajevo assassination, 95–96;
Galicians suspected of espionage,
226–27; Jandrić, Čedomil, spy
scandal, 85, 93; *Kundschaftsgruppe*,
83–84; Redl disaster, 84–89;
Russian, in Galicia, 26–28; Russian
radio intelligence, 96; Sarajevo
plot as failed intelligence analysis,
95–96; signals intelligence, 160,
227–28, 251, 262–63, 273–74, 278

"Srbe na vrbe" (Natlačen), 99

Standrecht (martial law), 110, 143, 148,
154

Stanisławów, 223

Stavka, 159

Stepanović, Stepa, 133–37; delivers
first Entente victory, 138

Stone, Norman, 152

Strafexpedition, 281–82

Stürgkh, Josef, 277

Stürgkh, Karl, 100

St. Vitus Day, 94

Styria/Styrians, 193; Forty-seventh
Regiment, 238; at Gródek, 231–33

Suchodoly, 174–75

suicide rate, 46

Świrz, 204

Syrmia (Croatia's easternmost
region), 129, 241, 269

Szeptycki, Stanislaus, 166

CPSIA information can be obtained at www.ICGtesting.com
Printed in the USA
LVOW08*0154251115

463871LV00009B/53/P

9 781612 347653

ednsabad@mc.com

Tr.

1 H

3 Mc